Using ...ve Lens tᴏ ᴸxplore Social Change and Organizations

Building a Theoretical and Research Foundation

ORGANIZATION AND MANAGEMENT SERIES
Series Editors
Arthur P. Brief
University of Utah
Kimberly D. Elsbach
University of California, Davis
Michael Frese
University of Lueneburg and National University of Singapore

Garud/Karnoe (Eds.): *Path Dependence and Creation*

Golden-Biddle/Dutton (Eds.): *Using a Positive Lens to Explore Social Change and Organizations: Building a Theoretical and Research Foundation*

Harris (Ed.): *Handbook of Research in International Human Resource Management*

Jacoby (Au.): *Employing Bureaucracy: Managers, Unions, and the Transformation of Work in the 20th Century, Revised Edition*

Kossek/Lambert (Eds.): *Work and Life Integration: Organizational, Cultural and Individual Perspectives*

Kramer/Tenbrunsel/Bazerman (Eds): Social Decision Making: Social Dilemmas, Social Values, and Ethical Judgments

Lampel/Shamsie/Lant (Eds.): *The Business of Culture: Strategic Perspectives on Entertainment and Media*

Lant/Shapira (Eds.): *Organizational Cognition: Computation and Interpretation*

Lord/Brown (Aus.): *Leadership Processes and Follower Self-Identity*

Margolis/Walsh (Aus.): *People and Profits? The Search Between a Company's Social and Financial Performance*

Miceli/Dworkin/Near (Aus): *Whistle-Blowing in Organizations*

Nord/Connell (Aus): *Rethinking the Knowledge Controversy in Organization Studies: A Generative Uncertainty Perspective*

Messick/Kramer (Eds.): *The Psychology of Leadership: Some New Approaches*

Pearce (Au.): *Organization and Management in the Embrace of the Government*

Peterson/Mannix (Eds.): *Leading and Managing People in the Dynamic Organization*

Rafaeli/Pratt (Eds.): *Artifacts and Organizations: Beyond Mere Symbolism*

Riggio/Murphy/Pirozzolo (Eds.): *Multiple Intelligences and Leadership*

Roberts/Dutton (Eds): *Exploring Positive Identities and Organizations: Building a Theoretical and Research Foundation*

Using a Positive Lens to Explore Social Change and Organizations

Building a Theoretical and Research Foundation

Edited by

Karen Golden-Biddle
Boston University

Jane E. Dutton
Univesity of Michigan

Routledge
Taylor & Francis Group
New York   London

Routledge
Taylor & Francis Group
711 Third Avenue
New York, NY 10017

Routledge
Taylor & Francis Group
27 Church Road
Hove, East Sussex BN3 2FA

© 2012 by Taylor & Francis Group, LLC
Routledge is an imprint of Taylor & Francis Group, an Informa business

Printed in the United States of America on acid-free paper
Version Date: 20120113

International Standard Book Number: 978-0-415-87885-2 (Hardback) 978-0-415-87886-9 (Paperback)

For permission to photocopy or use material electronically from this work, please access www.copyright.com (http://www.copyright.com/) or contact the Copyright Clearance Center, Inc. (CCC), 222 Rosewood Drive, Danvers, MA 01923, 978-750-8400. CCC is a not-for-profit organization that provides licenses and registration for a variety of users. For organizations that have been granted a photocopy license by the CCC, a separate system of payment has been arranged.

Trademark Notice: Product or corporate names may be trademarks or registered trademarks, and are used only for identification and explanation without intent to infringe.

Library of Congress Cataloging-in-Publication Data

Using a positive lens to explore social change and organizations : building a theoretical and research foundation / editors, Karen Golden-Biddle, Jane Dutton.
    p. cm. -- (Organization and management series)
    Includes bibliographical references and index.
    ISBN 978-0-415-87885-2 (hardcover : alk. paper) -- ISBN 978-0-415-87886-9 (pbk. : alk. paper)
    1. Social change. 2. Organizational change. 3. Sustainable development--Developing countries. 4. Developing countries--Social policy. I. Golden-Biddle, Karen. II. Dutton, Jane E.

HM831.U85 2012
303.4--dc23
                                         2012000344

Visit the Taylor & Francis Web site at
http://www.taylorandfrancis.com

and the Psychology Press Web site at
http://www.psypress.com

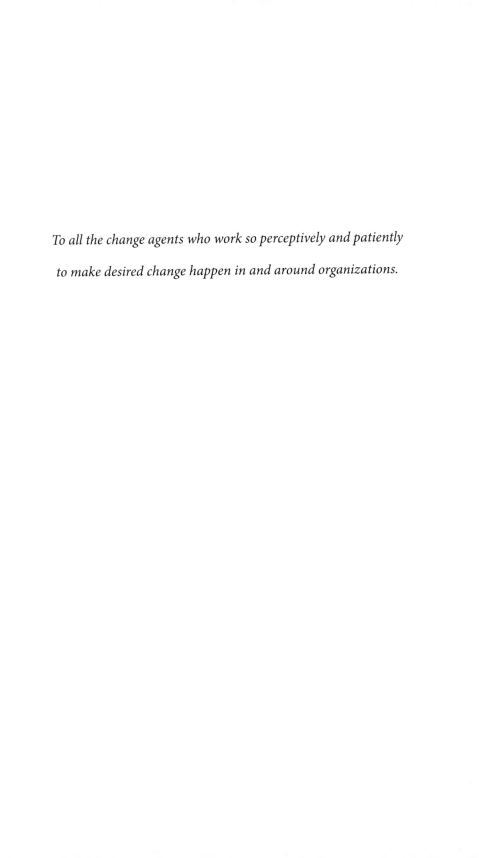

To all the change agents who work so perceptively and patiently

to make desired change happen in and around organizations.

Contents

PART I   Introduction

PART II   Change Agency

PART IV   Health Care

PART V Poverty and Low-Wage Work

PART VI Conclusion

Series Foreword

For way too long, the subject of social change largely has been ignored by management and organization scholars. Karen Golden-Biddle and Jane Dutton have taken a giant step toward remedying this embarrassing problem. We say "embarrassing" because the objects of social change, problems like health care and poverty for example, *should be* on our agenda. We are morally obligated to have these issues on the agenda. We commend Golden-Biddle and Dutton also for how they proceeded. They brought together a diverse and fascinating group of scholars and charged them with viewing the organizational aspects of social change through a positive lens. So, do not expect the language or tactics of a Che Guevara; rather, think Gandhi. We are pleased to have Karen and Jane join our Series.

Arthur P. Brief

Kimberly D. Elsbach

Michael Frese

Acknowledgments

This book has been a joyful project from its inception. It has been an adventure for the authors and for the editors, as we were exploring new theoretical territory in applying a positive lens to the context of social change. We are proud of the final product and grateful to the chapter authors and commentators who provided high quality contributions to this book.

Many people along the way have contributed to the creation and quality of this volume. First, we thank Carol Waldvogel, who made conference logistics seamless through her grace under pressure. She is also the designer of the lovely book cover. In addition, we benefited from the hosting of the conference, encouragement, and financial support from Boston University's School of Management and Organizational Behavior Department. We also sincerely thank Anne Duffy, from Psychology Press/Routledge at the Taylor & Francis Group, who has been an important supporter of this book, as well as of the other edited books in this series. Anne was the senior editor on the first book, *Exploring Positive Relationships at Work: Building a Theoretical and Research Foundation* (2007), as well as the book, *Exploring Positive Identities and Organizations: Building a Theoretical and Research Foundation* (2009). Anne has been a superb editor, encouraging and enabling us during every phase of this process. Our thanks also goes out to Elana Feldman, Steve Fellows, Jina Mao, and Jeff Yip, the outstanding doctoral students from Boston University who played important roles in the book building conference as memory keepers who traced ideas and other threads across the various discussions. Elana Feldman also joined as co-author of the introduction and conclusion chapters. She was a great contributor! We also thank Jane McGillicuddy who handled all proofing with patience and care. We thank Janet Max of the Center for Positive Organizational Scholarship for the various ways she has assisted in this process, and we express appreciation to the Center, and the Ross School of Business for lending financial support to our book building conference.

Finally, we wish to thank our partners in life, Mark and Lance, for abiding with us as we collaborated on the conference and the creation of this book. We are grateful for your support.

Karen Golden-Biddle and Jane Dutton

xix

About the Editors

Karen Golden-Biddle is Everett W. Lord Distinguished Faculty Scholar and Professor of Organizational Behavior at Boston University School of Management. She currently serves as Senior Associate Dean. Karen received her PhD from Case Western Reserve University. Her research interests focus on large-scale organizational change, cultural dynamics and micro-processes in change, and health system transformation. She also examines the process of theorizing in field-based research.

Jane E. Dutton is the Robert L. Kahn Distinguished University Professor of Business Administration and Psychology at the Ross School of Business, University of Michigan. She is currently Associate Director of the Center for Positive Organizational Scholarship. Jane received her PhD from Northwestern University. Her research interests focus on organizations and compassion, high quality connections at work, job crafting, and the dynamics of positive identities.

About the Contributors

Krista K. Badiane is a Doctoral Candidate in the School of Natural Resources and Environment at the University of Michigan. Krista is also a Graham Doctoral Fellow and Frederick A. and Barbara M. Erb Institute for Global Sustainable Enterprise affiliate. Her research interests include sustainability and social change in organizations.

Jean M. Bartunek is the Robert A. and Evelyn J. Ferris Chair and Professor of Management and Organization at the Carroll School of Management at Boston College. She is a past president and fellow of the Academy of Management, from which she received a career distinguished service award in 2009. She received her doctorate in social and organizational psychology from the University of Illinois at Chicago. Her research interests center broadly around organizational change and academic-practitioner relationships.

Julie Battilana is an Associate Professor of Business Administration in the Organizational Behavior unit at Harvard Business School. Julie holds a joint PhD in organizational behavior from INSEAD and in management and economics from Ecole Normale Supérieure de Cachan. Her research examines the process by which organizations or individuals initiate and implement changes that diverge from the taken-for-granted practices in a field of activity. Specifically, Julie's work examines (1) the conditions that enable actors to initiate change that diverges from the institutional status quo, and (2) the process by which they implement such change.

Christine M. Beckman is an Associate Professor of Organization and Management, and Chancellor's Fellow at The Paul Merage School of Business, University of California, Irvine, as well as co-director of both the Don Beall Center for Innovation and Entrepreneurship and the Center for Organizational Research. Christine received her doctorate from Stanford University. Her research focuses on collaborative relationships that facilitate organizational learning and change as well as the internal factors that enable and constrain learning.

Oana Branzei is the David G. Burgoyne Faculty Fellow, the Building Sustainable Value Research Fellow, and Associate Professor of Strategy at the Richard Ivey School of Business, the University of Western Ontario, London, Canada. Oana received her doctorate from the Sauder School of Business at the University of British Columbia. Her research interests, at the intersection of strategy and sustainability, include the pro-social foundations, forms, and functions of business as agents of positive social change and the relational micro-processes of value creation, capture and distribution.

Rodrigo Canales is an Assistant Professor of Organizational Behavior at the Yale School of Management. He is a Board Member of the Dalai Lama Center for Ethics and Transformative Values at the Massachusetts Institute of Technology and a co-founder of the Center's Mexico Chapter. He received a PhD and an MBA from the Massachusetts Institute of Technology Sloan School of Management. Rodrigo's work seeks to understand how individuals purposefully enact organizational and institutional change. In particular, Rodrigo explores how individuals' backgrounds, professional status, and organizational positions affect how they relate to existing structures and the strategies they pursue to change them.

Lisa Jones Christensen is an Assistant Professor of Strategy and Entrepreneurship at the Kenan-Flagler Business School at the University of North Carolina at Chapel Hill. She is also the research director for the Center for Sustainable Enterprise at Kenan-Flagler. She received her PhD in organizational behavior from Kenan-Flagler. Her research interests include commitment to change, sustainability (U.S. and international), social entrepreneurship, and microfinance.

Kathryn Correia is President and CEO of HealthEast Care System in St. Paul, MN. Previously, she was President of Appleton Medical Center and Theda Clark Medical Center, both part of ThedaCare, an integrated delivery system serving northeast Wisconsin. While at ThedaCare, Kathryn led the creation of the innovative and patented care model ("Collaborative Care"). She received her undergraduate degree from Denison University and her Masters degree from The Ohio State University.

Elana Feldman is a doctoral candidate in organizational behavior at the Boston University School of Management. Elana earned her BA from Brown University. Her research interests include work practices that enable fulfilling and balanced lives, as well as gender dynamics within organizations.

Martha S. Feldman holds the Johnson Chair for Civic Governance and Public Management and is a Professor of Planning, Policy and Design, Political Science, Management and Sociology at the University of California, Irvine. She earned her doctorate in Political Science from Stanford University. She is a Senior Editor for *Organization Science,* and she also serves on the editorial boards of *The Academy of Management Journal, The Journal of Management Studies, Organization Studies,* and *Advances in Organization.* Her research focuses on the study of organizational practices, such as routines, and organizational change. She has written four books and dozens of articles on the topics of organization theory, public management, and qualitative research methods. She received the 2009 Administrative Science Quarterly award for scholarly contribution and the 2011 Academy of Management Practice Scholarship Award.

C. Marlena Fiol received her MBA and a PhD in Strategic Management from the University of Illinois at Urbana-Champaign. She is currently Professor of Strategic Management and Health Administration at the University of Colorado Denver. Her research interests include managerial and organizational cognition, organizational learning/unlearning, and organizational identity.

Brooking Gatewood is a PhD student in Organization and Management at the Paul Merage School of Business at the University of California, Irvine. Her research interests include hybrid and social change organizations and inter-organizational cooperation.

Nardia Haigh is an Assistant Professor of Management in the Department of Management and Marketing at the University of Massachusetts Boston. Nardia's research focuses on business models and strategies that address large-scale sustainability issues, such as those associated with climate change and the management of environmental commons. She completed her PhD in business management at the University of Queensland Business School, in Brisbane, Australia.

Andrew J. Hoffman is the Holcim (US) Professor of Sustainable Enterprise at the University of Michigan, a position that holds joint appointments at the Stephen M. Ross School of Business and the School of Natural Resources & Environment. Within this role, Andrew also serves as Director of the Frederick A. and Barbara M. Erb Institute for

Global Sustainable Enterprise. Andrew received his doctorate from the Massachusetts Institute of Technology. His work uses a sociological perspective to understand the cultural, institutional, and managerial aspects of sustainability for organizations.

Jennifer Howard-Grenville is an Associate Professor of Management at the University of Oregon's Lundquist College of Business. Jennifer received her PhD at Massachusetts Institute of Technology. She studies processes of organizational and institutional change and has explored the role of routines, issue selling, and culture in enabling and inhibiting change.

Ellen Ernst Kossek is a University Distinguished Professor at the School of Human Resources & Labor Relations at Michigan State University and co-directs a National Center for Work, Family, & Health. She is a Fellow of the American Psychological Association, and the Society of Industrial Organizational Psychology, and recipient of the Academy of Management Gender and Diversity Division's Sage Scholarly Achievement award. Ellen received her doctorate from Yale University. Her research interests include positive work-family relationships and organizational change, workplace flexibility and innovation, and local and global international hr and multiculturalism.

Carrie R. Leana is the George H. Love Professor of Organizations and Management at the University of Pittsburgh, where she holds appointments in the Schools of Business Administration, Public Policy, and Medicine. She is also Director of the University's Center for Health and Care Work. Leana's PhD is from the University of Houston. Her current research is focused on organizational processes and employee outcomes, particularly for low-wage workers.

Johanna Mair is an Associate Professor of Strategic Management at IESE Business School, as well as the Academic Editor of Stanford Social Innovation Review. Johanna received her doctorate from INSEAD and was recognized as a "Faculty Pioneer" by the Aspen Institute. Her research interests center on how institutions stifle or enable social and economic progress and the role of entrepreneurial actors in this process.

Debra Meyerson is an Associate Professor of Organizational Behavior at the Stanford University School of Education and, by courtesy, the Stanford Graduate School of Business. She is the Faculty Co-founder and Co-director of the Stanford Center of Philanthropy and Civil Society.

Debra received her doctorate from the Stanford GSB. Her research interests include gender, diversity, and the scaling of educational and other social sector organizations.

Valerie Myers is an Assistant Professor of Management & Organizations at the University of Michigan in the School of Public Health's Department of Health Management & Policy and the Ross School of Business's Department of Management and Organizations, where she is affiliated with the Center for Positive Organizational Scholarship. Valerie earned a dual doctorate in Organizational Psychology and Social Work (Policy) from the University of Michigan, Ann Arbor. Her research interests include organizational culture and performance outcomes, diversity, and work ethics.

Edward J. O'Connor received his PhD in Industrial/Organizational Psychology from the University of Akron. He is currently a professor of management and health administration at the University of Colorado Denver. His research interests include physician–administration collaboration, leadership, and organizational cognition.

Paul Panico is the Executive Vice President and Chief Operating Officer at Cheyenne Regional Medical Center in Cheyenne Wyoming and a Fellow of the American College of Healthcare Executives. Paul received his doctorate in Industrial/Organizational Psychology from Colorado State University. His research interests include application of conflict management theory to the healthcare professions.

Jone L. Pearce is Dean's Professor of Leadership and Director of the Center for Global Leadership in The Paul Merage School of Business, University of California, Irvine, having received her PhD from Yale University. Her current research focus is on interpersonal processes, such as trust and status, and how these processes may be affected by political structures, economic conditions, and organizational policies and practices.

Paola Perez-Aleman is an Associate Professor of Strategy and Organization at McGill University's Desautels Faculty of Management. She holds a PhD from the Massachusetts Institute of Technology. Her research interests include business growth and economic development, innovation and enterprises in developing countries, and organizational and institutional change.

Michael G. Pratt is a Professor of Management and, by courtesy, Psychology, at Boston College. He is also a Winston Center for Leadership and Ethics Fellow and is finishing his term as the inaugural Associate Editor for Qualitative Research for the Academy of Management Journal. He earned his degree in Organizational Psychology at the University of Michigan. His research interests include how individuals connect with their work, organizations, and professions.

Trish Reay is Associate Professor at the University of Alberta School of Business. Trish received her PhD from the University of Alberta School of Business. Her research interests include inter-professional relationships, professional identity, and the dynamics of change with a current focus on the institutional context and organizations engaged in primary health care, mental health, and addictions treatment.

Darcy Riddell is a PhD Candidate in Social and Ecological Sustainability, Department of Environment and Resource Studies, at the University of Waterloo. She is an associate professional practitioner with Social Innovation Generation. Her scholarships include the SSHRC Joseph-Armand Bombardier Doctoral Scholarship and the University of Waterloo President's Graduate Scholarship. Darcy's research interests include sustainability, the relationship of human development to social innovation in complex systems, and multi-level theories of change.

Tomislav Rimac is an Assistant Professor of Management and Organization at the Faculty of Economics and Business Studies at the Autonomous University of Barcelona and a Project Officer for Spain for the European Union SELUSI project, an innovative multidisciplinary research investigating population of social ventures in the EU. Tomislav received his doctorate from IESE Business School, University of Navarra. His research is focused on entrepreneurship directed at social change, specifically on organizational mechanisms used in affecting dynamics and outcomes of social change.

Scott Sonenshein is an Assistant Professor of Management at the Jones Graduate School of Business, Rice University. He received his PhD in Management and Organizations from the Ross School of Business, University of Michigan. His current research interests include interpretive approaches to social and organizational change.

Erica Steckler is a doctoral candidate in the Management and Organization Department at Boston College. She received her MBA degree at Simmons School of Management. Her research interests include social change and organizations, authenticity, identity, and legitimacy within the global issue domains of corporate responsibility and sustainability.

Ola Tjörnbo is a PhD candidate in Global Governance at the Balsillie School of International Affairs, a Balsillie Fellow, and a McConnell Fellow at Social Innovation Generation, University of Waterloo. His main research focus is the role of social media in governing global problems, and he also looks at social change, power, and leadership.

Rebecca Wells is Associate Professor of Health Policy and Management at the Gillings School of Global Public Health, University of North Carolina at Chapel Hill, and a Fellow at the Cecil G. Sheps Center for Health Services Research. Rebecca received her doctorate from the University of Michigan School of Public Health. Her research focuses on cooperation within and across health and human service safety net organizations.

Laura Wernick is a postdoctoral fellow at the University of Michigan, School of Social Work. She recently completed her PhD in the Joint Doctoral Program in Social Work and Political Science at the University of Michigan, where she also received a Graduate Certificate in Women's Studies. Her research explores issues of diversity, power, pedagogy, and social justice within and across areas of community organizing, philanthropic institutions, and nonprofit organizations. Dr. Wernick is also engaged in research examining the use of performance as an empowerment and organizing tool among LGBTQQ youth.

Frances Westley holds the J.W. McConnell Chair in Social Innovation and is the Director for the Waterloo Institute on Social Innovation and Resilience at the University of Waterloo. Frances received her PhD in Sociology from McGill University (1978), her MA Sociology from McGill University (1975), and her BA in English Literature from Middlebury College (1970). Her research and consulting focuses on social innovation, strategies for sustainable development, strategic change, visionary leadership, and inter-organizational collaboration. She is on the editorial board of several journals, including *Journal of Applied Behavioral Science* and *Ecology and Society*. She is the recipient of several awards, including the Ulysses S. Seal award for innovation in conservation and the Corporate Knights Award.

Lynn Perry Wooten is a Clinical Associate Professor of Management, Organizations & Strategy. She previously served as the co-director of the Center for Positive Organizational Scholarship at the Ross School of Business. Lynn received her doctorate in Corporate Strategy from the University of Michigan. Her research interests include positive organizing practices in crisis situations, healthcare organizations, and the nonprofit sector. In addition, she studies how organizations leverage diversity and create inclusive environments that result in positive deviant outcomes.

Part I

Introduction

1

The Call: Why a Book Now on Using a Positive Lens to Explore Social Change and Organizations?

Jane E. Dutton
University of Michigan

Karen Golden-Biddle and Elana Feldman
Boston University

How can application of a positive lens to understanding social change and organizations enrich and elaborate theory and practice? This is the core question that inspired this book. It is a question that brought together a diverse and talented group of researchers interested in change and organizations in different problem domains (sustainability, healthcare, poverty alleviation, and education). The contributors to this book bring different theoretical lenses to the question of social change and organizations. Some are anchored in more macro accounts of how and why social change processes occur, while others approach the question from a more psychological or social psychological perspective. Many of the chapters in the book travel across levels of analyses, making their accounts of social change good examples of multi-level theorizing. Some scholars are practiced and immersed in thinking about organizational phenomena from a positive lens; for others it is a total adventure in trying on a new set of glasses. However, connecting all contributing authors is an excitement and willingness to explore new insights and new angles on how to explain and cultivate social change within or across organizations.

STARTING ASSUMPTIONS

Social Change and Organizations Are Fundamentally Intertwined

Social change has been a critical and enduring concern of organizational researchers since the field of organizational studies took root. Whether catalyzed by sociologists and their interests in social movements (e.g., Zald & McCarthy, 1979), social change organizations (Selznick, 1949), the social consequences of organizations (Blau & Scott, 1962), or prompted by psychologists' interests in how organizations and human welfare are intertwined (e.g., Argyris, 1957; Mayo, 1945), organizational studies have been central to understanding the processes and outcomes of social change. Today, interest in organizations and social change is more dispersed. The links between social change and organizations show up in a variety of topical areas including social entrepreneurship (e.g., Bornstein, 2007; Dees & Elian, 1998; Mair & Marti, 2006), social and corporate responsibility (e.g., Aguilera, Rupp, Williams, & Ganapathi, 2007; Tribo, Surroco, & Waddock, 2010), and under the broad umbrella of business and society (e.g., Carroll & Buckholz, 2009; Post, 2004; Waddock, 2009). In addition, there is focused interest by organizational researchers working on certain types of organizations (e.g., educational or healthcare organizations) or on certain large-scale issue domains (e.g., sustainability, diversity). However, to date there has been limited effort to look across these diverse research arenas to distill integrative insights about how social change and organizations come together in ways that enrich theory and practice. The time for integration and learning across research silos is particularly ripe given the call to researchers to more fully consider the links between organizations and society (Hinings & Greenwood, 2002; Margolis & Walsh, 2003) and the critique that organizational research is not having significant beneficial impact (Ghoshal, 2005).

Application of a Positive Lens Unlocks New Ways of Understanding and Enabling Change Processes

This book applies a positive lens to enrich theory and practice about social change and organizations. The use of a positive lens means there is an explicit focus on understanding the elements in the change process in and of organizations that build up, increase, enable, and foster beneficial outcomes associated with social change (Cameron, Dutton, & Quinn, 2003). A focus on these kinds of forces and processes at work in social change is particularly important given that most social efforts are directed toward producing outcomes that are viewed as beneficial or desirable. At the same time, application of a positive lens looks for instances of positive deviance involving social change (Pasquale, Sternin, & Sternin, 2010) and asks: How did that process work? Why did those outcomes happen? What were the roles of organizations or people connected to organizations in accounting for the social change? Application of a positive lens does not mean ignoring the role of negative states, processes, or outcomes in social change. In fact, the nature of social change means that negative conditions and states are endemic to activating social change efforts.

Application of a positive lens does mean keeping a particular eye on what are the processes and states which open up, build, strengthen, facilitate, and enable social change. Application of a positive lens is intentionally an appreciative scholarly stance. It is a lens which begins with inquiry about what is generative, life-giving, and worth noticing and appreciating in the way that this social change process is working and in the outcomes it produces (Cooperrider & Whitney, 2005).

As the chapters will reveal, the use of this eye discloses multiple new insights about the outcomes of change processes, new insights about change and resources, process insights about generativity and agency, and a host of other patterns that help to unlock the mystery behind social change. Thus, in contrast to accounts of social change that concentrate on barriers to change or accounts of change resistance, use of a positive lens directs attention to features and dynamics of processes and states that foster the change process or amplify beneficial results from the social change process. The book explicitly builds on previous efforts to elaborate and complicate organizational research using a positive lens (e.g., Cameron & Spreitzer, 2011; Dutton & Ragins, 2007; Nelson & Cooper, 2007; Roberts & Dutton, 2009). Like the efforts that have preceded this one, application of a positive lens stretches the boundaries of what we are able to see as important in explanatory theories and what we imagine for practical interventions.

Stories of Positive Social Change Unlock Wisdom but Also Inspire Scholarly Imagination Regarding What Is Possible With Respect to Organizations and Social Change

The chapters that compose this book contain compelling narratives of social change. These narratives reveal patterns of processes and practices that make a difference in the scale, scope, and impact of social change in a variety of realms. While these accounts can be analyzed for what they imply about organizations and social change, they are also carriers of imagined possibilities for the roles that individuals and organizations could play in social change. The potency of the stories transcends what they unlock for explanatory accounts. Individually and collectively, the stories elevate a sense of hope and possibility about the promise and the potential for social change when analyzed and viewed from an organizational lens.

GOALS FOR THE BOOK AND PROCESS OF BOOK BUILDING

We began this book with three clear goals in mind. First, we wished to enrich theories and practice through applying a positive lens to the study of social change and organizations. Our assumption beginning this project was that the majority of cases on social change in organizational studies tended to invite inquiry into failed or less-than-satisfactory change efforts. Second, we aspired to provide deeper inquiry into the processes and forms of change agency (at both the individual and collective levels) that play a role in social change processes and outcomes. The focus on agency as manifest in and of social change processes spotlights how engagement of different actors in different contexts transforms or alters structures and processes in response to a problem (Emirbayer & Mische, 1998). A focus on different forms and impacts of change agents in social change processes celebrates the variability in these critical activities, and how they matter in change processes serves to both enrich theory and broaden applications to practice. Third, we sought to foster linkages across important issue contexts where social change was active and desired (e.g., sustainability, healthcare, poverty, and low-wage work), exploring synergies and possibilities for cross-fertilization between these domains where organizational processes and practices matter for the accomplishment of social change. The book seeks to integrate ideas that arise from often seg-regated pockets of theory and practice that operate in siloed domains of inquiry in organizational and policy studies.

In meeting these goals, we used a different kind of book-building strategy than is typically used for composing edited books. We aspired to create this book in a way that foster the building of bridges across siloed areas of inquiry, as well as facilitate collective exploration of the value of applying a positive lens to the domain of organizations and social change. Accordingly, we gathered all book authors at Boston University in March 2010 to share chapter outlines and to foster building and helping each other with the outlines as the central conference activity. We also had sufficient group and collective time to wrestle with the meaning and the value of applying a positive lens. As a result of this book-building process, we believe the elements of the book cohere and speak to each other at a level that is not typically observed in edited volumes. We hope that you the reader will agree and will benefit from this integrating activity.

BOOK ROADMAP

The book is divided into six parts. After an introductory chapter by the edi-tors (Part I), the next four parts are composed of four chapters each plus a fifth commentator chapter that highlights themes and observations derived from the chapter contributions. Part II illustrates different takes on the role and form of change agency illuminated by applying a positive lens to social change and organizations. Part III includes four chapters that address the crucial issue of the natural environment and sustainability. Part IV addresses a similarly critical issue of social change in the domain of health care. Part V contains chapters that address the important but often invisible issue of poverty alleviation and low-wage work. Part VI comprises a response by the editors to the application of the positive lens to the study of social changes and organizations. To preview each chapter and to see how it contributes to the overall theme of the book, we next present appreciative summaries.

APPRECIATIVE SUMMARIES

Chapter 2: *Social Change Agency under Adversity: How Relational Processes (Re)Produce Hope in Hopeless Settings.* In this chapter, Oana

Branzei draws from life story interviews, visual ethnographies, and archival sources that document the lives and contributions of two individuals designated as Sawa Heroes. Sawa Heroes are inspirational individuals nominated by Sawa World who have made a difference in eradicating poverty. Branzei identifies the relational processes used by these two effective change agents to initiate and accelerate social change through creation and replenishment of hope. Through her study of these two leaders, Branzei shows us that change agency is deeply relational and can be a potent source to foster change through activating moral, social, and relational energies. Her chapter details three core relational processes of relating, revising, and rotating that account for hope (re)production during social change. Her chapter elevates theoretical and practical possibilities of how to unleash hope through relational connections to change agents' pasts and futures.

Chapter 3: *Being a Positive Social Change Agent through Issue Selling.* In this chapter, Scott Sonenshein draws on issue-selling theory to examine agency for social change inside organizations that foster goodness both in processes used and outcomes generated in the efforts. Drawing on vivid stories of such agency, Sonenshein portrays how efforts of even a few individuals can broaden over time to effect larger change for social good in organizations. Two particular issue-selling processes are highlighted: those that widen and enrich dialogue, and those that mindfully reclaim dead issues when the organizational context shifts or when individuals can use different meanings to sell the same issue. In addition to processes, the stories elucidate the importance of broadening the traditional range of issue-selling outcomes beyond the instrumental benefits to the individual change agent to include organization and good for society. Through the development of an endogenous model of social change agency incorporating these processes and outcomes, this chapter enriches understanding of social change, and elaborates and extends theorizing of issue selling.

Chapter 4: *Social Entrepreneurs, Socialization Processes, and Social Change: The Case of SEKEM.* In their chapter, Tomislav Rimac, Johanna Mair, and Julie Battilana transport us to the SEKEM initiative in Egypt, which has been ongoing as a living experiment of social change since its inception in the late 1970s. The authors provide a detailed analysis of how an everyday practice of congregating, holding hands as a circle at the beginning and the end of the day, coupled with a sharing of grace and the day's work and plan, contributes to the ongoing institutionalization of social change. They detail how the circle as a socialization practice creates and recreates a sense of dignity, respect, and worth that symbolically and instrumentally enacts inclusion at the beginning and end of each day. This practice introduces people to new beliefs and behaviors that are central to adopting other aspects of the societal innovations that are part of SEKEM. Their chapter grounds and elaborates the importance of everyday practices that cultivate ways of interrelating that create reciprocity and energy, and that are central to the solidarity necessary for initiating and guiding divergent social change.

Chapter 5: *Power Beyond the Purse: Philanthropic Foundations as Agents of Social Change.* In this chapter, Debra Meyerson and Laura Wernick use two cases developed through rich field methodology, "Ed Ventures" and "Resource Generation," to explore the role of two different types of philanthropic foundations in social change—"venture philanthropy" and "grassroots, or community-based social justice philanthropy." An intriguing case comparison, both foundations are similar in their intentional departure from a traditional philanthropic approach of funding established organizations, while at the same time they are differentiated by their respective innovative approaches. The authors enrich theorizing in social change by explicating these approaches and associated processes. The "breadth approach" of philanthropy for social change, used by venture philanthropy, focuses on funding new organizations with the promise of scalability in the targeted areas of change and holding them to standard, more quantitative metrics of impact. By contrast, a "depth approach," represented by grassroots social justice philanthropy, focuses on funding local grassroots efforts and working with them to build community capacity in the targeted areas of change and track both more quantitative as well as affective metrics of impact.

Chapter 6: *Revealing Themes: Applying a Positive Lens to the Chapters on Change Agency.* The *Change Agency* part concludes with Erica Steckler and Jean Bartunek's commentary, in which they describe positive social change agency as involving "a focused effort to impart social change in order to improve well-being and advance the public good." The authors first discuss three competencies that the change agents in the preceding chapters demonstrate: overcoming adversity, discerning alternate possibilities, and managing tensions. Second, they explore several contextual aspects of change agency work, including socialization influences, the locus of change, the locale, and the temporality of change. Finally, they discuss the theoretical and empirical implications of these competencies and contextual aspects.

Chapter 7: *Hybrid Organizations as Agents of Positive Social Change: Bridging the For-Profit and Not-for-Profit Divide.* Andrew Hoffman, Krista Badiane, and Nardia Haigh direct our attention to the expanding existence of hybrid organizations which blend features of for-profit and not-for-profit organizations, and the critical role they play in fostering social and environmental change. These hybrid organizational forms are social change organizations. Hybrid forms are generative in terms of both social and environmental change through bringing new products, practices, and services to market that enhance societal well-being. The chapter introduces a sustainability-driven model that illuminates how these forms of organizations promote social change agency through making social change a major objective, creating mutually beneficial relationships with suppliers and supplier communities, employers, and customers, and through creating progressive interactions with market competitors and industry institutions. Their chapter invites serious consideration of how the emergence of this organizational form is catalyzing and institutionalizing new possibilities for social change.

Chapter 8: *Agency and Innovation in a Phase of Turbulent Change: Conservation in the Great Bear Rainforest.* Darcy Riddell, Ola Tjörnbo, and Frances Westley unfold a complex case of social innovation involving the emergence of collaboration among sectors engaged in a divisive and conflictual situation in the Great Bear Rainforest. Their detailed analysis of the phases of the social innovation process reveals multi-layered processes of individual and collective agency that created intentional change at the personal, interpersonal, and systemic levels. Their account highlights how agency that occurred at the individual level enabled three more meso-level (e.g., group/relational) processes, which, in turn, facilitated the development of a vision that fostered the creation of a system-wide coalition that enabled a range of concrete solutions. Their chapter explains six processes of individual and collective agency which reached inside the heads and hearts of individual change participants (e.g., through the creation of powerful personal narratives), and also stretched across previously intractable divides (e.g., through the humanizing of opponents), creating caring and trusting relationships that facilitated the discovery of solutions across differences. Their chapter identifies tolerance of conflict and uncertainty as a form of agency that enabled the co-creation of an inclusive and powerful positive vision and a collective focusing on solutions that were enacted through new institutional mechanisms. Their story showcases the complex and multi-level processes that undergird change of this scope, scale, and magnitude, and the power of intentional expression of positive forms of agency to move large-scale change in the direction of generative relationships and innovative solutions.

Chapter 9: *Practicing Sustainability: A Generative Approach to Change Agency.* Martha Feldman draws on practice theory to examine change agency for environmental sustainability. Using two examples of practicing sustainability—turning cars off while waiting at traffic lights and drying hands with paper towels—she explores the use and design of artifacts as a generative mechanism that enables change in everyday practices through attuning people to the environmental impact of their actions. In the case of hand drying, a sticker becomes an artifact that mediates change when affixed to dispensers with wording that illuminates the connection between the production of paper towels and trees, for example, "Remember...these come from trees." It is the attunement created in this connection between actions and the implications for the natural world that generates alternative possibilities for practicing sustainability such as using only one not two towels for hand drying. Her chapter enriches theorizing on social change in environmental sustainability by identifying artifacts as mediators of changes in individual practices and individual practices as mediators of change agency.

Chapter 10: *Connecting Sustainability Movements and Enterprises in Developing Economies: Building Networks and Capabilities.* Paola Perez-Aleman draws our attention to the efforts of small, local producers in developing economies and their efforts to meet globally determined standards for reducing environmental degradation and improving ecological sustainability. Taking the reform for sustainability in the coffee supply chain as an important case in point, she shows that the adoption of standards and conduct codes for greening the coffee supply chain by purchasers and consumers does not automatically translate into change in production practices. Importantly, change to sustainable production is enabled by the active creation of new networks such as associations and cooperatives that provide local indigenous coffee producers with access to critical know-how and capability-building support. Her chapter enriches theorizing on social change in environmental sustainability by identifying the mechanism of creating local networks and how they operate to build capabilities of indigenous producers for implementing sustainable practices.

Chapter 11: *Revealing Themes: Applying a Positive Lens to the Chapters on Environment and Sustainability.* The *Environment and Sustainability* part concludes with a commentary by Jennifer Howard-Grenville. Howard-Grenville begins by tracing the history of organizational research on environmental issues, calling attention to the "normative thrust" of work in this domain as well as the need to acknowledge the complexity of specific situations. She then identifies and unpacks four different processes of positive change agency that emerged from the preceding chapters: experimentation and example-setting, transformation and amplification, design and attunement, and connecting and supporting. Painting these four processes as distinct but not mutually exclusive, Howard-Grenville suggests that they may all be essential to enacting change in areas of environmental concern. Finally, she suggests two directions for future research: exploring when and in what contexts the four change processes result in positive outcomes and considering whether loss—for individuals and/or systems—is required to trigger positive change processes.

Chapter 12: *Hope as Generative Dynamic in Transformational Change: Creating and Sustaining "Collaborative Care" in the ThedaCare Health System.* Karen Golden-Biddle and Kathryn Correia describe how leaders and clinicians collaboratively and effectively transformed care in a medium-sized healthcare system that mutually benefited patients, their families, and society. Their inspiring account elucidates how hope acted as a generative dynamic that enabled transformational change by both activating beliefs that change can make a positive difference and acting on belief to make this change happen. Their theorizing locates the initiation and perpetuation of this change inside the organizational system and it documents how hope operated as a generative force in enabling and sustaining collective beliefs about possibilities and expectations about desired outcomes for patients that built and sustained trust. Their theory of systemic change in one health care system showcases how a community of persons can look clearsightedly at current situations and, through interactions and genuine concern for the human condition and through learning and experimenting, collaborate in producing inventive and creative organizational solutions that transform the provision of care.

Chapter 13: *Promoting Positive Change in Physician–Administrator Relationships: The Importance of Identity Security in Managing Intractable*

Identity Conflicts. In this chapter, Michael Pratt, Marlena Fiol, Edward O'Connor, and Paul Panico draw on identity theory to unpack the intractable identity conflicts (IICs) that can dominate physician–administrator relationships and how such conflicts can be managed. The authors use a synthetic case comprising their collective experiences and perspectives as academic, consultant, and practitioner to develop a more nuanced conceptual rendering of identity security and its practical import for addressing IICs. Their elaboration of identity security as compared with identity strength involves expansion of group members' horizons beyond their group as well as the possibility for holding dual or multiple identifications concurrently, for example, own group and superordinate identity. Their chapter enriches understanding of social change by incorporating identity dynamics as a key intergroup mechanism of change agency, as well as the practice of social change by encouraging the use of more than structural solutions in reforming healthcare.

Chapter 14: *Amplifying Resources and Buffering Demands: How Managers Can Support Front Line Staff in Loving Action for Each Child.* Rebecca Wells' chapter redirects appreciation of how to improve services for children with mental health issues through understanding how management can direct action to increase the engagement of front line staff. Her chapter focuses on how management can direct engagement of front line staff toward enhancing loving action for each child. Wells' framing directs attention to how management in child-serving organizations can feed and protect line staff's love of children through buffering demands that create staff burnout and amplifying resources that foster staff engagement. Through her model of how management can foster front line employees' loving actions on behalf of each child, she opens up a range of pathways by which managerial actions can create conditions that foster the "good" in staff action toward children as well as minimize the "bad."

Chapter 15: *Generative Change in Health Care Organizations: Co-Creating Health to Reduce Health Disparities.* In this chapter, Valerie Myers and Lynn Wooten draw on two in-depth case studies from their larger investigation of health disparities to disclose and develop the central role of relationships in improving maternal child health outcomes. Their use of the verb "co-creating" signifies the generative function of relationships illuminated and so richly evidenced in these cases. Not only do people form relationships, but the particular way of forming them brings out the best of everyone involved to change delivery practices that reduce disparities and promote health. These relationships, for example, within and cross-sector partnerships, were constituted in high quality connections and fostered collective resourcefulness among those involved. More generally, Myers and Wooten enrich understanding of social change by drawing our analytic attention to relational mechanisms and how, when generative in nature, they are at the "core" of organizational change that seeks societal impact by improving human lives.

Chapter 16: *Revealing Themes: Applying a Positive Lens to the Chapters on Healthcare.* The *Healthcare* part concludes with a commentary by Trish Reay, who reminds us that change initiatives in healthcare often fail during implementation due to a lack of understanding of healthcare settings. Drawing on the preceding chapters, Reay offers several insights into these settings. First, she stresses that while most change efforts aim to achieve positive outcomes, the cases presented in the book differ in that they focus on positive outcomes for the patients/clients rather than for the organization. Second, she identifies four key ways that the chapters collectively advance our knowledge of the positive process of change in healthcare: the potential of relationships to serve as sources of energy, the role of professional conviction as a catalyst, the blurred distinction between top-down and bottom-up change, and the importance of power dynamics. Reay ends the commentary by underscoring that positive examples of change in healthcare "are right under our noses, but we have to have the desire to look for them."

Chapter 17: *Positive Change by and for the Working Poor.* Carrie Leana and Ellen Kossek draw from their experience with interventions designed to address needs of the working poor to theorize (and implement) changes that will benefit this critical group of employees. Their chapter documents the criticality of understanding employment of the working poor in the United States, explaining and illustrating both a top-down and bottom-up approach to internal organizational changes. The top-down approach highlights the beneficial role of family-supportive supervisory behaviors. The bottom-up approach shows the potential benefits of employee-initiated collaborative job crafting. These authors conclude that meaningful change that will benefit the working poor must be multi-level (targeting both individuals and the workplace context) and multi-pronged (avoiding unidimensional change tactics). Further, their chapter complicates the link between invisible and visible organizational and supervisor practices and the improvement of situations for the working poor.

Chapter 18: *Building Organizations to Change Communities: Educational Entrepreneurs in Poor Urban Areas.* Christine Beckman and Brooking Gatewood investigate charter schools founded to create access to quality education for children in high poverty, urban communities. They examine five different resources used by charter schools in Oakland, California to assess their contribution to school legitimacy (measured as survival) and to school accountability (measured as student academic performance). Their findings show that high student performance is an important predictor of charter school survival; that is, achieving accountability becomes a predictor of legitimacy. High performance itself is best predicted by school formalization. However, they also find that partnerships are beneficial elements of charter success and survival, especially in the absence of other predictors such as high test scores, financial resources, and formalization. Their findings imply the existence of multiple viable pathways for social change within an impoverished community context, and highlight the importance of partnerships for success and survival for organizations lacking other core resources.

Chapter 19: *Navigating Change in the Company of (Dissimilar) Others: Co-Developing Relational Capabilities with Microcredit Clients.* Lisa Jones Christensen's chapter introduces us to a vivid case study of how one business school partnered with a microcredit provider through a student field project designed to address poverty alleviation in Nairobi, Kenya. The case focuses on the processes by which the business school students partnered with the microcredit provider and students from African Nazarene University to create an entrepreneurial training program for microcredit clients. The case illuminates how deliberate efforts to embed themselves in the context through co-location, reflective thinking, enacting care in knowledge creation, and cultivating humility in the engagement were essential for the bi-directional learning necessary for creating effective change at multiple levels, and over the short and long term. The Christensen chapter reminds us of the importance of sequencing events in a learning process to enable relational capability building and co-creating of solutions. Further, the analysis provides a detailed account of how processes of social embedding are actually accomplished in ways that are deeply human and personal and that serve to foster knowledge creation and programs that can meaningfully contribute to poverty alleviation.

Chapter 20: *The Stranger as Friend: Loan Officers and Positive Deviance in Microfinance.* In this chapter, Rodrigo Canales draws on his rich, multiyear study of microfinance institutions in Mexico to explain structural conditions that lead some loan officers (LL–letter of the law) to strictly adhere to a set of defined rules for lending decisions and others (SL–spirit of the law) to bend or choose not to enforce these rules. While all loan officers seek to perform well in the context of uncertainty in microfinance, it is their understanding of what comprises performing well that differentiates their approach. This difference emerges most vividly in the types of client relationships they create. Whereas LL loan officers seek to perform well by maintaining professional distance from clients, SL loan officers consider personal relationships an important means of performing well because they get to know rich "soft" information significant to clients' situations. This chapter enriches understanding of social change by explicating the significance of positive relationships in enabling SL loan officers to bend rules in a way that generates new resources and repertoires for both the clients and their own organizations.

Chapter 21: *Revealing Themes: Applying a Positive Lens to the Chapters on Poverty and Low-Wage Work*. Part V, *Poverty and Low-Wage Work*, concludes with a commentary by Jone L. Pearce. Pearce first points out that, although academics in other disciplines such as sociology have long attended to issues of poverty, organizational scholars have been slow to follow suit, resulting in a poor understanding of organizations that address poverty. Pearce then explores two key questions that could benefit from attention by those who study organizations: How can we know if poverty-related change has been successful? How can organizations balance formality (accountability) and flexibility to meet clients' complex demands? Finally, Pearce suggests that organizational scholars could make unique contributions to poverty policy while also adding new insights to existing theories of change.

THE INVITATION

We invite you to engage these chapters with eyes and hearts wide open to imagining how your theories and practices regarding social change could be enriched and enlivened. We hope your theorizing and methodological repertoires, including concepts, constructs, questions, insights, and methods, are broadened through engagement with the diversity of contexts, of social issues, and of theoretical frameworks applied in these chapters. At the same time, we hope the promise of applying a positive lens to ideas about social change is crystal clear. Let the inquiry into this important domain of scholarship begin!

REFERENCES

Aguilera, R. V., Rupp, D. E., Williams, C. A., & Ganapathi, J. (2007). Putting the s back in corporate social responsibility: A multilevel theory of social change in organizations. *Academy of Management Review, 32,* 938–963.

Argyris, C. (1957). *Personality and organization: The conflict between the system and the individual.* New York: Harper.

Blau, P. M., & Scott, W. R. (1962). *Formal organizations.* San Francisco: Chandler.

Bornstein, D. (2007). *How to change the world: Social entrepreneurs and the power of new ideas.* Oxford, New York: Oxford University Press.

Cameron, K., Dutton, J., & Quinn, R. (2003). *Positive organizational scholarship.* San Francisco: Berrett Koehler Publishers.

Cameron, K., & Spreitzer, G. (2011). *Handbook of positive organizational scholarship.* New York: Oxford University Press.

Carroll, A., & Buchholtz, A. (2009). *Business & society: Ethics, sustainability, and stakeholder management.* Mason, OH: South-Western Cengage Learning.

Cooperrider, D. L., & Whitney, D. (2005). *Appreciative inquiry: A positive revolution in change.* San Francisco: Berrett-Koehler Publishers.

Dees, J. G., & Elias, J. (1998). The challenges of combining social and commercial enterprise. *Business Ethics Quarterly, 8,* 165–178.

Dutton, J. E., & Ragins, B. (2007). *Positive relationships and organizations: Building a theoretical and research foundation.* Mahwah, NJ: Lawrence Erlbaum, Inc.

Emirbayer, M., & Mische, A. (1998). What is agency? *American Journal of Sociology, 103,* 962–1023.

Ghoshal, S. (2005). Bad organizational theories are destroying good management practice. *Academy of Management Learning and Education, 4,* 75–91.

Mair, J., & Marti, I. (2006). Social entrepreneurship research: A source of explanation, prediction, and delight. *Journal of World Business, 41,* 36–44.

Margolis, J. D., & Walsh, J. P. (2003) Misery loves companies: Rethinking social initiatives by business. *Administrative Science Quarterly, 48,* 268–305.

Mayo, E. (1945). *The social problems of an industrial civilization.* Oxford: School of Industrial Administration.

Nelson, D., & Cooper, C. (2007). *Positive organizational behavior.* London: Sage Publications.

Pascale, R., Sternin, J., & Sternin, M. (2010). *The power of positive deviance.* Boston: Harvard Business Press.

Post, J. (2004). *Business and society: Corporate strategy, public policy, ethics* (11th ed). York, PA: McGraw-Hill Inc.

Roberts, L. M., & Dutton, J. E. (Eds). (2009). *Positive identity and organizations: Building a theoretical and research foundation.* New York: Psychology Press/Routledge.

Selznick, P. (1949). *TVA and the grassroots.* Berkeley, CA: University of California Press.

Tribo, J., Surroca, J., & Waddock, S. (2010). Corporate responsibility and financial performance: The role of intangible resources. *Strategic Management Journal, 31*, 463–490.

Waddock, S. (2009). *Leading corporate citizens: Vision, values, value added* (3rd ed.). New York: McGraw-Hill.

Zald, M., & McCarthy, J. P. (1987). *Social movements in an organizational society: Collected essays*. New Brunswick, NJ: Transaction Press.

Part II

Change Agency

2

Social Change Agency Under Adversity: How Relational Processes (Re)Produce Hope in Hopeless Settings

Oana Branzei
University of Western Ontario

INTRODUCTION

Most theories of social change are inherently hopeful (Ziegler, 2009): social change is possible, despite constraints, setbacks, and discontinuities (Hallinan, 1997). This chapter goes beyond the intuitive argument that hope can, and often does, enable social change (Snyder & Feldman, 2000) to reconceptualize social change agency work as explicitly relational efforts to (re)produce hope—even in hopeless circumstances (Davis, 2006; Seelos & Mair, 2009). To do so, I borrow and build on Tichy's (1978, p. 165) original conceptualization of social change agency as deliberate, recurrent efforts by which agents carefully employ and deploy different tools and skills to challenge and reconcile incongruencies between their image of a better future and (often persistent) inequitable circumstances that hinder or slow down progress toward this vision.

My main goal is to explain the generative functions of hope in initiating and accelerating positive social change. "Hopeful images of the future … become powerful catalysts for change and transformation by mobilizing the moral, social and relational energies needed to translate vision into reality and belief into practice" (Ludema, Wilmot, & Srivastava, 1997, p. 1025). Hopeful thought increases awareness, acceptance, and adoption of specific tools and skills (Branzei & Peneycad, 2008).

Hope is an inclusive act (Block, 1986). Hoping people "gain a sense of being carried and supported by others ... even if there is no chance that they themselves will witness the hoped for scenario, in relationship they can carry the fulfillment of their hopes beyond their own existence" (Ludema et al., 1997, p. 1043). Because it draws together an ever expanding number of participants (Dauenhauer, 1986, p. 99) and taps into the fundamental relatedness of all humankind, relating opens life-giving opportunities for the self and others (Marcel, 1951). Inclusiveness fosters generativity: relational processes "provide humanity with new guiding images of relational possibility [and] build new social architectures for human organizing and action" (Ludema et al., 1997, p. 1017).

This chapter adopts Ludema and his colleagues' definition of hope as a fundamentally relational construct: "always engendered in relationship to an 'other,' whether the other be collective or singular, imagined or real, human or divine" (1997, p. 1026). Relationships are essential in (re)producing hope (Snyder, 1994). They instill, buffer, and recover hopeful thought in the face of barriers, setbacks, and even chronic failure (Snyder, 2000a,b); they can also stall or reverse the learning of hopeless thought (Rodriques-Hanley & Snyder, 2000). High-hope individuals at first replicate the successful social inter-relating they first observed from their childhood role models (Snyder, 1994; Snyder, 2000b); they later learn by interacting with, accepting, and internalizing the beliefs of other formative audiences.

This chapter reconceptualizes social change agency work as a relational process that can endogenously (re)produce hope, even in hopeless circumstances. I start with a review of theories of social change to clarify the so far under-studied role of hope in social change agency work. I then revisit two different streams of hope theorizing to explain how relational processes enliven hope. The positive psychology lens, well-developed by Snyder and his colleagues, views hope as an individual process whereby individuals cycle between *will* (a sense and affirmation of individual agency) and *ways* (pathways to reach specific goals) as they persevere in the face of obstacles; this "narrow" view of hope is methodologically rigorous (Magaletta & Oliver, 1999), but inherently self-centered and static (Carlsen, Landsverk-Hagen, & Mortensen, 2011): relationships matter only in so far as role models help restore individual hopeful thought or ward off hopeless thought. I start with Snyder's work to understand how an individual's role models may inform and inspire deliberate efforts to (re)produce hope. I then elaborate on the relational processes underpinning the generative function of hope building on Ludema, Wilmot, and Srivastva's (1997) argument that we cannot experience hope outside of relationships (Marcel, 1951). Hope is "born, nurtured and sustained in relationships" (Ludema et al., 1997, p. 1030), "often inspired when one receives sustenance or nurturance in a time of difficulty or of growth, ... also enkindled when one gives sustenance or nurturance to another" (Ludema et al., 1997, p. 1032). The qualitative analyses presented in this chapter start at the theoretical intersection between Snyder's "narrow" view and Ludema and his colleagues' "relational" view of hope. This chapter explains how different types of relational processes contribute to generating the hope needed to initiate and accelerate positive social change.

THEORIES OF SOCIAL CHANGE

The past five decades explained social change using two distinct lenses—economic and emancipatory. The economic lens views social change as (gradual or indirect) improvements in productivity (Yapa, 1996), typically enabled by the provision of resources such as aid, income supplements, consumer goods subsidies, or social services to help the disadvantaged overcome a severe and persistent lack of economic means (Coleman, 1971, p. 638). The emancipatory lens focuses on the "disciplined efforts of individuals as the essential resource that produces change" (Coleman, 1971, p. 645). Social change requires and relies on individual emancipation: individuals develop new aspirations, tools, and skills by continuously confronting and transforming their goals, beliefs, and personalities. Individual agency is attributed to several different processes—need for achievement for McClelland; thrift for Weber; and release from passivity, custom, or traditional authority for Sartre. Hope is a common (if often implicit) premise in emancipatory theories of social change: "revolutionary action brings a goal and the hope of achieving that goal" (Coleman, 1971, p. 644).

Recent studies challenge the dichotomy between economic and emancipatory lenses, arguing that social change agency often requires both (Drayton, 2009; Ziegler, 2009). Social change agents recognize economic, political, and discursive opportunities, mobilize resources, and interpret change processes. My working assumption is that individual efforts—especially the relational processes that (re)produce hope—constitute an important micro-foundation of social change agency work when other resources are in short supply; but the effectiveness of these individual efforts is contingent on both meso (i.e., organizations, associations, networks, interactions) and macro (i.e., political, economic, institutional, and societal) conditions (Bies, Bartunek, Fort, & Zald, 2007).

How Hope Works

Snyder's theory of hope shares the underlying positive motivation approach inherent in other positive psychology theories[1] to explain how individuals hope within and across situations. The central premise is that individuals replenish hopeful thought as part of goal pursuit (Snyder, Rand, & Sigmon, 2005, p. 257). High-hope people restore hope in the face of setbacks simply because they believe they can adapt to potential difficulties and losses; thus they keep setting goals for themselves, view obstacles as challenges, and focus on successes rather than failure (Snyder, 1994; Snyder, 2000, p. 40). Everyone can feel temporarily hopeless, yet acquiring hopeless thinking requires the simultaneous depletion of one's energy and drive to pursue goals and chronic failure in achieving one's goals (Rodriquez-Hanley & Snyder, 2000). The sooner an individual works to replenish her agency (i.e., by identifying relational sources of security, nurturance, and developmental identification) or one devises alternative pathways (i.e., by learning new skills, emphasizing volition, and avoiding overload), the more quickly one restores individual hope. The longer hopeless thought lingers, the more likely the demise of hopeful thought; this typically happens sequentially, through stages of rage, despair, and ultimately apathy (Rodriguez-Hanley & Synder, 2000).

This "narrow" theory of hope (Carlsen et al., 2011) clearly acknowledges that relationships (i.e., modeling by childhood caregivers and early formative audiences) influence individual hope states both within and across situations. Relationships help individuals sustain hopeful thought and bounce back from hopeless thought. Understanding how relational processes (re)produce hope is important to hope theorists because high-hope individuals are not narcissistic (Snyder, 1994) but community-oriented

---

[1] This "narrow" view of hope (Carlsen et al., 2011) is part of a larger family of related positive psychology approaches that includes optimist attributions (Seligman, 1991), optimistic expectations (Scheier & Carver, 1985), self-efficacy (Bandura, 1997), esteem (Hewitt, 1998), problem-solving (Heppner & Hillerbrand, 1991), and interpersonal relations (Snyder, Cheavens, & Sympson, 1997).

(Cheavens, Feldman, Gum, Michael, & Snyder, 2006). "Shared goals, when accomplished by a large group of people, accentuate the sense of positive emotions and meaning in the lives of the group members" (Snyder & Feldman, 2000, p. 407). But Snyder and his colleagues largely overlook how hope evolves as one gives and takes sustenance and nurturance in relationships.

Ludema and his colleagues view hope as a collective accomplishment, as public property rather than individual states. People construct "textured vocabularies of hope—stories, theories, evidence, and illustrations—that provide humanity with new guiding images of relational possibility" (Ludema et al., 1997, p. 1016, emphasis in original). This "broader" definition of hope is explicitly generative: the act of hoping becomes a resource "necessary to build new social architectures for human organizing and action" (1997, p. 1017). Hope is also "intensely relational" (Carlsen et al., 2011): hope not only emerges and grows in relationships but also "promotes the reconstruction of relationships in ways that conform to collective images of the good" (Ludema et al., 1997, p. 1021).

My starting assumption is that the (re)production of hope hinges on relational processes because such relational processes can sustain high hope for individuals (Snyder, 1994; Snyder, 2000b) and they bring people together to achieve goals that would be impossible for any one individual—"the person as part of a collective unit can experience … a sense of meaning on a far grander scale" (Snyder & Feldman, 2000, p. 408). These relational processes are important because they can create new relational possibilities, through "the merging of self-interest with the interests of others that occurs when people hope allows them to participate more fully in relationships" (Ludema et al., 1997, p. 1033).

This chapter elaborates the role of relational processes in social change agency work starting at the intersection between Snyder and his colleagues' positive psychology theory of hope and Ludema and his colleagues' argument for exploring the relational underpinnings of hope. My goal is twofold. I first seek to understand which types of relational processes are important for social change agency work, based on the vocabularies employed by social change agents. Then I explain how social change agents combine multiple relational processes to help (re)produce hope for self and others. The main contribution is a grounded reconceptualization of social change agency as tri-dimensional relational work that (re)produces hope, even in hopeless settings.

Method

Sample

I was interested in social change agency work under extreme adversity because hope is critically important in such settings (Davis, 2006; Seelos & Mair, 2009). My sampling frame included individual difference-makers who completed multiple positive social change projects, despite many obstacles and few economic resources (Drayton, 2009; Ziegler, 2009). After exploring several organizations and initiatives that celebrate such "heroes" (e.g., Aga Khan, Ashoka, BBC's World Challenge competitions, Schwab), I focused on Sawa Heroes, an organization that recognizes and connects "individuals from the world's poorest countries who ... help others and ... with little or no outside support or resources ... have made an incredible impact in lifting their communities out of extreme poverty" (Sawa World, 2008). Sawa Heroes are selected through a rigorous process, which includes two criteria relevant for this study: Sawa Heroes "can clearly explain how they developed their project and found effective solutions to reduce extreme poverty with little resources" and their "work continues to have a significant and growing impact in local communities [which] they are able to keep track of ... and share ... with a global audience." These selection criteria provide homogeneity in the sample because the individual efforts of each Sawa Hero constitute an essential micro-foundation of their social change agency work and the influence of external contingencies was minimal within and across Sawa Heroes (Bies, Bartunek, Fort, & Zald, 2007)—that is, each Sawa Hero worked largely with their own skills and tools (Ticky, 1978), with few economic resources, organizations, or associations; they also worked in poor countries, having few local institutions to support their work; the platform organization provided a portal and networking opportunity to each other, and visibility of their work in the international community, but did not offer any economic or organizational resources. Publicly available documentation of the social agency work in situ, including summaries of social change projects and short video ethnographies, offered a quick and valuable introduction to sixteen different Sawa Heroes.

This chapter has two protagonists, Nadia Kanegai and Robert Kalyesubula, two Sawa Heroes. Both Nadia and Robert are internationally recognized for their social change agency work. Both participated in the September 2009 Connecting for Change (http://www.connectingforchange.ca), a forum that "brings together innovators from the business, social and philanthropic sectors to build connections and understanding about how to work together to create sustained social change."

Nadia Kanegai

Nadia Kanegai, who holds a masters in education science and has risen to occupy senior posts in both for-profit and non-profit organizations, was recognized by Sawa for her work with women, children, and marginalized constituencies in rural communities in Vanuatu. During the last 18 years, Nadia Kanegai has used her own salary and holidays to support community-based projects which directly touched over 10,000 lives. Nadia provided job training for 2,000 shopkeepers and taxi drivers; job skills to 1,000 single mothers and troubled youth; nutritional education for 5,000 women in rural communities; education for 1,000 children of low-income families; and recreational activities for 1,000 communities.

Robert Kalyesubula

A medical doctor and founder and executive director of the Nakaseke Community Development Initiative (NACODI) in Luwero (60 km from Kampala), Robert Kalyesubula was recognized by Sawa for his vision to create a fully self-sustainable program for his rural healthcare model and implement it across Uganda.[2] Robert also improved more than 10,000

---

[2] NACODI is a community based organization in Uganda that seeks to empower vulnerable groups in resource limited settings through innovative sustainable community based solutions. "To this end, we care and support people leaving with HIV-AIDS (PLWAs) together with orphans and other vulnerable children (OVC). We now have a medical center providing care for over 120 PLWAs and provide medical services to over 1,800 general patients per year. We have trained 66 community nurses who are currently working in over 7 Districts in Uganda providing care to thousands of Ugandans mostly in rural communities. With a grant from the Stephen Lewis Foundation (SLF) in 2006/2007 we supported 30 OVCs with income generation projects (IGA) in form of cows, start-up capital, chicken rearing, crop gardens and pigs in addition to medical care and school support (school fees, books, uniform, shows and lunch fees). An additional 40 families received a piglet each as start up support for poverty eradication from a small grant. In order to increase awareness and promote advocate for vulnerable members of the community, NACODI has 6 community support groups that work with the community healthworkers. The groups conduct shows, drama and sing songs that attract the community members to come and listen to messages on HIV prevention, care for PLWAS and OVCs, income generation and poverty eradication. It was therefore not so surprising that NACODI was voted the best performing CBO in Nakaseke District for the year 2006/2007 and 2007/2008 by the district NGO forum" (Kalyesubula, 2009).

lives. He provided medical care for over 6,000 HIV/AIDS patients in iso-lated communities; trained 73 nurses and volunteers in remote home care; offered livelihood means (a plot of land with corn and pigs) to 50 vulner-able families; built a school where 30 orphans are sponsored to attend; and organized health awareness education campaigns via theater plays for many communities.

Data

Early theorizing on social change agency (Tichy, 1974, 1978), the construc-tion of high-hope identities (McAdams, 1993), and the textured vocabular-ies of hope (Ludema et al., 1997) all emphasize "the stories we tell ourselves and others." These narratives may not always be true (McDermott & Hastings, 2000, p. 194; Rindova, Barry, & Ketchen, 2009) but are essential building blocks in my quest to understand how social change agents use "linguistic and moral resources ... to convert dreams into reality and pos-sibilities into practice" (Ludema et al., 1997, p. 1022). The importance of narratives as resources for action is well-accepted in organizational theory (Lounsbury & Glynn, 2001). Such relational vocabularies are also critical for broadening our evolving understanding of hope (Carlsen et al., 2011).

I first got to know Nadia and Robert virtually. I sampled their first-hand narratives from multiple sources (publicly available sources such as media articles, blogs, video ethnographies, speeches) and reviewed public accounts by people they had helped. We then met at the September 2009 Connecting for Change forum, where both Nadia and Robert volunteered deeply personal life-story narratives about themselves and their work and had also received substantial media coverage. I supplemented this data with in-depth interviews and several follow-ups. With their permission, I triangulated multiple data sources and re-analyzed their own narratives to isolate critical incidents (both setbacks and successes). For each criti-cal incident I developed a multisource summary account of their social change agency work and then looked for causal patterns, focusing on the role of relational processes in their work (Table 2.1).

Analyses

The narratives portray social change agency work as an inherently con-tinuous endeavor, consistent with earlier arguments that "when people

TABLE 2.1

Sample and Data

Social change agency episodes	Data sources	
	Episode-specific	Common
Nadia Kanegai		
Banks—*Telephone*	Press releases; local media.	Video-ethnography & profile, Sawa Web site
Luganville—*Group training*	Journal; local stories.	Life-story interview, Sept. 2009
Ambae—*Commercial complex*	Journal; local stories.	
Association—*Women in politics*	Online archival sources and association reports.	Public speech, Sept. 2009
Medical Clinics—*Solar power*	Media and online blogs.	Follow-up interview, Sept. 2009
Morris Ben Joseph—*Reintegration*	Video interview with Moris Ben Joseph; video interviews with youth.	Model validation, July 2009
		Phone interviews, Nov. 2010
Robert Kalyesubula		
Piglets—*HIV patient*	Online blogs, Web site, multiple stories of this experience.	Video-ethnography & profile, Sawa Web site
Cows & Bulls—*Income generation*	Local stories and reflections on why the project was unsuccessful.	Video-clips & media interviews (2009–2010) Blogs (2009)
Project Set-up—*Individual ownership*	Blogs with different examples; reflection on what made these successful.	Life-story interview, Sept. 2009 Public speech, Sept. 2009 Radio & TV interviews, Canada, Sept. 2009
Volunteering—*Individual problems*	Personal reflections. Follow-up on specific examples of problems and solutions.	Follow-up interview, Sept. 2009 Model validation, July 2009 Phone interviews, Nov. 2010

hope, their stance is not only that reality is open, but that it is continually becoming.... hoping people prepare the way for possible futures to emerge" (Ludema et al., 1997, p. 1035). The critical incidents I isolated and analyzed were not seen as discrete events, but rather as natural transitions (Adam, 1990; Bates, 2006)—for example, Nadia felt she kept working to meet the same need for different communities: "and then, I continue in other areas." Robert felt that he kept working with the same community to meet different needs: "then you know that it's time for you to go and start something else."

Relationships were an important source of continuity in Nadia's and Robert's narratives: although their social change agency work kept evolving as they developed new tools and skills (Tichy, 1978), both Nadia and Robert deliberately replicated several relational patterns that gave meaning and consistency to their efforts over projects and over time. My analyses of Nadia's six and Robert's four social change agency episodes identified seven relational themes, each recurrent across multiple episodes.

FINDINGS

One theme, *modeling*, was shared among the three relational processes and consistent with received wisdom in the theory of hope: as Snyder and his colleagues' hope theory would predict, Nadia and Robert initially mirrored their childhood caregivers and formative audiences. These patiently coached the young Nadia and Robert how they could help others (even before they could fully understand the meaning of their actions). Modeling also had a pervasive and persistent influence on their later work as well. Both Nadia and Robert periodically referred back to their role models and contrasted their efforts in each consecutive social change agency episode to the earlier examples set by Nadia's grandmother and Robert's mentor, Ray Barnett.

I iterated between the data and the theory to identify six additional relational themes: *Morphing, Mapping, Moral Dialogue, Moral Vision, Mutuality,* and *Mobilization*. Table 2.2 defines and illustrates each of the seven relational themes. I then examined sequences and complementarities among different themes and identified three relational processes, each anchored by modeling but also uniquely described by two other distinct themes: (1) **Relating**—social agents kept going back and forth to their role model through time to (re)affirm their sense of purpose; (2) **Revising**—social agents periodically (re)focused on deeply internalized values and themes to help infuse the future with generative power (Ludema et al., 1997, p. 1039); and (3) **Rotating**—social agents shared and spread their hope to others by emphasizing mutuality of purpose and mobilizing others to initiate and accelerate social change projects. Because modeling underpins all three relational processes, I introduce this relational theme first. Then I explain how the remaining six themes endogenously (re)generate hope through these distinct relational processes.

TABLE 2.2

Relational Themes and Processes

Nadia Kanegai	Robert Kalyesubula	Definition	Relational Themes	Relational Processes	Definition	Example
"If you respect and if you help other people, you are recognized by the elders, ... it gives motivation when they recognize that you do things for them." (Sept. 2009)	"When I got empowered to be a doctor through the help that I got, I knew that really I had to do something also to try and address the problems that were there." (Sept. 2009)	Repeated reference to role models (childhood care-givers and formative audiences)	*Modeling*	*Relating*	Social agents go back and forth through time and refer to role models which provide a relatively stable anchor as they undertake social change agency work.	"I would sit back and observe them, you know, observing the community and my grandma. And, we would be talking in the evening around the fire and she would say; oh, I saw something today that I need to help. At first I didn't pick up because I was so young, but as years went by I picked it up because I could feel it myself because it touched my heart. [....] When I visit people, I go around and I see things. And, you can see very clearly. If you have a heart to help, to contribute to the community, instantly it will come." (Nadia explains how she relates back and forth to the example set by her grandmother.)
"As years went by I picked it up because I could feel it myself because it touched my heart [....] I go around and I see things." (Sept. 2009)	"Role models also give you independence. And, of course, it's a different generation and a different problem all the time" (Sept. 2009)	Deliberate efforts to understand who needs help & what help is needed	*Morphing*			
"I call him. ... He actually calls me [....] And, I always sit by his side and learn from him." (Sept. 2009)	"Do I draw from the experience of having had Ray Barnett come? It always inspires me. I always think about that." (Sept. 2009)	Comparing one's way against the example/advice of role models	*Mapping*			

continued

TABLE 2.2 CONTINUED

Relational Themes and Processes

Nadia Kanegai	Robert Kalyesubula	Definition	Relational Themes	Relational Processes	Definition	Example
"I just tendered my resignation; sorry, I'm not going to be in this committee. I've decided it's against my values; thank you for giving me the opportunity." (Sept. 2009)	"I ask myself what have I done to make someone else's life better. So, that's how I reflect [....] And, yes, I reflect on [my own], but I also always engage the community." (Sept. 2009)	Ultimate concerns which sustain and give meaning to life and transcend transitory experience	*Moral Dialogue*		Social agents identify and leverage the moral foundations of their social change agency work.	"I ask myself what have I done to make someone else's life better. So, that's how I reflect [....] And, yes, I reflect on [my own], but I also always engage the community. And, we do evaluations and the evaluations are by the community [....] Other problems are going to come. Other people will say you are thinking too much, but this is [about] the problems that have come. And, you react to the problems that have come and you sit with the community and reflect back." (Robert compares the cows & bulls with the piglets project.)
"We concentrate on our values, ... respecting the elderly; helping them when they need one or they need assistance. ... these things are the most valuable." (Sept. 2009)	"You can never guarantee the sustainability; but if you have the community at your hand, they will always look back and say, oh, why did we do this and why did we fail in this [....] the solutions will come later." (Sept. 2009)	A deeper and broader base of wisdom, which infuses images of the future with generative power	*Moral Vision*	Revising ↑		

	Mutuality		
"The grassroots, the people. Sit down with them. That is when you know exactly what the needs are." (Sept. 2009) "You see how they participate ... they will be all the time asking you questions and coming attached to you." (Sept. 2009)	"You have to belong to a community. You have to understand them in order to give them the solutions." (Sept. 2009)	Identifying a deep connection, often based on similar formative experiences	

Mobilization → **Rotating**

"The greatest thing you can do is to have someone take over your responsibility and learn what you can do and they do it on their own." (Sept. 2009)	Nurturing this deep connection to co-create the future	Social agents initiate and accelerate different projects by forming new relationships (which eventually replace them in each project).	"And, at the end ... I gave them a little bit of money to start their association and off they went. They flew like a bird. And, that was brilliant. And, now, they do things on their own. I just go in there once in a while [....] If you need help, give me a call[....] So, now, they're doing it themselves and it's a multiplying effect [....] I slowly let go. And then, I continue in other areas." (Nadia reflects on the success of the Luganville project.)

Modeling

"Children truly hunger for models of hope" (Snyder, 2000b, p. 34), and one important way is by taking others' views and examples. Hope theorists agree on the relevance of two distinct relationships: childhood role models and formative audiences. These often complement (Snyder, 1994; Snyder et al., 2005), and can even compensate for delays in the natural learning of hopeful thought in early childhood (Snyder, 2000b). "Caregivers play many significant roles—mentor, nurturer, fortifier and instructor—in imparting pathways and agentic thinking. Without this mentor, a child can feel that there is no one to 'show the way'" (Rodriguez-Hanley & Snyder, 2000, p. 44). As the child becomes the instigator of specific actions, childhood caregivers and formative audiences help the child formulate agentic thoughts by drawing attention to their ability to "author" their own goals and then to devise paths to meet these goals.

Modeling was a central and recurrent theme in Nadia's and Robert's narratives. Both emphasized the relational aspects of modeling: after observing first-hand how their role models related to others, they were driven to form and replicate similar bonds over time. As an orphan displaced in post-conflict Uganda, Robert met his life-time mentor, Ray Barnett, in 1984 (CNN.com, 2010) after he had dropped out of school. Robert pursued his dream to become a medical doctor (he was one of only three nephrologists practicing in Uganda), but Ray's example motivated him to return to his natal village, where he kept looking for every opportunity to give back to others; among his social change projects, he sponsored 30 orphans (like himself) by providing education and community. For Nadia, the time spent with her grandmother kept motivating her to help others:

> I spent a lot of time with my grandmother. And, my grandmother would take me around, taught me ... to respect the elderly, taught me things that I would do to help communities ... helping other people is something that ... I grew up into it. And, when my grandmother told me when we were sitting around the fire one evening said, 'to live is to help others'. ... I sort of moved around with her everywhere she went. I saw the things that she would do. And, I would, sort of, do the same things to help the community when I was young. [These] grounded values ... brought up myself to be in this way.

Modeling was a recurrent theme, which anchored and connected three processes: *Relating, Revising,* and *Rotating*. Figure 2.1 visualizes modeling as a common origin which grounds hopeful thought in the example

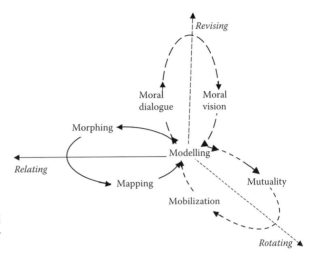

FIGURE 2.1
A tri-dimensional model
of social change agency
work.

of one's early role models, as proposed by Snyder and his colleagues. Modeling is essential to the endogenous (re)production of hope because it facilitates transitions among these three relational processes—either to restore confidence in one's social change agency work (for example, when the social change agent lost track of their core values, relating back to one's role models prompted **Revising** by engaging in *Moral dialogue* and/or rearticulating their *Moral vision*) or to initiate or accelerate action on deeply internalized values (for example, relating back to one's role models encouraged **Rotating** from one project to another and the formation of new relationships through *Mutuality* and *Mobilization*).

Relating

Modeling

Modeling was the starting point for both Robert and Nadia and a recurring theme in how they related to others over time. Modeling kept alive their will to help others (Snyder et al., 2000, p. 257; Snyder, Irving, & Anderson, 1991, p. 287), but also gave them the independence to find their own way to do so. Robert explains: "Do I draw from the experience of having had Ray Barnett come? It always inspires me because whenever I remember what I could have been and what I am today, I always think about that.… I always draw from that inspiration that he was able to come and make that difference." However, precisely how Robert chose to make a difference kept evolving over time: "Now, it is my time to make that difference [but] the current problems of my community are actually different."

Morphing

Rather than simply mirroring the social change agency work of their role models, both Robert and Nadia made deliberate efforts to understand who needed their help and what help was needed. To Nadia, this understanding came gradually and naturally, as a seamless extension of earlier modeling her grandmother: "I would sit back and observe them, you know, observing the community and my grandma. And, we would be talking in the evening around the fire and she would say, oh, I saw something today that I need to help. At first I didn't pick up because I was so young, but as years went by I picked it up because I could feel it myself because it touched my heart. ... When I visit people, I go around and I see things. And, you can see very clearly. If you have a heart to help, to contribute to the community, instantly it will come." Robert shared the same feeling: "I think most of it is instinctive. It comes with time."

Mapping

Both Nadia and Robert habitually reflected on their social change agency work, comparing and contrasting their efforts with the approach they initially modeled and had deeply internalized. Morphing was important, but always referenced their earlier role models, and the internalized values developed in their childhood. Nadia related back to her grandmother who is no longer alive: "For me I relate back all the time. ... I'm in my early forties and I still relate back. And, it's very vivid in my mind. ... It's like a map of my life. So, when I do something, I relate back to see am I on track? ... if my grandma was alive, would she, you know, give me the advice to say, yes, you are on track or no, you are not on track. Sometimes I did things, I said, oh, maybe I'm not on track. ... And, I said to myself, no, I'm not in the right place. It was because I looked back and I saw how my grandma was advising me, encouraging me to mix with the elderly, encouraging me to follow my uncles and help them out." Robert similarly relates back to his mentor, taking every opportunity to check-in and spend time together, so he can keep learning from him: "I always go back to [Ray Barnett]. I call him. I learn from him. ... He actually calls me ... I'm one of those special people who always come to celebrate at the anniversaries. And, I always sit by his side and learn from him." Both Nadia and Robert held frequent encounters with their role models. Many of these encounters were imaginary: the agents evoked past interactions and reflected back on the advice they had received at earlier points in their life to map and remap their current work relative to these initial goals (will and ways). These maps were not constraining: both Nadia and Robert kept growing in different directions, and taking new projects; however, relating back and forth through time to their early role models provided useful guidance about which projects were particularly worthwhile as well as why they ought to keep doing social change agency work. Essentially, mapping (re)kindled the original hopefulness they had experienced by being helped and helping others, and sustained hopeful thought when the going got tough.

Revising

Revising became necessary when social change agents felt they were no longer on track—typically because mapping identified a discrepancy between their efforts and the (evoked) advice of the role models. In such cases, social change agents fell back on the formative relationships that helped scaffold their hopeful thoughts, and reflected on the deeply internalized values that motivate their agency work, consistent with Ludema and his colleagues' emphasis on the moral dimension of hope (1997, p. 1036). The analyses surfaced two relational themes that enlivened hope—social change agents *dialogued* with themselves, (re)establishing their own source of hope and meaning and drawing on this source to (re) kindle the will to help others; or they sought to engage themselves and others in (re)imagining the future, through *Moral vision*.

Moral dialogue sustained social change agents as they avoided or overcame setbacks by helping them (re)focus on broader and deeper relational possibilities (Ludema et al., 1997). For Nadia, moral dialogue revolved around respect for the elders, which she considers the foundation of her growth; she valued and safeguarded this foundation because it helped restore her motivation for social change agency work: "The core in our society is the values that we have. You know, we have responsibilities in the society. As young children all the time we need to respect the people; we need to carry out the responsibilities as per expectation of society.... you do things out of your way to help the society.... Those became the foundation of my growth in my society."

Moral vision is an act of hoping that draws on the past to (re)imagine what the future can bring, dually motivated "by anticipations of the future and by the question of what makes the future possible. Future is then found in the past and possibilities in what has been" (Moltmann, 1991, p. 265). For Nadia and Robert, (re)imagining the future was a relational endeavor. They worked closely with the communities to understand what the future could bring and how past activities, resources, and people might work together to realize this possibility. Robert illustrates how relationships enabled moral visioning by recalling what worked and what did not work in the past: "So, we sat back and said, what should we do? Then people said you need to give smaller, individual income generation activities tailored to those particular people's needs. They identified the people. They [contacted] the people. Let them tell you what they want to do.... And, when we did that and gave it to the individuals, they flourished, but we learnt a lesson." "It's not that we have all the answers all the time," Robert further explained, "I can't even tell you today what will happen tomorrow, but what I know is that we have created systems that [help us] to be here today. And, our programs continue."

Rotating

Communities were often ready for social change—but social change remained latent because there were no outsiders willing to help and no insiders willing to try. Robert recalls "that if you don't do anything about it, then no one else will do anything about it." Nadia and Robert drew on their own role models as they searched for "even more vital possibilities" (Ludema et al., 1997, p. 1035), consistent with Kast's (1991, p. 136) suggestion that "by hoping, we walk toward a light that we do not see but sense somewhere in the darkness of the future."

One of Nadia's narratives vividly illustrates that she deliberately rotates in and out of projects: "That's only Santo, a thousand five hundred. On Ambae there's another thousand.... Now, Ambae is concluded.... and then, the last one would be Tafea, the group of islands in the south. Then I've completed my mission in the different areas." Nadia clarifies that her role is to initiate and accelerate, but neither substitute nor complete, others' social change agency work: "So, today, they have the market house. They have the shop. They have the restaurant or the food area. And, it's making money. It's self sustaining even though I had to start them, to show them how to record their money, how to place the order for the goods, how to do the cooking. … that was where the training came in. And, now they flourished." Nadia further explains how she decides when it is time for her to let others take over and continue her work. "How do I know that it's coming to an end? It's when I train somebody to take over … I'm not that capable of doing it, then I slowly let go; but, I still hold their hand until I know that they can fly on their wings and their wings are strong to fly. I can't let them fly on their own. But, now, with Santo, Ambae, they're flying up in the sky. Yeah, so, it's great. And, it's great satisfaction."

Modeling reminded Nadia and Robert that they had once been selected and groomed to the task by their role models and motivated them to actively search for the right people, as Robert explains: "your task will be finding that right person to do that. And, usually, there is that person. … there's usually that connection. You find that right person who's going to do that work, who has that contact with that community."

Two additional relational themes explained how Nadia and Robert rotated in and out of specific projects. The first theme referred to *Mutuality*, which was critical to initiating new projects—they identified "the right people" based on a deeply felt sense of shared purpose and reciprocated personal affinity. The second theme dealt with *Mobilization*, an important step for accelerating and eventually passing on and/or letting go of a given project.

Mutuality. A deep sense of connection based on past experiences and/ or a shared purpose (often both) were starting conditions for recruiting others and working with them to create a better future. The right people to join forces with on a new project are those "who usually have someone with a similar problem"—which for Robert meant "they have an orphan. They've had an experience and they have that commitment to know because they can identify … Beyond their gratification, they have that thing within themselves that they want to help." Robert further explains that it typically took him some time to "see it. You see it after dealing with them over a long time." Such mutuality helped by tapping into a shared and deeply internalized will for social change, even when the way to accomplish the desired change was unclear or demanding, as Robert illustrates: "But, if someone has never had an experience, it's usually very difficult to impress it upon them because most times we do what we do because of the experiences we went through. Maybe if my dad was around, I would not be doing these things, but I grew up as an orphan. I dropped out of school at one time. And, so, I can relate to orphans. I know the problems they have. And, if I can advocate for them, yes, because I know. And, when I go and talk to them I tell them, yes, you have a disadvantage, but here, we're offering you an opportunity. And, they listen."

Mutuality is quickly and often intuitively discovered. For Robert, the "right person" was "usually that person who belongs to that community and probably had something that attracted them to find that problem in the first place and have a vision to want to do something about it." For Nadia, "It's the relationship. You know, some people … have a relationship with you for the sake of the project to be achieved, but it's not a genuine relationship. A genuine relationship builds a very strong foundation. … When there is a fake relationship because that is my objective. I've got to achieve that and I'm going for that. And, I'm just setting up a relationship with you because I want to achieve that. That won't work."

Mutuality is inherently and intensely relational—it is about the connection between the agent and the "right person," rather than the tools and skills that either may be able to bring to the table. As Nadia eloquently explains: "You don't follow somebody because somebody has a degree because it will take you nowhere. You follow your heart … that says this is the person. And, always you'll go right. And, I've done that so many times. I've never gone wrong yet. Maybe one day, but to date I haven't gone wrong." Mutuality can only be discovered by letting oneself get very close to others in the first place. Robert, for example, worked with "these fellow people … on a daily basis." Similarly, Nadia was getting "back to the grassroots, the people. Sit down with them. … That's why I always make an effort to go there at least six times a year. If I can make it more than that, fine, but if I can't, my minimum is six times a year."

Mobilization explains how relationships can accelerate social change agency work. A vivid illustration of mobilization comes from one of Nadia's training programs which eventually provided skill training to more than 4,000 women in Vanuatu. Nadia worked daily with smaller cohorts of several hundred women: "we did that for four months continuously. One month, training, the following month, practical. … By the third month these people completed their practical. Now, they can go out and do their little businesses while the second group goes in for their practical." As soon as the first batch of trainees completed their full program,

Nadia enlisted them to guide the next cohort through their practical; this enabled Nadia to work with more groups and to move on faster to the next phase of the project.

Robert makes a similar point. For him, relationships were more important than the project itself because relationships helped agents move toward the future they wanted: "you can never guarantee the sustainability, but I think if you have the community at your hand, they will always look back and say, oh, why did we do this and why did we fail in this. And then, the solutions will come later." Robert further explained that mutuality precedes and enables mobilization by reaching to "the emotion of the people.... Once someone sees that you want to care and you're paying attention, you want to listen to their problem, then they will tell you.... And, getting people to air out their views is really important. And, once they start it becomes familiar. And, when they know you are willing to listen, they volunteer their problems .... So, it is a cycle which you have to work at to create."

HOW RELATIONAL PROCESSES (RE)PRODUCE HOPE

There is no shortage of examples of social change agency. Well-respected institutions like the Aga Khan, Ashoka, and Schwab explicitly recognize and publicize outstanding examples of positive social change. There is also no lack of introspection: many change agents have written memoires (Yunus, 2008), published collections of speeches (Aga Khan, 2008), or collaborated closely with researchers to document ongoing case studies (e.g., Seelos & Mair, 2009). All of these provide us with an intuitive appreciation for the role hope may play in initiating and accelerating social change. However, systematic theorizing on the role of hope in social change agency has not kept pace with practice (Drayton, 2009). Several researchers have noted a larger theoretical gap in understanding the micro-processes of social change agency work (Hjorth & Steyaert, 2010; Ziegler, 2009). This chapter takes one step toward addressing this gap by providing a thick description of hope-full social change agency work. Specifically, it enriches theories of social change agency work with specific relational themes and processes and explains how these may endogenously sustain and restore hope in the face of setbacks.

Contribution

The main theoretical contribution is a relational understanding of social change agency work: three distinct relational processes periodically overlap and intertwine to (re)produce hope. The findings offer a theoretical combination and elaboration of two theoretical lenses on hope—one well-developed but largely under-relational and a competing but underdeveloped perspective which portrays hope as an inclusive and generative process. The combination portrays hope as a deeply relational engine of human organizing toward better, if often highly uncertain, futures.

This elaboration is important in at least two ways. First, it develops the intersection between two different approaches of theorizing hope to anticipate and advocate an explicitly relational understanding of hope in organization studies (Carlsen et al., 2011). Although the present effort is limited to understanding how hope influences social change agency work, the relational themes and processes emerging from the data could be operationalized and tested as more general sources of hope (Magaletta & Oliver, 1999); this approach could build on, and enrich, the individual hope state approach promoted by Snyder and his colleagues. They also provide an application and illustration of several conceptual points introduced earlier by Ludema and his colleagues in their 1997 *Human Relations* theoretical review piece, the only relational approach to hope theorizing in over a decade. In so doing, this chapter suggests that social change agency work requires and relies on hope—in some cases only on hope (Coleman, 1971; Davis, 2006). By isolating other factors, this study takes a first step to suggest that relational processes can endogenously (re)produce hope. Specifically, hope is (re)produced in three distinct ways: by relating back and forth through time to one's earlier role models; by revising one's moral ground in and through relationships with others; and by rotating in and out of projects in order to identify and nurture future role models. These three processes are self-referential, in that they cycle back to deeply internalized values and advice which triggered social change agency work in the first place, and guide it through time. However, these three processes are also "life-giving [constantly] moving persons in the direction of transcending the status quo" (Ludema et al., 1997, p. 1038). This generative function of relational processes, I argue and show, enables social change agency work by (re)kindling hope.

Second, reconceptualizing social change agency work as relational possibility draws explicit attention to how social relationships transform our reality and move us toward imagined, but uncertain futures. Prior work showed that small actions can amplify into "something much greater than the originators of the change or the actors taking the amplifying actions intended" (Plowman et al., 2007, p. 519). Relational processes provide an important explanation for why such generative processes happen: social change agents work to nurture and replenish relational possibilities; they do not seek to effect positive social change on their own, nor is social change per se their ultimate goal. Their actions are instead anchored by a deeper sense of relational possibilities and a clear pattern of intertwining relational processes to (re)produce hope, one relationship at a time. The focus on relationships and relational possibilities complements the emancipatory view of social change agency work in general (Coleman, 1971; Tichy, 1978) and more recent arguments that individual emancipation is an important ingredient in all aspects of social action, especially positive social change (Rindova et al., 2009). Relational processes, albeit so far largely overlooked, can add explanatory power to these theories, and work collectively toward the larger projects of developing "textured vocabularies of hope" in organizational studies (Carlsen et al., 2011; Ludema et al., 1997).

Limitations

The findings are subject to several limitations. Conceptually, this chapter stays within the positive range (building and growing hope, Snyder, 2000a) rather than its negative range (i.e., the demise of hope, Rodriguez-Hanley & Snyder, 2000). This chapter does not explain why high-hope individuals may think, feel, or act differently than low-hope individuals; it simply offers one intriguing starting point for understanding how high-hope individuals create new relational possibilities. Empirically, I rely on two positively deviant cases—agents who succeed despite the odds—in part because I expect hopeful thought to play a greater role in such social change journeys and in even greater part because positively deviant agents have much to teach us about whether or how hope propels social change when other means may be scarce (Seelos & Mair, 2009). Furthermore, this chapter views social change primarily through the narratives of individual agents, as they tell and re-tell different interventions; I rely on archival sources, media, blogs, and accounts by others, whenever possible, but my analyses are mainly focused on how individuals approach social change agency work.

FUTURE RESEARCH

The focus on relational possibilities can enrich the rapidly growing literature on positive social change (Hjorth & Steyaert, 2010; Rindova et al., 2009), but much more remains to be done. Future research needs to take a closer look at how hope drives different paths to positive social change, especially when other resources are scarce (Davis, 2006). We also need better theories of communal hope (Cheavens et al., 2006; Snyder & Feldman, 2000), which remains largely untapped in research and practice, yet offers an important engine of positive social change. In so doing, we can collectively begin to fulfill the great promise hope theory might hold "for the many, rather than the few" (Snyder & Feldman, 2000).

CONCLUSION

Hope cannot but grow in its pursuit (Aga-Khan, 2008; Yunus, 2008). Working with the premise that hope is generative even in hopeless circumstances, this chapter recasts social change agency work through an explicitly hope-full lens (Carlsen et al., 2011; Ludema et al., 1997; Snyder, 1994; Snyder, 2000a). It suggests that relationships initiate and accelerate social change because they help (re)produce hope in the face of uncertainty, adversity, and setbacks.

ACKNOWLEDGMENTS

Financial support from the Richard Ivey School of Business and from the Social Sciences and Humanities Research Council is gratefully acknowledged.

REFERENCES

Adam, B. (1990). *Time and social theory*. Cambridge: Polity Press.

Aga Khan (2008). *Where hope takes root*. Vancouver: Douglas &McIntyre Ltd.

Bandura, A. (1997). *Self-efficacy: The exercise of control*. New York: Freeman.

Bates, S. R. (2006). Making time for change: On temporal conceptualizations within (critical realist) approaches to the relationship between structure and agency. *Sociology, 40*, 143–161.

Bies, R. J., Bartunek, J. M., Fort, T. L., & Zald, M. N. (2007). Introduction to special topic forum: Corporations as social change agents: Individual, interpersonal, institutional, and environmental dynamics. *Academy of Management Review, 32*, 788–793.

Block, E. (1986). *The principle of hope* (N. Plaice, S. Plaice, & P. Knight, Trans.). Cambridge, MA: MIT Press.

Branzei, O., & Peneycad, M. (2008). Weaving sustainable partnerships in Zanzibar: The social fabric of women entrepreneurship. In R. Hamann, S. Woolman, & C. Sprague (Eds.), *The business of sustainable development in Africa: Human rights, partnerships, and new business models*. Pretoria: Unisa Press.

Carlsen, A., Landsverk Hagen A., & Mortensen, T. F. (2011). Imagining hope in organizations: From individual goal-attainment to horizons of relational possibility. In K. Cameron & G. Spreitzer (Eds.), *The Oxford handbook of positive organizational scholarship*. New York: Oxford University Press.

Cheavens, J. S., Feldman, D. B, Gum, A., Michael, S. T., & Snyder, C. R. (2006). Hope therapy in a community sample: A pilot investigation. *Social Indicators Research, 77*, 61–78.

CNN.com. (2010, January). *Singing to Success*, Inside Africa. Retrieved July 2010 from http://edition.cnn.com/video/#/video/interntaional/2010/01/05/ia.cing.success.bk.b.cnn

Coleman, J. S. (1971). Conflicting theories of social change. *The American Behavioral Scientist, 14*, 633–650.

Dauenhauer, D. H. (1986). *The politics of hope*. New York: Routledge & Kegan Paul.

Davis, M. (2006). *Planet of slums*. London: Verso.

Drayton, W. (2006). Everyone a changemaker: Social entrepreneurship's ultimate goal. *Innovations: Technology, Governance, Globalization, Winter*, 1–32.

Hallinan, M. T. (1997). The sociological study of social change: 1996 presidential address. *American Sociological Review, 62*, 1–11.

Heppner, P. P., & Hillerbrand, E. T. (1991). Problem-solving training implications for remedial and preventive training. In C. R. Snyder & D. R. Forsyth (Eds.), *Handbook of social and clinical psychology: The health perspective* (pp. 681–698). Elmsford, New York: Pergamon Press.

Hewitt, J. P. (1998). *The myth of self-esteem: Finding happiness and solving problems in America*. New York: St. Martin's Press.

Hjorth, D., & Steyaert, C. (2010). *The politics and aesthetics of entrepreneurship*. Cornwall, UK: MPG Books Group.

Kalyesubula, R. (2009). NACODI brings hope to those in need in Uganda. Retrieved September 2009 from http://www.connectingforchange.ca/cadoi

Lounsbury, M., & Glynn, M. A. (2001). Cultural entrepreneurship: Stories, legitimacy, and the acquisition of resources. *Strategic Management Journal, 22*, 545–564.

Ludema, J. D., Wilmot, T. B., & Srivastva, S. (1997). Organizational hope: Reaffirming the constructive task of social and organizational inquiry. *Human Relations, 50*, 1015–1052.

Magaletta, P. R., & Oliver, J. M. (1999). The hope construct, will and ways: Their relations with self-efficacy, optimism, and general well-being. *Journal of Clinical Psychology, 55,* 539–551.

Marcel, G. (1951). *Homo viator* (E. Craufurd, Trans.). Chicago: Henry Regnery.

McAdams, D. P. (1993). *The stories we live by: Personal myths and the making of the self.* New York: Morrow.

McDermott, D., & Hastings, S. (2000). Children: Raising future hopes. In C.R. Snyder (Ed.), *Handbook of hope: Theory, measures, & applications* (pp. 185–199). Academic Press: San Diego.

Moltmann, J. (1991). *Theology of hope* (J. W. Leitch, Trans.). New York: Harper Collins.

Plowman, D. A., Baker, L. T., Beck, T. E., Kulkarni, M., Solansky, S. T., & Travis, D. V. (2007). Radical change accidentally: The emergence and amplification of small change. *Academy of Management Journal, 50,* 515–543.

Rindova, V., Barry, D., & Ketchen Jr., D. J. (2009). Entrepreneuring as emancipation. *Academy of Management Review, 34,* 477–491.

Rodriquez-Hanley, A., & Snyder, C. R. (2000b). The demise of hope: On losing positive thinking. In C. R. Snyder (Ed.), *Handbook of hope: Theory, measures, & applications* (pp. 39–52). San Diego: Academic Press.

Sawa World (2008). Blog #23: Sawa World and their positive impact. Retrieved July 8, 2010 from http://sawaworld.org/blogs/blog-23-sawa-heroes-and-their-positive-impact-40000-people%E2%80%99s-lives-improved

Scheier, M. E., & Carver, C. S. (1985). Optimism, hoping and health: Assessment and implications of generalized outcome expectancies. *Health Psychology, 4,* 219–247.

Seelos, C., & Mair, J. (2009). Hope for sustainable development: How social entrepreneurs make it happen. In R. Ziegler (Ed.), *An introduction to social entrepreneurship: Voices, preconditions, contexts* (pp. 228–246). Cheltenham, UK: Edward Elgar.

Seligman, M. E. P. (1991). *Learned optimism.* New York: Knopf.

Snyder, C. R. (1994). *The psychology of hope: You can get there from here.* New York: Free Press.

Snyder, C. R. (2000a). Hypothesis: There is hope. In C. R. Snyder (Ed.), *Handbook of hope: Theory, measures, & applications* (pp. 3–18). San Diego: Academic Press.

Snyder, C. R. (2000b). Genesis: The birth and growth of hope. In C. R. Snyder (Ed.), *Handbook of hope: Theory, measures, & applications* (pp. 25–36). San Diego: Academic Press.

Snyder, C. R. (2002). Hope theory: Rainbows in the mind. *Psychological Inquiry, 13*(4), 249–275.

Snyder, C. R., Cheavens, J., & Sumpson, S. C. (1997). Hope: An individual motive for social commerce. *Group Dynamics: Theory, Research and Practice, 1,* 107–118.

Snyder, C. R., & Feldman, D. B. (2000). Hope for the many: An empowering social agenda. In C. R. Snyder (Ed.), *Handbook of hope: Theory, measures, & applications* (pp. 389–412). San Diego: Academic Press.

Snyder, C. R., Irving, L., & Anderson, J. R. (1991). Hope and health: Measuring the will and the ways. In C. R. Snyder & D. R. Forsyth (Eds.), *Handbook of social and clinical psychology: The health perspective* (pp. 285–305). Elmsford, New York: Pergamon Press.

Snyder, C. R., Rand, K. L., & Sigmon, D. R. (2005). Hope theory: A member of the positive psychology family. In C. R. Snyder & S. J. Lopez (Eds.), *The Oxford handbook of positive psychology* (pp. 257–276). New York: Oxford University Press.

Tichy, N. M. (1978). Current and future trends for change agency. *Group & Organization Management, 3*, 467–482.

Tichy, N. M. (1974). Agents of planned social change: Congruence of values, cognitions and actions. *Administrative Science Quarterly, 19*(2), 164–182.

Yapa, L. (1996). What causes poverty? A postmodern view. *Annals of the Association of American Geographers, 86*(4), 707–728.

Yunus, M. (2008). *Creating a world without poverty: Social business and the future of capitalism.* New York: Public Affairs.

Ziegler, R. (2009). Introduction: Voices, preconditions, contexts. In R. Ziegler (Ed.), *An introduction to social entrepreneurship: Voices, preconditions, contexts* (pp. 1–18). Cheltenham, UK: Edward Elgar.

3

Being a Positive Social Change Agent Through Issue Selling

Scott Sonenshein
Rice University

Business academics have increasingly turned attention to the role of organizations in fostering social change. One way in which organizations become engaged with social change is through issue sellers, individuals who act as change agents inside mainstream business organizations by trying to convince others to direct attention and resources to issues (Dutton & Ashford, 1993; Howard-Grenville, 2007; Sonenshein, 2006). This chapter unpacks not simply how individuals sell social issues, but more specifically, how individuals engage in issue selling as *positive* social change agents. By positive, I refer to goodness and generativity in terms of both processes and outcomes (Roberts, 2006). I highlight how shifting the examination of the process of issue selling to a more positive perspective can help identify more positively oriented methods for social change agents to use to foster social change (positive issue-selling processes) and accomplish more positive outcomes (positive issue-selling outcomes).

Shifting our perspective of issue selling to a positive one is important for several reasons. First, while issue selling was originally theorized as having both instrumental and symbolic properties (Dutton & Ashford, 1993), most issue-selling research has historically taken the instrumental approach in which change agents factor the potential for benefits versus harm to their careers as they determine whether or not to sell an issue (e.g., Ashford, Rothbard, Piderit, & Dutton, 1998). As a consequence, change agents facing work contexts inhospitable to the change they are trying to foster are more likely to abandon their plans (e.g., Dutton, Ashford, Lawrence, & Miner-Rubino, 2002; Dutton, Ashford, O'Neill, Hayes, & Wierba, 1997). However, social change agents often make great sacrifices in pursuit of their causes despite the likelihood of failure or professional damage. A positive perspective on issue selling helps explain this resiliency by unpacking how social change agents persevere even within inhospitable contexts.

Second, existing conceptions of social change often conjure images of rancorous discourse dominated by the harsh criticisms of radicals operating outside the focal organization. Popular examples include Greenpeace's confrontation with Shell Oil over Brent Spar (Zyglidopoulos, 2002) and the media's hostile coverage of Chiquita (Were, 2003). However, by unpacking issue selling from a positive perspective, I reveal how social change agents may foster more generative and effective dialogues from *inside* organizations.

Third, by applying a positive issue-selling perspective onto social change, new questions about issue selling, such as its outcomes, are brought to light and the multiple levels in which social change can be positive—such as for the change agent, the organization, and society—are emphasized. This allows for a focus on outcomes that transcends the immediate self-interests of the social change agent, thus advancing issue-selling research beyond its frequent focus on instrumental motivations to include a more complex set of drivers (see also Ashford & Barton, 2007).

BRIEF REVIEW OF ISSUE-SELLING RESEARCH

To understand the relevance of issue selling for social change agency requires both a rudimentary understanding of the extant issue-selling research as well as details of how core properties of this literature must shift to accommodate a more positive view.

In brief, issue-selling research originated in the study of upward influence attempts of middle managers working for the attention of top managers for strategic issues (Dutton & Ashford, 1993). Middle managers are theorized to "sell" issues to top managers using tactics including building consensus by talking to others about the issue or logic (Piderit & Ashford, 2003). A key principle of issue selling is that organizations are a marketplace of ideas (Dutton, Ashford, O'Neill, & Lawrence, 2001). However, with a finite amount of attention to dole out (Ocasio, 1997), top managers give attention to issues they find most compelling.

While issue-selling research originated with a focus on upward selling, the concept now also recognizes downward and lateral influence (e.g., Sonenshein, 2006). This expanded focus is important for theorizing issue selling because it extends the designation of "change agent" (and by extension, "social change agent") to individuals outside middle management. For example, top managers can sell issues downward to subordinates by using an arsenal of issue-selling tactics similar to that of a middle manager. While these top managers may opt to exercise their positional power to garner support, issue-selling research reminds us that effective change comes from how the meanings of issues are shaped by change agents and not the formal power of the change agent alone.

Another important innovation in the issue-selling literature is the move from a primary focus on strategic issues to include social issues. As a result of this expansion, scholars have focused on a range of issues with important implications for social change, such as the natural environment (Andersson & Bateman, 2000; Bansal, 2004; Howard-Grenville, 2007) and gender equity (Ashford et al., 1998). This move makes sense from an issue-selling perspective because, by definition, no issue is inherently "strategic." Rather, through issue-selling processes, any issue can be viewed as strategic as the meaning of issues is malleable. Put another way, issues do not have inherent meanings but are given meaning through the claims-making process (Best, 1995; Spector & Kitsuse, 1977). Individuals make claims about the meaning of an issue using language to construct it in a manner that weaves the issue into a dominant organizational logic, thereby increasing its perceived legitimacy (Sonenshein, 2006). For example, because economic logic dominates many work organizations, issue sellers may highlight the "business case" of an issue to increase its perceived legitimacy (Dutton et al., 2001).

One of the key limitations of existing issue-selling research in respect to social change is the motivational model implicit in this body of research. As suggested earlier, issue selling takes primarily an instrumental approach, with change agents making calculative assessments of the career implications of selling a particular issue. As Figure 3.1 illustrates, issue sellers make calculations based on the relative career benefits and risks of a particular issue, therefore potentially thwarting action if this calculus turns negative. As a result, in its current form, issue-selling research struggles to explain why social change agents might nevertheless attempt social change when the calculations predict a harmful impact on the change agent.

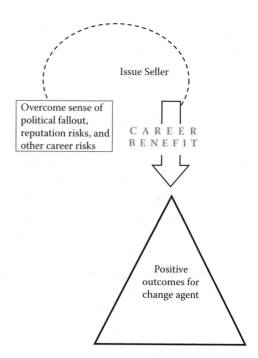

FIGURE 3.1
Internal social change agent as an
issue seller.

ISSUE SELLING AND SOCIAL CHANGE: STARTING PREMISES FROM A POSITIVE PERSPECTIVE

Issue-selling research examines the processes by which individuals at work draw attention to issues (Dutton & Ashford, 1993). Presumably, these issues may include even those issues viewed by some as tangential to an organization's strategy including corporate social responsibility initiatives. To include such types of social responsibility initiatives, it is important to recall the premise that a key process of issue selling is the construction of an issue in a way that weaves the issue into the dominant logic of an organization, thereby increasing the perceived legitimacy of the issue (Sonenshein, 2006). However, to do so, particularly in light of desired outcomes of social change raises the question—what is positive about issue selling?

To answer this question requires rethinking the role of the social change agent. As previously mentioned, much of the social change research involves external, and often antagonistic, critics exerting pressure on business organizations to engage in social change, such as through social movements (e.g., Davis & Anderson, 2008) or via social activists (Den Hond & De Bakker, 2007). Figure 3.2 provides a visual depiction of this, in which external change agents seek to impact societal-level outcomes through hostile discourse with organizations. While this approach can lead to dramatic social change (Marquis, Glynn, & Davis, 2007), it suggests that the resources (such as change agents and the meanings they use) must be external to the entity that is the center of change. Such an approach has an intuitive appeal as it is difficult—but not impossible (Reay, Golden-Biddle, & GermAnn, 2006)—for individuals within a social system to change that very system (Battilana, Leca, & Boxenbaum, 2009; Meyerson, 2001) and our beliefs about social change have historically privileged the external social critic over the internal one (Sonenshein, 2005).

Conversely, an issue-selling perspective firmly plants the origins of social change *inside* the social system that is the focus of change, therefore extending social change agency from a singularly exogenous perspective to include an endogenous change agent. Similar to other internal social

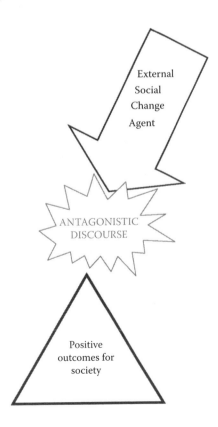

FIGURE 3.2
External social change agent.

change perspectives (Meyerson, 2001; Meyerson & Scully, 1995; Scully & Segal, 2002), issue selling can explain how, despite the challenges, individuals internal to a social system, particularly an organization, can change that system. This shifts the research from examining how social forces exogenous to the organization impact social change by instead spotlighting the often relentless efforts of those inside the business organization, with a specific emphasis on how these change agents construct meanings that balance the need for conformity and stability with the desire for social change (Battilana et al., 2009; Meyerson, 2001).

To appreciate how social change can unfold endogenously, consider Bollier's (1996) telling of how five employees at Inland Steel confronted a culture of workplace discrimination and successfully advocated for the implementation of company-wide diversity initiatives. The issue-selling process began when four minority employees shared stories with one another of the subtle stereotyping each had experienced during their tenure and discussed the pervasive feeling that minorities were passed over for promotion. After meeting, the employees approached an upper-management sales executive, Steve Bowsher, to convince him that Inland's culture prevented minority workers from excelling. As with many issue-selling attempts, the social change agents directed their efforts at upward influence (Dutton & Ashford, 1993). The social change agents described to Bowsher their predicament of "never getting the opportunity to succeed in a job ... being called names, being told racists jokes." In addition, the issue sellers framed the meaning of the issue in terms they believed would resonate with Bowsher. As one change agent told him, "We can multiply [our] profitability twice if we had all of our people in power to move ahead ... particularly our minority employees" (Bollier, 1996, p. 113). This is a classic example of a meaningful construction process in which the issue seller crafts the meaning (in this case, diversity) in a way that is likely to be viewed as legitimate by top managers (Sonenshein, 2006).

At the outset, Bowsher, who was white, struggled to grasp the meaning and ramifications of the issue. Undeterred, the social change agents began sending workplace diversity reading materials to him, eventually sending a brochure for a race relations seminar, which Bowsher decided to attend on his own time and with his own funds. This seminar served as a turning point for Bowsher—he was the only white upper-level manager and the participants were primarily African American. Bowsher recalls his experience: "For two days, they basically ignored me. They would not respond to my questions, they wouldn't listen to me … it clearly opened my thinking so that I could understand what [my employees] had been telling me" (Bollier, 1996, p. 114).

Bowsher returned to Inland transformed by the experience and by extension and became an issue seller himself, thereby illustrating an upward spiral as the issue selling spread (Cameron, Dutton, & Quinn, 2003). Having taken on the role of a social change agent, he used his more formal power to continue the upward sell of social change to top management, eventually convincing Inland president Robert Darnall of the importance of promoting diversity and cultural understanding at the organization. He did this by getting Darnall to attend the same diversity seminar that had given meaning to the issue for him. By the experience of participating in the seminar as a racial minority, Darnall returned similarly changed as Bowsher and with a much better understanding of the plight of his minority workers. Taking it a step further, Darnall also constructed the economic meaning of the issue and became convinced that, with minorities comprising 40% of Inland's employee population, managing diversity was essential not just to stay competitive, but to attract and retain quality employees as well. Put another way, Darnall constructed the issue of diversity as a vital competitive advantage for Inland. This facilitated resources that trickled from the bottom up to top managers through the way in which internal social change agents translated important social issues into something that resonated inside the organization, thereby continuing the upward spiral in which more and more members of the organization began to embrace the same meanings as the original four employees who served as social change agents. In the end, what started as a grassroots effort by a few social change agents percolated up to top managers, who helped reposition Inland as an organization that valued diversity.

Positive Issue-Selling Processes

Generative Dialoguing

While issue selling holds the promise of a theory of social change agency that unfolds endogenously, there are important shifts that must occur in theorizing how social change agents engage in issue selling from a positive perspective that departs from how scholars usually understand social change. As previously mentioned, research on social change often depicts a rancorous process complete with activists engaging in disruptive activities and hostile discourse. In fact, research suggests that for external social change agents, negative emotions—including anger—can motivate change agents, such as through how they denigrate the out-group (i.e., the organization they are trying to change). Conversely, negative emotions are detrimental to the internal social change agent as they can narrow their creativity (DeCelles, Sonenshein, & Hoffman, 2010). Accordingly, a shift in theorizing offers the promise of clarifying positive processes around social change by examining the generative (versus antagonistic) dialogues stimulated by social change agents. *Generative dialogue*—discourse that "brings into being a mutually satisfying and effective organization" (Gergen, Gergen, & Barrett, 2004, p. 45)—can lead to a more sustained engagement with social change. The Inland Steel example shows how issue sellers, by engaging in generative dialogues and making connections between positive social outcomes and business objectives, can expand the opportunities and benefits afforded an organization and create change that benefits both the organization and society. The following example illuminates another aspect of generative dialogue—*productive differences*—which sustains or extends debate about an issue in a positive manner (Gergen et al., 2004).

When Barbara Waugh (Anonymous, 2004) was a personnel director for HP labs, she learned that HP would not be extending domestic partnership benefits (DPBs) to its gay and lesbian employees. Her first reaction was to initiate a non-generative dialogue; responding to the organization by demonizing it and casting it as an "evil corporation." This type of response is a conversation stopper that, while making the point that the social change agent is angry about a decision, usually curtails debate and may even stymie the change agent. Upon further consideration, she opted for a more generative approach—Waugh sought to *extend* the conversation rather than shut it down. She first *widened* the conversation by collecting stories from HP employees about how homophobia impacted their productivity. Furthermore, she *enriched* the dialogue by engaging in "narrative and temporal integration," an approach using accounts of the past to create compelling, reliable, and significant portraits of reality (Gergen et al., 2004). More specifically, she turned the stories she collected into a play. When top management learned of the play, they responded to her efforts by affirming the dialogue. In fact, top management encouraged Waugh to stage the play across the company and supported 60 performances in the following six months. While top management had been confident and firm in their decision to not extend DPBs, Waugh's use of generative dialogue successfully engaged both other employees and senior management and kept the issue alive. In doing so, she contributed to HP's reversal of its decision and helped lead HP to become the first Fortune 500 company to offer DPBs to gay and lesbian employees. Instead of following her initial reaction that would have closed debate, Waugh widened and enriched the dialogue and, in turn, management joined in, leading to social change happening through the collective activities of both the change agent and the top management team. Similar to what unfolded at Inland Steel, the issue seller successfully invited others to join a generative dialogue.

Reclaiming "Dead" Issues

Another way of theorizing social change from a positive perspective is through the process of reclaiming "dead" issues. While social change is difficult, issue selling assumes that meanings inside organizations are always in flux and that there are always several ways to construct the meaning of an issue (Dutton & Ashford, 1993; Sonenshein, 2006). This allows for at least two different ways to reclaim a dead issue. First, as the organizational context shifts, the original meanings used to sell the issue may become more legitimate. In this case, the organization "catches up" to the issue seller because the larger environment has shifted (e.g., other companies offer DPBs). As the environment or context changes, the values of past meanings change and the opportunity to revisit previously unsuccessful issue-selling attempts and to renew social change processes arises. A second and perhaps more powerful approach is for the issue seller to reframe the meaning of the social issue, thereby attempting a new issue-selling approach for the same issue. While current conceptualizations of issue selling tend to view the construction of meaning as a single event, it is possible to theorize issue selling as a succession of attempts to exert influence over the meaning of change. By doing so, social change agents can attempt to sell the same issue using a different set of meanings to infuse thwarted conversations about social change with new energy, excitement, and perspective.

A good example of reclaiming dead issues comes from a group of employees at "Metropolitan Healthcare" (Githens & Aragon, 2009; a pseudonym representing events at two healthcare organizations) who approached management with a number of concerns and ideas about how the company could foster a more positive culture for its gay, lesbian, and bisexual workers. The employees described to management the unwelcoming attitudes and unfavorable conditions they had encountered in the workplace and asked that the company alter its non-discrimination statement to include "sexual orientation" as a protected class. In addition, the employees requested that management extend its DPBs to unmarried partners. Although the request to alter the non-discrimination statement was granted within two years of the request, the issue of DPBs was a problem. The social change agents met with upper management many times but were unable to make headway. The social change agents, frustrated with their lack of progress, tried a new strategy: they formed a coalition with union leaders who agreed to support DPBs in its negotiations with management. Despite this, almost eight years after presenting the issue, no progress had been made. In 2000, a new opportunity to sell the issue arose: the company's diversity manager suggested the group become a formal "employee network." The LGBT and Allies Network became an officially recognized employee network—a position that provided leverage as they renewed their efforts to advocate for DPBs. The group continued to sell the issue to management and, thanks to a number of efforts including a benchmark analysis comparing Metropolitan Healthcare to other U.S. employers who had instituted DPBs, as well as continued support from the unions and other allies within the organization, in 2004, Metropolitan Healthcare approved the debut of DPBs. This case shows that, particularly over time, the meanings and support structures (in this case, a coalition of individuals) of issues are malleable. In other words, meanings about an issue, and meanings about an individual or entity selling that issue, are in flux. In this sense, an issue is never dead but instead just dormant. With persistence, resilience, and creativity, social change agents can reinvigorate a dormant issue by changing its meaning (as in this example by transforming an informal group to an "employee network" and building bridges to new allies) as they reevaluate and reconstruct the meanings of their issue.

Positive Outcomes

I now turn to unpacking three positive outcomes—two of which the issue-selling literature has previously considered (positive outcomes for the organization and positive outcomes for the issue seller), and a third that is relatively absent in the literature (positive outcomes for society).

Positive Outcomes for the Organization

As stated, existing research in issue selling often takes an instrumental view proposing that individuals are more likely to engage in issue selling if they perceive career benefits (Dutton & Ashford, 1993). An extension of this reasoning suggests that the selling of certain issues might result in benefits to the organization (and, in turn, the issue seller). These positive organizational outcomes can indirectly create a positive social impact. For example, a major cost savings for an organization may also translate to less environmental waste. Such "win-win" scenarios for organizations and society can further encourage organizational support of social change as they legitimize social change advocacy by creating not only concrete examples of successful social change attempts but blueprints for how to do so as well.

One example of a win-win outcome comes from the story of Barbara Roberts (Bollier, 1996) who, as president of the stock photography firm FPG International, was committed to promoting diversity within the company she was hired to run. Roberts observed an opportunity for FPG to distinguish itself in the industry by promoting multicultural stock photography—photographs depicting individuals, groups, and situations that, at the time, were underrepresented in stock photography (such as photos depicting minorities, battered wives, the physically challenged, etc.). Roberts, who describes herself as committed to eradicating stereotypes and promoting a realistic and multicultural view of society, linked her ideas for social change to her plan to create a competitive advantage for FPG. FPG's 1994 catalog, filled with a diverse array of subjects and situations, led to strong sales. Ultimately, Roberts' decision to link social change with business decisions led to success for FPG (now Getty Images), which is regarded as "the artistic, technological, and commercial pacesetter for stock photography." More generally, however, it also shows that an organization can actually *advance* their profit objectives through social change—a meaning that issue sellers can exploit when they advocate for change.

Positive Outcomes for the Social Change Agent

In addition to positive organizational outcomes, a positive perspective on issue selling also offers opportunities to examine dependent variables that are positively deviant with respect to the issue seller (Spreitzer & Sonenshein, 2004). These may include how engaging in social change can lead to the increased courage of social change agents—individuals willing to risk their careers to champion a speculative, but nevertheless important, social issue—or ways that engaging in social change can build an issue seller's competencies—competencies necessary to make social change happen.

Consider Julia Stasch (Bollier, 1996) who, while employed by real estate development company Stein & Company, was instrumental in developing and implementing programs to provide equal employment opportunities for women and minorities. When Stasch joined the firm, she was "openly committed to a civic and social agenda of racial justice and gender equity" and determined to enact social change by promoting new and innovative business practices. From within, Stasch advocated that Stein & Company could distinguish its contract bids, attract better workers, and attract more business by including affirmative action plans and, more generally, embracing equal employment opportunities. After her firm won a major bid to build AT&T's regional headquarters, Stasch proposed assembling a task force to ensure the representation of minority- and women-owned firms on the job site. The project, as well as Stasch's efforts to promote the use of minority- and women-owned firms, was a success. Not only were Stasch's social objectives met but the values she espoused were becoming an increasingly important part of the firm's identity as noted by a customer, "The firm won this plum contract in part by using its signature technique: distinguishing itself in the area of affirmative action" (Bollier, 1996, p. 129). Stasch next turned her sights to helping tradeswomen succeed in an industry notoriously unwelcoming of females. By building on the lessons learned in the previous project, Stasch was able to persuade contractors to support her goals, including recruiting and hiring women. Ultimately, Stasch's initiatives were successful not only in creating opportunities for females and minorities in the construction industry, but also in bolstering her company's reputation and ability to secure contracts. Stasch, a former high school teacher, experienced personal positive outcomes beyond just the satisfaction of her social advocacy goals. Starting her career at Stein & Company as a secretary, she was promoted to project coordinator, executive vice president, and chief administrative officer before taking on the role of chief operating officer.

Positive Outcomes for Society

While much research has focused on trying to link social change to economic performance (Margolis & Walsh, 2003), it is also important to understand the (positive) impact such initiatives have on society. A positive perspective on issue selling reminds scholars and practitioners of the outcomes designed to benefit society, not just the social change agent or their organization.

An example of societal impact comes from Chris Weeks (Rigoglioso, 2006), a DHL International logistics manager who was on loan to the Disaster Resource Network as part of DHL's corporate responsibility program. It was after a 2003 earthquake in Iran that Weeks experienced firsthand the challenges of coordinating the logistics of disaster relief. Because the earthquake had immobilized much of Iran's infrastructure, Weeks was unable to direct a substantial amount of relief aircraft and supplies into the country to help the Iranian people. Recognizing that more could be done, Weeks went to Bob Bellhouse, then the executive director of the Disaster Resource Network, to pitch an idea: an organization staffed by volunteer logistics experts that could be rapidly mobilized to help airport managers in disaster-ravaged locations coordinate incoming relief planes and the aid they contained. With Bellhouse's support, Weeks sold the idea to DHL as a way to connect to the world community by utilizing their logistics expertise to provide quick and specialized help after disasters. With DHL committed to the effort, Weeks approached other global shipping companies including TNT, Aramex, Dnata, and Emirates Air, with similar proposals. Weeks' brainchild, the Airport Emergency Team, is now a volunteer team of personnel who—with the blessings and support of their employers—are able to fly anywhere at a moment's notice to help coordinate disaster logistics. In addition, DHL has expanded on the idea with its own disaster response teams and emphasizes disaster relief as one of its key initiatives as an organization. While this example highlights a substantial positive outcome for society, his efforts earned Weeks a position in keeping with his personal social principles: Director of Humanitarian Affairs at DHL.

TOWARD A MODEL OF POSITIVE SOCIAL CHANGE AGENCY

Figure 3.3 contains a summary and integration model for theorizing social change agency as issue selling from a positive perspective. It integrates the

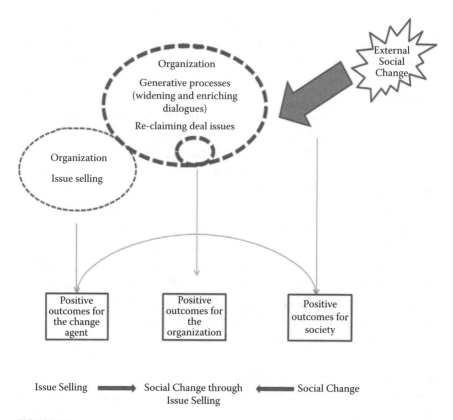

FIGURE 3.3

Summary model of social change agency from positive issue selling perspective.

previously discussed Figures 3.1 and 3.2 to show how the model of positive social change agency I presented builds off of existing research in issue selling and social change, while also extending these literatures. Starting from the top right, the big arrow signifies external social change in which social change agents from the outside of organizations attempt to foster social change by interjecting external arguments (such as fundamental values that may differ from those of the organization) to pressure organizations to change.

These social change agents, often activists, are primarily concerned with positive outcomes for society (represented with an arrow from external social change to positive outcomes for society) with little concern for what is best personally or best for the organization they are trying to influence. In fact, their discourse may even need to create these binaries (i.e., change agent benefit versus societal benefit; social good versus organizational good) to emphasize the sacrifices they must endure in order to be accepted by other activists or to denigrate the business organization to motivate action.

The circle on the left represents a traditional issue-selling perspective: a perspective that has not historically focused on either social change or positive processes of change. The processes of change represented here are internal to the organization and the emphasis on outcomes is primarily focused on what is best for the change agent.

The circle in the center represents the recasting of issue selling from a positive perspective focused on social change. The circle representing the organization is both wider (to signify a widened dialogue that accounts for a broader range of stakeholders) and thicker (to signify a richer dialogue) than the traditional issue-selling circle. The circle nested within it represents reclaiming dead issues that can be re-introduced to the broader dialogue about social change inside an organization. The view of issue selling from a positive perspective is also concerned with all three types of outcomes—for society, the change agent, and the organization—as represented by the arrows linking this circle with all three types of outcomes. In sum, the model depicts how a theory of social change agency as issue selling from a positive perspective draws from both social change's historical emphasis on positive outcomes for society as well as from issue selling's emphasis on positive outcomes for the issue seller and internal meaning construction processes. This combination, along with theorizing positive processes such as generative dialogues and reclaiming dead issues, grounds a perspective on social change agency that locates the resources (such as meanings and change agents) as endogenous to the organization.

Discussion

Implications for Theory

This chapter contributes to the literature on both social change agency and issue selling. For social change agency, issue selling adds an important emphasis to meaning construction processes, particularly those internal to the organization. These internal processes suggest that the raw materials for making social change happen can be endogenous to the organization itself (e.g., Sonenshein, 2005) and contrast with the more traditional perspective of organizations being pressured by outside activists or non-governmental organizations to conform to some external standard (e.g.,

Argenti, 2004; Mirvis, 2002; Zyglidopoulos, 2002). Instead of creating tension and using external standards that pit social interests versus organizational interests, a positive perspective on issue selling illustrates how internal social change agents can foster generative dialogues that widen and enrich discussion about social change. Through opening up debate by enlisting new and different players and meanings (such as arguments about an issue), issue sellers use processes likely to lead to a greater variety of morally imaginative solutions that can provide a host of positive outcomes (Werhane, 1999). In fact, a key question in research in positive social change (and positive organizational scholarship more generally) is, *"Positive to whom?"* summing up the sense that one person's or entity's benefit can only come at the expense of another. While this is certainly true in some cases, it is not universal. In fact, one of the common threads uniting the social change agents introduced in this chapter is their ability to create positive outcomes across a wide range of domains—for society, their organizations, and themselves. Artificially created binaries that separate "business" and "society" obstruct scholars and practitioners from seeing that these different types of outcomes need not be mutually exclusive. Issue selling, through how it allows for social change to be malleable and how it fosters generative dialogue, enables the transcendence of these artificial boundaries. For the issue seller, social change can be constructed and subsequently enacted as a beneficial process that can have a positive impact on society, the organization, and the change agent collectively.

Similarly, issue-selling processes can bring new life to previously thwarted attempts at social change through unearthing new ways of understanding social change and its impact. In short, positive social change agents view their focal organization not as their adversary, but rather as their partner in trying to make social change happen, using (but also repackaging) the meaning of its discursive resources (Hardy, Palmer, & Phillips, 2000). Yet, advocating positive social change through issue selling is not a naïve process either—social change agents can use sophisticated tactics to influence and persuade others inside their organization to adopt social change (Piderit & Ashford, 2003). The basic shift, however, is from viewing the focal organization as a battleground to the perception of the organization as a repository of meaning resources—such as compelling arguments (Sonenshein, 2006) or collective identities (Creed & Scully, 2000; Dutton & Dukerich, 1991)—from which issue sellers can frame the meaning of social change for themselves, their organization, and society at large.

While issue selling is a useful framework for theorizing change agency, this research has largely narrowed its focus to the instrumental perspective of the change agent (Ashford & Barton, 2007), thereby obscuring how issue selling can ground a more encompassing view of change agency that includes with it positive outcomes for society. For example, by rethinking issue selling as a positive process and applying it to social change, the manner in which issue selling captures the important processes and outcomes that transcend the narrow interests of the change agent unfolds. Issue selling need not always be a contingent, career building process. Fundamentally, issue selling can instead be about asking questions that make the world a better place (Margolis & Walsh, 2003). A near exclusive focus on the instrumental benefits bestowed upon change agents obscures important positive outcomes, particularly those most relevant to society. Accordingly, this chapter suggests that issue-selling research broaden its study of dependent variables beyond its usual constructs (Ashford et al., 1998; Dutton et al., 2002) to include the potential for social impact as well as independent variables that explain why social change agents, despite formidable personal challenges, nevertheless persist in trying to make social change happen through constructs such as identity (Ashford & Barton, 2007) or positive meaning (Sonenshein, DeCelles, & Dutton, 2010).

This chapter also contributes to two distinctly positive processes of issue selling—generative processes (widening and enriching dialogues) and reclaiming dead issues. Issue-selling research has predominately focused on processes that involve coalition building, framing, controlling demeanor, and timing (Piderit & Ashford, 2003). While these processes are important, they supplant opportunities to view issue selling as an ongoing effort to create new ideas by enriching debates and revisiting past change attempts. On this latter point, by theorizing social change agency as issue selling from a positive perspective, issue selling is recast as an ongoing conversation that can create upward spirals, such as when new dialogues yield incremental social change that, in turn, serves as the foundation for social change for a larger constituency.

Implications for Practice

Social change agents can be internal change agents who work to advance social outcomes, benefit their focal organizations, and seek personal gains—not just the external, rancorous change agent that engages in hostile discourse sometimes at great sacrifice. While not all three constituencies can always benefit from change, social change agents can take advantage of malleable meanings to increase the chances of achieving a host of positive outcomes. This can lead to new opportunities as the social change agent examines issues, including those previously deemed dead, in new ways.

This research also suggests that being a social change agent need not involve a contentious battle with others, a role that can lead to burnout from the exhaustion of trying to make change happen (Maslach, 1982). Instead, a social change agent can find a viable voice by working with an organization to create change from the inside (e.g., Meyerson, 2001). Tools such as enriching and widening debates can help along these lines and reframe social change as a partnership between the social change agent and the organization.

CONCLUSION

Perhaps more than ever, the world needs business organizations to participate in meeting society's demands. While there are a variety of motivations for and consequences of engaging in social change, there has been limited attention to the ways in which individuals go about being social change agents inside business organizations. This chapter has examined but one possibility: that of the internal social change agent as molding the meaning of an old or new issue to foster generative dialogues. In doing so, I take an important step in recognizing internal change agents and the power they hold in making a positive, impactful difference for themselves, their organization, and society.

ACKNOWLEDGMENT

I thank Kim Jones Davenport for her valuable research assistance.

REFERENCES

Andersson, L. M., & Bateman, T. S. (2000). Individual environmental initiative: Championing natural environmental issues in U.S. business organizations. *Academy of Management Journal, 43,* 548–570.

Anonymous. (2004). A personal dilemma turns into collective action. *Stanford Social Innovation Review, 2,* 23.

Argenti, P. A. (2004). Collaborating with activists: How Starbucks works with NGOs. *California Management Review, 47,* 91–116.

Ashford, S. J., Rothbard, N. P., Piderit, S. K., & Dutton, J. E. (1998). Out on a limb: The role of context and impression management in selling gender-equity issues. *Administrative Science Quarterly, 43,* 23–57.

Ashford, S. J., & Barton, M. A. (2007). Identity-based issue selling. In C. Bartel, S. Blader, & A. Wrzesniewski (Eds.). *Identity and the modern organization.* Mahwah, NJ: Lawrence Erlbaum.

Bansal, P. (2004). From issues to actions: The importance of individual concerns and organizational values in responding to natural environment issues. *Organization Science, 14,* 510–527.

Battilana, J., Leca, B., & Boxenbaum, E. (2009). How actors change institutions: Towards a theory of institutional entrepreneurship. *The Academy of Management Annal., 3,* 65–107.

Best, J. (Ed.). (1995). *Images of issues: Typifying contemporary social problems* (2nd ed.). New York: Aldine De Gruyter.

Bollier, D. (1996). *Aiming higher: 25 stories of how companies prosper by combining sound management and social vision.* New York: AMACOM.

Cameron, K., Dutton, J., & Quinn, R. (2003). *Positive organizational scholarship.* San Francisco: Berrett-Koehler Publishers.

Creed, W. E. D., & Scully, M. A. (2000). Songs of ourselves: Employees' deployment of social identity in workplace encounters. *Journal of Management Inquiry, 9,* 391–412.

Davis, G. F., & Anderson, P. J. J. (2008). Social movements and failed institutionalization: corporate (non) response to the AIDS epidemic. In R. Greenwood, C. Oliver, K. Sahlin, & R. Suddaby (Eds.), *The Sage handbook of organizational institutionalism* (pp. 371–388). London: Sage.

DeCelles, K., Sonenshein, S., & Hoffman, A. (2010). The radical with a temper: The varied experience of negative emotion and its effects on social change performance (working paper).

Den Hond, F., & De Bakker, F. G. A. (2007). Ideologically motivated activism: How activist groups influence corporate social change activities. *The Academy of Management Review, 32,* 901–924.

Dutton, J. E., & Ashford, S. J. (1993). Selling issues to top management. *Academy of Management Review, 18,* 397–428.

Dutton, J. E., Ashford, S. J., O'Neill, R. M., Hayes, E., & Wierba, E. E. (1997). Reading the wind: How middle managers assess the context for selling issues to top managers. *Strategic Management Journal, 18,* 407–425.

Dutton, J. E., Ashford, S. J., O'Neill, R. M., & Lawrence, K. A. (2001). Moves that matter: issue selling and organizational change. *Academy of Management Journal, 44,* 716–736.

Dutton, J. E., Ashford, S. J., Lawrence, K. A., & Miner-Rubino, K. (2002). Red light, green light: Making sense of the organizational context for issue selling. *Organization Science, 13,* 355–369.

Dutton, J. E., & Dukerich, J. M. (1991). Keeping an eye on the mirror: Image and identity in organizational adaptation. *Academy of Management Journal, 34*, 517–554.

Gergen, K. J., Gergen, M. M., & Barrett, F. J. (2004). Dialogue: Life and death of the organization. In D. Grant, C. Hardy, C. Oswick, & L. Putnam (Eds.), *The Sage handbook of organizational discourse* (pp. 39–59). London: Sage Publications.

Githens, R. P., & Aragon, S. R. (2009). LGBT employee groups: Goals and organizational structures. *Advances in Developing Human Resources, 11*, 121–135.

Hardy, C., Palmer, I., & Phillips, N. (2000). Discourse as a strategic resource. *Human Relations, 53*, 1227–1248.

Howard-Grenville, J. A. (2007). Developing issue-selling effectiveness over time: Issue selling as resourcing. *Organization Science, 18*, 560–577.

Margolis, J. D., & Walsh, J. P. (2003). Misery loves companies: Rethinking social initiatives by business. *Administrative Science Quarterly, 48*, 268–306.

Marquis, C., Glynn, M. A., & Davis, G. F. (2007). Community isomorphism and corporate social action. *Academy of Management Review, 32*, 925–945.

Maslach, C. (1982). *Burnout: The cost of caring.* Englewood Cliffs, NJ: Prentice Hall.

Meyerson, D. E., & Scully, M. A. (1995). Tempered radicalism and the politics of ambivalence and change. *Organization Science, 6*, 585–600.

Meyerson, D. E. (2001). *Tempered radicals: How people use difference to inspire change at work.* Boston: Harvard Business School Press.

Mirvis, P. H. (2002). Transformation at Shell: Commerce and citizenship. *Business and Society Review, 105*, 63–84.

Ocasio, W. (1997). Towards an attention-based view of the firm. *Strategic Management Journal, 18*, 187–206.

Piderit, S. K., & Ashford, S. J. (2003). Breaking silence: Tactical choices women managers make in speaking up about gender-equity issues. *Journal of Management Studies, 40*, 1477–1502.

Reay, T., Golden-Biddle, K., & GermAnn, K. (2006). Legitimizing a new role: Small wins and micro-processes of change. *Academy of Management Journal, 49*, 977–998.

Rigoglioso, M. (2006). Shipping companies to the rescue. *Stanford Social Innovation Review, 4*, 64–65.

Roberts, L. M. (2006). Shifting the lens on organizational life: The added value of positive scholarship. *Academy of Management Review, 31*, 292–305.

Scully, M., & Segal, A. (2002). Passion with an umbrella: Grassroots activists in the workplace. In M. Lounsbury & M. Ventresca (Eds.), *Social structure and organizations revised*, Vol. 19 (pp. 125–168). Amsterdam: Elsevier.

Sonenshein, S. (2005). Business ethics and internal social criticism. *Business Ethics Quarterly, 15*, 475–498.

Sonenshein, S. (2006). Crafting social issues at work. *Academy of Management Journal, 49*, 1158–1172.

Sonenshein, S., DeCelles, K., & Dutton J. (2010). *It's not easy being green: The role of positive self-meanings in facilitating environmental change* (working paper).

Spector, M., & Kitsuse, J. I. (1977). *Constructing social problems.* Menlo Park, CA: Cummings.

Spreitzer, G., & Sonenshein, S. (2004). Toward the construct definition of positive deviance. *American Behavioral Scientist, 47*, 828–848.

Were, M. (2003). Implementing corporate responsibility–The Chiquita case. *Journal of Business Ethics, 44*, 247–260.

Werhane, P. (1999). *Moral imagination and management decision-making.* Oxford: Oxford University Press.

Zyglidopoulos, S. C. (2002). The social and environmental responsibilities of multinationals: evidence from the Brent Spar case. *Journal of Business Ethics, 36,* 141–151.

4

Social Entrepreneurs, Socialization Processes, and Social Change: The Case of SEKEM

Tomislav Rimac and Johanna Mair
University of Navarra

Julie Battilana
Harvard University

Implementing social change often requires diverging from existing institutions that define how things are done in a given environment (Mair & Marti, 2006). This is a daunting task since institutions are patterns of acting and organizing that often become so taken-for-granted that actors perceive them as the only possible ways of acting and organizing (Douglas, 1986). Social entrepreneurs face several significant challenges in trying to implement change that diverges from existing institutions, hereafter referred to as divergent change. They have to create new ways of thinking and acting that deviate from or are at odds with the prevailing institutional environment and then convince others to both abandon institutionalized practices and adopt new ones.

While research on the conditions that enable actors to implement divergent change has highlighted the importance of discourse in convincing others to adopt practices that diverge from the existing institutional environment, we do not know much about other aspects of the change implementation (Battilana, 2011; Battilana, Leca, & Boxenbaum, 2009). In this chapter, we argue that the everyday practices of people involved in and targeted by the social change efforts might provide an important but understudied mechanism for implementing social change. More specifically, we contend that socialization processes, which are meant to introduce and reinforce desired behaviors and values in organizational members (Van Maanen & Schein, 1979), likely play a key role in implementing change as they influence how organizational members enact institutions in their everyday practices (Battilana & Dorado, 2010). When engaging in social change, social entrepreneurs face the challenge of socializing people in ways that depart from the prevailing institutional environment in which they are embedded without jeopardizing social entrepreneurs' legitimacy in that environment. This chapter explores processes employed by social entrepreneurs to maintain this delicate balance while implementing divergent change. How can they possibly simultaneously balance these tensions and accomplish significant social change?

To address this question, we use an in-depth case study of SEKEM. Dr. Ibrahim Abouleish founded SEKEM in 1977 in Egypt with the mission to create a society "where every human being can unfold his or her individual potential" (SEKEM, 2010, p. 6). We illustrate how, by adopting an inclusive model of organizing that integrates economic, social, and cultural activities, SEKEM created a cocoon within which it managed to socialize people in ways that departed from the prevailing institutional environment in Egypt. SEKEM's model enabled its organizational members to increase their perception of self-worth, sense of personal responsibility, and respect for other organizational members and to potentially take an active role in social change processes. To understand the mechanisms at play, we concentrate our analytical efforts around the widely used practice of employee circles. The circle serves as our empirical window to illustrate how everyday practices are part of the change agency repertoire and create an important mechanism for social change.

The remainder of this chapter is organized in the following way. We first provide an overview of SEKEM and then present the prevailing institutional context in Egypt in the 1980s and 1990s. Next, we introduce and interpret the practice of the circle. We situate the practice within the process of social change envisioned by SEKEM by analyzing both what it does and what it means. We conclude by discussing this chapter's contribution to the literature on agency and social change and by offering avenues and suggestions for future research.

THE SEKEM INITIATIVE

After 19 years of living in Austria, first as a student at the University of Graz, then as a scientist and a director of a pharmaceutical research center, Dr. Ibrahim Abouleish went back to Egypt in 1975 to show his children his native country. However, the Egypt he encountered during his visit was different from his memory of the country during his childhood and adolescence. Reflecting on overpopulated cities, widespread poverty, and a fragile health system, he observed:

> With shock I realized that the old one was often better than the new—but in a life orientated toward the future the new should have been better than the old. Here it was different—such a decline in twenty years! (Abouleish, 2005, p. 60)

Concerned and moved by his experience, in 1977 Dr. Abouleish returned to Egypt. Guided by the spiritual inspiration that he found in Islam and anthroposophy—a human oriented spiritual philosophy—he set out to develop a new and ambitious holistic model of sustainable development for Egypt.

Immediately following his arrival, Dr. Abouleish purchased 70 hectares of desert near Cairo with the intention of addressing many of his country's problems (Seelos & Mair, 2004). Two years later, he founded the SEKEM Initiative and set in motion an improbable experiment: he engaged in biodynamic[1] agriculture aimed at transforming the desert into productive farmland. However, his ambition did not stop there. His objective was to pursue social change by transforming the economic, social, and cultural reality of people living in nearby communities and ultimately, of Egyptian society.

Though the first three years were difficult, SEKEM made considerable progress. It planted 120,000 trees to protect the soil from erosion, increased fertility through composting, and negotiated disputes over the land with the Egyptian army. Most notably, despite significant local resistance from both farmers and the Egyptian government, it began

---

[1] A type of organic farming based on the ideas of anthroposophy. It looks upon the farm and the soil as strong, self-sustaining, and vibrant living organisms that recognize and respect the basic principles at work in nature.

cultivation according to international biodynamic standards. By setting standards and establishing trust and awareness among employees, farmers, and support organizations, SEKEM was able to help legitimize biodynamic cultivation in Egypt. In 1990, SEKEM established the Centre for Organic Agriculture, which the Egyptian government later appointed as the independent inspection body for international organic certification. SEKEM also created the Egyptian Biodynamic Association to promote organic agriculture and provide training, research, and advisory services. SEKEM's early success with medicinal plant products in local and international markets led to a collaboration with the ministry of agriculture to develop a system of pheromone plant protection for cotton, and eventually a ban on pesticide crop dusting throughout Egypt. By 2000, the approach promoted by SEKEM was applied to 80% of the country's cotton crop, and this change contributed to more than a 90% decline in chemical pesticide use in Egyptian cotton fields (Seelos & Mair, 2006; 2007). Today, Egypt is one of the top ten global producers of organic cotton (Organic Exchange, 2009). With annual revenues of EGP 193 million (approximately US$ 34 million) (SEKEM, 2010), SEKEM is one of the leading organic producers in the Middle East.

Though they were established as for-profit organizations, SEKEM companies follow the principles associated with "social businesses" or "social purpose organizations." They strictly comply with fair trade standards, are deeply committed to the well-being of employees and the communities with which they engage, and reinvest 10% of their profits in the SEKEM Development Foundation to finance community projects to improve education, health, and cultural development (SEKEM, 2010, p. 43). From its inception, Dr. Abouleish has thought of it as more than a conglomeration of for-profit and not-for-profit organizations engaged in biodynamic agriculture. His vision for SEKEM was to create a thriving initiative committed to the holistic development of its employees, the local community, and ultimately Egyptian society. His belief was that society's problems were complex and therefore required a holistic approach that addressed all of the economic, social, and cultural spheres of life. This belief led to the creation of SEKEM's integrative development methodology, which is composed of a multitude of interrelated components such as literacy, vocational training, primary healthcare, community outreach, arts, and education. To implement this methodology, SEKEM created three nongovernmental organizations (NGOs) providing health, education, and cultural services to SEKEM employees and to the surrounding communities. Overall, SEKEM employs over 2,000 people in its eight for-profit businesses and NGOs and provides health, education, and cultural services to approximately 40,000 people (Abouleish & Abouleish, 2009).

In 2003, SEKEM was awarded the Right Livelihood Award, which stated in the press release (cf. Seelos & Mair, 2004):

> SEKEM (Egypt) shows how a modern business can combine profitability and engagement in world markets with a humane and spiritual approach to people and respect for the natural environment. The Jury sees in SEKEM, "a business model for the 21st century in which commercial success is integrated with and promotes the social and cultural development of society through the economics of love."

Today SEKEM's accomplishments[2] in Egypt are widely recognized by a number of international organizations such as World Economic Forum, Arab Sustainability Leadership Group, the Ford Foundation, the Acumen Fund, and One World Award. SEKEM is credited with contributing to the reduction of widespread poverty, fulfillment of elementary human needs such as education and healthcare, prevention of violations of basic human liberties and political freedoms, shaping of national policies and business practices, and effective handling of increasing threats to the environment. However, the path toward these outcomes has often required overcoming tough challenges.

In a society where individual responsibility is often relinquished to a higher level of authority—be it the family, the government, or God—one of the key challenges that SEKEM faced was to initiate and support change in people's attitudes and behaviors. Within the boundaries of the organization, it aimed to remove attitudes of powerlessness and dependence by inculcating attitudes of proactiveness and self-efficacy that would enable people not only to imagine different social arrangements, but also to act on them. How did SEKEM approach this challenge? It employed a social change repertoire involving a number of tools and processes. In this chapter, we focus on the circle, which is one of the socialization practices that SEKEM used to try to transform its employees into social change agents by replacing their existing attitudes and behaviors with new ones.

---

[2] For a detailed list of accomplishments, please refer to SEKEM's reports on sustainable development (SEKEM, 2010).

INSTITUTIONAL CONTEXT AND
SOCIAL CHANGE IN EGYPT

Some of the largest impediments to SEKEM's social change efforts arose from the persistence of attitudes and behaviors shaped by the dominant institutions in Egypt, such as religion, family, and the social class system. A German-born managing director of one of SEKEM's companies told us about the obstacles he encountered when he started working for SEKEM in the mid-1980s:

> I had to work with people I found not having a sense of responsibility for what they were doing ... Here [In Egypt], the responsibility always belonged to somebody else. People always said that things were outside of their control and power—often it was interpreted as the will of Allah. This has caused a lot of problems. (personal interview, 2008)

The challenge in implementing SEKEM's vision of inclusive development was to change these deeply ingrained patterns of beliefs and behaviors while staying respectful to existing institutions in order to maintain legitimacy. To understand the complexity of the task, we provide a snapshot of the rules, traditions, and ways of thinking and acting determined by religion, family, and the social class system in Egypt at the time when SEKEM was created. We base our review on sociological accounts of the social, economic, and cultural changes taking place in Egypt since the early 1950s (Amin, 2006; Shamir, 1995).

Changes in the social and cultural conditions of Egypt and its evolution as a state cannot be decoupled from Islam (Winter, 1995). The Qur'an, the central religious text of Islam, is simultaneously a religious text and a legal code. In addition to ethical and faith-based teachings, it provides guidance for interpersonal relationships and an all-encompassing legal code that "deals with forming a just society, government, economic principles, laws, schools and conducting business" (Nydell, 2006, p. 82). Consequently, Islam was pervasive in all aspects of Egyptian society during the 1980s and 1990s, from daily greetings such as *Allahu Akbar* ("God is great") to state laws that, according to the constitution, have to at a minimum implicitly agree with Islamic laws. In addition, many Egyptians developed behaviors that reflected their deep religious beliefs. For example, a strong belief in predestination, the belief that everything that occurs in life is due to the will of Allah, was particularly common among the rural population. This belief resulted in a norm in which expressing too much self-confidence in controlling events was considered a sign of arrogance that bordered on blasphemy (Nydell, 2006).

In addition to religion, family was another key institution. In Egypt, the extended family system created a stable social order and provided an indispensable material and emotional support system (Al-Krenawi & Graham, 2003). Family was one of the most prominent loci of socialization of children that traditionally emphasized integration among the kin group, taught profound respect for adults, and focused on maintaining power relations within existing networks of kin. The opinion of the family elders held considerable weight in the family and status in a family increased with age. A person's dignity, honor, and reputation were of paramount importance and often viewed as reflective of the entire family or group. Therefore, one was responsible for upholding not only individual honor, but also the honor of the family. This sense of responsibility for family members influenced a variety of decisions from hiring a new employee to selecting a spouse.

Although other factors played a role, family origin was the most important factor influencing social class and status in society. One could improve one's status through education, professional position, and acquired wealth; however, Egyptians tended to readily accept the social class into which they were born and, therefore, class mobility and class tensions were uncommon. In addition, each social class had a distinct set of norms that reinforced class boundaries. For instance, members of the upper class did not publicly engage in manual labor.

A system of authority and hierarchy among and within social classes emerged from this institutional context. Through the imposition of an absolute personal obedience (i.e., to family elders and to the will of Allah), this strict hierarchical and authoritarian social structure achieved comprehensive control over individual lives. Consequently, personal responsibility and the ability to plan, prevent, and respond proactively were foreign concepts for many in Egypt. Overall, submitting to authorities had become a norm and precluded agency; specifically, it inhibited people from proactively seeking opportunities to participate in social change that directly and indirectly affected Egyptian society.

THE CIRCLE

Given the societal norms of Egypt in the early 1980s, how could SEKEM ignite social change processes aimed at creating a society where sustainable development and individual agency would be a norm? What practices did SEKEM use to generate the necessary change in peoples' attitudes and behaviors so that they themselves might become the agents of change?

SEKEM's socialization practices played an important role in its social change efforts. In this section, we center our analysis on employee circles, one representative socialization practice. During our visits to SEKEM as part of our fieldwork,[3] we were able to both observe and participate in four circles. We filmed an additional four circles and analyzed archival data, such as videos about SEKEM and the founder's autobiography. In addition, we conducted 29 interviews during which we explicitly asked each interviewee about the history and meaning of the circle.

The practice. It is Thursday afternoon, just 10 minutes before 4 p.m. The lush vegetation that surrounds us at SEKEM's mother farm in Balbeis, an oasis in the middle of the Egyptian desert, offers little respite from scorching July sun. In a few hours, as it has been done for centuries, calls for prayer from the minarets of surrounding mosques will mark the end of the workweek. At the same moment 60 kilometers away in Cairo, people are swarming out of offices and factories making their way home. However, the workweek ends very differently at SEKEM. Suddenly, as if they were pulled by some invisible force, groups of people from different parts of the farm start to congregate in the landscaped area between three of SEKEM's factories. Deserted and peaceful just a few minutes ago, the area now fills with colors and the lively sounds of human chatter. People gather and start forming circles. The scene develops in an orderly and almost scripted manner and there is a palpable energy in the air. At exactly four o'clock, the chatter is replaced by complete silence. Standing side by side in several concentric circles are young women wearing headscarves, unshaven men in traditional galabias, men in more formal outfits, disabled children attending SEKEM's special needs education programs, schoolchildren attending SEKEM School, and young adults attending

---

[3] The data for this chapter comes from an ongoing, larger research project about SEKEM conducted by IESE Business School (Instituto de Estudios Superiores de la Empresa) that included field trips to Egypt in winter of 2003 and summer of 2008.

FIGURE 4.1
SEKEM employees' end-of-the-week circle. Source: SEKEM Report on Sustainable Development 2008.

SEKEM's vocational training programs. Figure 4.1 shows one of the end-of-the-week circles.

The voice of a man breaks the silence. In Arabic, he reports what his organization did this week and what they plan to do the following week. Then, people in the circle take the hand of those standing on either side and recite in Arabic:

> Admire what is beautiful, preserve the truth. Honor what is noble, choose what is good. Guide humans in their lives toward goals, in their actions toward what is right, in their heart toward peace, in their thoughts toward the light; and teach them to trust in divine leadership with respect to all that is: in the expansive universe, in the their own soul. (Verhag, 2007)

The circles begin to unravel. People say goodbye to one another as an unwinding human spiral passes by the members of the Abouleish family and other managers who shake hands with each one of them. In small groups, people head home through SEKEM's gates. Once on the other side of the gate, they quickly light cigarettes. SEKEM's strict no-smoking policy does not apply there.

Each morning more than 2,000 people (employees, schoolchildren, and vocational trainees) from nearby towns and villages pass through SEKEM's gates. In their respective work units, they start the day with a ritual similar to the end-of-the-week circle. For instance, in the middle of SEKEM's head office in Cairo, there is a blossoming garden providing a refuge from the hectic energy of the streets—a rare luxury in the city. At about 10 minutes before 9 a.m., people start to congregate in the garden. They greet each other with a handshake or simply with the Arabic greeting *Salaam Alaykum* translated as "Peace be upon you." Lively conversation continues until about one or two minutes before 9 a.m., when people start forming a circle. Everyone takes a random position in the circle and holds hands with his or her neighbors. A female senior manager may be holding hands with a male cafeteria worker, a female research engineer, or a foreign visitor. Exactly at 9 a.m., without much prompting, an almost meditative peace and silence descends upon the group. After a few seconds, the most senior person in the circle calls on one randomly selected individual to ask for the date and the day of the week, and then on another person, to ask about the previous day's work and plans for the day that is about to begin. This is followed by a joint recitation of a non-denominational grace after which the circle dissolves and the workday begins.

At the same time, at SEKEM's mother farm, students of the SEKEM School form their circles. Their circles resemble unwinding spirals where students and teachers, girls and boys, Muslims and Copts[4] hold hands and recite the following grace:

> The sun with loving light makes bright for me each day. The soul with spirit power gives strength unto my limbs. In sunlight shining clear, I revere, oh God, the strength of humankind, which Thou so graciously hast planted in my soul that I with all my might, may love to work and learn. From Thee stream light and strength. To Thee rise love and thanks.[5]

Once the circle dissolves, students head to their classrooms. At the entrance, they greet the teachers by shaking their hands and by looking them directly in their eyes.

Interpreting the Practice

How and why did the circle emerge as a practice? Primarily, the circle was developed to replace the existing institutionally shaped modes of beliefs and behaviors and to create new ones in order to address two key problems that were impeding SEKEM employees from actively participating in the change processes envisioned by Dr. Abouleish. First, punctuality and planning were unfamiliar concepts for many of SEKEM's employees. Second, they lacked a sense of equality and personal dignity that was necessary to develop respect for others, self-efficacy, and a sense of personal responsibility. A German-born female senior manager with extensive and diverse experience at SEKEM described it in the following way:

---

[4] Native Egyptian Christians
[5] Translation by Verhaag (2007)

> We have a practice of circle to develop a tradition and a daily practice of punctuality, sense of togetherness, awareness of yesterday and tomorrow ... people here do not have a sense of time ... This is why linking what one has been doing yesterday with what one is going to do today is essential.

The idea of the circle as a socialization practice that aspires to introduce people to new modes of belief and behavior originated from Dr. Abouleish's observations about Egyptian people (Abouleish, 2005, p. 97–114). He noticed that they were not effective workers without supervision and that they were even appreciative of inspection; they perceived supervision as an indication of attention and acceptance. In one of our conversations, Dr. Abouleish elaborated further on the objectives associated with the introduction of the circle:

> The circle is a very social form. We form a circle and people can see each other. But the equality and the equal opportunity is something we have been missing for a long time in this culture. Not everyone here is having comparatively equal opportunities—girls and boys, women and men. Also there are all levels of workers standing together in a circle so that they can experience that they are equal. Equality is very, very important for everybody in order to feel their dignity as human beings. I see people in Egypt—they go to their offices and to their companies without having experienced that dignity. (personal interview, July 2008)

Throughout our visits, we never encountered people arriving late to the circle, nor did we notice people deliberately skipping the practice. By all indications at our disposal, punctuality and participation had become norms of the group. The norm of punctuality was developed by instituting the circle at the beginning of the workday. In order to arrive at SEKEM in time for the circle, every employee was required to plan. This practice gradually caused their concept of time to change. Furthermore, it is easy to notice if someone is absent or arrives late since the shape of the circle enables any person to observe everyone else. By design, the circle enabled the adoption of new modes of belief and behavior as well as monitoring and reinforcing of the adoption process.

Unlike punctuality, participation in the circle is voluntary, and there are no official sanctions for those who choose not to participate. However, participation is part of a tacit obligation to one's coworkers who do not have formal authority over one another. By choosing to participate and by arriving on time, one demonstrates respect toward other employees regardless of their social status, education, or gender, and a readiness to participate in collective efforts. Participation and punctuality set in motion a virtuous circle whereby participants demonstrate and reciprocate respect for others, thereby amplifying the participants' sense of worth as human beings.

By developing mutual respect among participants, the circle has become a space for inclusion. A newly hired engineer, a native Egyptian who recently finished her doctoral studies in Germany, described how her attitude toward the circle changed from initially being reluctant to participate to fully embracing the practice due to its inclusive nature:

> When I joined SEKEM as a contractor, I was invited to join [the circle], but I didn't. They laughed and told me that I became too German … Actually, I found it to be a very innovative idea to keep different employees together, regardless of their education, responsibility levels, and seniority. And not only the circle—you can see this also when you go for the break to the cafeteria where all people are using the same dining area … not too many people outside of SEKEM are used to it … I am working also at the engineering faculty [University of Cairo] and people there are not used to such a civilized behavior. (personal interview, July 2008)

The diversity that characterized participants in the circle is unusual for social and professional gatherings in Egypt. In a country where subway cars are gender segregated, having female and male workers stand side by side and hold hands represents an important change in attitudes and behaviors. In addition to changing attitudes and behaviors between genders, having disabled students participate in the same activity with other students represents an important step toward their acceptance, integration, and the development of their self-respect at SEKEM. In an institutional context characterized by authority and strict hierarchy, the participation of SEKEM's managers in the circle serves as a clear indication of the importance of treating others with respect. Our interviews as well as our field observations revealed that the circle as a relational socialization practice has contributed to a high level of "generalized reciprocity" (Baker & Dutton, 2007), that is, people treating each other with respect, irrespective of their differences. Our observations further suggest that participants believe that regardless of their social status, education, and family background, they deserve respect as human beings. They also believe that they should regard others as equal and reciprocate respect.

Over the years, attitudes and behaviors have changed and participants have started to attribute specific meaning to the circle, thus transforming it into a symbolic practice. Our interviews and observations revealed that the circle not only became a symbol of group membership, but it also motivated individuals with the emotional energy of a "collective effervescence" (Collins, 2004) that has become embodied in sentiments of group solidarity and individual emotional energy. During our visit, one of the informers told us the following story that illustrates how the circle assumed vital relational and emotional roles for initiating and guiding divergent change processes.

As the number of SEKEM's employees started to grow, the logistics of circles were becoming increasingly complicated. Eventually, SEKEM officially abandoned the practice in the late 1990s. However, some employees continued the practice in smaller groups inside their factories. When management discovered employees continuing the practice, the employees asked for the practice to be formally reestablished arguing that circles distinguished SEKEM from other companies in Egypt. Only a few months after abandoning the practice, the management decided to reinstate the circle.

This anecdote suggests that the employees as a community had assumed ownership of the practice. It reveals that through its daily practice, participants developed an underlying emotional attachment to the circle. It defined participants' identity as SEKEM workers, motivated them to organize and redefine relationships with others (Kohut, 2009). It served as a symbol of the collective with a special status that participants protected and reinforced even if it meant disobeying the management orders. Group disobedience required confidence, trust, and energy among the participants—durable resources generated through participants' individual and collective emotional investment in the practice (Goffman, 2005). Furthermore, it required participants to see themselves as belonging to the group and to feel a sense of solidarity. Their actions became synchronous and conscious. One of the male teachers at the SEKEM School described the community building aspect of the circle in the following way:

> What do I feel when I participate in the circle? Is it just a part of my work? Yes, but this is not the most important thing. I can do my work only if people around me do their work correctly. So, I feel like a link in a chain. Only by working together we can succeed. (personal interview, 2008).

Providing participants a sense of inclusiveness and acceptance, the circle helps to demarcate the boundary of life inside and outside SEKEM. By enacting the circle every morning (when joining the organization) and on Thursday afternoon (when taking a temporary leave from the organization), the circle becomes a "rite of passage"—a ritual that accompanies the passage of a person from one environment to another and marks recognized points in the passage (Van Gennep, 2004). Thus, the circle seems to serve as an emotional and cognitive tool that participants use to manage the transition from the cocoon of SEKEM to the outside world.

The meaning assigned to the circle varies across individuals within SEKEM. For example, some of our interviewees emphasized a certain routine aspect associated with the practice, while others described the circle as a purely instrumental tool that changes people's sense of time and develops a sense of social equality. Some, such as young employees who had been part of SEKEM since their kindergarten days, even attached strong positive emotional connotations to the practice. In its extreme, it defines who they are and serves as a validation of the system of personal values, beliefs, and attitudes that have been instilled in them over their lives at SEKEM. A recently hired SEKEM School employee who joined SEKEM as a four-year-old boy and remained with SEKEM until his university age, told us:

> For people who believe in SEKEM and its ideas, it [the circle] is not a routine. I leave everything and run for the circle. For me it is not a routine. I feel I cannot start the day till I go to the circle. It is a part of me. (personal interview, July 2008)

This heterogeneity of meanings is congruent with the circle as a socialization practice that has different objectives, places where socialization occurs, and methods of implementation.

SOCIALIZATION PRACTICES AND THE PROCESS OF SOCIAL CHANGE AT SEKEM

Building on the description of the circle as a socialization practice, in this section we concentrate on the role of socialization practices in social change processes. Organizational theorists have long acknowledged the importance of socialization practices on various outcomes such as group performance and newcomers' commitment (e.g., Ashforth & Saks, 1996), or positive social capital, capacities, and outcomes (e.g., Baker & Dutton, 2007). In our analysis, we build upon prior research on socialization practices by using an institutional perspective to assess the role of organizational socialization within a social enterprise initiative in fueling processes that may generate social change.

SEKEM's vision offered an alternative to prevalent modes of organizing and acting in Egypt that facilitated initiating and implementing social change. Often, implementing social change entails pursuing divergent changes such as creating new patterns of organizing (e.g., Egyptian Biodynamic Association), breaking with existing ways of thinking and acting (e.g., replacing chemical pesticides with biodynamic cultivation methods), and/or challenging and changing attitudes and behaviors shaped by the dominant institutions such as religion, family, and social class system. Efforts to change existing attitudes and behaviors that oppose the envisioned change processes entail socializing people in unique ways. In our example, SEKEM used the socialization practice of the circle to introduce its employees to new modes of belief and behavior, such as punctuality and respect for diversity. Through its consistent and continual enactment, the circle not only contributed to change of taken-for-granted attitudes and behaviors, but also acquired a symbolic meaning for the participants (e.g., creating a collective identity). Gradually, the practice evolved to include important relational and emotional processes that fostered community building. As the practice grew beyond its immediate socialization goals, participants assumed ownership. The response of participants to management's attempt to abandon the practice suggests that some of these consequences of this evolution were unanticipated. Overall, the circle was instrumental in creating new attitudes and behaviors of equality, self-efficacy, and initiative for its participants.

Since it is still unfolding, it is unclear whether the change processes started by SEKEM and introduced at the organizational and community levels will spread widely. SEKEM's social change efforts were not intended to be limited to the boundaries of the organization or even a local community; they are focused on generating a model that could be applied by Egyptian society. The ban of the use of chemical pesticides in cotton cultivation and many other accomplishments provide anecdotal evidence that SEKEM has been successful in initiating changes that have affected the entire Egyptian society. However, we lack systematic data and evidence to demonstrate how SEKEM's efforts in socializing and empowering people to participate in social change have directly affected Egyptian society.

While a number of indicators suggest that SEKEM's socialization practices, such as the circle, will have a lasting impact, future research will need to account for possible effects of over-socialization. Some of our interviewees repeatedly pointed out that SEKEM's practices might contribute to the isolation of its employees in the Egyptian society. They shared with us their perception of SEKEM as an almost utopian socio-economic oasis that is radically different from the rest of Egyptian society. In a personal interview (2008), two young SEKEM employees, who have been part of SEKEM since their early childhood, told us:

> *Male employee:* Till the high school, I didn't have any friends outside the SEKEM School. At the University, I found myself isolated. So I started to go out and relate to other people.... I still feel that there are things missing between me and (the) few friends I have outside of SEKEM.
>
> *Female employee:* SEKEM is my home, actually. I just found everything I wanted here. I do not need anything from outside. I also don't believe that I can live in another place in Egypt.

CONCLUSION AND FUTURE DIRECTIONS

This chapter set out to explore the role of agency in the process of social change. We have done so by investigating how social enterprise organizations, such as SEKEM, can socialize people in ways that radically depart from the institutional environment in which they are embedded while being respectful to existing institutions. Specifically, using SEKEM's employee circles as an example of one of its socialization practices, we examined how everyday practices are part of the change agency repertoire of social entrepreneurs and constitute important mechanisms for implementing social change at the individual and organizational level.

Our analysis has provided several intriguing insights into the role of agency in social change First, we demonstrated that divergent change often requires social entrepreneurs to mobilize and empower intended beneficiaries to facilitate social change. By widely distributing agency, social entrepreneurs can transform a social change effort into a collective effort. In other words, in order to understand the role of agency in social change processes, we focused our analysis not on the entrepreneur, but on the organizational members affected by the socialization practices created by the entrepreneur. We demonstrate how socialization processes that create clusters of small everyday interactions can change organizational members' behaviors and beliefs. Through analyzing the structural and social aspects of these interactions, we shed light on how the values enacted by these ritualistic behaviors may change the way the participants relate to themselves and to others. We showed that though these changes may initially seem small, they can be self-reinforcing with participants playing an active role in facilitating change through processes such as monitoring and reinforcing norms. Our data suggests that these self-reinforcing cycles can cause significant changes in behaviors and beliefs over time. By actively participating in and supporting these practices, organizational members may become agents that play a key role in enacting new institutions within the organization. Indeed, our analysis suggests that these practices may even develop far beyond their original socialization purposes and create shared identities and emotional ties among organizational members. Overall, our analysis contributes to the broader literature on divergent change implementation by revealing a mechanism by which socialization practices can facilitate the creation of new norms and broader social change for individuals and organizations.

Second, we demonstrate one way in which social entrepreneurs are able to socialize people to norms that depart from the prevailing institutional environment while trying to remain respectful to it. Instead of taking an oppositional approach by directly changing institutions or creating completely new ones, social entrepreneurs may focus their efforts on socialization practices to create opportunities for organizational members to be exposed to new beliefs through ritualistic behaviors. We show how over time these behaviors and beliefs become self-sustaining within the organization and have the potential to expand beyond its boundaries. In our analysis, one of the critical elements for successfully implementing this type of change is the physical and temporal separation of the socialization practices from the prevailing institutional environment. By creating this clear separation, social entrepreneurs can create a space that does not directly challenge the prevailing norms. However, our data suggest that there may be a risk that this separation may lead to an over-socialization of organizational members that could lead to their isolation from the institutional environment. This situation may hamper efforts to diffuse practices outside of the organization and into society.

The findings of this study suggest a number of future directions for research. First, in our analysis we focused on social changes that are widely regarded to be positive. Indeed, scholars, practitioners, and policy makers increasingly see social entrepreneurship as a desirable approach to solving important socio-economic problems that plague our societies. However, over the last decade, we have realized that some interventions once regarded as panaceas for these problems may sometimes produce unintended effects. We also know that social change disrupts the status quo and threatens the associated system of power and privileges. Those who benefit from the status quo often actively resist change. Consequently, when analyzing social change, we need to examine different social and cultural dimensions of the change and take into consideration the perspective of all the constituencies involved.

Second, it is essential that we recognize that how social change is perceived is socially constructed. The perception of "positivity" of social change depends not only on the agents' points of view, but also on the point in time at which agents evaluate the change. Although a change initially may be seen as negatively deviant behavior, it eventually may become accepted and even used as a model of highly desirable, "positively" deviant behavior depending on the evolution of the institutional environment. Hence, it would be interesting to explore the factors influencing adjustments in the perception of social change over time.

Third, in order to understand social change more completely, it is necessary to analyze the effects of different processes and modes of organizing on implementing social change and on individual lives. SEKEM's inclusive form of organizing that integrates economic, social, and cultural activities with its socialization practices may have been successful in initiating its desired social change; however, the same practices may also have caused unintended effects that undermine its success. For instance, the inability to imagine life without SEKEM may indicate a significant over-socialization problem. On the other hand, we can see this problem as a transient one, likely to disappear once the social change becomes firmly entrenched in the society. Therefore, we may ask if over-socialization is a necessary step (or a necessary risk) for implementing social change. If so, under what circumstances do social entrepreneurs take that step or risk?

Finally, we argue that social change is an expansive process that, once ignited, diffuses and self-reinforces. Thus, understanding social change requires studying not only instances of and conditions for ignition but also the unfolding of social change processes experienced and shaped by the various actors involved in the process. Thirty-three years ago, Dr. Abouleish embarked on an ambitious journey of social change. The antecedents, process, and outcomes of this journey have provided rich material for our effort to relate agency and social change. Yet our study provides only a snapshot. For scholars interested in the dynamics of social change, SEKEM and other organizations involved in social change efforts provide excellent research settings. We still know far too little about the intended and unintended consequences of social change efforts. A portfolio of studies examining social change efforts across geographies and social settings will be an important step toward enhancing our understanding of social change.

REFERENCES

Abouleish, I. (2005). *SEKEM: A sustainable community in the Egyptian desert*. Edinburgh: Floris Books.

Abouleish, I., & Abouleish, H. (2009). Garden in the desert: SEKEM makes comprehensive sustainable development a reality in Egypt. *Innovations: Technology | Governance | Globalization*, 125–152.

Al-Krenawi, A., & Graham, J. R. (2003). Principles of social work practice in the Muslim Arab world. *Arab Studies Quarterly, 25*, 75–101.

Amin, G. A. (2006). *Whatever happened to the Egyptians? Changes in Egyptian society from 1950 to the present* (9th ed.). Cairo, Egypt: The American University in Cairo Press.

Ashforth, B. E., & Saks, A. M. (1996). Socialization tactics: Longitudinal effects on newcomer adjustment. *Academy of Management Journal, 39*, 149–178.

Baker, W., & Dutton, J. E. (2007). Enabling positive social capital in organizations. In J. E. Dutton & B. R. Ragins (Eds.), *Exploring positive relationships at work: Building a theoretical and research foundation* (pp. 325–346). Mahwah, NJ: Erlbaum.

Battilana, J. (2011). The enabling role of social position in diverging from the institutional status quo: Evidence from the U.K. National Health Service. *Organization Science, 22*, 817–834.

Battilana, J., & Dorado, S. (2010). Building sustainable hybrid organizations: The case of commercial microfinance organizations. *Academy of Management Journal, 53*, 1419–1440.

Battilana, J., Leca, B., & Boxenbaum, E. (2009). How actors change institutions: Toward a theory of institutional entrepreneurship. *Academy of Management Annals, 3*, 65–107.

Collins, R. (2004). *Interaction ritual chains*. Princeton, NJ: Princeton University Press.

Douglas, M. (1986). *How institutions think*. Syracuse, NY: Syracuse University Press.

Goffman, E. (1961). On the characteristics of total institutions: Staff-inmate relations. In D. R. Cressey (Ed.), *The prison: Studies in institutional organization and change* (pp. 68–106). New York: Holt, Rinehart and Winston.

Kohut, H. (2009). *The restoration of the self.* New York: University of Chicago Press.

Mair, J., & Marti, I. (2006). Social entrepreneurship research: a source of explanation, prediction, and delight. *Journal of World Business, 41,* 36–44.

Nydell, M. K. (2006). *Understanding Arabs: A guide for modern times* (4th ed.). Boston: Intercultural Press.

Organic Exchange (2009). *Cotton Farm and Fibre Report.*

Seelos, C., & Mair, J. (2004). *The SEKEM Initiative,* IESE Case Study 2004. Barcelona, Spain: IESE Business School (Instituto de Estudios Superiores de la Empresa)

Seelos, C., & Mair, J. (2006). Social entrepreneurship. The contribution of individual entrepreneurs to sustainable development. *The ICFAI Journal for Entrepreneurship Development, March,* 30–46. Hyderabad, India: Institute of Chartered Financial Analysts of India (ICFAI) University Press. ISSN: 0973-2659.

Seelos, C., & Mair, J. (2007). How social entrepreneurs enable human, social, and economic development. In V. Rangan, J. Quelch, G. Herrero, & B. Barton (Eds.), *Business solutions for the global poor: Creating social and economic calue* (pp. 271–294). San Francisco: Jossey-Bass.

SEKEM (2010). *Report on Sustainable Development 2009.* SEKEM, Cairo, Egypt. Retrieved from http://www.sekem.com/Files/PDFs/SEKEM%20%20Report%20 on%20Sustainable%20Development%202009.pdf

Shamir, S. (Ed.). (1995). *Egypt from monarchy to republic: A reassessment of revolution and change.* Boulder, CO: Westview Press.

Van Gennep, A. (2004). *The rites of passage.* London, UK: Routledge.

Van Maanen, J., & Schein, E. H. (1979). Toward a theory of organizational socialization. *Research in Organizational Behavior, 1,* 209–264.

Verhaag, B., director. (2007). *SEKEM: Born of the sun.* (DVD). DENKmal-Film GmbH, Munich, Germany.

Winter, M. (1995). Islam in the state: Pragmatism and growing commitment. In S. Shimon (Ed.), *Egypt from monarchy to republic: A reassessment of revolution and change.* Boulder, CO: Westview Press.

5

Power Beyond the Purse: Philanthropic Foundations as Agents of Social Change

Debra Meyerson
Stanford University

Laura Wernick
University of Michigan

INTRODUCTION

As an institution, philanthropy in the United States and throughout the world has become increasingly prominent in addressing social problems and effecting social change to improve the public good. According to the Foundation Center (2009), charitable giving by the 1,300 largest foundations in the United States rose in 2007 by 13.2% to $21.6 billion. Giving USA (2008) estimated that total charitable spending in the United States reached $307.65 billion in 2008, a sum that included $229.3 billion from individual donations, $14.5 billion from corporate donations, $41.2 billion from all foundations, and $22.6 billion from charitable bequests. The number of registered foundations has also expanded rapidly over the past century. Whereas in 1930 approximately 200 foundations with endowments that totaled $13 billion (in current dollars) were registered in the United States, by 2008, that number had expanded to 75,000 foundations with assets totaling more than $565 billion (Giving USA, 2008; Lawrence & Mukai, 2010).

The role of philanthropic organizations as agents and partners in social change efforts has not escaped the attention of scholars and observers from a variety of social science disciplines. Analyses by historians (e.g., Lagemann, 1989) and sociologists (e.g., DiMaggio, 1991) have documented the influential role of philanthropy in establishing and legitimating new fields, shaping social movements (e.g., McAdam, 1982; McCarthy & Zald, 1977), and creating and legitimating new organizational forms (Meyerson, Quinn, & Tompkins-Stange, 2010; Morrill, Forthcoming). Despite this acknowledgment of foundations' influence, less scholarly attention has been paid to the variety of ways that foundations approach their work, how they relate to grantees, and how they affect social change. Analyses of philanthropy's role in social change efforts offered by scholars and activists have focused on particular forms of philanthropic foundations, such as feminist foundations (e.g., Ostrander, 2004), social justice and grassroots foundations (e.g., Korten, 2009), or family foundations (Oelberger, 2010). Studies like these suggest that foundations' approach to grant-making—the assumptions they express, the processes and practices they engage, and the power relations they enact—as well as the selection and effectiveness of their grants, matter a great deal; however, these studies lack a comparative approach to understanding how different forms of foundation support effect change.

In this chapter, we build on the authors' independent empirical projects to compare and contrast the assumptions, values, and social change processes engaged by two different types of philanthropic foundations—"venture philanthropy" and "grassroots, or community-based, social justice philanthropy"—to illustrate how different forms of foundations may assume distinct roles as agents of positive social change. Both approaches focus on improving the public good by drawing upon the strengths of leaders to empower communities to create positive social change; however, each approach draws upon different assumptions about the source of agency and power, which manifest themselves in their missions, strategies and expertise, and decision making and accountability processes to impact change. Most generally, venture philanthropy begins with a "top-down" approach to change, emphasizing big bets on novel and scalable solutions offered by bold *entrepreneurs* (Letts, Ryan, & Grossman, 1997), whereas social justice (or grassroots) philanthropy is decidedly bottom-up, favoring processes that originate in, are partially controlled by, and build capacity within a local community even as they grow (Korten, 2009).

The contrasting approaches raise different, yet complimentary dilemmas that can help us shed light on the strengths and limitations of each approach. We will begin this chapter with a selective review of prior research on philanthropy and social change, focusing on main currents in organization theory and sociology. We then describe the two empirical projects that ground our analysis. Following this description, we use a positive lens to draw attention to what it is about each approach that most benefits those funded and creates beneficial social change. We will bring this forward at the end as well. We conclude with a discussion of the differences between approaches and their implications for positive social change and change agency.

PREVIOUS RESEARCH ON FOUNDATIONS AND SOCIAL CHANGE

The effects of foundation support on the trajectory of social change efforts have been at the center of a long-standing debate. Most academic scholarship has focused on the top-down approach to grant making, which is exemplified in the venture philanthropy approach. Among social movement scholars, early versions of resource mobilization theory contend that the success of social movements depends on securing the sponsorship of elites who "control large resource pools" (McCarthy & Zald, 1977, p. 1121). Critics of this view argue that elite sponsorship of social movements results in the cooptation or cooling out of radical elements of a movement by channeling protest activities toward more conservative goals and strategies (e.g., Haines, 1984; Jenkins & Eckert, 1986; McAdam, 1982; Skocpol, 2003). Other scholars of social movements have complicated this debate by showing how foundations' efforts can simultaneously support radical action while also channeling elements of a social movement toward more conservative strategies and goals. As one example, Tim Bartley (2007) showed how a handful of foundations enrolled a disparate set of actors to create the new field of forest certification. In so doing, foundations channeled the social movement organizations without eliminating the radical protest activities. More generally, Bartley's study illustrated the variety of processes utilized by foundations to advance social change for which movement scholars had not yet accounted.

In addition to the research on philanthropy in the context of social movements, foundations' efforts have been the subject of study by organizational sociologists, who demonstrate foundations' roles in field building and professionalization (e.g., DiMaggio, 1991; Morrill, Forthcoming). DiMaggio's research on the construction and professionalization of the U.S. art museum field highlighted the role of the Carnegie Corporation. More recently, Khurana (2007) demonstrated foundations' influence in professionalizing and legitimatizing business schools through their support of core research activities. In their study of the professionalization of the non-profit field, Hwang and Powell (2009) conclude that foundations exert influence on non-profit organizations not only through the funds they provide, but more importantly through the mindsets and attendant practices they stipulate in grant agreements they impose on non-profit organizations.

In contrast, a handful of academic scholars (Korten, 2009; Odendahl, 1990; Ostrander, 1995; Silver, 1998), along with industry watchdogs and professional associations within the field of philanthropy, such as the National Committee for Responsive Philanthropy, Grantmakers for Effective Organizations, Grantcraft, and Urban Institute, have engaged in studies that highlight those foundations that take a more "grassroots," or bottom-up, approach to social change philanthropy, and that emphasize the need for including the knowledge, expertise, and experiences of community members who are most impacted by social injustices into the grant-making process. Ostrander (1995), for example, highlights this approach through her study of Haymarket People's Fund, where the decision-making process is shifted to those in the community who have been historically marginalized, thereby drawing upon the knowledge and experience that comes from living within the social conditions that are being addressed and increasing the accountability to grantees. However, this approach is not without critics. Today, only a small percentage of social change funding takes this grassroots approach (Jenkins & Halcli, 1999; National Committee for Responsive Therapy, 2005). Moreover, Odendahl (1990) and Silver (1998) both suggest that wealthy donors often still have a disproportionate amount of power by virtue of their ability to withdraw funding.

Based on a study of 1,992 foundations, Ostrower (2004, 2006) concluded that foundations are most commonly categorized by type (corporate, community, or independent), assets, or staff size. However, she argues that:

"[T]o capture broader elements of foundation approaches to philanthropy, we also need to develop ways of categorizing foundations that reflect differences in how they approach their work and the underlying philosophies that inform their philanthropy" (2006, pp. 510–511). Ostrander's (1999, 2004) research suggests that a foundation's approach to grant making shapes the processes it engages and the outcomes it seeks to effect. While professionals in the field of philanthropy and a few comparative studies attend to the variation in philanthropic approaches, there remains much to learn about the significance of these differences for processes of social change and change agency. In this spirit, this chapter compares two approaches to philanthropy, venture and grassroots social justice philanthropy, paying particular attention to the qualities of each approach that have the potential to catalyze positive social change processes.

TWO APPROACHES, TWO PROJECTS

In order to provide a more complete context, we will briefly describe the two projects and sources from which we have extracted the principles and examples. Our description of venture philanthropy draws on data from a larger project on philanthropy and education led by the first author and her colleagues (Meyerson, Quinn, & Oelberger, 2010; Meyerson, Quinn, & Tompkins-Stange, 2010). As part of that project, the team examined the practices and principles of the NewSchools Venture Fund (2009), a venture philanthropy firm that has been integrally involved in what informants referred to as "the entrepreneurial reform movement" in U.S. education, by sponsoring the expansion of charter school systems and other promising organizational, technological, and human resource innovations.

NewSchools Venture Fund was founded in 1998 by two prominent Silicon Valley venture capitalists who, in the course of doing research into a potential investment in an educational technology company, were shocked by the appalling state of public schools in California. Their founding aspiration was to apply principles of venture capital to identify and support entrepreneurial organizations that would address the ills of public education. With their own funds and backing by other prominent high technology investors and entrepreneurs, they founded NewSchools Venture Fund and hired their first CEO, a Stanford business school student and member of the founding team of Teach for America, to lead their effort (Dees & Anderson, 2001a; 2001b).[1]

For 15 months beginning in January 2008, Meyerson and colleagues periodically observed and participated in NewSchools Venture Fund partner and staff meetings, retreats, and invitation-only conferences. They had access to supporting documents, such as grant agreements, presentations, and staff memos that contained assessments of grantees and the metric by which partners of NewSchools Venture Fund assessed the current and prospective organizations in its portfolio. They supplemented these data with formal interviews with four partners of NewSchools Venture Fund. In addition, as part of the larger project, the research team interviewed 30 of NewSchools Venture Fund's grantees, primarily leaders and founders of charter school systems funded by NewSchools Venture Fund. The purpose of these interviews was to learn about grantees' priorities and challenges and their relationship with different foundation sponsors. Although these interviews did not focus on grantees' relationship with NewSchools Venture Fund, our inferences about NewSchools Venture Fund's approach and relations with grantees were informed by these conversations.

Our portrait of the second approach to philanthropy relies on data from Wernick's (2009) dissertation project on social justice philanthropy and young donor organizing, ongoing observations of a professional network of social justice foundations, and secondary case reports. Wernick studied Resource Generation (RG), a national organization with over 1,200 members who participate in regional chapters throughout the United States. RG attempts to bridge the worlds of philanthropy and grassroots community organizing through their organizational relationships as well as through individuals' participation in the philanthropic and grassroots sectors.

Wernick began her collection in 2005 with participant observation, and she continued to engage in periodic observation of various activities through the first half of 2010. During this period, she attended conferences, workshops, and meetings of social justice philanthropists that included delegates from RG. She also conducted 25 semi-structured interviews, a document analysis, and a web-based survey of RG's current and

---

[1] Because NewSchools Venture Fund, like many other venture philanthropy firms, relied on monies it raised from other sources, including major foundations, it was technically considered a public charity rather than a foundation under the 501(c)(3) code. Nonetheless, the firm's primary function was philanthropic and thus, for this purpose, we refer to it as a foundation.

former staff, constituents, board members, facilitators, and community allies. In addition, Wernick participated in a series of events organized by a network of funders that self-identified as social justice philanthropists, including members of the Funding Exchange, a network of 16 public foundations, such as North Star, Haymarket, and Headwaters, each of which funds grassroots community organizations, as well as the Twenty-First Century Foundation (21CF), a social justice foundation aimed at improving Black communities. The description of social justice philanthropy that follows blends examples from Wernick's observations with secondary source reports and foundations' publicly available materials.

PHILANTHROPY AND SOCIAL CHANGE

Venture Philanthropy

Mission and Assumptions

Over the last two decades, a small set of new actors in the U.S. philanthropic field have attempted to distinguish themselves from "traditional" philanthropy by adopting the language and ideology of the venture capital industry. Commonly referred to as venture philanthropy, the approach focuses on funding what are perceived to be innovations and start-up non-profit organizations rather than supporting traditional methods and established organizations. Proponents of the venture philanthropy approach argue that non-profits are often undercapitalized by traditional foundations. In order to address this, venture philanthropists favor "big bets" whereby a smaller number of organizations are provided with greater funds, as opposed to supporting a range of organizations, but providing fewer resources to individual groups.

Reflecting this orientation, the mission of NewSchools Venture Fund has been to "transform public education through powerful ideas and passionate entrepreneurs so that *all* children have the opportunity to succeed in the 21st century" (NewSchools Venture Fund, 2009, p. 4). Every document we consulted and person we interviewed concurred with the organization's publicly stated mission. To the founders of NewSchools Venture Fund and many of its partners, the inequities in public education represented the greatest and most pressing social injustice of the time. One of the founders explained her commitment to the organization's mission: In

a just society, a "child's zip code should not determine his or her opportunities in life" (Ed Ventures, 2009, p. 4). NewSchools Venture Fund was
established to remedy this injustice.

A core assumption underlying NewSchools Venture Fund's approach to
change was the potential for entrepreneurs and entrepreneurial solutions to
address social problems. An internal strategy document explained the firm's
focus on entrepreneurs: "entrepreneurs exploit innovative ideas, focus on
the needs of customers, act with urgency, and are accountable for results." In
answering the hypothetical question, "Why entrepreneurs?" the same document explained, "entrepreneurs are [not afraid] to *compete* or collaborate
with the established system to bring about change," and they are not afraid
"to build independent organizations that are immune from policy changes."[2]

Strategy and Expertise

Venture philanthropists profess to a more engaged relationship with their
grantees, as compared to "traditional" philanthropy. Beyond the provision of 12-month grants, venture philanthropists agree to a multiyear
commitment that may include technical assistance on long-term organizational stability issues, board development, and executive director coaching. Since many self-proclaimed venture philanthropists acquired their
wealth in the business world, they may favor business talent and experience to lead the organizations they fund, and provide support for a more
business-oriented strategy in organizations they support.

NewSchools Venture Fund pursued its mission through three pillars
of activities, which together comprised the firm's strategy or "theory of
change." The first pillar, reflecting its core assumption about the promise
of entrepreneurs, was to "identify the most promising education entrepreneurs" (Ed Ventures, 2009, p. 15) from business, education, and other
fields. These were people who had thoughtful and ambitious plans to build
innovative organizations that would alter existing practices or challenge
traditional educational institutions; in short, the people and organizations
NewSchools Venture Fund sought to support were "not beholden to the
status quo. They [brought] fresh thinking to the problems of public education, and invent[ed] ways of organizing schooling around the needs of

---

[2] Summarized statement extracted from internal strategy document (NewSchools Venture Fund,
2009).

students rather than the interest of adults" (NewSchools Venture Fund, 2009, p. 15). In founding NewSchools Venture Fund, they explicitly sought to harness that same energy and ingenuity to remedy the problems of established educational institutions.

NewSchools Venture Fund's preference for supporting entrepreneurs who brought fresh approaches to entrenched problems was illustrated in its start-up investment in 2000 in a bold plan to create New Leaders for New Schools, a national organization to build an alternative pipeline of talented principals for K-12 schools. NewSchools Venture Fund backed Jon Schnur, who conceived of the organization as the winning entry to a Harvard business plan competition. He proposed to build an organization of sufficient scale and quality that it would challenge the grip of the traditional institutions that had held control of the training and credentialing of school leaders. With NewSchools Venture Fund's ongoing support, by 2009 New Leaders for New Schools had grown to recruit and train 565 principals in 9 cities.

The second pillar of their strategy was to apply "engaged venture philanthropy," which they took to mean to support entrepreneurs and "help fund [them] from an early stage" so that they could "grow to scale high-impact education organizations." Implicit in this statement is NewSchools Venture Fund's adherence to venture philanthropy's emphasis on growing organizations to a scale that allows them to maximize impact and sustainability. For example, they enacted this pillar in their choices to fund organizations that had the potential to efficiently replicate schools within or across communities. As a result, grantees and potential grantees reported that an intention and compelling plan to scale was the price of securing funding. In response to a question about the origins of his push to replicate charter schools, a founder of a charter school system and an early grantee of the NewSchools Venture Fund responded:

> We had to raise some money [for our original school] locally and so where was the money? The money was in scale. [The NewSchools Venture Fund partner] told me point blank when he visited my school, "Sam, I'm not going to give you money [for one school], but if you [plan to] create ten schools, I'll give you money."

Our informant was not alone in his response to funders' push to scale. As we have argued elsewhere (Meyerson, Quinn, & Tompkins-Stange, 2010), the emphasis on scale by some funders has resulted in the rapid growth of charter systems that have built a capacity to replicate schools.

"Engaged venture philanthropy" was also practiced by NewSchools Venture Fund through their ongoing involvement and input in organizations they were funding. This was accomplished through board participation and monitoring, strategic advice from NewSchools Venture Fund's partners or hired consultants, and sustained investment contingent on ongoing monitoring of grantees' performance.

The third pillar of NewSchools Venture Fund's strategy went beyond the traditional principles of venture philanthropy. As an important part of its efforts to build a new field, NewSchools Venture Fund devoted significant resources to building a network of thoughtful leaders across the business, education, and non-profit and policy communities (NewSchools Venture Fund). The firm led these efforts by sponsoring a variety of forums, many of which were invitation only and established clear criteria of inclusion in an emerging professional community (Meyerson, Quinn, & Tompkins-Stange, 2010). In these forums, grantees and other like-minded funders shared knowledge and best practices and cultivated relationships across sectors. These networking activities were, according to NewSchools Venture Fund leaders, pivotal to their overall strategy of building a new field of "educational entrepreneurship."

In this way, NewSchools Venture Fund's approach to change helped legitimate an emerging preference for managerial forms of knowledge and expertise, particularly through its support of an educational entrepreneurship field and by supporting programs that could be replicated across communities. Leaders in the NewSchools Venture Fund identified that existing problems in education emerged from the present system of institutions, communities, and educational professionals. Responding to this, the foundation sponsored programs and organizations that would incorporate the spirit of managerial professions—specifically, organizations that valued efficiency and scalability. Sometimes these priorities conflicted with the acceptance by community members and their expressed needs and desires for educational change.

Decision Making and Accountability

Venture philanthropy attempts to address the issues of effectiveness and accountability by drawing from the methods of venture capitalists who, particularly during the high-tech boom, conducted due diligence to screen out poor investment decisions, provided long-term financial commitments, and offered ongoing advice and consulting on the management of startups. Venture philanthropists argue for the tracking of social return on investment (SROI) by their grantees. Even when not employing an SROI framework, the emphasis is on tangible and measurable results. Venture philanthropists argue that the traditional foundation model does not include a strategy for withdrawing funding, which can lead to the continued funding of underperforming and ineffective organizations.

NewSchools Venture Fund (2009) decision-making structure and process were systematic, careful, and unambiguously top-down. Although the size of investment determined the specific decision-making processes, partners and members of the board of directors were primarily responsible for deciding on investments. Individual partners took leadership of evaluating potential grantees based on evaluation of the entrepreneurial team, the "market," and potential for scalability and impact. That same individual partner was also responsible for presenting the organization to the partner team, who could then approve a project outright (if the investment was small enough), or send the project to the investment committee of the board for approval.[3] NewSchools Venture Fund's board is comprised of elite outsiders who are representatives of other foundations or venture capitalists. As a result, entrepreneurs that made their way through NewSchools Venture Fund's rigorous screening process not only received material support, but gained access to NewSchools Venture Fund growing network of funders, business people, politicians, and educational entrepreneurs—they became "part of an elite national club," as one grantee explained.

In addition, venture philanthropy emphasizes close monitoring of grantee performance through explicit metrics to which they hold grantees accountable. For example, NewSchools Venture Fund monitored each of its grantee organizations using a set of educational measures that could be applied to most of its organizations. Those measures included, but were not limited to, dimensions such as gains in student test scores, the "managerial and operational" qualifications of a grantee's leadership team, and the viability of a grantee's "replication model" or its capacity to grow to scale. Metrics were articulated as time-stamped milestones, and NewSchools Venture Fund held grantees accountable to these by tying funding to measured performance against milestones. Although, a number of grantees acknowledged that they had some voice in the specific metrics to which

---

[3] Based on summary contained within internal documents (NewSchools Venture Fund, 2009).

they were held accountable, the balance of performance metrics were defined and monitored by NewSchools Venture Fund as expressions of the organization's strategy of change.

As is generally the case in philanthropy, NewSchools Venture Fund controls a resource pool that grantees have come to rely on. This suggests that these firms favor (or "cherry pick") grantees that adhere to the principles and ideology of market efficiency and business rationality endorsed by venture philanthropists. The drawback, of course, is that effective organizations that embody alternate ideologies are in danger of falling by the wayside. As organizations with considerable material resources and the ability to confer legitimacy to non-profit organizations through the grant-making process, venture philanthropy firms can shape new ideas around organizational structure and practice that, eventually, may become standard. While a venture philanthropy framework may be an efficient way to disperse capital and expertise, particularly where large-scale impact is a goal, it is not the only way.

Grassroots Social Justice Philanthropy

Mission and Assumptions

While venture philanthropy may seek to address the manifestations of institutional and social inequalities—unemployment, the achievement gap, poor access to healthcare—grassroots, or community-based, social justice philanthropy aims to address the root causes of those inequalities and to challenge the practices and institutions that reproduce them. Instead of accountability to donors, this approach suggests that foundations need to be accountable and transparent to the public, grantees, and constituents throughout each step in the philanthropic process. For this reason, organizations that adhere to the principles of grassroots social justice philanthropy seek to render funds in ways that challenge and alter the asymmetric power relation inherent in foundation-grantee relationships, modeling the vision of the change they want to promote (National Committee for Responsive Philanthropy, 2009).

For example, community-based public foundations such as Haymarket in Boston, North Star Fund in New York, and Headwaters from the Funding Exchange Network utilize activist-led grant-making strategies to alter these power relationships. According to its 2010 Web site, "Haymarket People's Fund is an anti-racist and multicultural foundation that is committed to strengthening the movement for social justice in New England. Through grant making, fundraising and capacity building, we support grassroots organizations that address the root causes of injustice. Haymarket also organizes to increase sustainable community philanthropy throughout our region" (Haymarket People's Fund, 2010). Similarly, the Twenty-First Century Foundation (21CF), a fund dedicated to promoting new models of Black philanthropy that work with and serve local Black communities, also illustrates this approach. "Our mission is to lead, innovate and influence giving for Black community change. As one of the few, endowed, Black foundations in the U.S., Twenty-First Century Foundation (21CF) works to advance the welfare of the Black community through strategic and collective grant making ..." (Twenty-First Century Foundation, 2010).

The principles and practices of social justice philanthropy rest on the assumption that the individuals and communities who are most negatively impacted by social and economic injustices have critical knowledge, experiences, and other resources that are essential to address the roots of injustice. Following this belief, grassroots social justice philanthropy strives that those most impacted are integrally involved in the decision making that affects their communities and the philanthropic process generally. Adherents to the principles of the grassroots approach to social justice philanthropy assume that the inclusion of community members not only reflects core democratic principles, but also that the participation of these people enhances decision making, implementation, and accountability.

Strategy and Expertise

Following from these working assumptions, the organizations that self-identify as social justice foundations pursue their social justice missions through strategies that seek to privilege the expertise, knowledge, and experiences of people and organizations who are the intended beneficiaries of grants, by ensuring that their decision-making structures incorporate members of the community they are meant to serve—those who have been most affected by social and economic injustices. This insistence on local and diverse representation is designed to create solutions that speak to the needs of a community and build on its local resources and talent. Working with local community members has served to both identify and cultivate within the community a pool of talented, well-trained activist leaders. These leaders have the knowledge and expertise to address the structural roots of inequalities that afflict the community. By focusing on community-based talent and leaders, social justice foundations operation-alize a wide variety of "expertise," allowing for a range of specialists— local business people, trained social workers, local organizers—who are able to build a complex and comprehensive understanding of the social problems, and therefore, more complete solutions.

Moreover, the promotion of and dependence on local expertise shapes how social justice foundations work with members of the local communi-ties they are trying to serve. In particular, trust takes a prominent role in the approach of these organizations. Rather than depending on the systematic and lengthy vetting process that is characteristic of venture philanthropy, social justice philanthropists are more likely to depend on community rela-tionships and institutional trust to guide which projects they fund. This trust building often includes a program officer who has personal ties to the community and/or has taken the time to educate themselves about the community (McGarvey & Mackinnon, 2008; National Committee for Responsive Philanthropy, 2009). "It really means continuing to be curious and ask us as many questions as possible," explained Tara Seeley of Central Indiana Community Foundation, "it's getting out in the neighborhood and listening" (Buteau, Buchanan, & Chu, 2010, p. 12). By building trust and institutional relationships, grantees and funders are able to determine col-laboratively the effectiveness of the foundations' support. Most often, grant-ees are the experts on the issues that the funder wants to address and the funder needs to be willing and open to learn from them. Furthermore, this trust can be developed through longer term sustained contact and when calls and e-mails are returned in a timely and respectful manner (Buteau et al., 2010; McGarvey & Mackinnon, 2008). Trust allows and is reinforced by funding relationships that provide multiyear grants, general operating funds, unrestricted funding, and, importantly, rapid response grants.

Rapid response grants, a common practice among social justice phi-lanthropists, provide the latitude for foundations to support community-based organizations through political, social, economic, or environmental crises. The application process for these grants has been simplified dra-matically to shorten the approval cycle, which allows for organizations that are in the most need of funding to receive it—sometimes within days or hours of the request. For example, North Star Fund in New York City enabled "groups to organize strategic events or initiatives that could not have been anticipated in their regular program work," while the Alaska

Conservation Foundation provides funds to address fast-breaking, unforeseen environmental issues that arise and require immediate attention (Alaska Conservation Foundation, 2010; North Star Fund, 2010). For example, North Star Fund and others had been funding Domestic Workers United (DWU), a New York City-based organization that had been organizing domestic workers to fight for power, respect, and fair labor standards, over a period of eight years. In that time, North Star also provided them critical rapid response grants for emergencies that included last-minute convenings, mobilizations to Albany, and city hall vigils. Ai-Jen Poo, DWU's lead organizer explained, "There's always twists and turns as we do our work, as power shifts and things unfold. The Rapid Response grant allows for organizers to have access to a pool of resources to be able think on their feet in changing times" (North Star Fund, 2009).

In addition to the small-scale flexibility of rapid response grants, another way social justice funders encourage creative and innovative efforts for social change is through funding clusters of organizations such as creative collaborations, coalitions, and networks to expand their impact and build on the resources and expertise of other communities. For example, following Hurricanes Katrina and Rita in 2005, the Twenty-First Century Foundation (21CF) helped form the STEPS coalition, a group of more than 40 organizations along the Mississippi Gulf Coast to promote cooperative, proactive, and equitable rebuilding strategies. In this way, social justice philanthropy is able to support wide-scale action, while still concentrating and focusing on supporting community-based and grassroots organizations. (As a result of their organizing, Mississippi doubled STEPS' federal dollars [$50,000 to $100,000] for lower-income residents to rebuild their homes [Twenty-First Century Foundation, 2007].)

Decision Making and Accountability

As described earlier, social justice foundations strive to include members of local communities, specifically those who are directly impacted by structural inequalities, throughout the decision-making processes. This serves as a means to expand conceptions of expertise as well as a direct challenge to the traditional power relations that underlie and recreate the inequalities philanthropists are attempting to change (Ostrander, 2004). Additionally it functions as a means to increase foundations' accountability to local communities.

Beyond the decision-making structures and processes of any one organization, social justice philanthropy places value on collaboration between organizations and funders, which influences foundations' decision making. A good example of the increased role collaboration has in large-scale decision making is Gulf Coast Funders for Equity. This group consists of more than 100 funders—including the 21CF—all of which employed a bottom-up grant-making approach by including in the decision making those with the least access to resources (Gulf Coast Funders for Equity, 2010; Twenty-First Century Foundation, 2007). Together, these groups mapped the flow of philanthropic dollars, established collaborative funding strategies, engaged foundations as advocates, and expanded philanthropic opportunities in areas such as community organizing, mental health, immigration, and refugee policy (Twenty-First Century Foundation, 2007).

Grassroots social justice philanthropy recognizes that addressing the root causes of social injustice is a protracted, challenging, and community-specific project. As funders who see themselves as accountable primarily to local communities, the metrics used to evaluate grantees have tended to vary, reflecting the goals and criteria the grantee set up for themselves—in both the short and long term. Unlike the venture approach, there is recognition that one size does not fit all. While these metrics are developed at the beginning of a grant process, there is an understanding that these may shift in accordance with the situational context. By allowing grantees to develop their own standards to measure their success, and including those who are most impacted in decision-making processes, social justice philanthropy allows funders and organizations to share a comprehensive and complete view of the progress and struggles of an organization.

Moreover, because much of social justice philanthropy relies on community organizing as a means of systemic change, in addition to measuring concrete policy and institutional changes, these funds measure the development of local capacities and leadership, particularly among those who are disenfranchised. For example, metrics also access various aspects of organizational capacity building including: grantees' increase in capability and diversity in their membership, developing skills, and building community-based leadership that represents the diversity of people within the community. Moreover, metrics access the organization's capacity to work collaboratively and form coalitions. This approach to accountability metrics may be less objectively verifiable and comparable to other organizations than the quantitative metrics applied by venture philanthropy;

however, grassroots social justice foundations have weighted more heavily less tangible criteria, such as the building of trust, hope, and community engagement. Social justice philanthropists believe that these measures are significant indicators of an organization's success. The search for appropriate and credible metrics is therefore an ongoing challenge and one that is at the center of lively debates among grantees and funders (Alexander, Brudney, & Yang, 2010; Suarez, 2010).

Social justice philanthropy allows for accountability and community involvement, as well as the ability for communities to be active agents in controlling their own social justice projects; however, this approach requires a significant dedication of time, resources, energy, and relationships for each funded project. Likewise, there has been historically fewer dollars that have gone to grassroots social justice philanthropy (Independent Sector and The Foundation Center, 2005; National Committee for Responsive Philanthropy, 2005). Social justice philanthropy is thus limited in its ability to affect organizations on the same scale that venture philanthropy can.

DISCUSSION AND CONCLUSION

Both the venture and grassroots social justice approaches intend to advance public good by seeking to effect positive social change; however, they do so through different processes based upon different assumptions about their role as agents and with different targets of impact. Most profoundly, they engage in different power relationships with grantees and, thus, the communities they serve. While the grassroots social justice approach takes a bottom-up approach, with organic growth that starts with local knowledge and experience as a means to frame the funding approaches and priorities, the venture philanthropic approach utilizes a more top-down model with centralized growth.

These differences have broad implications for how they engage grantees, conceptualize expertise, and practice accountability and decision making, and whose voices are represented and listened to in the process. As we saw earlier, venture philanthropy firms bring material, professional, and symbolic resources to grantees from the outside, whereas grassroots social justice foundations fund grantees and work with them to locate, enhance, and build on the expertise and resources within their organizations and communities (National Committee for Responsive Philanthropy, 2009). Whereas venture philanthropy firms track return on investments and hold grantees accountable to measureable outcomes, grassroots social justice foundations track "hard" quantitative outcomes as well as "softer" or affective measures of impact, such as the level and extent of trust and hope within a community and leadership and organizing capacity (National Committee for Responsive Philanthropy, 2009). While venture philanthropists are accountable to their funders, who are often represented on their boards, the grassroots philanthropic approach attempts to hold themselves accountable to local communities.

Using a positive lens, we show how each approach points to ways that are beneficial to those who are funded and creates valuable social change. Differing from "traditional foundations," each is trying in unique ways to address the limitations of traditional philanthropy. While the venture and grassroots approaches to philanthropy each have dilemmas, indicating that one form cannot accomplish all, both also incorporate interesting processes that benefit those they fund. Venture philanthropists take the approach that big problems often need immediate and large scale solutions. Thus, they provide a great deal of new resources—both funding and expertise—that they believe the community needs in order to address the breadth of these problems. Expertise comes from a variety of sources, focusing greatly on business elites, politicians, funders, and other entrepreneurs to assist them in taking their project to scale and create an impact. Therefore, instead of funding a single organization, for example, they are more likely to fund a larger scale project such as charter schools. Along with this funding, they hold local organizations accountable to broad metrics. This allows them to hold all the organizations to the same standard.

The grassroots social justice philanthropic approach also attempts to take on big problems, but they attempt to address the root causes to provide more systemic change from the bottom up. They focus on identifying and building resources and capacities within communities both to solve problems on the local level and to collaborate with other communities to address broader systemic issues. While they fund a variety of tactics and strategies, including advocacy and policy change, they focus mostly on community organizing. Because they are more grassroots focused, the goals, processes, and metrics can vary to match specific practices of each community. Thus, program officers often take time to build trust with and across local communities in order to direct their funding in ways that foster organizational interdependence and collaboration as well as internal capacity building.

The venture and other high engagement and agentic approaches to philanthropy have greater access to resources and can more easily and rapidly take projects to scale, thus positioning themselves as central actors in social change efforts, often partnering with key institutions. But, at the same time, they do so at a cost—they become more disconnected from and less accountable to local communities most impacted by the programs and policies they are creating. Additionally, by maintaining a top-down approach, they often recreate the power dynamics that are played out in the injustices they are fighting against. Grassroots social justice philanthropy consciously challenges this notion of elite outsiders as central agents and instead actively engages grantees as influential partners, often following their leadership in their struggle to address the root causes of social injustices. However, this process is much slower compared to the venture approach. Through the combination of the lack of larger funds and the localized grassroots change process, this makes it more difficult to quickly and successfully bring projects to scale.

Trying on one hand to have the broadest effect and the other the deepest effect, the jury is out as to which is most beneficial and impactful. Venture and grassroots social justice philanthropy are just two of many types of philanthropic approaches that are trying to have an impact on creating positive social change. Other types include family, community, strategic, corporate, and individual philanthropy, which has the largest share of the philanthropic sector. However, these cases allow us to differentiate and consider the implications of each approach in terms of their social change processes.

ACKNOWLEDGMENT

The authors would like to thank Rand Quinn, doctoral candidate at Stanford University School of Education, for his invaluable contributions to this chapter.

REFERENCES

Alaska Conservation Foundation. Rapid Response Grants. (2010) Retrieved July 19, 2010, from http://alaskaconservation.org/strategic-funding/rapid-response-grants/.

Alexander, J., Brudney, J. L., & Yang, K. (2010). Symposium: Accountability and performance measurement: The evolving role of nonprofits in the hollow state [special issue]. *Nonprofit and Voluntary Sector Quarterly, 39.*

Bartley, T. (2007). How foundations shape social movements: The construction of an organizational field and the rise of forest certification. *Social Problems, 54,* 229–255.

Brenner, R. (1988). *American philanthropy.* Chicago: University of Chicago Press.

Buteau, E., Buchanan, P., & Chu, T. (2010). *Working with grantees: The keys to success and five program officers who exemplify them.* Cambridge, MA: Center for Effective Philanthropy.

Dees, J. G., & Anderson, B. B. (2001a). *New school's venture fund (A).* Cambridge, MA: Harvard Business School.

Dees, J. G., & Anderson, B. B. (2001b). *New school's venture fund (B).* Cambridge, MA: Harvard Business School.

DiMaggio, P. (1991). Constructing an organizational field as a professional project. In W. W. Powell & P. DiMaggio (Eds.), *The new institutionalism in organizational analysis* (pp. 267–292). Chicago: University of Chicago Press.

Foundation Center (2009). *Foundation giving trends.* New York: Foundation Center.

Giving USA (2008). *The annual report on philanthropy.* Indianapolis, IN: American Association of Fundraising Counsel.

Gulf Coast Funders for Equity (2010). About us. Retrieved July 18, 2010, from http://gulf coastfunders.org.

Haines, H. H. (1984). Black radicalization and the funding of civil right: 1957–1970. *Social Problems, 32,* 31–43.

Haymarket People's Fund (2010). Haymarket People's Fund: 35 years of social change 1974–2009. Retrieved August 1, 2010, from http://www.haymarket.org.

Hwang, H., & Powell, W. W. (2009). The rationalization of charity: The influences of professionalism in the nonprofit sector. *Administrative Science Quarterly, 54,* 268–298.

Independent Sector and The Foundation Center (2005). *Social justice grantmaking: A report on foundation trends.* Washington, DC: Independent Sector & The Foundation Center.

Jenkins, J. C., & Eckert, C. M. (1986). Channeling black insurgency: Elite patronage and professional social movement organizations in the development of the black movement. *American Sociological Review, 51,* 812.

Jenkins, J. C., & Halcli, A. (1999). Grassrooting the system? The development and impact of social movement philanthropy, 1953–1990. In E. C. Lagemann (Ed.), *Philanthropic foundations: New scholarship new possibilities* (pp. 229–256). Bloomington, IN: University Press.

Khurana, R. (2007). *From higher aims to hired hands: The social transformation of American business schools and the unfulfilled promise of management as a profession.* Princeton: Princeton University Press.

Korten, A. E. (2009). *Change philanthropy.* San Francisco: Jossey-Bass.

Lagemann, E. C. (1989). The plural worlds of educational-research. *History of Education Quarterly, 29,* 185–214.

Lawrence, S., & Mukai, R. (2010). *Foundation giving trends: Update on funding priorities.* New York: Foundation Center.

McAdam, D. (1982). *Political process and the development of black insurgency.* Chicago: University of Chicago Press.

McCarthy, J. D., & Zald, M. N. (1977). Resource mobilization and social movements: A partial theory. *American Journal of Sociology, 82*, 1212–1241.

McGarvey, C., & Mackinnon, C. A. (2008). *Funding community organizing: Social change through civic participation.* New York: Grantcraft.

Meyerson, D., Quinn, R., & Oelberger, C. (2010). The emergence of the charter management organization: A social movement account (unpublished manuscript).

Meyerson, D., Quinn, R., & Tompkins-Stange, M. (2010). Elites as agents of institutional change: The case of philanthropic foundations in the california charter school movement (unpublished manuscript).

Morrill, S. (Forthcoming). Institutional change through interstitial emergence: The growth of alternative dispute resolution in American law, 1965–1995. In W. W. Powell & D. L. Jones (Eds.), *How institutions change.* Chicago: University of Chicago Press.

National Committee for Responsive Philanthropy (2005). *Social justice philanthropy: The latest trend of the lasting lens for grantmaking?* Washington, DC: National Committee for Responsive Philanthropy.

National Committee for Responsive Philanthropy (2009). *Criteria for philanthropy at its best: Benchmarks assess and enhance grantmaker impact.* Washington, DC: National Committee for Responsive Philanthropy.

NewSchools Venture Fund (author). 2009. Investing in a revolution: NewSchools Venture Fund and America's education entrepreneurs. Retrieved from http://www.newschools.org/publications/investing-in-a-revolution San Francisco, CA.

North Star Fund (2009). *Three lessons from three decades: 2009 Annual Report.* New York City: North Star Fund.

North Star Fund (2010). Grant categories. Retrieved July 19, 2010, from http://northstarfund.org/grants/grant-categories.php.

Odendahl, T. (1990). *Charity begins at home: Generosity and self-interest among the philanthropic elite.* New York: Basic Books.

Oelberger, C. (2010). Families and philanthropy: A proposed typology of endowed foundation organizational structures (unpublished manuscript).

Ostrander, S. A. (1995). *Money for change: Social movement philanthropy at Haymarket People's Fund.* Philadelphia: Temple University Press.

Ostrander, S. A. (1999). When grantees become grantors: Accountability, democracy, and social movement philanthropy. In E. C. Langemann (Ed.), *Philanthropic foundations: New scholarship, new possibilities.* Bloomington: Indiana University Press.

Ostrander, S. A. (2004). Moderating contradictions of feminist philanthropy: Women's community organizations and the Boston women's fund, 1995 to 2000. *Gender & Society, 18*, 29–46.

Ostrower, F. (2004). *Attitudes and practices concerning effective philanthropy: Survey report.* Washington, DC: The Urban Institute: Center on Nonprofits and Philanthropy.

Ostrower, F. (2006). Foundation approaches to effectiveness: A typology. *Nonprofit and Voluntary Sector Quarterly, 35*, 510–516.

Salamon, L. M. (1992). *America's nonprofit sector: A primer.* New York: Foundation Center.

Silver, I. (1998). Buying an activist identity: Reproducing class though social movement philanthropy. *Social Perspectives, 41*, 303–321.

Skocpol, T. (2003). *Diminishing democracy: From membership to management in American civic life.* Norman: University of Oklahoma Press.

Suarez, D. F. (2010). Street credentials and management backgrounds: Careers of nonprofit executives in an evolving sector. *Nonprofit and Voluntary Sector Quarterly, 39*, 696–716.

Twenty-First Century Foundation (2007). *After the deluge: Fighting the impacts of Katrina and Rita*. New York: Twenty-First Century Foundation.

Twenty-First Century Foundation (2010). Giving for black community change. Retrieved August 1, 2010, from http://www.21cf.org/about/history.php.

Wernick, L. J. (2009). How young progressives with wealth are leveraging their power and privilege to support social justice: A case study of social justice philanthropy and young donor organizing. Unpublished doctoral dissertation. University of Michigan.

6

Revealing Themes: Applying a Positive Lens to the Chapters on Change Agency

Erica L. Steckler and Jean M. Bartunek
Boston College

INTRODUCTION

Chris Weeks, a DHL international logistics manager, designed ways to leverage the company's logistics expertise to help airport managers in disaster-ravaged locations coordinate relief planes and the distribution of aid resources (Sonenshein, Chapter 3). Dr. Ibrahim Abouleish created an innovative organic farming initiative committed to the holistic development of employees, the local community, and Egyptian society more generally (Rimac, Mair, & Battilana, Chapter 4). The Central Indiana Community Foundation, a grassroots social justice philanthropy, focuses on trust-building by engaging with the local neighborhood, asking questions, and listening to the concerns of the constituencies they are trying to serve (Meyerson & Wernick, Chapter 5). For 18 years, Nadia Kanegai has used her personal salary and holidays to support community projects that have touched over 10,000 lives in Vanuatu, an island nation in the South Pacific (Branzei, Chapter 2).

The wide range of significant change agency recognized in these chapters is striking. It is also instructive. There is much to learn from these change agents' practices and the contexts in which they work. Our purpose in this commentary is to highlight characteristics in the chapters that are particularly generative for future theoretical and empirical exploration and constructive for supporting the practice of positive social change agency.

The domain of change agency is typically informed by the experience of a focal actor or set of actors around a particular change effort, often (though not necessarily) within the context of a formal organization (e.g., Bartunek, Austin, & Seo, 2008). *Social* change agency deals more explicitly with change efforts that target broad social issues, such as public health, housing, poverty, gender or racial inequality and injustice, education, economic development, and environmental threats. As evidenced in the preceding chapters, the arena of *positive* social change agency involves a focused effort to impart social change in order to improve well-being and advance the public good, and highlights the generative processes and outcomes in which change agents and change stakeholders engage and by which they are influenced.

These chapters demonstrate that positive change agency can be practiced by a wide array of individuals, groups, and organizations. Practitioners of change agency can include issue sellers, social entrepreneurs, philanthropic organizations and foundations, and just about any actor who harbors hope for achieving change. Positive change agents' work may take place within for-profit and non-profit organizations and organizational units, within grantor-grantee partnerships, and more generally within constellations of relational others. Further, their work can be discussed from conceptual lenses including issue selling, hopefulness, institutional theory, and social movements, among others.

Our commentary focuses on key themes in the accounts of positive social change presented in the four preceding chapters. Table 6.1 provides an overview of the basic attributes of the change agents and the particular change agency contexts introduced in these chapters, as well as a summary of some fundamental dimensions of positive social change agency that we identify and discuss in greater detail. First, we elaborate on some of the *competencies* that positive social change agents demonstrate, including overcoming adversity, discerning alternate possibilities, and managing tensions. Then we suggest some important *contextual aspects* of their work, including socialization, the locus of change, and the locale and temporality of change. Finally, we address implications for theoretical and empirical exploration.

TABLE 6.1

Key Themes of Positive Social Change Agency

Themes	Sonenshein	Branzei	Rimac, Mair, & Battilana	Meyerson & Wernick
Basic Attributes & Contexts				
Focal change agents	Issue sellers	Hope-full individuals	Social entrepreneurs	Philanthropic foundations
Level of analysis and context	Individual, within existing organizations	Individual, within constellation of relational others	Individual, within for-profit social purpose organization and Egyptian society at large	Organizational, within grantor-grantee partnerships
Theoretical lens	Issue selling	Hope functions	Institutional theory	Stakeholder engagement
Explicit or implicit challenges to social change	Organizational environment inhospitable to change	Hopelessness	Resistance by traditionalists	Resource constraints
Competencies				
Overcome adversity through processes of	Meaning-making through dialog	Relationships to produce, reproduce, and sustain hope	Socialization to change dominant attitudes and behaviors in national context	Resource distribution, guided by project specificity (grassroots) or scalability (venture)
Discern alternate potentialities	Experience and articulate current problems and propose future possibilities instead	Inspired by role models, see problems and initiate change actions	Influenced by experience as an outsider, envision a more egalitarian and efficient Egyptian society	Given philanthropic mandate to serve society, identify ways to improve and solve an array of local or scalable social issues

continued

TABLE 6.1 CONTINUED

Key Themes of Positive Social Change Agency

Themes	Sonenshein	Branzei	Rimac, Mair, & Battilana	Meyerson & Wernick
Manage tensions	Business case for addressing a social issue	Social change to improve productivity (economic view) and to help the disadvantaged (emancipatory)	Personal obedience, gender segregation vs. personal responsibility, desegregation	Scalability and external managerial expertise (venture) vs. project specificity and local community experts (grassroots)
Contextual Aspects				
Socialization	Of issue sellers by organization to propose social change through appropriate channels	Of change agents by role models; of subsequent change agents by originating change agents	Of employees by SEKEM	Of funding recipients by venture philanthropy
Locus of change	Endogenous Exogenous Bottom-up	Endogenous Exogenous Bottom-up	Endogenous Exogenous Top-down	Endogenous Exogenous Bottom-up & Top-down
Locale of change	Issue seller, organization, society	Specific projects, adjacent communities, change agent	SEKEM and Egyptian society	Grantee entities and local communities
Temporality of change	Multi-year and across changing organizational context	Continuous over the lifetime of a change agent, indefinite thereafter	Founding of SEKEM (1977) through very long term	Multi-year

Positive View

Positive social change agency involves	Goodness and generativity of social change processes and outcomes	Participative and relational efforts to initiate and accelerate social change	Advancement of individual agency through the enactment of sustainable institutions	Ability to catalyze social change processes to advance the public good
POS assumptions	Positions different perspectives as potentially positive and productive within conventionally antagonistic contestations	Even in dire circumstances, advances the benefits of a glass-half-full perspective by actors who proactively recognize opportunities and move toward an imagined future	Extends ideas of individual potentiality and cultures of possibilities to socio-cultural context where embedded members might not see themselves or others in this manner	Foundations as social change agents are essentially generative with the potential to spark exponential positive impacts; and, given two contrasting approaches to social change funding, finds that both can be beneficial
Positive to whom?	Individual, organization, society	Individual, relational others, communities, society	Employees, communities, environment, Egyptian society	Grantees, community members, generalized public

COMPETENCIES OF POSITIVE SOCIAL CHANGE AGENTS

Competencies generally refer to skills and abilities that enable a focal actor to be effective within a given context. Despite the diverse examples of social change agency presented in these chapters, a core set of competencies, including abilities to overcome adversity, discern alternate possibilities, and manage tensions, emerged as shared across all of them. These commonalities highlight important considerations for research and practice.

Overcoming Adversity

The capacity of change agents to overcome adversity is a dominant theme in the discourse of positive social change agency. Branzei's chapter about social change agency in hopeless settings highlights how relational processes reproduce and build hope as an important mechanism of social change. Sonenshein focuses on the issue-selling processes of meaning making and dialogue requisite to navigating and advocating for social change in inhospitable organizational environments. Meyerson and Wernick consider a broader social change context of adversity in terms of the actors involved in the distribution of scarce resources. By comparing two kinds of philanthropic foundations—venture and grassroots social justice—the authors provide a nuanced view of how different forms of foundations effect social change through processes and actions that guide resource distribution and "investment" in change. Rimac, Mair, and Battilana call attention to the daunting task of divergent change, where social change agents choose to break with existing institutions and work to convince others to do the same in order to implement new practices. Taken together, these chapters provide evidence for how positive social change agency provides an opportunity to explore how adversity can be transformed into essential inputs to and resources of change through processes such as issue selling, hope, philanthropic approaches to resource distribution, and socialization.

Discerning Alternate Potentialities

Positive social change agency entails sensitivity to different and implicitly better alternatives to an existing social situation. The change agents in these chapters are inherently possibilities-oriented, discerning between "what is" and "what might be." According to Rimac et al., on his return to Egypt following an extended period abroad, SEKEM's founder, Dr. Abouleish, advanced a vision to model a more egalitarian and efficient Egypt. Meyerson and Wernick frame how philanthropic foundations, in partnership with the organizations to which they provide resources and stewardship, recognize, confront, and provide solutions to social problems. Individual grassroots change agents such as Nadia Kenegai and Robert Kalyesubul in Branzei's chapter are inspired by the values of their role models to—as Ghandi said—be the change they wish to see in the world, with particular attention to communities of marginalized people. As Sonenshein details, individual social change agents within established organizational contexts motivate change by effectively articulating the problem of "now" and the promise of alternate potentialities. In effect, the change agents in these chapters see opportunities to enact change by actively and creatively engaging in processes of discernment and meaning making (Cameron, Dutton, & Quinn, 2003) around a social issue.

Managing Tensions

Tensions surface repeatedly in the arena of positive social change agency. The social change agents in these chapters struggle to some degree with a tension between business and social justice values, in which rationality, efficiency, return on investment, and objectivity are at least potentially at odds with "doing good" for society. Meyerson and Wernick contrast the values driving venture and grassroots social justice philanthropic initiatives. For example, where venture philanthropy preferences scalability and external managerial expertise, grassroots philanthropy values project specificity and locally embedded experts. Branzei acknowledges contradictions between an economic view of social change agents in an organizational context to advance social issues by nesting them within conventional arguments. For example, change agents might advocate for diversity in the workplace by framing the issue within an economic rationale that diversity is good because it is good for business. Sonenshein shows a tendency for social change agents in an organizational context to nest social issues, for example, diversity is good, within a business argument, for example, diversity is good because it's good for business. Rimac et al.'s account of the SEKEM initiative highlights polarities between traditions such as personal obedience and gender segregation and more contemporary business values of personal responsibility and greater gender equality. A key competency of social change agency is the ability to navigate and overcome such contrariety.

CONTEXTS OF POSITIVE SOCIAL CHANGE AGENCY

There can be a tendency to focus only on individual change agents, such as social entrepreneurs (Bornstein, 2004), when considering social change initiatives. However, their work always takes place within particular contexts. In this section, we highlight four contextual aspects of positive social change agency: socialization influences, and the locus, locale, and temporality of change.

Socialization Influences

Socialization plays an explicit or implicit role in the chapters. For example, Ms. Kenegai and Mr. Kalyesubula are socialized by their role models, and subsequently socialize the "next generation" change agents. SEKEM serves as an instrumental vessel for socializing employees (to be on time, to value equality, to work hard, etc.). Venture philanthropists socialize prospective change agent organizations towards values of efficiency and scalability. Finally, issue sellers in organizations pursue their social change agendas by engaging in dialogue and sharing their vision, i.e., socializing others. We often think of change agents as full-blown change leaders without paying adequate attention to how they emerged as such. The chapters make evident that this attention is inadequate; the content and process of learning about change possibilities and potential roles is also very important to the actions and impacts of change agents.

Internal and External Loci of Change

The chapters position positive social change agency as a likely domain for endogenous change initiatives, where change is motivated, influenced, and implemented by internal actors (Livne-Tarandach & Bartunek, 2009).

The pervasiveness of endogenous change is embedded in examples in all four chapters. Actors such as grassroots social justice philanthropy foundations, organizational members and founders, and community leaders rely on their hyper-local and highly nuanced understanding of context, community, and capacities to see and implement opportunities for creating social change.

However, the important influence of exogenous perspectives, wherein external actors influence and drive social change, is also apparent in these accounts. For example, it is instructive that SEKEM's Egyptian founder lived abroad for decades (a kind of outside socialization experience) prior to returning to Egypt and feeling inspired to establish his social change initiative. Sonenshein describes an upper management white executive who couldn't "grasp the meaning and ramifications" of discrimination toward minority employees until he attended a race relations seminar and felt discriminated against himself by other participants. At the organizational level, philanthropic foundations are inherently, at least initially, outsiders to the organizations they support. In particular, venture philanthropy has gained a strong foothold as an effective agent of social change through its preference for bringing in professionally trained outside managers as leaders. Finally, the Sawa Heroes that Branzei highlights spark change from the outside even as they advocate change from the inside of the projects they steward. These examples suggest that an "exogenous" orientation for an endogenous change agent may be beneficial, if not integral, to recognizing the potential for a different and improved social situation. Further, these accounts are instructive for considering how both endogenous and exogenous factors may be vital to the process of positive social change agency.

Locales of Change

As illustrated by Lewin's (1951) unfreeze, change, refreeze model, organizational change is sometimes described as relatively discrete, contained within a period of time, a particular setting, or among a certain group of people. In a positive social change context, by contrast, there appears to be no such thing as a "one-off" change effort. The change initiatives in these chapters are characterized as spurring a spiral of other positive effects, with the potential to transcend a limited organizational space. Sonenshein's model of social change agency frames social issue selling by organizational insiders as a generative process with the potential to widen and enrich dialogue, and with positive outcomes not only for the organization, but also for the change agent and society more broadly. Branzei's tri-dimensional model of social change agency accounts for an iterative, expansive, and interrelational process of change that involves the change agent, role models, and particular community beneficiaries. The SEKEM Initiative is comprised of successful for-profit and NGO components that are local in nature yet remain governed by their founding principle to bring about holistic social change to all of Egyptian society. Finally, philanthropic foundations routinely measure their impacts as change agents in terms of spiral effects in the communities they are active in.

In addition, the efforts of change agents in these chapters seem to be informed by and fundamentally integrated with other change actors. As characterized by individual protagonists in Sonenshein's and Branzei's accounts, as well as the organizational level change agency of SEKEM and philanthropic foundations, the work of a social change agent is not solitary or static, but is inherently shared and mutual. While positive social change can be initiated by a focal agent, these chapters reinforce how such efforts tend to be tightly interwoven with other individuals or entities and can ultimately result in a shared enactment of change.

Temporality of Change

In addition to the positive spirals that expand beyond a limited organizational space, the positive change agency work in these chapters appears to have the potential to transcend a particular period of time that might characterize more traditional change efforts. The chapters suggest that social change agents' efforts are frequently inter-temporal and operative through continuous and dynamic cycles. For example, Branzei's examples of Nadia and Robert's experiences of being inspired by early role models to effect social change, and the continual evolution and revisiting of their visions, strategies, and actions for change, illustrate how the work of positive social change agents can "simmer" and adapt, gaining potency over time. Venture and grassroots philanthropic foundations make multiyear commitments to the change initiatives they get involved with, frequently revisiting needs and goals. SEKEM's mission to change pieces of the social and cultural fabric of Egypt, including issues deeply embedded within dominant religious and family traditions, is expected to occur over very long periods of time and within the evolving historical context at the community, national, and global levels. Sonenshein details a change initiative to foster a more positive culture for gay, lesbian, and bisexual workers that unfolds over 12 years of raising and then reclaiming the issue. These examples highlight how social change agency work might proceed iteratively across long periods of time, and not necessarily in discrete, contained time units. Positive social change is treated in these chapters as unfolding in a continuous process (Weick & Quinn, 1999) as issues become prevalent and prominent in a given context with an agent to steward a change.

IMPLICATIONS FOR THEORETICAL AND EMPIRICAL EXPLORATION

The competencies and contexts detailed in these chapters have both empirical and conceptual implications. We will suggest some of these below.

Competencies of Positive Social Change Agents

Some of the adversities that positive social change agents must address, such as organizational environments that are inhospitable to change, resistance, hopelessness, and resource constraints, are familiar to most change agents (cf. Cummings & Worley, 2009). But how they address adversity is not usually considered a property of the change agent as much as of pre-developed processes aimed at countering it. The change agents depicted in these chapters encounter adversity and severe resource constraints, and manage tensions as human beings. Their doing so draws attention to their own capacities, something that is rarely addressed in writing about planned change in organizations (e.g., Burke, 2011).

Thus, the chapters make evident that, contrary to much organizational scholarship, attention to change processes themselves is not adequate. Rather, it is important, as positive organizational studies emphasize (cf. Cameron & Spreitzer, 2011), to understand positive characteristics and competencies of agents who lead change. These include the ability to be courageous and tenacious, and not intimidated by adversity, in pursuing a change agenda. They also include a creative capacity to consider multiple alternative possibilities for action, rather than following one pattern rigidly both within a particular context and over time. Finally, they include the ability of change agents to demonstrate equanimity to remain above the fray and cope with tensions. This usually comes with a conviction and confidence, for better or worse, that the change itself and the change agent's approach is the correct one.

Contexts of Change

Socialization

The chapters also provoke several questions regarding the larger contexts of change. For example, what is the relationship between change agency and socialization practices and influences, and why or when would such a relationship matter? We were struck by the suggestion that long-term socialization may play a role in the development of change agents and their subsequent change initiatives. When organizational scholars discuss socialization, their focus is almost always on adult socialization within organizations (cf. Van Maanen & Schein, 1979). As the SEKEM example makes evident, such socialization does occur. But the protagonists in Branzei's chapter, as well as the account of SEKEM, also show that socialization in a social change context likely starts in early childhood.

Planned and Emergent Change

Before our reading of these chapters, we might have been tempted to match positive social change agency with bottom-up efforts, in which change spirals from the bottom (Cameron, Dutton, & Quinn, 2003) of a structure of social relations toward the top, as illustrated by issue selling. While many of the change efforts highlighted in these chapters are bottom-up, there is also a notable presence of top-down change. SEKEM's influential culture and venture philanthropy's rigid investment protocol both employ top-down influence, where difference-making efforts flow from positions of power and resources to the less-powerful and under-resourced. The presence and importance of both endogenous and exogenous orientations as well as top-down and bottom-up social change efforts detailed in these chapters positions positive social change agency as an ideal arena for scholars to move beyond the perennial locus of change debate (cf. Beer &

Nohria, 2000; Livne-Tarandach & Bartunek, 2009) and instead consider the importance of diverse reference points and perspectives in motivating and sustaining change efforts.

Spatial and Temporal Boundaries

The positive social change agents in these chapters effect change that ripples beyond specific target beneficiaries to strengthen and improve communities in proximity and society at large, both in the "now" and into the future. In this sense, the boundaries of space and time of positive social change agency are both expansive and inclusive. For example, in some of these chapters the role of the originating change agent shifts over time, with an implicit goal of making this actor redundant once the desired process of change takes effect. At the individual level, Branzei identifies the role of a social change agent to "initiate and accelerate, but neither substitute nor complete, others' social change agency work." At the organizational level, Meyerson and Wernick describe the emphasis that grassroots social justice foundations place on the internal capacity-building of grantees, such as developing community-based leadership and then relinquishing decision-making power to local leadership.

Studies of organizational change rarely pay attention to emergent ripple effects; they more often focus on how well pre-established goals are accomplished (e.g., Andriessen, 2007). Attention to expansive effects requires a broader attention than is usually afforded to change phenomena, and obliges scholars to be able to maintain a dual-focus on the actions and experiences of the change agent as well as on the change itself that may extend well beyond any one agent of change and across long periods of time (Bartunek, 2003; Bond, 2008).

The Importance of POSITIVE Social Change Agency

It would be easy, and more standard in most discussions of organizational change agency, to focus on problems to the exclusion of the positive possibilities. In the majority of teaching cases, for example, the focus is on problems that need to be solved, and, implicitly if not explicitly, what wrong has been done so far by the leader or change agent (e.g., Ellet, 2007). The conventional emphasis in organizational scholarship is on the 70% of cases that are failed examples of change. But these chapters challenge taken-for-granted assumptions of change as a process that is often negatively characterized as fraught with conflict, likely to fail, and exhausting or even corrosive for the change agent and others involved. Instead, these scholars advance a view of and provide models of change agency as distinctly generative, empowering, beneficial, enabling, and ennobling for the change agent and a host of other change-stakeholders. Sonenshein's chapter spotlights the goodness and generativity of issue-selling processes and outcomes. Branzei highlights the positive participative and relational efforts that agents engage in to initiate and accelerate social change. Rimac and colleagues emphasize the ideas of individual potentiality and cultures of possibilities in a socio-cultural context where embedded members might not see themselves or others in this manner. Finally, Meyerson and Wernick explore two types of philanthropic foundations and find that even with contrasting approaches to catalyzing change and serving the public service, both can be effective agents of social change and inherently generative in terms of their potential to spark exponential positive impacts. Determining what goes right in a change sometimes happens by accident, for example, in studies that make use of process models that focus on how an unexpected end was achieved (e.g., Elsbach & Sutton, 1992). However, there is little empirical research and even less theorizing that starts out by wondering how change agent virtues and competencies such as courage and creativity combine to effect changing over time that is generative for the recipients of change, perhaps in a way that goes beyond what could have been envisaged at first. The chapters here suggest the value of this type of theorizing and study.

Interestingly, in order to frame and initiate their efforts, many of the change agents we have read about in these chapters seem to position their perspective and approach as categorically "right" and others' as lacking or wrong. This strategy is evident in the case of SEKEM where the organization's dogma seems to be that others in Egypt are doing things backwards and they need to change to the SEKEM model to succeed. Similarly, Meyerson and Wernick depict how venture philanthropy foundations adopt the view that scaling charter schools is the one best way to accomplish educational improvements. The protagonists in Branzei's chapter articulate the "right" kind of people they seek to enroll in their social change efforts, which implies that they differentiate among people they perceive as lacking the potential to help create their vision of a better future. Finally, Sonenshein illustrates how social change issue sellers within organizations often take the approach that their organization is impeded by an archaic (bad) culture that must be adapted to the new (good) vision in order for the company to survive. This also raises important issues for inquiry. Does positive change require some sort of villain it can overcome? Does it, perhaps or necessarily, tend to form dynamic cycles with negative events? What kinds of lenses, perhaps paradoxical ones (cf. Smith & Lewis, 2011), are necessary to appreciate positive change as fully as possible?

CONCLUDING REMARKS

We have been grateful for and humbled by the opportunity to revisit and revise our own assumptions about change agency through the accounts and analyses presented here. Sonenshein's chapter has contributed to our understanding of resilience, persistence, and the creativity of change agents, has focused our attention on outcomes that expand beyond a focal change agenda, and has positioned issue selling as more than just an instrumental practice. Branzei's contribution highlights the role of hope in change agency, emphasizing hope as inclusive, participative, relational, and developmental. Rimac et al. tackle "divergent" social change in their case study of SEKEM to explore norm-breaking around traditional socio-cultural power dynamics through holistic socialization processes. In addition, these authors present a unique organizational case of a collective as change agent. Finally, in their comparative study of philanthropic foundations, Meyerson and Wernick advance the positive values of creativity, innovation, community engagement, and trust-building as they explore power relations in the distribution of funding for public betterment. In particular, their account of grassroots philanthropy offers an expanded notion of legitimate expertise and acknowledges ripple-effects from smaller-scale capacity building efforts. Each chapter has expanded and inspired our thinking about who and what constitutes social change agency, what competencies are needed, and how and under what conditions positive social change agency might occur. We hope these chapters may inspire others' imaginations and thinking about these important issues as well.

REFERENCES

Andriessen, D. (2007). Designing and testing an OD intervention: Reporting intellectual capital to develop organizations. *Journal of Applied Behavioral Science, 43,* 89–107.

Bartunek, J. M. (2003). *Organizational and educational change: The life and role of a change agent group.* Mahwah, NJ: Lawrence Erlbaum Associates.

Bartunek, J. M., Austin, J. R., & Seo, M. (2008). The conceptual underpinnings of intervening in organizations. In T. G. Cummings (Ed.), *Handbook of Organization Development* (pp. 151–166). Thousand Oaks: Sage.

Beer, M. & Nohria, N. (2000). Cracking the code of change. *Harvard Business Review,* May-June, 133–141.

Bond, M. A. (2008). *Workplace chemistry: Promoting diversity through organizational change.* Hanover, NH: University Press of New England.

Bornstein, D. (2004). *How to change the world: Social entrepreneurs and the power of new ideas.* New York: Oxford University Press.

Burke, W. W. (2011). Organization change: Theory and practice (3rd ed.). Thousand Oaks, CA: Sage.

Cameron, K. S., Dutton, J. E., & Quinn, R. E. (Eds.). (2003). Positive organizational scholarship: Foundations of a new discipline. San Francisco: Berrett-Koehler.

Cameron, K. S. & Spreitzer, G. M. (Eds.). (2011). *The Oxford handbook of Positive Organizational Scholarship.* New York: Oxford University Press.

Cummings, T. G. & Worley, C. G. (2009). *Organization development & change* (9th ed.) Mason, OH: South-Western Cengage Learning.

Ellett, W. (2007). *The case study handbook: How to read, discuss, and write persuasively about cases.* Boston: Harvard Business School Press.

Elsbach, K. D. & Sutton, R. I. (1992). Acquiring organizational legitimacy through illegitimate actions: A marriage of institutional and impression management theories. *Academy of Management Journal, 35,* 699–738.

Lewin, K. (1951). *Field theory in social science: Selected theoretical papers.* D. Cartwright (Ed.). New York: Harper & Row.

Livne-Tarandach, R., & Bartunek, J. M. (2009). A new horizon for organizational change and development scholarship: Connecting planned and emergent change. In R. Woodman & W. Pasmore (Eds.), *Research in organizational change and development,* (17: pp. 1–35). Bingley, UK: Emerald.

Smith, W. K. & Lewis, M. W. (2011). Toward a theory of paradox: A dynamic equilibrium model of organizing. *Academy of Management Review, 36,* 381–403.

Van Maanen, J. E. & Schein, E. H. (1979). Toward a theory of organizational socialization. *Research in Organizational Behavior, 1,* 209–264.

Weick, K. E. & Quinn, R. E. (1999). Organizational change and development, *Annual Review of Psychology, 50,* 361–386.

Part III

Environment and Sustainability

7

Hybrid Organizations as Agents of Positive Social Change: Bridging the For-Profit and Non-Profit Divide

Andrew J. Hoffman and Krista K. Badiane
University of Michigan

Nardia Haigh
University of Massachusetts, Boston

INTRODUCTION: BRIDGING ORGANIZATIONAL BOUNDARIES

Addressing sustainability issues in a globalized world requires the emergence and diffusion of new organizational forms and new forms of governance (Ehrenfeld, 2008; Elkington, 1998). In this chapter, we note how the traditional distinctions between for-profit and non-profit sectors are blurring, and explore the emergence of a new form of organization in that intervening space: termed the hybrid organization. We explore this new organizational form and identify a sustainability-driven business model that hybrids use to create and diffuse positive social change within the social and environmental contexts they operate. Drivers of this model include concepts familiar to scholars of positive organizational scholarship, such as organizational virtuousness (Cameron, Bright, & Caza, 2004), positive meaning-making, positive relationships (Dutton & Glynn, 2008), and thriving at work (Spreitzer, Sutcliffe, Dutton, Sonenshein, & Grant, 2005). The social change agency of hybrid organizations is further enabled by positive leadership (Cameron & Lavine, 2006).

Our primary interest in this chapter is to explain this model, and to describe some of the positive social, environmental, and economic outcomes it has enabled. We begin by introducing sustainability issues, hybrid organizations, and the linkages between the two that lead to positive social change. We then develop a theoretical model to explain the behaviors and outcomes of hybrid organizations as agents that drive social change. We also provide a descriptive account of this model through a case study of one hybrid organization: Maggie's Organics. Finally, we conclude with contributions to theory and practice as well as recommendations for future research. Our aim is to lay the foundation for further research in this interesting and emergent area.

HYBRID ORGANIZATIONS AND THE ISSUES AND OPPORTUNITIES OF SUSTAINABILITY

The environmental and social sustainability challenges that hybrid organizations seek to address, such as poverty, environmental destruction, and climate change, have received a great deal of attention in recent years as trends measuring them become more alarming. For instance, the world economy has enjoyed tremendous success over the past century. Economic activity has increased by a factor of fourteen (Thomas, 2002), global per capita income tripled (World Business Council on Sustainable Development, 1997), and average life expectancy increased by almost two-thirds (World Resources Institute, 1994). However, proponents of sustainability call attention to the fact that this success has been accompanied by tremendous environmental abuses and that the benefits of this development are not shared equitably. For example, according to the United Nations, the richest 20% of the world's population consume 86% of all goods and services while the poorest 20% consume just 1.3%. Of the 4.4 billion people in the developing world, almost 60% lack access to safe sewers, 33% do not have access to clean water, 25% lack adequate housing, and 30% have no modern health services (Crossette, 1998).

Hybrid organizations use the market system as the tool for rectifying these problems.[1] Built upon the assertion that traditional business models are no longer adequate to address the social and environmental problems of our day (Alexander, 2000; Draper, 2005), hybrid organizations call for mission-centered business models that employ market tactics to address social and environmental issues. In effect, they are practicing sustainable development as it was defined by the Brundtland Commission Report and are showing that economic development can proceed by meeting "the needs of present generations without compromising the ability of future generations to meet their own needs" (World Commission on Environment and Development, 1987, p. 51).

Hybrid Organizations in Practice

The phenomenon of hybrid organizations is emerging at a time when the role of the state as the principal agent of environmental governance is declining and "private alternatives" (e.g., market and voluntary mechanisms) are proliferating (Bernstein & Cashore, 2007; Cashore, 2002; Donahue, 2002; Lemos & Agrawal, 2006; Liverman, 2004). Nongovernmental organizations (NGOs), corporations, trade unions, religious groups, and a host of other entities have emerged to develop sustainability solutions that have import for national competitiveness, global development, and trade flows. Within this context, there is a concurrent evolution in the purpose, form, and role of the for-profit and non-profit sectors.

Consider how corporations are now engaging in activities that would have once seemed implausible. For example, the Anglo-American Corporation is engaged in a comprehensive program that covers HIV/AIDS prevention and care for its employees and local communities in its African operations. Walmart, the world's largest retailer, announced in 2008 that it would require suppliers to make major appliances that use 25% less energy within three years. Emblematic of the redefinition of the

---

[1] It is important to note that this tactic is not without controversy. In fact, a schism within the environmental non-governmental organization (NGO) world sees two positions on the role of the market in solving environmental and social problems (Conner & Epstein, 2007; Hoffman, 2009; Schwartz & Shuva, 1992). The *dark green* NGOs—such as Greenpeace USA and Friends of the Earth (FOE)—see the market as the problem and seek radical social change to solve environmental problems, often by confronting corporations and the market. The *bright green* NGOs—such as Conservation International and the Environmental Defense Fund (EDF)—see the market as the solution and work within the system, often in close alliance with corporations, to solve environmental problems.

social role of the corporation (Post, 2002), CEO Lee Scott proclaimed, "We live in a time when people are losing confidence in the ability of government to solve problems… [But, Walmart] does not wait for someone else to solve problems" (Barbaro, 2008, p. WK3).

Non-profit organizations also play new, emergent, and influential roles in the global marketplace. They act as policy advisers to governments, strategy advisers to corporations, thought leaders for public opinion, and catalysts for action by bankers, investors, suppliers, customers, and even religious organizations. The Environmental Defense Fund (EDF), for example, participated in the 2007 leveraged buyout of the energy company TXU Corporation and hired Perella Weinberg Partners, a boutique investment bank, to advise it on using Wall Street tactics in negotiating mergers and acquisitions. The Bill and Melinda Gates Foundation, the world's largest foundation with assets of $30 billion, now rivals most governments in its annual disbursements of over $3 billion to address global health challenges.

With this evolution of the form and function of the for-profit and non-profit sectors, there is a blurring of boundaries between them such that a new vocabulary becomes necessary to recognize a hybrid form. These hybrid organizations defy traditional categorizations employed by organizational theorists; categorizations that are often applied a priori. Alternatively described as fourth sector, blended value, for-benefit, values driven, mission driven, or B-corporations (Alter, 2004; Boyd, Henning, Reyna, Wang, & Welch, 2009), hybrid organizations can lie on either side of the IRS for-profit/non-profit classification scheme. On one side, some are non-profit organizations that adopt the practices of a for-profit firm. For example, Ten Thousand Villages is a volunteer run 501(c)(3) non-profit organization that operates a for-profit retail operation to provide fair income to artisans from more than 30 countries by selling their fair-trade goods. On the other side, some are for-profit companies operating according to social and environmental sustainability agendas. For example, Stonyfield Farms is a for-profit agricultural company, but it also takes sustainability seriously in the development of its organic dairy products. Therefore, does Stonyfield Farms have more in common with Cargill (a for-profit agricultural company) or the Rainforest Alliance (a non-profit organization dedicated to sustainable agriculture)? As hybrids, these organizations are "both market-oriented and mission-centered" (Boyd et al., 2009, p. 1).

This is a growing market segment. Indicative of its increasing prevalence and importance, a recent Maryland law creates a new legal class of company, called "benefit corporations," that grants hybrid organizations greater protection from shareholder lawsuits that demand that management put profits above social and environmental missions (Tozzi, 2010). To qualify as a benefit corporation, the company must define its nonfinancial goals in its charter and obtain approval of two-thirds of the shareholders. In this chapter, we will focus on hybrid organizations that occupy the for-profit classification by the IRS.

Given such growing importance, hybrid organizations offer an interesting empirical domain for study; one that we believe will produce an ongoing stream of research. However, at this point, research on hybrid organizations is notably lacking, and has primarily focused on the topics of corporate social responsibility (CSR) or social entrepreneurship (Alter, 2004; Haugh, 2005; Smallbone et al., 2001). In the next section, we go beyond a CSR perspective and use a positive lens to elaborate a sustainability-driven business model by which hybrid organizations couple economic profitability with social and environmental sustainability.

THE SUSTAINABILITY-DRIVEN BUSINESS MODEL

Recent research on hybrid organizations is offering insight into the specific aspects of the business models they employ (e.g., Boyd et al., 2009; Neville, 2008). By applying a positive lens to the hybrid organization form, we expand on this preliminary work to identify a sustainability-driven business model that elucidates how they are able to create positive social outcomes at multiple levels. Depicted in Figure 7.1, the model has three basic elements: (1) social change as organizational objective; (2) mutually beneficial relationships with suppliers and communities, employees, and customers; and (3) progressive interaction with markets, competitors, and industry institutions. In the following sections, we describe each element of the business model in detail, and identify ways in which they are informed by (and may inform) concepts within the positive organizational scholarship literature.

Social Change as Organizational Objective

By applying a positive lens to hybrid organizations, it becomes evident that hybrid organizations construct and enact sustainability in a distinctly different way than businesses following a purely economic rationale—in

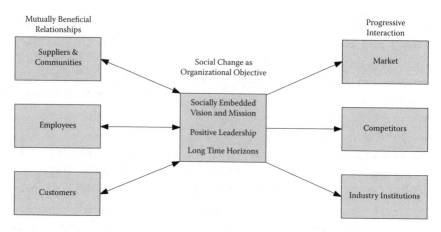

FIGURE 7.1
The hybrid organization's sustainability-driven business model.

that they see sustainability as imperative to the viability of the business. This positive meaning (Dutton & Glynn, 2008) attributed to sustainability is institutionalized through three core firm-level qualities that drive and facilitate hybrids' social change agency.

Socially and Environmentally Embedded Mission

Hybrid organizations "have values-based missions baked in" (Boyd et al., 2009, p. 1). Like other for-profit organizations, hybrid organizations aim to supply high quality, differentiated goods to satisfy a specific market demand in order to remain economically viable. However, hybrid organizations maintain a unique view of their role within the social and environmental systems in which they are embedded, and seek to use the market system to rejuvenate those systems for mutual benefit of the business, the environment, and society. Their products promote some form of socially or environmentally positive outcome consistent with the organizational mission. For example, Sun Ovens produces solar cooking equipment, not just to cook food, but also to "radically decrease the developing world's dependence on fuel wood and dung as the primary cooking fuels while benefiting the environment, raising the standard of living and improving the health of the poor worldwide" (Boyd et al., 2009, p. 33). Similarly, Guayakí sells organic, fair trade Yerba maté and is also devoted to creating "economic models that drive reforestation while employing a living wage" for farmers and indigenous communities (Boyd et al., 2009, p. 64), rather than industry averages which often only provide for poor quality of life. Such products, driven by socially and environmentally embedded missions, exemplify how hybrid organizations challenge the traditional notion that the primary goal of the corporation is to increase its profits (e.g., Friedman, 1970). Rather, hybrids consider economic profitability as a means to achieve its sustainability goals.

Longer Time Horizons for Patient and Autonomous Growth

The social change objectives that hybrid organizations adopt—potentially taking several generations to realize—often drive them to operate on a longer time horizon than traditional for-profit businesses. As such, hybrids often equate slow, stable growth with sustainable growth. For instance, Clif Bar has an aspiration to "grow slower, grow better and stick around longer" (Boyd et al., 2009, p.147), and Guayakí CEO Chris Mann acknowledges that his company could expand faster if it were willing to compromise its mission and source maté in ways that neither promote prosperity among suppliers nor protect the Atlantic rainforest (Boyd et al., 2009).

Concurrent with longer time horizons, hybrid organizations often seek to operate with a higher degree of autonomy than traditional businesses. To ensure that they remain true to their mission, hybrid organizations avoid traditional venture capitalists who often want more control and a greater focus on profit as the overriding objective. To many, "joining forces with venture capitalists, would mean selling out the very essence of [being sustainable]: small, alternative and individualistic" (Mills, 2009, p. 4). Instead, hybrids seek sources of "patient capital" and "below market-rate" equity or debt from friends or sustainability motivated investors (Boyd et al., 2009). For example, early investors in Ben & Jerry's Ice Cream signed waivers that they expected to receive no financial gain; rather, the expected return was social and environmental capital. Such choices can limit growth, though the investors they attract attribute as much or more value to the sustainability mission than to the rate of financial return.

Positive Leadership

Although leadership is an important aspect of any business, it is particularly relevant to the development and operation of a hybrid's values-based mission and objectives. Much like a non-profit organization, there are strong links between the objectives and mission of the organization and the deeply held personal values of its employees. Employees often feel a sense of calling or purpose through their work in a hybrid organization. For that reason, leaders of hybrid organizations must generally embody the culture and the strong social values that drive their organization's mission; they must authentically and completely enact the values of the organization through their everyday activities and approach to management.

Survey results show that 75% of hybrid organization leaders are participative or transformational in their leadership style (Boyd et al., 2009). Their style exemplifies positive leadership through a strong emphasis on ethics, participative management, positive culture, and exceptional and transformational achievement (Cameron & Lavine, 2006; Flynn, 2008). For example, Honest Tea founder and CEO Seth Goldman, quit his job at Calvert Group to brew tea in his home, dreaming of a future when "his tea would not only succeed but would also establish honest, mutually beneficial relationships with suppliers and customers while being true to the environment" (Hoffman et al., 2010, p. 3). With this start, Goldman grew his company with a strong emphasis on social responsibility, bringing a high degree of personal commitment and values to the business. In much the same way, many hybrid leaders link their business mission tightly with their personal mission or vocation.

Mutually Beneficial Relationships

While most businesses seek to externalize the costs of community health and environmental protection (Lazlo & Cooperrider, 2008), hybrid organizations actively seek to internalize the enrichment of natural environmental systems and develop close relationships with external constituents. In fact, they treat these relationships, which are marked by mutuality, positive regard, trust, and vitality (Dutton & Heaphy, 2003), as assets to be developed for mutual prosperity (Rousseau & Ling, 2007). Positive relationships are foundational to organizational resilience (Dutton, Worline, Frost, & Lilius, 2006; Gittell, Cameron, Lim, & Rivas, 2006), learning, and innovation (Carmeli & Spreitzer, 2009). The creation of mutually beneficial relationships enables hybrid organizations to create positive social change among suppliers and supplier communities, employees, and customers. We next describe these relationships in detail.

Mutually Beneficial Relationships with Suppliers and Communities

Rather than sourcing from suppliers on the basis of price alone and maintaining a strictly economic and transactional relationship, hybrid organizations invest in deep personal relationships with suppliers, and develop an intimate understanding of what is required for the relationship to be mutually beneficial. These relationships both drive renewal within the social and environmental systems, and assure that high quality supplies are available to meet specific market expectations. With practices such as fair trade sourcing, paying living wages, and investing in supplier education, hybrid organizations demonstrate a commitment to their suppliers and supplier communities beyond those of mainstream competitors. For instance, rather than seeking the lowest price suppliers that pay minimum wages and have no regard for the sustainability of their farming practices, Guayakí pays its farmers above market living wages and devotes significant resources into training them in the sustainable farming techniques necessary to meet the organization's mission. The strong relationship that results is central to the company's business model, while such strong and lasting relationships also show that hybrids' approach is one of organizational virtuousness, demonstrating that moral goodness for positive human impact and social betterment supports financial prosperity (Cameron et al., 2004).

Mutually Beneficial Relationships with Employees

Hybrid organizations select employees who possess the sustainability values of the organization, ensuring that the organization's sustainability identity (Hamilton & Gioia, 2009) is maintained. Once hired, hybrid organizations socialize employees into the social change objective and establish close relationships based on mutual respect, compassion, and cooperation. For example, employees at Green Mountain Coffee Roasters (GMCR) are taken to the communities that supply its coffee to enable them to gain a more holistic view of key raw ingredients, the people who cultivate it, and the natural environment in which it is grown. Further to this, executives have been known to extend personal kindnesses, such as interest-free loans to employees suffering hardship (Neville, 2008), and share company decision-making rights through its employee stock option plan (GMCR, 2009). Research has shown that when information is shared, trust and respect are cultivated, and decision making is inclusive, both employees and the organization thrive (Spreitzer et al., 2005). Employees experience greater workplace satisfaction and the company enjoys low staff turnover and high levels of employee loyalty. Further, GMCR's approach displays aspects of compassionate organizing through the increased empathetic concern in addition to the creation of credible trusting relationships (Dutton et al., 2006).

Mutually Beneficial Relationships with Customers

Hybrids develop a line of products that represent far more than simply the utility they provide. To their customers, these products are a projection of the values that they mutually share and an opportunity to express themselves through the companies' positive sustainable identity (Hamilton & Gioia, 2009). The class of customers that are drawn to this connection has been named "cultural creatives" or LOHAS—lifestyles of health and sustainability. These customers seek design, health, and ecological sustainability in the products they purchase. Rather than valuing achievement, style, and economic progress, cultural creatives value authenticity, nature, and community. They are "careful consumers" who reject "fake, imitation, poorly made, throwaway, cliché style or high fashion." They read labels and want to know "where a product came from, how it was made, who made it, and what will happen to it when they are finished with it" (Ray & Anderson, 2007, p.35).

As a result, a deep trusting relationship develops between the hybrid organization and its customers, who in turn grow these markets and help hybrids meet their social change objectives. It is a mutually reinforcing, virtuous cycle. Conversely, if the hybrid breaks that relationship, the outcome has more significant consequences than for other companies. For example, in 2006, Seventh Generation customers described feeling "betrayed" when the company changed the ingredients of its baby wipes because its suppliers were unable to meet demand and they switched suppliers. To respond to what amounted to a deep crisis of trust and restore its relationship with customers, the company allowed the existing stock of reformulated product to clear the shelf space, and then waited for its regular supplier to provide product based on the original formula. Giving up this valuable shelf space, even for a short period of time, is something that a traditional for-profit company would never do (Goldstein & Russo,

2006), but for the hybrid organization, a demonstrated commitment to its values is paramount.

Progressive Interaction with Markets, Competitors, and Industry Institutions

Hybrid organizations do not simply develop this successful business model for their own use. Unlike traditional for-profit business models that use competition and political activity for individual gain and market protection, hybrid organizations use them to promote the diffusion of sustainable products and practices. These efforts are driven in three primary directions: markets, competitors, and institutions.

Building Markets for More Sustainable Products

Hybrid organizations produce products for a sustainable market segment they seek to grow, not simply for their own benefit, but also for other firms who are in associated markets. Rather than make their core competency opaque and their value-adding capabilities inimitable (Barney, 1991), hybrids value transparency and use an open source model that others can follow. Seventh Generation, for example, publishes the ingredients for all of its products on the Web rather than protecting such formulations as confidential. Its customers demand this transparency, and its market is growing. In 2006, the LOHAS demand "for goods and services focused on health, the environment, social justice, personal development and sustainable living" represented an estimated $209 billion U.S. industry (LOHAS, 2010). In 2001, it was estimated that this class represented 50 million people, and by 2003 that figure had grown to 68 million Americans, or about 33% of the adult population (Cortese, 2003).

Rousing Competition

The growing success and profitability of hybrid organizations and the markets they help to build has made them targets for competition with dominant incumbent firms that develop sustainable product offerings of their own. For example, following the market success of Seventh Generation, Clorox developed a line of green cleaners, and Kimberly Clark developed a line of recycled content bathroom tissue (Wong, 2008). Further, many hybrids have become attractive acquisition targets and been absorbed by larger conglomerates.[2] For many hybrids, this prospect is anathema, as it threatens the desire for autonomy in maintaining sustainable operational and investment practices. However, some have speculated that acquisition can help hybrids reach larger markets and may even create an opportunity for change within the portfolios and practices of the acquiring parent companies.

Changing Industry Institutions

Similar to other for-profit organizations, hybrid organizations seek a leadership role within their industry. However, while other companies seek to influence institutions to reduce regulation and external costs to protect their competitive advantage, hybrid organizations seek to influence institutions to draw other companies into emulating them. Put another way, where other companies seek to create barriers to entry to their markets, hybrids actively encourage entry. In fact, emulation by other companies signals the success of their mission. Toward that end, hybrids act as catalysts for positive social change by working with industry groups and government agencies to create industry standards for more sustainable products and practices. In this respect, hybrid organizations act as institutional entrepreneurs (Fligstein, 1997; Lawrence, 1999), changing the rules of the game for all organizations.

In sum, the sustainability-driven business model explains how hybrid organizations drive change at the firm and industry levels, promoting sustainable products and practices that will eventually become established as industry norms that all must follow. The following case study illustrates how one firm embodies the elements of this model.

CASE STUDY: MAGGIE'S ORGANICS (CLEAN CLOTHES, INC.)

Maggie's Organics, founded in 1992 in Ann Arbor, Michigan, is the oldest organic apparel company and one of the oldest hybrid organizations in the United States. Its track record exemplifies the three elements of the sustainability-driven business model leading to positive social change.

---

[2] For example, Ben & Jerry's was acquired by Unilever in 2000; Stonyfield Farms was acquired by the Danone Group in 2003; and Burt's Bees was acquired by Clorox in 2008.

Social Change as Organizational Objective

Maggie's Organics is driven by a passionate founder and leader, Bená Burda, who began her career in the organics industry in 1978. Like many leaders, Burda embodies the values that her company espouses. She humbly states, "At this point I feel that I actually *am* both a fair trade person and socially responsible. But I did not start out to be either of those, nor a philanthropist. I don't like the labels, but instead feel that at Maggie's we have simply created a logical, sustainable, and rewarding business model" (author interview, August 9, 2010).

The company has an expressed mission to "…restore, sustain, and enhance the resources, including human, from which they [the apparel] are made" (Boyd et al., 2009, p.107). In particular, the company was founded with a goal of saving land from the devastation of conventional cotton production and developing new agricultural practices that exclude the use of toxic chemical pesticides. To remain true to its mission, Maggie's is a privately held company preferring to maintain its autonomy without the influence of traditional investors. Burda initially financed Maggie's along with a business partner, but she remains the majority-owner today with two friends holding minority (10%) ownership.

Mutually Beneficial Relationships

Burda's dedication is central to the organization's culture and has resulted in lasting friendships with employees. Further, to carry out its mission, Maggie's Organics has created supplier partnerships that are based on interpersonal connections, and recognizes that their prosperity is tightly linked with its own. For example, Maggie's has created new types of suppliers in the formation of 100% worker-owned sewing cooperatives in both Nueva Vida, Nicaragua (known as the Fair Trade Zone Sewing), and North Carolina (Opportunity Threads). Burda is committed to supporting these cooperatives and pays them a higher living wage for their sewing services. She has vowed she will not discontinue business with the cooperatives, and works with them to continually improve their operations in an effort to avoid quality issues and missed deadlines.

At home, Maggie's Organics prides itself on a culture of respect and equality; there is a relatively small difference between the salaries of the highest and lowest-paid employees. The company's culture attracts employees that share its values of environmentally progressive think-ing. In fact, the company (while small in number with only 14 employ-ees) screens potential employees for knowledge of organics and organic cotton.

Progressive Interaction with Markets, Competitors, and Industry Institutions

Maggie's Organics has been consistently profitable since 2004, and with this success as a platform, Burda has dedicated her career to acting as a "positive deviant" within the apparel industry (Spreitzer & Sonenshein, 2004). Burda has not been satisfied only to instill sustainable practices at Maggie's, but she is also creating institutional change by altering the apparel industry's sourcing and production practices. Specifically, Burda and Maggie's Organics have played a central role in developing the U.S. Organic Cotton Apparel Industry and the Organic Trade Association's (OTA) American Organic Fiber Processing Standards. Maggie's is also the first apparel company worldwide to achieve the Fair Labor Practices and Community Benefits Certification standard, a global, third-party certi-fied standard that certifies that all workers in the production process are treated fairly with safe and healthy working conditions.

Indicative of the ultimate goal of the company as promoting broad social and environmental change, Burda reflects "if the entire apparel industry were to adopt Maggie's organic practices, I would be satisfied with our suc-cess and might consider my job done" (author interview, August 9, 2010).

IMPLICATIONS AND FUTURE RESEARCH

The contributions of this chapter lie in the areas of theoretical develop-ment and practical consideration. We will cover each in turn and offer suggestions for future research.

Implications for Theory

Hybrid organizations provide scholars with insights into how organiza-tions can act as institutional entrepreneurs, and add to our understanding of the literatures on both positive social change and sustainability.

Positive Social Change

In this chapter, we have described ways in which new forms of for-profit and non-profit organizations act as agents for social change. Hybrid organizations present positive organizational scholars with a new domain in which to study their phenomena of interest. Hybrids present a novel and exciting attempt to break the "mythical fixed pie" (Bazerman & Hoffman, 1999), challenging traditional notions of the win-lose relationship between economic and environmental or social goals (Hoffman, 2000). As such, firms can have a positive role to play in social change, rather than the negative role they have had in the past and are generally assumed to have in future. The positivity of the model we have identified here is enabled by hybrids looking past the need for compliance or reducing negative social impacts, and identifying opportunities to restore community prosperity and environmental integrity. As hybrids bridge for-profit and non-profit domains to accomplish these goals they offer an interesting empirical site for linking theories of social movements, management, and positive social change.

Institutional Entrepreneurship

In creating positive change, hybrid organizations are sustainable businesses (Lazlo & Cooperrider, 2008) but go further. They not only create value for their owners, society, and the environment, but also reach beyond their specific supply chains with the aim of changing the institutionalized rules of the markets in which they operate. As such, they act as institutional entrepreneurs (DiMaggio, 1988), "exploiting cultural discontinuities...across multiple societal sectors... [and] discovering ways to innovate through structural overlap, thus blurring their primary roles and activities by moving from one societal sector to another" (Thornton & Ocasio, 2008, p. 129). Understanding the role of institutional entrepreneurs in shaping the discourse, norms, and structures that guide organizational action is of key importance in analyzing the success of hybrid organizations. In fact, this is the ultimate goal and success metric by which many hybrid organizations measure themselves. This is a significant deviation from traditional business practice and demonstrates a new form of social movement beyond a strict focus on NGOs. By choosing positive institutional change as their primary objective, hybrid organizations demonstrate how many positive concepts, such as positive deviance (Spreitzer & Sonenshein, 2004), organizational virtuousness (Cameron et al., 2004), positive leadership (Cameron & Lavine, 2006), positive meaning, and positive relationships (Dutton & Sonenshein, 2008) not only apply to individuals and dyads but also to the firm, inter-organizational, and industry levels of analysis.

Sustainability

The sustainability literature is emerging as a field of its own with a rich body of research work and key findings and assumptions. At its core, the challenge of sustainability represents far more than an incremental advancement of corporate greening initiatives or environmental management. It is a fundamental shift in society and a concurrent shift in the management and strategic frameworks by which business is conducted. These shifts challenge prevailing dominant conceptions of the role of business within society. According to Ehrenfeld (2011, p. 614),

> ... the criticality of creating sustainability lie[s] in the alternate pathway. This choice poses a huge challenge. The offerings and operations of these firms must not only produce a different kind of customer satisfaction, they must also employ a positive strategy to change the culture inside and outside of the firm. Deliberately changing culture inside a firm is not new although experience teaches that such change is difficult (Schein 1984). Deliberately changing the outside culture in which the firm is embedded is a new challenge and departs from traditional models that define roles for business within a political economy. Taking on culture change is about as far as one can get from Milton Friedman's (1970) famous assertion that, "The social responsibility of business is to increase its profits."

Hybrid organizations are an answer to Ehrenfeld's call; striving not simply to reduce their impact on the environment and their communities, but rather to develop positive and generative social and environmental change. This represents a phenomenological shift (Hoffman & Haigh, 2011) from a focus on organizations being less unsustainable to becoming more sustainable (Ehrenfeld, 2008), and a theoretical shift from addressing *deficit* gaps to instead addressing *abundance* gaps (Cameron, 2007). Within this fundamental shift of focus lie innovative solutions and cues to future market shifts toward addressing sustainability problems.

Implications for Practice

The model we have identified also has implications for practitioners. First, the model itself offers a template for the development of a hybrid strategy. Beyond that, we will discuss how hybrid organizations challenge conventional business assumptions, bridge two ends of a dichotomy, and risk extinction by bringing sustainability into the mainstream.

Challenging Conventional Business Assumptions

Hybrid organizations are driven by a goal to alter the taken-for-granted assumptions of business management that lead to unsustainable behavior and outcomes. While much of management literature promotes the externalization of social and environmental costs as wise strategy, hybrid organizations actively internalize them for the very same reasons. This is just one of the dominant business assumptions that hybrids challenge (Capra, 1982; Daly & Cobb, 1994; Daly, 1991; Gladwin, Kennelly, & Krause, 1995). Hybrid organizations also call for a reconsideration of business principles to see:

- The firm as socially and physically connected to the ecosystem and other societies.
- The profit motive as reconfigured to just one of many prime objectives of the firm.
- Economic growth as redefined to include concerns for information intensiveness, community consciousness, and the experiential quality of economic activity, rather than merely its material-energy intensiveness.
- Nature as having social, cultural, and spiritual value beyond immediate interests in economic value.
- Supplier, customer, and employee relationships as having dimensions far beyond being primarily transaction in nature.

By challenging these taken-for-granted beliefs of business management and succeeding as business ventures, the sustainability-driven business model that hybrids develop offers clues to the future direction of business practice more generally.

Bridging Two Ends of a Dichotomy

Hybrid organizations present a bridge between two ends of a dichotomy previously seen as incommensurable (economic profit, and social and environmental mission). This means that success for a hybrid organization requires serving two or even three masters, in that they need to manage the three E's of the triple bottom line (Elkington, 1998): economic, environment, and (social) equity. It is difficult to do this well; however, by developing a negotiated order among them, hybrids represent an important breakthrough in what has traditionally been seen as a win-lose relationship (Hoffman, 2000). They show that the relationship can be win-win-win with a reassessment of the definition of win in each category. By charting a course in this direction, hybrid organizations offer a means to explore whether a breakthrough in positive social change is possible (Hampden-Turner, 1994).

Risking Extinction by Mainstreaming the Sustainability Mission

Hybrid organizations have created niches for themselves, and in the process have enjoyed increasing competitive benefits. But those niches are becoming mainstream, and while many hybrids were the first-movers in their field and will retain leadership positions, they will continue to be challenged by dominant players. This represents a strange tension for hybrids. On the one hand, this is a victory for the company's efforts at driving social change. On the other hand, it raises the question of whether hybrids are undermining their own competitive viability through their diffusion of practices. As for-profit companies, they seek to capitalize on their market segment. As social entrepreneurs, they seek to entice others into joining their market segment. In the end, is the ultimate goal of a hybrid also its extinction?

Directions for Future Research

The metaphorical bridge that hybrid organizations create among economic, social, and environmental priorities offers a rich array of possibilities for future research spanning sustainability and positive organizational scholarship.

First, it will be important to understand the ways in which hybrid organizations impact industry-wide standards. How do they act as institutional entrepreneurs (DiMaggio & Powell, 1983), and what insights can they provide into these dynamics? For example, existing literature attends to issues of size, power, and network connections as critical attributes for allowing organizations to exercise control over their environments. However, hybrid organizations rarely possess such attributes. As small businesses attempting to change the norms of larger entities (competitors, communities, institutions), hybrid organizations often deal with organizations and systems of disproportionate power. And yet, they are often able to promote significant shifts. This raises the question of what the power differential means for traditional studies of institutional change, and whether other forms of power (i.e., the power of legitimacy driven by a moral purpose) are at play.

In a related domain, there is a vast area of research to be conducted into the dynamics around the acquisition of hybrids by larger incumbent forms. Acting as a metaphorical Trojan horse, questions emerge around how hybrid organizations can promote social change from within a dominant incumbent. First, is it universally true that acquisition threatens the autonomy and ability of hybrids to maintain sustainable operational and investment practices? Second, under what conditions can acquired hybrid organizations change the portfolios and practices of the acquiring parent companies?

Finally, this chapter has sought to be an example of the benefits of problem-based research (Biggart & Lutzenhiser, 2007; Davis & Marquis, 2005) which draws on theoretical principles for providing deeper and richer explanations of critical problems in our world. Rather than seeing the only merit of academic scholarship in theory development (Hambrick, 2007), this chapter builds on the presupposition that social science research has a valid and critical role in providing scholarly analysis of contemporary social issues. Few contemporary issues warrant social and cultural analysis by problem-focused researchers more than sustainability, and such analysis can aid in providing greater "rigor and relevance" in the assessment of our research questions (Tushman & O'Reilly, 2007).

CONCLUSION

Questions around the role of the market and the firm in addressing societal issues are particularly salient today given the growing distrust of the for-profit sector, and their contribution to environmental and social problems (Braudel, 1982; Lemos & Agrawal, 2006; Perrow, 1991; Polanyi, 1944; Smith, 1994). In this chapter, we sought to apply a positive lens to hybrid organizations, and through that lens we examined ways in which the hybrid form fosters positive social and environmental change. By doing so, we identified a model of social change agency that hybrid organizations develop that uses the market system to yield positive social and environmental outcomes. In this way, hybrid organizations offer exciting insights into possibilities for sustainability outcomes.

ACKNOWLEDGMENTS

The authors would like to thank Bená Burda for her assistance with the Maggie's Organics case study and acknowledge the financial support of the Frederick A. and Barbara M. Erb Institute for Global Sustainable Enterprise at the University of Michigan.

REFERENCES

Alexander, J. (2000). Adaptive strategies of nonprofit human service organizations in an era of devolution and new public management. *Nonprofit Management and Leadership, 10*, 287–303.

Alter, K. (2004). *Social enterprise typology.* Seattle, WA: Virtue Ventures LLC.

Barbaro, M. (2008, February 3). Wal-Mart: The new Washington. *New York Times.* Retrieved October 24, 2010, from http://www.nytimes.com/2008/02/03/weekinreview/03barb.html.

Barney, J. (1991). Firm resources and sustained competitive advantage. *Journal of Management, 17*, 99–120.

Bazerman, M., & Hoffman, A. (1999). Sources of environmentally destructive behavior: Individual, organizational and institutional perspectives. *Research in Organizational Behavior, 21*, 39–79.

Bernstein, S., & Cashore, B. (2007). Can non-state global governance be legitimate? An analytical framework. *Regulation and Governance, 4*, 347–371.

Biggart, N., & Lutzenhiser, L. (2007). Economic sociology and the social problem of energy efficiency. *American Behavioral Scientist, 50*, 1070–1086.

Boyd, B., Henning, N., Reyna, E., Wang, D., & Welch, M. (2009). *Hybrid organizations: New business models for environmental leadership.* Sheffield: Greenleaf Publishing.

Braudel, F. (1982). *The wheels of commerce: Civilization and capitalism 15th–18th century* (S. Reynolds, Trans.) Vol. 2. New York: Harper and Row.

Cameron, K., Bright, D., & Caza, A. (2004). Exploring the relationships between organizational virtuousness and performance. *American Behavioral Scientist, 47*, 1–24.

Cameron, K., & Lavine, M. (2006). *Making the impossible possible: Leading extraordinary performance: The Rocky Flats story.* San Francisco: Berrett-Koehler Publishers.

Capra, F. (1982). *The turning point.* New York: Bantam Books.

Carmeli, A., & Spreitzer, G. (2009). Trust, connectivity, and thriving: Implications for innovative work behavior. *Journal of Creative Behavior, 43,* 169–191.

Cashore, B. (2002). Legitimacy and the privatization of environmental governance: How non-state market driven (NSMD) governance systems gain rule-making authority. *Governance, 15,* 503–529.

Cortese, A. (2003, July 20). Business: They care about the world (and they shop, too). *New York Times.* Retrieved October 24, 2010, from http://query.nytimes.com/gst/fullpage.html?res=9E01E3D8103CF933A15754C0A9659C8B63.

Crossette, B. (1998, September 27). Kofi Anna's astonishing facts. *New York Times, 4,* 16.

Daly, H. (1991). *Steady-state economics.* Washington DC: Island Press.

Daly, H., & Cobb, J. (1994). *For the common good.* Boston: Beacon Press.

Davis, G., & Marquis, C. (2005). Prospects for organization theory in the early twenty-first century: Institutional fields and mechanisms. *Organization Science, 16,* 332–344.

DiMaggio, P. (1988). Interest and agency in institutional theory. In L. Zucker (Ed.), *Institutional patterns and organizations* (pp. 3–2). Cambridge, MA: Ballinger.

DiMaggio, P., & Powell, W. (1983). The iron cage revisited: Institutional isomorphism and collective rationality in organizational fields. *American Sociological Review, 48,* 147–160.

Donahue, J. (2002). Market based governance and the architecture of accountability. In J. Donahue & J. Nye (Eds.), *Market-based governance: Supply side, demand side, upside, and downside.* Cambridge: Brookings Institution Press.

Draper, L. (2005). Tapping overlooked sources of support for nonprofits. *Foundation News & Commentary, 43,* 27–32.

Dutton, J., & Glynn, M. (2008). Positive organizational scholarship. In J. Barling & C. L. Cooper (Eds.). *The SAGE handbook of organizational behavior* (pp. 693–712). Los Angeles: Sage.

Dutton, J., & Heaphy, E. (2003). The power of high-quality connections at work. In K. Cameron, J. Dutton, & R. E. Quinn (Eds.), *Positive organizational scholarship* (pp. 263–278). San Francisco: Berrett-Koehler Publishers.

Dutton, J., & Sonenshein, S. (2008). Positive organizational scholarship. In S. Lopez & A. Beauchamps (Eds.), *Encyclopedia of positive psychology.* Oxford, UK: Blackwell Publishing.

Dutton, J., Worline, M., Frost, P., & Lilius, J. (2006). Explaining compassion organizing, *Administrative Science Quarterly, 51,* 59–96.

Ehrenfeld, J. (2008). *Sustainability by design: A subversive strategy for transforming our consumer culture.* New Haven: Yale University Press.

Ehrenfeld, J. (2011). Over the rainbow: Business for sustainability. In T. Bansal & A. Hoffman (Eds.), *The Oxford handbook of business and the environment* (pp. 611–619). New York: Oxford University Press.

Elkington, J. (1998). *Cannibals with forks: The triple bottom line for 21st century business.* Oxford: Capstone.

Fligstein, N. (1997). Social skill and institutional theory. *American Behavioral Scientist, 40,* 397–405.

Flynn, G. (2008). The virtuous manager: A vision for leadership in business. *Journal of Business Ethics, 78,* 359–372.

Friedman, M. (1970, September 13). The social responsibility of business is to increase its profits. *The New York Times Magazine*, pp. 32–33, 122, 124, 126.

Gittell, J., Cameron, K., Lim, S., & Rivas, V. (2006). Relationships, layoffs and organizational resilience: Airline industry responses to September 11th. *Journal of Applied Behavioral Science, 42*, 300–329.

Gladwin, T., Kennelly, J., & Krause, T. (1995). Shifting paradigms for sustainable development: Implications for management theory and research. *Academy of Management Review, 20*, 874–907.

Goldstein, D., & Russo, M. (2006). *Seventh generation: Balancing customer expectations with supply chain realities* (case study). University of Oregon.

Green Mountain Coffee Roasters, Inc. (2009). Retrieved October 18, 2010, from http://www.gmcr.com/csr

Hambrick, D. (2007). The field of management's devotion to theory: Too much of a good thing? *Academy of Management Journal, 50*, 1346–1352.

Hamilton, A., & Gioia, D. (2009). Fostering sustainability-focused organizational identities. In L. M. Roberts & J. E. Dutton (Eds.), *Exploring positive identities and organizations: Building a theoretical and research foundation.* New York: Routledge.

Haugh, H. (2005). A research agenda for social entrepreneurship. *Social Enterprise Journal, 1*, 1–12.

Hoffman, A. (2000). *Competitive environmental strategy: A guide to the changing business landscape.* Washington DC: Island Press.

Hoffman, A., & Haigh, N. (2011). Positive deviance for a sustainable world: Linking sustainability and positive organizational scholarship. In K. Cameron & G. Spreitzer (Eds.), *The Oxford handbook on positive organizational scholarship* (pp. 953–964). Oxford, UK: Oxford University Press.

Hoffman, A., Paynter, E., Senecal, E., Start, L., Tam, T., Weinglass, D., Whisnant, R., & Jongejan, A. (2010). *Honest tea—Sell up or sell out?* Case study 1–428–947. Ann Arbor, MI: Erb Institute/William Davidson Institute, University of Michigan.

Lawrence, T. (1999). Institutional strategy. *Journal of Management, 25*, 161–188.

Lazlo, C. & Cooperrider, D. (2008). Design for sustainable value: A whole system approach, *Advances in Appreciative Inquiry, 2*, 15–29.

Lemos, M., & Agrawal, A. (2006). Environmental governance. *Annual Review of Environmental Resources, 31*, 1–29.

Lifestyles of Health and Sustainability. (2010). Retrieved October 18, 2010, from http://www.lohas.com/.

Liverman, D. (2004). Who governs, at what scale, and at what price? Geography, environmental governance, and the commodification of nature. *Annals of the Association of American Geographers, 94*, 734–738.

Mills, S. (2009, August 19). Organic foods: Big companies swoop in to capitalize on lucrative market. *Chicago Tribune.* Retrieved October 24, 2010, from http://articles.chicagotribune.com/2009–08-19/news/0908180620_1_organic-foods-cascadian-farm-small-planet-foods.

Neville, M. (2008). Positive deviance on the ethical continuum: Green Mountain Coffee as a case study in conscientious capitalism. *Business & Society Review, 113*, 555–576.

Perrow, C. (1991). A society of prganizations. *Theory and Society, 20*, 725–762.

Polanyi, K. (1944). *The great transformation.* New York: Rinehart.

Post, J. (2002). *Redefining the corporation: Stakeholder management and organizational wealth.* Stanford, CA: Stanford University Press.

Ray, P., & Anderson, S. (2007). *Lifestyles of the cultural creatives.* Retrieved October 24, 2010, from http://culturalcreatives.org/lifestyles.html.

Rousseau, D., & Ling, K. (2007). Following the resources in positive relationships. In J. Dutton & B. Ragins (Eds.), *Exploring positive relationships at work: Building a theoretical and research foundation* (pp. 373–384). Mahwah, NJ: Lawrence Erlbaum, Inc.

Smallbone, D., Evans, M., Ekanem, I., & Butters, S. (2001). *Researching social enterprise. Report to the Small Business Service.* Retrieved October 24, 2010, from http://www. bis.gov.uk/files/file38361.pdf.

Smith, A. (1994). *The wealth of nations.* New York: Modern Library.

Spreitzer, G., & Sonenshein, S. (2004). Toward the construct definition of positive deviance. *American Behavioral Scientist, 47*, 828–847.

Spreitzer, G., Sutcliffe, K., Dutton, J., Sonenshein, S., & Grant, A. (2005). A socially embedded model of thriving at work. *Organization Science, 16*, 537–549.

Thomas, W. (2002). Business and the journey towards sustainable development: Reflections on progress since Rio. *Environmental Law Reporter,* June, 10873–10955.

Thornton, P., & Ocasio, W. (2008). Institutional logics. In R. Greenwood et al. (Eds.), *The Sage handbook of organizational institutionalism* (pp. 99–129). Los Angeles: Sage.

Tozzi, J. (2010, April 13). Maryland passes "benefit corp." law for social entrepreneurs. *Businessweek.* Retrieved October 24, 2010, from http://www.businessweek.com/ smallbiz/running_small_business/archives/2010/04/benefit_corp_bi.html.

Tushman, M., & O'Reilly, C. (2007). Research and relevance: Implications of Pasteur's quadrant for doctoral programs and faculty development. *Academy of Management Journal, 50*, 769–774.

Wong, E. (2008). Seventh Generation strikes back. *Brandweek.* Retrieved October 13, 2010, from http://www.brandweek.com/bw/content_display/news-and-features/ packaging-and-design/e3i397aa99d2932d77d18d4dc9daa147187.

World Business Council on Sustainable Development (1997). *Exploring sustainable development: WBCSD global scenarios.* London: World Business Council on Sustainable Development.

World Commission on Environment and Development (1987). *Our common future.* New York: Oxford University Press.

World Resources Institute (1994). *World resources.* Oxford: Oxford University Press.

8

Agency and Innovation in a Phase of Turbulent Change: Conservation in the Great Bear Rainforest

Darcy Riddell, Ola Tjörnbo, and Frances Westley
University of Waterloo

CONSERVATION IN THE GREAT BEAR RAINFOREST: AGENCY AND INNOVATION IN A PHASE OF TURBULENT CHANGE

The rallying cry for a new generation of activists, from the words famously famous attributed to M. K. Gandhi, proclaims that "we must be the change we wish to see in the world." This is a call both to enact change and to embody a desired future in one's current way of life. Yet, when impersonal political and economic structures and large-scale cultural forces are implicated in systemic problems such as poverty, climate change, or species loss, what power do individuals truly have to create positive social and organizational change? So-called messy, wicked, or complex problems refer to problems whose very definition is contested, and for which solutions are unknown, multiple, and emergent. Organization- or leadership-based theories can be inadequate to explain change in these complex problem domains: those with convoluted overlaps of authority, institutions operating at multiple scales, and a multiplicity of actors with clashing beliefs that frame the problem differently and generate competing knowledge claims. Yet individuals *are* enacting change, and impacting on large-scale problems—with both positive and negative consequences.

Many cases describe how courageous individuals and collections of people can catalyze social innovations through their own agency and tenacity (e.g., Bornstein, 2007; Hawken, 2007; Westley et al., 2006). Given the increasing complexity of the problems in our world, theories of agency that illuminate, without privileging, the role of individual change makers in addressing complex problems, are an important part of theorizing change. Such theories, when consistent with complexity theory, suggest that positive change has an emergent process: that change at the individual level can change group dynamics which in turn can change broader system dynamics (Westley et al., 2006). A complexity- and agency-based approach contrasts with heroic leadership-based theories of organizational change, and is more appropriate for theorizing in complex social-political domains. This chapter looks at these dynamics of change in a case of social innovation, and focuses on the question: what are the individual and collective processes of agency that catalyze systems change? By applying a positive lens, we enrich our exploration of the processes of agency that enabled system change to emerge.

This chapter describes the case of forest conservation in the Great Bear Rainforest, where the passion and purposeful action of individuals created conditions for greater social justice, sustainability, and community resilience. In the process, these individuals met circumstances that called forth their own transformation, which in turn supported their ability change relationship dynamics, and through this process, to enlist conflicted sectors into collaboration toward a shared vision. This group of actors and organizations successfully established a globally significant conservation agreement that protected 33% of the Great Bear Rainforest, caused a radical reorientation of forest policy and management regimes, raised conservation capital to support innovation in communities, and enshrined a powerful new legal role for First Nations. After introducing the case, we frame it as an example of social innovation in a complex problem domain, emphasizing the phase of turbulent change (Westley et al., 2006). We describe six processes of individual and collective agency that led to innovation, drawing from socio-cognitive (Bandura, 2001; 2006) and sociological theories of agency (Emirbayer & Mische, 1998) to better understand these aspects of agency. We suggest that social change agency can be understood as a multilevel process of creating intentional change, where actors must attend to transformation at personal, interpersonal, and systemic levels in order to be successful. We identify positive dynamics at each of these levels, whereby individuals experience growth and harness compassionate motivation, which in turn supports generative relationships and new forms of problem-solving between actors in conflict, finally contributing to emergent, innovative solutions that support human development and are more just and sustainable. We highlight some new lines of sight offered by the case, and propose future areas of research.

CONFLICT AND SOCIAL INNOVATION IN THE GREAT BEAR RAINFOREST

Forest Conflict on British Columbia's Coast

Heated controversies over the large-scale clear-cutting of old growth forest—dubbed "the War in the Woods"—made headlines in the province of British Columbia, Canada (BC), for over a decade. The Great Bear Rainforest on BC's west coast was the largest unprotected coastal temperate rainforest remaining worldwide in the 1990s, and a coalition of environmental non-governmental organizations (ENGOs) was determined to protect it. Located between the Alaska panhandle and the northern tip of Vancouver Island, the 6.4 million hectares Great Bear Rainforest is about the size of Ireland, encompassing hundreds of intact valleys of temperate rainforest (Figure 8.1). About 22,000 people live in the Great Bear Rainforest, and it is home to the unique white "spirit bear," grizzly bears, and cedars over 2000 years old. First Nations (aboriginal people) make up about half of the population, and the region includes the traditional territories of 25 culturally distinct Nations, who face a loss of languages and traditional cultures, serious social problems, and limited economic opportunities as a result of being excluded historically from the economic benefits of forestry, fishing, and other extractive industries (Prescott-Allen, 2005; Smith & Sterritt, 2007). During the period of conservation battles, First Nations were claiming rights and title over their traditional territories, and winning key battles against the provincial government in the Canadian Supreme Court. The provincial government controlled the majority of land in BC, and granted long-term forest tenures to a handful of forest companies operating on the coast, in turn reaping logging fees (Wagner, 2003). Forestry was historically of vital importance to BC's economy, and the changing softwood lumber market had the coastal forest industry struggling.

Aware of looming controversy, in 1997, the province created a multi-stakeholder land use planning process for the central coast region, and

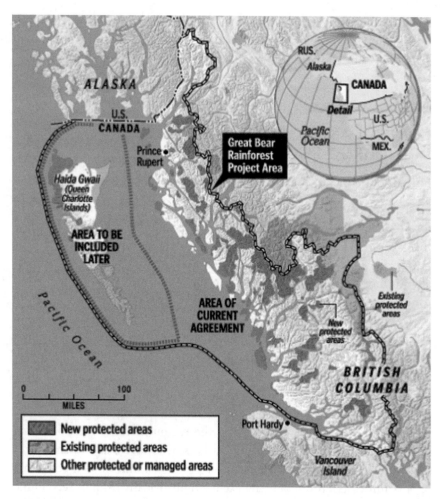

FIGURE 8.1
Map of the Great Bear Rainforest area including Haida Gwaii, British Columbia, Canada.

later the north coast, and invited stakeholders from all sectors to participate (Tjornbo et al., 2010). The process was undermined from the outset,
as environmental organizations boycotted the process—labeling it as inca-
pable of legislating meaningful conservation, and First Nations attended
as observers, unwilling to be considered merely "stakeholders" in an area
they believed to be under their jurisdiction. In 1997–1998, as the planning process proceeded, 13 rainforest valleys were roaded and logged, and
almost every valley in the region was scheduled for clear-cutting within
decades (Sierra Club of BC, 1999). A coalition of ENGOs consisting of

ForestEthics, Greenpeace, the Sierra Club of BC, and Rainforest Action Network launched international and provincial campaigns to protect the Great Bear Rainforest. Their vision was of large-scale rainforest conservation, new forest practices, recognition of First Nations title and rights, and new sustainable economic opportunities for the region. Public and marketplace campaigns targeted wood and paper products originating from endangered forest regions worldwide, using the Great Bear Rainforest as the "poster child."

The ENGOs' campaigns fueled intense conflict between the forest industry, government, forest workers, First Nations, and environmentalists in both the media and political arenas—but they proved to be powerful strategies in catalyzing change. Campaigns targeted customers of BC wood products in U.S., European, and Japanese markets worth roughly one billion dollars (Smith & Sterrit, 2007). Over 80 companies made commitments to phase out endangered forest products, including Home Depot and Lowe's, the world's largest wood retailers, IKEA, and Fortune 500 companies Nike, Dell, and IBM (Riddell, 2009; Smith & Sterrit, 2007). Over $200 million in contracts were cancelled with forest companies logging in the Great Bear Rainforest, and German and U.S. buyers registered concerns with the government and industry, signaling that a solution to the conflict had to be found. As a result of this financial pressure and the related controversy, forest companies operating in the Great Bear Rainforest entered into bi-lateral negotiations with ENGOs, and the province lifted restrictions so that ENGOs would agree to join official land-use planning processes.

Negotiations and Coalition-Building

In 1999, senior forest company representatives met, agreeing that they would redefine their approach to the coastal conflict and seek a negotiated resolution to the War in the Woods (Smith & Sterrit, 2007). Clearcut logging and markets campaigns continued, while the two sides found their footing in tense negotiations. A skilled facilitator, hired by forest companies, supported the negotiations. The ENGO leaders negotiating with industry were the same individuals who were leading the much-hated markets campaigns, and there was strong personal animosity on both sides. The negotiators on the ENGO side had faced threats of violence and backlash in the media and logging-dependent communities.

The premier of British Columbia had publicly labeled environmentalists as the "Enemies of BC" (Hoberg, 2001). Early negotiations were polarizing and uncomfortable, with environmental and industry representatives hurling bitter recriminations across the board table (Tjornbo et al., 2010). The industry negotiators were largely male, and had previous negotiating experience, whereas the women leading negotiations on the ENGO side had never undertaken such a role. During this time, ENGO leaders sought training and delved deeper into collective strategizing and visioning processes, as well as embracing new dialogue and learning approaches with their opponents.

In 2000, after over a year of negotiations, the parties created a "Standstill Agreement" whereby the markets campaigns would be suspended, and the forest companies agreed to a voluntary moratorium of logging in over 100 valleys, so future negotiations could proceed without battles in an atmosphere of "solutions space." The logging moratorium was an extraordinary milestone, as nothing like this, let alone on such grand scale, had ever been negotiated in BC—and certainly not without government involvement. The two sides had to "sell" the agreement to government, First Nations, and the land use planning table, and endured significant backlash from rural mayors, forest workers, and disgruntled members of their own camps when news of the agreement was leaked.

During this time of negotiations, coalitions were formalized both on the ENGO side (Rainforest Solutions Project—RSP) and the Forest Industry side (Coast Forest Companies Initiative—CFCI). After successfully negotiating the Standstill, CFCI and RSP created the Joint Solutions Project (JSP) as a structure for communication and further negotiations, and to advance dialogue with First Nations, the BC government, labor groups, and local communities. JSP became a venue for sharing information, discussing new policy and regulatory models, and problem solving (Smith & Sterrit, 2007). This ushered in an era of coalitions, where First Nations formalized their relationships with one another in the Coastal First Nations alliance, and government and coastal communities also established vehicles for collaboration, experimental thinking, and piloting new approaches.

Joint Solutions Emerge

In 2001, these multilateral negotiations led to a joint solutions framework, which maintained the logging deferrals and created new vehicles for knowledge generation, developing alternative management regimes, and supporting economic transition. The framework included an independent scientific panel—the Coast Information Team (CIT), which was set up to determine which areas needed protection, and how logging could take place in the region within the highest conservation standards. Parties agreed to embrace ecosystem-based management (EBM) principles and goals, which are based in the recognition that healthy ecosystems form the basis of healthy communities and economies—representing a significant shift from the extractive industrial forestry mindset. They also agreed to pursue efforts at economic diversification away from natural resource extraction toward a "conservation-based economy," which included a $35 million transition package for displaced workers, and the idea for a $120 million conservation investment fund. Finally the BC government and First Nations signed historic government-to-government protocol agreements with eight Coastal First Nations, acknowledging their shared jurisdiction.

Turning this framework into a substantive plan took five years, over a dozen committees, and thousands of hours of meetings (Smith & Sterrit, 2007). The CIT conducted ecological and socio-economic research, developed recommendations for the land use planning tables, and created a framework and guide for the new forest management regime. Individual First Nations pursued land use planning, and the Coast Investments and Incentives Initiative (CIII) was created as a joint initiative between the First Nations, ENGOs, and government, with ENGOs taking the lead to raise $60 million of philanthropic capital for conservation investments. Pilot projects were initiated in Coastal First Nations communities to apply new business concepts and EBM forestry. In 2004 the land use planning tables of the central and north coast came to consensus recommendations regarding protected areas and EBM forestry. In a parallel process, First Nations were completing their land use plans and preparing for government-to-government negotiations.

At last, by February 2006, the final Great Bear Rainforest Land Use Decisions were announced, formalizing the multifaceted new policies and legal agreements developed through ongoing collaboration. The final policy package represented a significant institutional shift to ecosystem-based forest management, with over 33% of the region (two million hectares) protected from logging. New legal designations were created to allow First Nations cultural uses in protected areas. The conservation fund of

$120 million was raised successfully, with half the funds supporting a permanent conservation endowment to finance ecosystem protection and management on public lands, and the other half to support ecologically sustainable First Nations businesses and economic development (Price et al., 2009). Finally, in March 2009, after tough negotiations on EBM implementation, the full agreement entered into force—a startling example of system transformation whose full effects on the province of BC are still to be felt.

The final agreements are touted by all parties as a world-class example of positive change, conserving large areas of rainforest, enshrining a more just relationship with First Nations, supporting community economic development needs, meeting forest industry requirements for certainty, and alleviating conflict. The parties agree that such a multidimensional solution would not have come about without participation and input from such diverse coalitions of interest (Smith & Sterritt, 2007). Inevitably, the parties involved continue to disagree on important aspects of implementation, and conflicts and competition for influence still characterize the policy arena, albeit in the context of these new institutional arrangements. As with all complex problems, change unfolds, the context shifts, and there is no true end to the process.

PHASES OF CHANGE IN THE GREAT BEAR RAINFOREST CASE

Social Innovation and the Adaptive Cycle

Social innovation is an emerging concept at the nexus of change efforts in civil society, business, philanthropy, government, and the emerging "fourth sector" of hybrid organizations, describing the myriad ways social and environmental value can be generated, and deep-rooted problems can be addressed. We define social innovation as a product, process, initiative, or program that profoundly changes the basic routines, resource and authority flows, or beliefs of any social system (Westley & Antadze, 2010). When a social innovation has a broad or durable impact, it will be *disruptive*—it will challenge the underlying system and institutions, changing the distribution of power and resources, and altering beliefs (Antadze & Westley, 2010).

According to the definition, social innovation occurred in the Great Bear Rainforest in many ways. The positive changes that took place required disruptions in social systems and institutions, redistributions of power and resources, new forms of governance, and a revolution in the management regime and assumptions guiding forest practices. The new legislation and parks designations, combined with the EBM approach, may be the largest of its kind globally. It is also likely the largest such region to have aboriginal co-management and highly transparent and adaptive governance structures (Price et al., 2009). On a global scale, markets campaigns have shifted the ways that wood and paper purchasing occurs, ushering in new supply chain management regimes (Riddell, 2009).

One of the ways social innovation theory illuminates complex change processes is by applying the concept of the adaptive cycle. The adaptive cycle describes four phases of change in a complex system, and suggests that a given system cycles continually through these stages as it responds to fluctuations in the internal and external environment (Gunderson & Holling, 2002). It provides a heuristic to understand processes of social innovation because by understanding the rhythms of different cycles and influences across scales, it is possible to identify points where the system can accept positive change, and to anticipate points of vulnerability (Holling, 2001; Westley et al., 2006). In this case, we apply the adaptive cycle to better locate and understand how phases of social innovation occurred and to analyze processes during each phase.

The four phases of change are depicted in Figure 8.2. The "front-loop" of the adaptive cycle is a relatively stable phase of predictable, incremental growth where production and accumulation are maximized—moving from the *exploitation phase* where new configurations grow in the system, and competition for resources increases, toward the *conservation phase* where a mature system is sustained, with little flexibility. The "back-loop" is an unpredictable phase of turbulent change and variation, where reorganization and invention are maximized, and transformative change is possible. This is characterized by the *release phase,* where the system undergoes a process of "creative destruction" and structures, processes, and/or function are disrupted. Changes release resources, dissolving the connection or coherence between existing systems parts. Dominant beliefs and understandings are called into question and novelty may emerge. In the *reorganization phase* that follows, a process of exploration and renewal occurs, enabling growth, resource accumulation, and storage. Ideas and adaptations proliferate. The system then moves along the front-loop toward

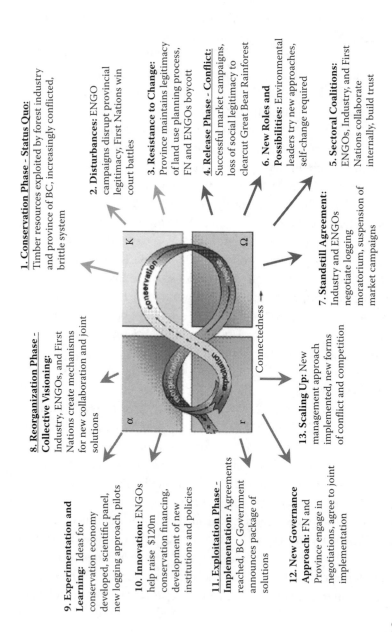

1. Conservation Phase - Status Quo: Timber resources exploited by forest industry and province of BC, increasingly conflicted, brittle system

2. Disturbances: ENGO campaigns disrupt provincial legitimacy, First Nations win court battles

3. Resistance to Change: Province maintains legitimacy of land use planning process, FN and ENGOs boycott

4. Release Phase - Conflict: Successful market campaigns, loss of social legitimacy to clearcut Great Bear Rainforest

5. Sectoral Coalitions: ENGOs, Industry, and First Nations collaborate internally, build trust

6. New Roles and Possibilities: Environmental leaders try new approaches, self-change required

7. Standstill Agreement: Industry and ENGOs negotiate logging moratorium, suspension of market campaigns

8. Reorganization Phase - Collective Visioning: Industry, ENGOs, and First Nations create mechanisms for new collaboration and joint solutions

9. Experimentation and Learning: Ideas for conservation economy developed, scientific panel, new logging approach, pilots

10. Innovation: ENGOs help raise $120m conservation financing, development of new institutions and policies

11. Exploitation Phase - Implementation: Agreements reached, BC Government announces package of solutions

12. New Governance Approach: FN and Province engage in negotiations, agree to joint implementation

13. Scaling Up: New management approach implemented, new forms of conflict and competition

FIGURE 8.2

Adaptive cycle in the Great Bear Rainforest case. This figure describes the phases of change in the case, and highlights the "back-loop" of turbulent change (underlined numbers 4–10), from conflict, through negotiations, collective visioning, experimentation, and innovation. FN, First Nations.

exploitation again. Adaptive cycles of change operating at different scales have been observed in ecosystems (Gunderson & Holling, 2002), institutions (Ostrom, 1992), societies (Westley, 1995), economies (Whitaker, 1987), and the production of scientific knowledge (Kuhn, 1962).

Using the adaptive cycle as a lens to interpret events in the Great Bear Rainforest case (Figure 8.2), different phases of change can be observed. In the **conservation phase**, forestry institutions became increasingly brittle and locked-in, making them vulnerable to economic pressures from changing markets and from the deliberately disruptive actions of environmentalists (numbers 1–3). Initially, conservative forces resisted change, but a release and reorganization was catalyzed by successful environmental campaigns and the changing status of First Nations resulting in a loss of legitimacy for the status quo of forest policy and the beginning of a transformative back-loop. During the **release phase** (numbers 4–7), sectors had to overcome conflict and collaborate more closely, and environmental leaders experimented with new strategies to navigate change. The standstill agreement created a foundation for the **reorganization phase** (numbers 8–10), a time of experimentation and learning, where the building blocks of the solution were generated including attracting new capital, creating political buy-in, and developing the economic, scientific/ecological, and human cases for change. New policy and economic and management mechanisms were developed and scaled up, leading to the **exploitation phase** (numbers 11–13), where the BC government announced a solutions package supported by all parties; new institutional arrangements with First Nations were established, and new battle lines were drawn between sectors as they jockeyed for position and power in defining implementation details of the complex new agreements. Of particular interest in this chapter is the phase of change through the turbulent back-loop, when the system moved from conflict to innovation. The next section highlights the role of agency in this turbulent phase, and identifies six processes of agency that influenced systemic change.

AGENCY IN THE GREAT BEAR RAINFOREST

Understanding Agency in Phases of Turbulent Change

While the adaptive cycle illuminates the phased process of social innovation and provides a lens for understanding the trajectory of change that took place in the Great Bear Rainforest, the cycle alone does not tell us how it was possible for such change to occur. We now look more closely at the agency social change actors expressed during the back-loop, from release to reorganization, to help move the system toward social innovation. Emirbayer and Mische (1998) suggest that upheaval stimulates particular aspects of agency, and have called for further research into how different aspects of agency are related to periods of stability and/or change. High levels of disorganization—manifesting as antagonism and open conflict— marked the release phase in the Great Bear Rainforest case. Despite the hostile environment, it was possible for the actors involved to build new partnerships and generate change. The lens of agency reveals dynamics across multiple levels (from micro-individual, to meso-relational/ organizational, to macro-systemic) which actors deliberately cultivated to generate social innovation. What is also revealed is that many of the expressions of agency involved positive processes. The macro-process of social innovation in the Great Bear Rainforest led to positive outcomes for human and community well-being, increased justice for First Nations, and more adaptive, sustainable forest practices and protection. The six micro- and meso-processes we have identified involve generative personal experiences, and the transformation of relationships from conflict to constructive engagement, which were framed as positive by the individuals involved. Taken together, these multilevel processes provide greater clarity into the kinds of individual and collective agency that are effective during times of turbulent change.

Social innovation concerns the interplay between intentionality and complexity and portrays change as occurring simultaneously at different scales. Because social innovators operate in fields of uncertainty, agency involves attending to and influencing the context in a manner that enables the success and extension of innovations. The agency involved in this kind of systems change has been described as institutional or systems "entrepreneurship" (Garud et al., 2007; Westley & Moore, 2009). Many social innovators describe the paradox that wanting to change others means also accepting profound change in oneself (Westley et al., 2006). This self-transformation is dependent on learning and reflection, as an individual realizes how they are implicated by and participating in the system they seek to change. Bandura (2001, 2006) understands humans as both producers and products of their life circumstances, recognizing that agents and systems/structures are mutually dependent and co-evolving.

Following Bandura we define agency as intentional action to influence one's functioning and life circumstances or environment (2001, 2006). Drawing on the definition of social innovation, we define social change agency as intentional action to influence profound change in the basic routines, resource and authority flows, or beliefs of a social system.

Bandura's socio-cognitive approach identifies key elements of agency, including *self-reflectiveness*, which is the meta-cognitive capacity to reflect on (and change) one's purposes, thoughts, and actions, and *self-efficacy*, which is the belief that one has the power to effect change. Self-efficacy is a primary determinant of which challenges people will undertake, how long they persevere in the face of obstacles, and how they interpret failure (Bandura, 2001). Bandura (2001, 2006) describes other elements of agency including *intentionality*—the formation of intentions and commitment to a course of action by individuals or collectivities, and *forethought*—the visualization of futures as motivators that provide direction, coherence, and meaning to actions. Emirbayer and Mische's (1998) sociological conception of agency echoes these elements, and emphasizes the temporal nature of agency in its past (*iterational*), present (*practical-evaluative*), and future (*projective*) aspects. Emirbayer and Mische (1998) emphasize the importance of collective agency in responding to the structural and emergent demands of real-time problem contexts. *Collective agency* refers to the interdependent efforts of people acting in concert, pooling knowledge, skills, and resources in order to shape their future (Bandura, 2001). Bandura's (2001) research suggests that groups with strongly perceived collective efficacy have higher aspirations and motivation, more perseverance, stronger morale and resilience to stressors, and greater performance accomplishments. Taken together, these elements of agency imply an array of positive or generative processes both individually and collectively, including individual reflection and transformation, establishment and maintenance of motivation, and perseverance in pursuit of a future vision. Next, we will explore how these processes of agency operated in the Great Bear Rainforest case, showing how social change agency operated at individual and collective levels, and ultimately led to broader systems change.

Six Processes of Agency

Many individuals played significant roles in generating the final agreements; however, it can be argued the social conflict over the region's fate was instigated by ENGO leaders, and they continued to advocate most strongly throughout the process (Riddell, 2009). Several sector representatives interviewed, including First Nations leaders, government representatives, and forest company executives indicated that it was the ENGO leaders' commitment and tenacity that maintained momentum toward the ultimate solution. For this reason, and because early in the process ENGO representatives outlined a vision encompassing the central elements of the eventual solution package, it is instructive to look at the Great Bear Rainforest case through the lens of the agency expressed by the ENGO leaders. Other actors or sectors did not call for a solution of this scope, as they were generally looking for minor modifications of the status quo in their own interests (with the exception of the large-scale legal challenges of First Nations). It is clear that the agency of the ENGO leaders played a large role in enabling social innovation in this case, and that is where we begin.

Analysis of interview data in the Great Bear Rainforest case revealed six generative processes of individual and collective agency that were critical to the transition from release to reorganization and innovation in the back-loop: (1) creating powerful personal narratives; (2) humanizing opponents; (3) tolerating conflict and uncertainty; (4) focusing on solutions; (5) building an inclusive vision; and (6) understanding the dynamics and psychology of change. While these processes interweaved, they also acted as emergent dynamics that allowed for the subsequent processes to build on them. Taken as a whole, these processes of agency describe the stages of the ENGO leaders' journey, beginning with three processes that primarily happened at the micro-level (self), which enabled shifting perceptions of others and new relationships to be forged with former opponents, developing into three meso-level (group/relational) processes enabling development of a broad vision for the region that became the touchstone for a system-wide change coalition, and a range of concrete solutions. These six processes demonstrate links between the micro-level processes of individuals, meso-level group interactions, and the macro-systemic context, and show that positive personal transformations gave rise to new relationships and laid the groundwork for system transformation.

Creating powerful personal narratives: "... *what I am learning is that it is 'as above, so below'—everything is completely connected and we can't pull things apart from each other. My personal process is mirrored back to me* *through this campaign, and the more that each of us does our personal work and integrates that into this broader campaign the more it becomes whole, and this whole journey has been about becoming whole, and it has been about finding peace."* ENGO campaigner.[1]

The ENGO leaders came to the negotiating table as political activists steeped in their sector's perception of the problems of the Great Bear Rainforest. However, in order to spark a social innovation they had to alter their perspective to encompass the concerns of the other actors. While environmentalists were committed to the idea of social justice for First Nations, there were conflicts when First Nations perceived that conservation was placed in opposition to human well-being and economic opportunities. First Nations leaders made clear to environmental leaders that any solution must address the realities their communities faced, including social dysfunction and up to 80% unemployment rates (Smith & Sterritt, 2006). The Sierra Club of BC and Greenpeace campaigners went back to their respective organizations and initiated a mission statement change, reflecting the commitment to advance conservation and just resolution of First Nations rights and title simultaneously. Through such encounters the ENGO leaders engaged their self-reflective capacities (Bandura, 2006) and the campaign was experienced, among other things, as a journey of personal development. One campaigner described the Great Bear Rainforest campaign as a "crucible for personal development and transformation," and emphasized her sense of responsibility to future generations, "There was this intentional fusion of what does this mean to each of us individuals personally in terms of our life story. There is a story that is being created, what do we want to tell our grandkids about this, and tell them we were working for more than just saving the trees; we are thinking about how communities are going to survive, and we have to address this." This personal focus also led to a re-evaluation of their role in negotiations. Another campaigner had a breakthrough when realizing her power in negotiations did not come from being an "ice queen," likening early negotiations to a battle where each side shot bullets and then hid behind riot shields, not letting any of their opponent's words hit them. In her previous role as a video producer and interviewer, she had an ability to open people up and

---

[1] All quotations in this section come from personal interviews with the authors, conducted between 2009 and 2011.

listen to their perspectives to gain deeper understanding. She resolved to integrate that part of herself into the environmentalist role, and began to make progress with her opponents.

Individuals underwent transformations as they developed emotionally meaningful personal narratives of the change they were seeking, reflecting on and re-evaluating their purposes and roles. This set the stage for the building of different kinds of relationships with other stakeholders. Instead of a battle of opposing and warring factions, the campaigners began to define their work as a journey of mutual discovery and understanding.

Humanizing opponents: *"Respect costs you nothing."* ENGO negotiator. *"Leaders who spent the time and care to understand interests and aspirations were much more able to envisage and achieve an outcome that could work."* Representative of Environmental Foundation.

When individuals understood that their vision needed everyone's contribution, they began to see the humanity in their opponents, treating them with greater respect, compassion, and curiosity. In an approach that became known, somewhat tongue-in-cheek, as "the Love Strategy," ENGO negotiators shifted their engagement with opponents, working to see them not just as enemies, or as corporate representatives, but as people. One negotiator says this originated from the strong caring relationships that existed between members of the ENGO team. This group participated in training retreats that emphasized negotiation, leadership, and strategic skills, and introduced campaigners to new approaches, including the idea of sourcing action from love, not anger or animosity. Over time, genuinely friendly personal relationships developed between some initial "enemies." This shift is described by one ENGO negotiator as shifting from "not having a crack of compassion" toward becoming genuinely curious, and when roadblocks in negotiations were hit, persevering and always "digging deeper" to find solutions. This led to new conversations and new possibilities from what seemed to be impasses, "It's about being curious...OK now we have to ask them a bunch more questions—'what is it the contractor needs?' and we really had to understand the consequence of what we were asking for and to understand it so that we could either defend or position or we could actually come up with ideas to try to mitigate some of the fallout." As ENGO leaders deliberately redefined and humanized their interactions with forest industry representatives, trust and engagement increased, and more information about the needs and interests of each group surfaced. This provided more material for solutions, but it also revealed more grounds of conflict. Fortunately, the individuals involved and the relationships being cultivated were becoming resilient enough to absorb considerable increases in tension and uncertainty.

Tolerating conflict and uncertainty: "*You need to stay in that proximate place and engage.*" ENGO negotiator.

With positive processes of self-change and relationship building as the foundation, conflict could be made to serve the process of social innovation, rather than derail it. The lead ENGO negotiators identified the ability to sit in both conflict and uncertainty as being central to finding solutions. The external power that the markets campaign provided was essential to creating an equal playing field of negotiations, and they enabled negotiators to engage in more powerful yet dialogical ways, maintaining their bottom line, but looking for alternative options. One negotiator described the challenge of sitting in conflict: it was uncomfortable to have people angry at her, but she deliberately cultivated a sense of staying anchored and empowered, noticing but not giving in to, the urges to run away, lash out, or compromise in order to be liked. One strategy she used to stay engaged through conflict included being very frank with company executives, explaining positions and countermoves they could anticipate from more radical members of the coalition ("good cop-bad cop tactics"). This ability to remain empowered while in conflict was generative, enabling participants in the negotiations process to focus on gaining more information about the situation, learn together, and look for alternatives.

Another ENGO negotiator described how fruitful it was for her to learn to be comfortable in uncertainty. "My natural tendency up until that point had been to find what's wrong. It is so much more challenging to find what is right or to make right." She gradually learned to accept her own internal feelings of conflict and "stuckness" for long enough to allow new alternatives to emerge. This practice also helped her to be patient and allow collaborative processes to remain "stuck" until there could be collective learning, without bypassing the important experience of uncertainty, and the natural resolutions that emerged.

These first three processes of agency (creating new narratives, humanizing opponents, building tolerance for conflict and uncertainty) reveal many generative micro-dynamics of self-development and transformation that were key to moving creatively through the release phase of turbulent change. In this case, we see how this process began by transformations in personal identity and meaning making but grew to include a transformation of relationships. Dominant beliefs and ways of interacting were called into question, and new generative patterns of interacting emerged. Here we can see how individual social change agency was expressed first through self-development and then through enlisting others in a change process—linking individual agency to collective agency. In terms of the adaptive cycle, this allowed the problem domain to move from the release phase to a reorganization phase. This in turn gave rise to the emergence of an integrated vision and concrete and innovative solution building.

> **Building an inclusive vision:** *"This campaign felt more whole, it felt healthy, that the best of each of us was being mixed into it, and the best of us was being asked for...The questions that were being asked within this campaign and the ways we were building it were much bigger and broader."* ENGO campaigner.

The ENGO leaders' vision was founded on a belief in people's capacity to create a better future for the benefit of the whole. The personal work that ENGO leaders did supported effective action in service of this larger goal: "The most effective leadership was egoless—people who were most effective were less concerned with their role or the perception of their role and more about the big picture or the big outcome we were working for." This founding ENGO commitment to the health of the whole rippled out into a compelling narrative in the Great Bear Rainforest Campaign. Later, when the First Nations challenged ENGOs to "put their money where their mouth is," they tried something never done before and successfully raised $60 million in private philanthropic capital to invest in conservation-based economic development on public lands. It became clear to those involved that solutions would require a vision of profound change that addressed many sectors' concerns for the region.

This greater collective vision and the strong personal identification with it created a powerful sense that anything was possible (self- and collective efficacy, Bandura, 2001), and people were motivated to create innovative approaches to accomplish the vision. One campaigner in particular is credited with fueling this efficacy belief, and she was able to build confidence in the ENGO team over time—in their ability to create the future, to "pull rabbits out of hats," and to accomplish the previously unthinkable. One of her colleagues reports that, "a lot of people have begun to believe it…it is a mystique, and we still have it 10 years later." She described it as building up a "powerful intentional field," and that, "After a couple of times doing the impossible, discovering that it was possible against the odds, this built on itself." She gave the example of the creation and strong outcomes from the CIT science panel, which ultimately called for 44–70% protection, saying, "we never would have predicted we could accomplish that." This sense of the possible expanded over time to include other sectors, and was referred to in terms that conjure the presence of a supportive field, a "mystique" supporting success. One of the foundation representatives reflected on the power of the founding vision created by sector leaders pursuing conservation financing initiatives (the CIII):

> I looked over the diagram we made during the original brainstorm, and it's remarkable how much actually came to pass 8 years later. For me, there were a number of pivotal CIII discussions, when the deputy minister of the Premier looked at the dialogue papers, and said, if we could actually pull this off, it would be magic. And, this word over 5 years became a touchstone for the discussions—are we really creating the magic?

One of the forestry executives observed that nobody had the power to force anyone to agree to a vision, and "this new path forward, is uncertain, but we have to believe in it—there's a whole thing about believing which is hard to articulate…you have to believe that you have the power as an individual and within your team, to achieve the goal that you set out." It was described as "alchemy" by one of the forest industry negotiators, bringing together forces, and coming up with innovations between them that could never have been done alone. By deliberately co-creating an inclusive and positive vision, ENGO leaders invited broad participation and a powerful sense of collective efficacy.

Focusing on solutions: *"We realized we needed to keep driving the solutions forward, and we needed a forester, an economist, scientists, we needed professionals to help us design solutions so we stayed one step ahead of everybody."* ENGO leader.

The shift in role from campaigner to negotiator required ENGO leaders to embrace a new mindset as architects of change, and invite others into that mindset. While the ENGOs successfully initiated change through their campaigns, they realized that the path to solutions required a maturation of strategy. Instead of demanding that others change, ENGO leaders took the onus upon themselves to "figure out the path," consciously shifting tactics to deepen their analysis of the obstacles facing forest companies and communities. In negotiating the Standstill Agreement, tenure agreements and obligations to contractors required creative solutions, and ENGOs participated with industry in generating novel approaches to get around policy and contractual obstacles. This focus on solutions also became a hallmark of the work done across sectors in bilateral coalitions. For example, a foundation representative who was collaborating with ENGOs described his role: "I was focused on process so that all the relevant actors were moved along, with the endgame in mind, and also building the institutions to oversee investments and ensure tools we were bringing to table had viable delivery vehicles, for example the Coast Opportunities Fund, which could continue to grow, evolve and add more benefit over time."

Through the coalitions, negotiations processes, and other institutional vehicles that were established, sector leaders within the ENGOs, forest companies, First Nations, foundations, and government began to work out the elements of the solution. Several pilots were initiated as proving grounds for new ideas generated from the CIII, on EBM, and co-management, which built people's belief in the new approach. One of the ENGO negotiators stated, "It is very holographic, you don't have to make the change at the largest scale—the whole idea of piloting—the ripple effect is profound."

In the reorganization phase of the adaptive cycle, new innovations occur through a combination of experimentation, partnerships, and new ideas joined together. We have seen how this was made possible by positive processes of trust and engagement engendered by personal transformation during the release phase. Mutual understanding and tolerance for conflict allowed for the surfacing of the diversity necessary for building innovative solutions. Finally, an inclusive vision created the space and capacity to move solutions into new institutional arrangements. Equally interesting, however, from the perspective of understanding social change agency, is the fact that the first five processes unfolded within a growing and strategic awareness by participants that understanding the psychology and dynamics of change in itself contributed to facilitating change.

Understanding the dynamics and psychology of change: *"Humans always require drama when changing underlying belief structures else they fall back into the old patterns. They need an excess of pain, joy, strong emotion, or new experience, to impress the change upon the dull recording medium between their ears."* Asher (2010), quoted by ENGO negotiator.

The Great Bear Rainforest conflict raised high levels of emotion on all sides, as it called into question people's deep beliefs about the purposes of society and what constituted moral action. One campaigner shared her recognition of the emotional experience of exclusion experienced by the forest industry when they were targeted as destructive "bad guys." She observed that "humans don't want to be excluded, and they don't want to be bad. They needed to hear us say 'there is a place for you, you can be gold star good.'" This accompanied the shift toward discussing *how* and *where* logging might take place, as opposed to an outright ban. She observed that this process took time (about five years), and though at first the companies were pushed into participating in the solutions structure, over time they recognized that the region was of global significance and that they *could* do things differently, culminating in them proudly taking joint credit for the solutions package.

ENGO representatives intentionally cultivated the role of drama and conflict in the process of human change and politics (including among their own allies). Upon reflecting on the success of the campaign, one ENGO leader quoted Asher (2010), and described the deliberate use of both rational and irrational tactics to create this sense of drama in order to facilitate change. Environmental campaigners strategically engaged different aspects of their identity—from the threat of direct action groups protesting and hanging banners, to strategic suit-wearing and inclusion of economists, professional foresters, and MBAs on their team. The campaigner observed, "I think a lot about the psychology of change. This is not about policy. You want to know how to be a change agent? It is how humans change psychologically that you have to master." Another way the ENGOs successfully harnessed and influenced the psychology of change was by advancing the Coast Investments and Incentives Initiative. First Nations, forest company executives, and senior government officials have all acknowledged the shift in perception that occurred when environmental leaders initially delivered $9 million in seed funding for the CIII, and then quickly raised their half of the $120 million fund from private donors in Canada and the United States. It was surprising and compelling to have ENGOs delivering tens of millions of dollars to support community transitions and calling on government to match their contribution—not the least because it became difficult to dismiss them as economically naïve or self-interested.

SUMMARY AND CONCLUSION

This chapter analyzes the individual and collective actions of key leaders, and uses a positive lens to understand processes underlying social change agency, particularly during periods of turbulent change. The narrative arc that the data presents is one of positive, system-wide changes emerging from personal transformation, through transformed group relationships to system-wide transformation. The ENGO leaders first disrupted the current system through the markets campaign and helped to trigger a release phase. This created a phase of turbulent change bringing the forestry industry to the table. However, with mistrust and animosity at very intense levels, the challenge was to keep all players there long enough for innovative solutions to emerge. The individual and collective processes of agency that led to solutions involved positive processes of self-reflectiveness and transformation, motivation, relationship building, and persevering in pursuit of an inclusive future vision. Strong individual agency expressed in these positive processes gave rise to collective agency, forging a powerful coalition of shared action. Both conflict and collaboration are hallmarks of this process of emerging innovation and change.

The markets campaign got the ENGOs to the negotiating table with the forestry industry and ensured that they were taken seriously. However, when they got there the two sides were adversaries and it would have been easy for negotiations to deadlock. Instead, the individual ENGO negotiators underwent a period of self-reflection and redefined their expectations for the system (Bandura, 2001), developing powerful personal narratives. This transformation was triggered by their encounter with the First Nations, which encouraged ENGO leaders to shift from their role as traditional environmental activists. Their own process of change, and their deep bonds of trust in each other, in turn led to a reevaluation and transformation of their perception of forest industry opponents, through the "Love Strategy." By humanizing their opponents, they turned a phase of uncertainty and conflict into a generative space for solution building. Such work required the joint effort of all of the major actors in the system and was motivated by the ENGOs' ability to communicate and co-create an inspiring vision of success and potential for all the region's major players. The strong self-efficacy of environmental leaders built on successes and led to a collective sense that this vision was possible. Finally, a conscious cultivation of the psychology and dynamics of change is a critical part of social change agency. The data demonstrates that while some of the success depended on a complex series of opportunities and dynamics far removed from the negotiations, the intentional expression of positive forms of agency, spread from environmental leaders to other sectors, enabled the emergence and the flowering of generative relationships and innovative solutions.

This process incorporated activities such as vision building, sense making, and collective learning, which led to the development of new collaborations and innovations that helped to transform the system. In this way, a close analysis of the Great Bear Rainforest case corroborates other findings in social innovation theory (Westley et al., 2006). This data also shows that successful social change agency in the release and reorganization phase involves the positive micro-processes of self-transformation and profound changes in relationships. These six processes of agency enabled collective social change agency to emerge and guide solution-building. This analysis highlights how personal change engendered positive outcomes, allowing the conflict and confusion typical of the release phase to give way to a positive alliance for change. It also helps to enrich social innovation theory by answering the question of how individual agents are able to enact more abstract strategies such as sense making, visioning, and collaboration during times of turbulent change.

These positive processes involved the ENGO leaders' recognition of the limits and narrowness of their own perspective of the system, and an active effort to overcome these limitations by incorporating both the perspectives of other groups and parts of their own persona that were being neglected into creating a new role for themselves in the system. Moreover, there was an active effort to transmit this change to others partly by using a compelling vision of change and partly by being sensitive to the perceptions and internal changes taking place in other actors. Such hard won perspectives, when linked to opportunities presented by the larger system dynamics, resulted in positive social and ecological outcomes. Through these forms of generative, intentional action, individuals were able to "be the change" they wished to see in the world.

In the Great Bear Rainforest, social change agency played a crucial role in navigating a complex change through a period of disruption to allow for the emergence of a collective process of innovation and solutions building. Although structural forces shaped the evolution of this process, they did so in relation with individual and collective agency, which both responded to and acted to direct these forces. By incorporating a socio-cognitive perspective on agency, this case highlights positive processes of social change agency that operated at personal and relational scales, complementing and advancing efforts to create profound systems change. Social change agency can therefore be understood as a multilevel process of creating intentional change, where actors must attend to transformation at personal, interpersonal, and systemic levels in order to be successful.

Further Research

This has been an exploratory chapter, where we engage the neglected topic of the co-emergence of individual and broader system transformation in response to complex problems, specifically during times of turbulent change. More research is needed to describe these micro-meso-macro interactions, to understand the role of social change agency in social innovations, and to further illuminate the positive dynamics underlying change at different scales. This chapter has drawn on social-psychological theories of agency and applied them to a case of social innovation, but it should be seen only as a first step in this direction. The authors hope that more systematic studies can be conducted in the future. Such studies would explore social change agency as a multilevel process of creating intentional change in complex systems, deepening our understanding of linkages between personal, interpersonal, and systemic change. Further research could also describe in more detail the interlinked processes, individual and collective agency, and the role of positive dynamics in developing and extending social change agency. Specifically, studies could ask questions about the importance of the individual capacity for accepting conflict and uncertainty (especially its' primary role during the "back-loop" of turbulent social change) and how this relates to self-perception, personal power, self-efficacy, and perseverance/resilience (Lichtenstein &

Plowman, 2009). They would also look at the importance of the humanizing dynamic observed in this case, including shifts in perception toward architect of change from advocate or agitator. What are the dynamics underlying this change, how is it fostered (what conditions/contexts), and how does it spread from individual to collective form? Further research is also warranted on the role and dynamics of vision in its individual and collective forms, and how this may strengthen social change agency. Finally, in exploring all these questions, we anticipate, based on the findings of this chapter, that self-transformation may play a more important role in social transformation than has been previously thought.

REFERENCES

Allen, R. P., (2005). Coast information team review report. Retrieved November 15, 2010, from http://www.citbc.org/c-citreview-jan05.pdf.

Antadze, N., & Westley, F. W. (2010). Funding social innovation: How do we know what to grow? *The Philanthropist, 23*, 343–356.

Asher, N. (2010). *The technician*. London: Tor UK.

Bandura, A. (2001). Social cognitive theory: An agentic perspective. *Annual Review of Psychology, 52*, 1–26.

Bandura, A. (2006). Toward a psychology of human agency. *Perspectives on Psychological Science, 1*, 164–180.

BC Stats. (2009). Retrieved March 2009 from http://www.bcstats.gov.bc.ca/pubs/exp/exp0011.pdf.

Bornstein, D. (2007). *How to change the world: Social entrepreneurs and the power of new ideas*. New York: Oxford University Press.

Emirbayer, M., & Mische, A. (1998). What is agency? *American Journal of Sociology, 103*, 962–1023.

Garud, R., Hardy, C., & Maguire, S. (2007). Institutional entrepreneurship as embedded agency: An introduction to the special issue. *Organization Studies, 28*, 957–969.

Gunderson, L., & Holling, C. S. (Eds.) (2002). *Panarchy: Understanding transformations in human and natural systems*. Washington, DC: Island Press.

Hawken, P. (2007). *Blessed unrest*. New York: Viking.

Hoberg, G. (2001). Policy cycles and policy regimes: A framework for studying policy change. In W. B. Cashore (Ed.), *In search of sustainability: British Columbia forest policy in the 1990s* (pp. 3–30). Vancouver: UBC Press.

Holling, C. S. (2001). Understanding the complexity of economic, ecological, and social systems. *Ecosystems, 4*, 390–405.

Kuhn, T. (1962). *The structure of scientific revolutions*. Chicago: The University of Chicago Press.

Lichtenstein, B., & Plowman, D. (2009). The leadership of emergence: A complex systems leadership theory of emergence at successive organizational levels. *The Leadership Quarterly, 20*, 617–630.

Ostrom, E. (1992). *Crafting institutions for self-governing irrigation systems.* San Francisco: Institute for Contemporary Studies Press.

Persky, S. (2000). *Delgamuukw: The Supreme Court of Canada decision on Aboriginal title.* Seattle: University of Washington Press.

Rao, H. (1998). Caveat emptor: The construction of non-profit consumer watchdog organizations. *American Journal of Sociology, 103*, 912–961.

Riddell, D. (2009). Evolving approaches to conservation: Integral ecology and Canada's Great Bear Rainforest. In S. Esbjörn-Hargens & M. E. Zimmerman (Eds.), *Integral ecology: Uniting multiple perspectives on the natural world* (pp. 454–475). Boston: Shambhala Publications.

Sierra Club of British Columbia. (1999). *Canada's ancient rainforest: Home of the great bears and wild salmon.* Victoria, BC: Sierra Club of British Columbia.

Smith, M., & Sterritt, A. (2007). From conflict to collaboration: The story of the Great Bear Rainforest. Retried June 2010 from http://www.forestethics.org/section.php?id=19.

Tjornbo, O., Westley, F., & Riddell, D. (2010). *Great Bear Rainforest case study.* Social Innovation Generation case study. Retrieved November 15, 2010 from http://www.sig.uwaterloo.ca/sites/.../SiG%20GBRF%20Web_Feb2%202010.pdf.

Wagner, W. L. (2003). Tenure reform in British Columbia? Model, trust, and charter forests. *Small-scale Forest Economics, Management, and Policy, 2*, 423–439.

Westley, F., & Antatze, N. (2010). Making a difference: Strategies for scaling social innovation for greater impact. *The Innovation Journal: The Public Sector Innovation Journal, 15*, article 2.

Westley, F., & Moore, M. L. (2009). Surmountable chasms: The role of cross-scale interactions in social innovation. Social Innovation Generation working paper no. 001. Retrieved November 15, 2010 from http://sig.uwaterloo.ca/research-publications.

Westley, F., Zimmerman, B., & Patton, M. Q. (2006). *Getting to maybe: How the world is changed.* Toronto: Random House Canada.

Westley, F. W., Carpenter, S., Brock, W., Holling, C. S., & Gunderson, L. (2002). Why systems of people and nature are not just social and ecological systems. In L. H. Gunderson & C. S. Holling (Eds.), *Panarchy: Understanding transformations in human and natural systems* (pp. 103–119). Washington, DC: Island Press.

Whitaker, John K. (1987). Marshall, Alfred (1842–1924). In J. Eatwell, M. Milgate, & P. Newman (Eds.), *The new Palgrave: A dictionary of economics* (1st ed.). The New Palgrave Dictionary of Economics Online. Palgrave Macmillan. Retrieved November 15, 2010, from http://www.dictionaryofeconomics.com/article?id=pde1987_X001413; doi:10.1057/9780230226203.3045.

9

Practicing Sustainability: A Generative Approach to Change Agency

Martha S. Feldman
University of California, Irvine

INTRODUCTION

This chapter introduces practice theory as a way of thinking about change agency. Though there are many ways that practice theory is implicated in change, I focus specifically on the relationship between designed artifacts and environmental sustainability. The emphasis on environmental sustainability is motivated by personal commitment and experience. The focus on practice theory and artifacts is motivated by both theoretical intuitions and empirical understandings. It is related to a theoretical intuition about the potential for conceptualizing change agency as distributed across interconnected assemblages of people, artifacts, and ideas. It is related to an understanding of the empirical context of sustainability as an area of social change in which there is a need for continuous updating of patterns of action. In the course of this chapter, I endeavor to develop and articulate these ideas and their connections.

Organizations and organizational scholars are well aware that adopting new practices is important to promoting greater environmental sustainability. A recent review of the literature catalogues and assesses a wide variety of proposed and adopted sustainability practices (Bertels, Papania, & Papania, 2010). The adoption of practices is influenced by a variety of external and internal factors (Howard-Grenville, Nash, & Coglianese, 2008). Though it is important to understand what practices work in particular contexts and to disseminate these practices, research has shown that the development of best practices is problematic and that transfer is an inaccurate metaphor for the movement of practices from one context to another (D'Adderio, 2010). The metaphor of transfer assumes that practices are unified and independent entities. An alternative approach to understanding practices and how they move involves conceptualizing practices as assemblages of interconnected actions, human actors, and non-human actants or artifacts and the process of movement across time and space as translation (Czarnaiwska & Hernes, 2005; Czarniawska & Sevon, 1996; D'Adderio, 2010; Latour, 1996, 2005).

In this chapter, I use this conceptualization of practices in relation to environmentally sustainable practices to explore the generative nature of change agency. Specifically, I suggest that one way of thinking about change is to focus on our ability to change interconnections between people, artifacts, and ideas through the actions we take. This approach to change encourages orienting to already existing connections and their potential to resource new ways of interacting with the environment and to the nature of environmental sustainability as an ever-emergent end in view. I suggest that it is useful for organizations, scholars, and individuals who wish to promote environmental sustainability to become attuned to the networked nature of practice. By orienting their actions within these networks these various actors are more able to activate or resource parts of the network that support sustainability.

In exploring this conceptualization, I draw on the increased attention to the dynamic nature of practices and routines (Feldman & Pentland, 2003; Feldman & Rafaeli, 2002; Howard-Grenville, 2005), to the constitutive nature of practices (Brickson & Lemmon, 2009; Feldman, 2004; Howard-Grenville, 2007; Quinn & Worline, 2008), as well as to the entangled nature of artifacts and practices (D'Adderio, 2010; Gherardi, 2006; Orlikowski, 2009; Suchman, 2007). In the following pages, I introduce this material and some thoughts about how it relates to practicing sustainability. First, however, I introduce an example of a practice that illustrates the entangled or networked nature of practice.

A Networked Practice

In the summer of 2009, I visited St. Gallen University in Switzerland. Professor Johannes Ruegg took me for a drive in the surrounding countryside. I noticed that when he stopped at traffic lights he often turned his car off. When I asked about this practice, he told me that it saves gas. I care enough about reducing my carbon footprint to have invested in solar panels that provide all the electricity for our household use even though the economic analysis was not overwhelmingly supportive. Yet after returning home, I did not start turning my car off at traffic lights. Until recently, I had not even done a simple Web search about this practice to see if others agreed that it would constitute a green practice.

I have now done the Web search and found that there is research that shows that if the car will idle for more than 10 seconds, turning the engine off will save gas and is a green practice. The belief that starting a car engine uses lots of gas is, apparently, based on old car technology. Yet the practice still seems difficult to enact.

Scholars have recently argued for the necessity of looking at practices from a sociomaterial perspective because of the entangled nature of action and physical objects (Orlikowski & Scott, 2008; Suchman, 2007). Orlikowski and Scott propose the following challenge: "consider doing anything in the world (whether at home, on the road, or in organizations) that does not in some way or another entail material means (e.g., bodies, clothes, food, spectacles, buildings, classrooms, devices, water pipes, paper, telephones, email, etc.) ... " (2008, p. 455). They further point out that these material means are not only tools used to accomplish tasks but also means to social constructs such as identity. The entangled nature of practices and the material means used in their enactment can help us understand my reluctance to engage in the "turning off the car" behavior.

I live in Southern California where many of the city streets are multilane with a posted speed limit of 50 mph. Cars tend to go like bats out of hell between traffic lights, taking off quickly when the light turns green. The roads Professor Ruegg was driving on were fairly narrow, and the traffic was slower than in Southern California. Restarting the car did not appear to take much time, though it likely requires a fair amount of attentiveness. Driving in Southern California also requires a fair amount of attentiveness, but the streamlined design of the roads suggests that most of this attention can be focused on moving quickly along with the other cars on the road. On the freeway, this takes the form of what one friend refers to as "bumper to bumper at 70 mph" (C. Morrill, January 21, 2008, personal communication). It is no secret that streets in my part of the world are generally designed for speed and "safety." It is interesting to note, however, how the collection of objects and social norms affects driving practices.

I wonder if there are artifacts that could promote the practice of turning off my engine when idling for more than 10 seconds. What if the California *Driver Handbook* included this as a safe driving practice? The current version of the *Handbook* is oriented entirely to safety so promoting this practice for conservation reasons might be inappropriate, but acknowledging it as a practice that can be safely accommodated could be within the scope of this document. Another object that might be useful is a countdown timer on red lights, which would cue drivers of the amount of time they will be idling. Of course, every new object has multiple implications for practices. The countdown timer, for instance, could encourage people to focus even more intently on when the light will change and distract attention from what else is going on in and around the road that might need to be accommodated.[1]

This example of driving practices helps us to see the networked nature of driving practices. Figure 9.1 depicts some of the features of the driving example. Various ways of driving are listed on the left-hand side of the figure and various patterns that are enacted through these ways of driving are listed in the ovals on the right-hand side of the figure. Some of the artifacts that mediate these relationships are shown in the boxes in the middle. The arrows connecting the left-hand side to the right-hand side indicate the constitutive nature of how we do things (like driving). The actions (driving quickly, using seat belts, turning the car off rather than idling) on the left-hand side constitute patterns of action (speed, safety, sustainability—or at least conservation) when they are repeated over time. The multiple ovals on the right-hand side of the figure show that our actions produce many patterns of action at the same time. We can drive in ways that achieve speed, safety, and sustainability—or at least higher mpg—all at the same time, though these patterns may be interdependent in complicated ways. The arrows are labeled "actions produce patterns" and "patterns support actions" and indicate the recursive nature of the relationship between actions and patterns.

In the middle of the figure are the artifacts. Placing the artifacts in the middle helps to depict that actions and patterns of action are entwined/ entangled with the material world. Note that the same artifact (in this case,

---

[1] Recent experiments removing traffic signals from intersections have found that the intersections become safer presumably because drivers are forced to look around and assess whether it is safe to proceed. While these experiments began in Europe, there are instances of them in the United States (McNichols, 2004).

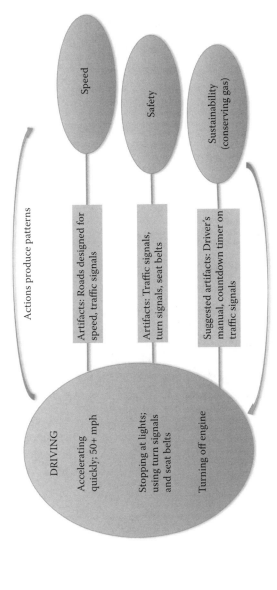

FIGURE 9.1
Resource driving practices.

traffic signals) may be associated with many different patterns of action. Of course, only a few of the artifacts involved in driving practices are listed in Figure 9.1.[2] Nonetheless, the figure indicates the entangled nature of the artifacts with the patterns of action and suggests that such artifacts may be an important part in taking these actions and creating these patterns.

The pattern of action that relates to turning the car off at traffic signals is labeled sustainability (conservation of gas). The addition of the parenthetical phrase is to indicate the unusual nature of the sustainability pattern. Of course, changing this small practice will not produce enough change to produce a sustainable balance of energy use. Moving in the direction of sustainability will require changes to many practices. Exploring the possibility of change in this and similar practices, however, may be able to help us understand how we can support practicing sustainability.

ENVIRONMENTAL SUSTAINABILITY

Environmental sustainability is not a fixed state, but an ever emergent "end-in-view" (Dewey, 1916; Joas, 1996) or journey (Milne, Kearins, & Walton, 2006). Thinking about environmental sustainability as a journey without a fixed destination can be used in a cynical way to avoid making important changes (Milne et al., 2006). The emergent nature of sustainability, however, is an unavoidable feature of the current context (Ehrenfeld, 2008). As an "end-in-view," sustainability is similar to democracy, about which Flyvbjerg (1998, p. 5) states, "Democracy is not something a society 'gets'; democracy must be fought for each and every day in concrete instances, even long after democracy is first constituted in a society." Though conceptually sustainability relates more to equilibrium than does democracy, in practice there are many reasons to treat sustainability as an end in view rather than a fixed state. For one thing, what

---

[2] Among the missing are several without which no driving would happen, such as cars, engines, accelerators, and brakes. These are important omissions. The conserving gas pattern associated with turning off the car while stopped, for instance, may be achieved differently with different types of cars. Changes in the way cars start is important to whether turning the car off and back on uses less gas than allowing it to idle, and some older cars that may still be on the road would not conserve gas if the engine were turned off and on frequently. Hybrids provide another way of enacting the same pattern because they essentially turn themselves off, running only on the battery, when stopped (Carr, 2007).

constitutes a sustainable pattern of actions for a global population of the three billion people who lived on earth in 1960 may not be sustainable for a global population of the nearly seven billion who live on earth today or the nine billion projected to live on the earth in the early 2040s. Moreover, in many domains we may be so far from sustainability that action we take now to move in the direction of sustainability simply opens new possibilities for yet more (or less) sustainable future actions rather than achieving equilibrium. It is the focus on the emergent nature of future possibilities that draws me to the end-in-view or journey metaphor and, indeed, to the potential of practice theory as a way of articulating the enacting of an ever-emergent web of increasingly sustainable connections.

PRACTICE THEORY

Practice theories are particularly appropriate for thinking about sustainability as an end-in-view or an emergent outcome. At the core of practice theories is the relation of mutual constitution between actions and patterns (Bourdieu, 1990; Feldman & Orlikowski, 2011; Gherardi, 2006; Giddens, 1984). The patterns may be called a variety of different names, including "structures," "institutions," and "routines," but they are always enacted. Further, the enactment of patterns is consequential for the actions that are taken both in that the patterns help to define past and current actions and that the patterns constrain and enable future actions. As such, practice theories draw attention to the internal dynamics of practices (Feldman & Pentland, 2003; MacIntyre, 2007) and to the importance of theorizing processes as they relate to outcomes.

In particular, practice theories draw attention to processes of endogenous unintended change. While accomplishing a specific task (e.g., driving from one location to another, photocopying a document, hiring personnel, or creating a budget) may be the intended or articulated reason for engaging in the actions, the way these actions are enacted may result in additional outcomes that are often unintended (Feldman, 2004; Giddens, 1984; Merton, 1949/1968; Sewell, 1992). In the driving example, the intended outcome of leaving the car running at a stop light is to be able to go quickly once the light turns and any contribution to global warming is presumably unintended. Yet both patterns are enacted through the same action.

Resourcing and Practice Theory

Studying the process of what patterns are being enacted has been studied as a theory of resourcing (Feldman, 2004; Howard-Grenville, 2007). Based on practice theory, resourcing theory emphasizes the importance of practices for turning potential resources into resources in use (Feldman & Quick, 2009; Feldman & Worline, 2011; Howard-Grenville, Golden-Biddle, Irwin, & Mao, 2011). Potential resources include not only material resources but also nonmaterial resources such as effort, emotion, or identity (Brickson & Lemmon, 2009; Quinn & Worline, 2008). Practices turn potential resources into resources in use by taking up potential resources and using them to energize patterns. From this perspective, more attention to what patterns are being resourced would produce different outcomes from the same potential resources. Drawing again on the driving example, driving practices can resource a variety of different patterns, including speed, safety, or sustainability and different combinations of these depending on what practices are enacted.

Consistent with the recursive nature of practice, engaging in actions that resource a particular pattern can also enable or constrain other actions. For instance, turning off the car while idling at a traffic signal may enable other actions related to conserving gas. This effect occurs partly through reflexive self-monitoring, the ability of actors to "maintain a continuing 'theoretical understanding' of the grounds of their activity" (Giddens, 1984, p. 5) or to maintain or develop a practical consciousness about the connection between our actions and what we accomplish or resource through our actions. Routines and practices are notable for their ability to make and alter such connections (Feldman & Rafaeli, 2002).

Many patterns, however, are created through the same actions (Sewell, 1992) and our practical consciousness may be more or less oriented to these patterns. When we go about our daily activities, for instance, we are more or less oriented to the environmental cost of our actions. Unless the cost of an environmentally unsustainable action is very high, however, this aspect of the activity is often not the primary intention. Thus, when I buy groceries my primary goal is to have food to eat; when I throw out my trash my primary goal is to clean my immediate living space; when I drive my primary intention is to move from origin to destination. How these activities affect the environment is often an unintended consequence. Yet I can do these activities in ways that are more or less sustainable. How can we think about the potential for intervening in our everyday routines in ways that promote or resource more sustainable activities? How can we orient practical consciousness both to what patterns are being resourced and to what patterns could be resourced?

Artifacts and Resourcing

The design of tools or artifacts can be used to orient and re-orient practical consciousness (Ehrenfeld, 2008). "Physical artifacts are defined by the Oxford dictionary as 'artificial products, something made by humans and thus any element of a working environment'" (Vilnai-Yavetz & Rafaeli, 2006, p. 10). Artifacts can play a part in the assembling, disassembling, and reassembling of practices as they are enacted in everyday life and in organizational contexts (D'Adderio, 2010). They participate in the deconstruction and reconstruction of routines, both by destabilizing existing patterns and by providing the glue that can hold these patterns together.

Artifacts can act as either intermediaries or mediators (Latour, 2005). Intermediaries mask connections, resulting in the conjunction of two or more things appearing to be innate, natural, and the only possibility. Mediators draw attention to connections and the multiple possible ways in which the conjunction of things work out. Intermediaries produce black boxes that appear to have no parts and no dynamics. Mediators produce connections between things that are indeterminate; they may work out in a variety of different ways. Beveridge and Guy describe an intermediary as a "neutral vessel passing between two actors" (2009, p. 83). Mediators "are seen as having a more transformative role in their passage between actors" (Beveridge & Guy, 2009, p. 83).

Whether an artifact acts as a mediator or an intermediary is not just a feature of the artifact's design but how it is used and seen. Take a light switch as an example. The switch operates to connect a person wanting to light a room with a highly complex network of people and equipment. For many of us, such a switch masks everything on the other side of the switch and becomes simply a way of producing light. Rheostats that allow us to increase or decrease the amount of light may create a somewhat more complex connection. Few of us, however, will see beyond the object on the wall and its connection to the light fixture. An electrician, by contrast, is likely to be attuned to the way the switch connects to the wires within the walls of the house that carry electricity and the possible configurations of those wires. Others (perhaps people working for the electric company or STS scholars studying the electric grid) may also be attuned to the vast electric grid and the many technical and social connections that make it possible for us to flip a switch and have light. Thus, the light switch primarily performs as an intermediary. Under certain circumstances, however, and for certain people, the light switch may operate as a mediator reminding them of the multiple connections that are masked for most of us.

While for Latour the concepts of mediator and intermediary distinguish different approaches to studying the social (2005, p. 40), it is not just people who study the social (e.g., sociologists) who are engaged in the kinds of conceptualizations he discusses. I argue that when people (whether or not they study these things for a living) become attuned to the connections underlying what appear to be stable entities, there is the potential for their actions to be affected in ways that may produce more environmentally sustainable practices. When artifacts operate as intermediaries in routines, the practical consciousness of participants is limited to just one pattern of action and just one way of producing that pattern. When artifacts operate as mediators in routines, the practical consciousness of participants is attuned to a multiplicity of possibilities. While actions can be affected in many other ways (Goldstein, Cialdini, & Griskevicius, 2008), being attuned to connections increases not only the ability to alter actions in that particular context but also in other related contexts. For instance, becoming attuned to the connections between turning the car off and saving gas has altered my actions when I go to pick someone up and need to wait for them to arrive. Whereas it used to seem not worth the effort to turn the car off, thanks to the example of Professor Ruegg's practice, I have become attuned to a different set of connections and the possibility of a different way of acting. In particular, the ignition has changed from an intermediary to a mediator, connecting me not only to making the car move but also to the potential for me to use the ignition to enact other patterns such as gas conservation. Thus, shifting the orientation from artifacts as intermediaries to artifacts as mediators that are part of webs of interconnected actants is an important part of enabling change agency.

Resourcing Sustainability Example

One of my favorite examples of resourcing sustainability through the interaction of artifacts is related to a sticker that can be affixed to paper towel or napkin dispensers. A picture of the sticker is shown on the following page.

The simple language on the sticker links the paper products with the trees that are required to make them. Additional language points out that each sticker saves 100 lbs of paper, but the primary impact of the simple straightforward message enmeshed in a green leaf is to link the practice of using the paper product with the impact on the trees that are used to create the product. When I first encountered one of these stickers, I was washing my hands. As I reached for the paper towels, I noticed the sticker. My general practice had been to take two towels to dry my hands as thoroughly as possible. The sticker re-oriented this practice, and I tried using a single towel. It turns out that my hands were sufficiently dry with one towel and within seconds they were completely dry. This simple re-orientation of practice not only influenced how many towels I used that time but in my case influenced how many towels I used as a general practice to dry my hands. The Web site listed on the sticker provides evidence that I am not alone in these reactions.

Figure 9.2 is a diagram showing that as with the driving practices, multiple patterns can be resourced by the same action. In this case, the sticker helps to create a resourcing pattern that includes not only drying hands but also conserving trees. As before the patterns also support actions and, in this case, the pattern of conserving trees can be resourced not only in the context of drying hands, but also in other contexts in which paper towels or other paper products are used.

The potential for resourcing patterns in different contexts is important and one of the reasons for using practice theory to think about the relationship between actions, artifacts, and sustainability. Intrinsic to a notion of practice are the consequentiality of action and relationality of mutual constitution (Feldman & Orlikowski, 2011). According to this view, an important feature of a practice is that the action of engaging in it

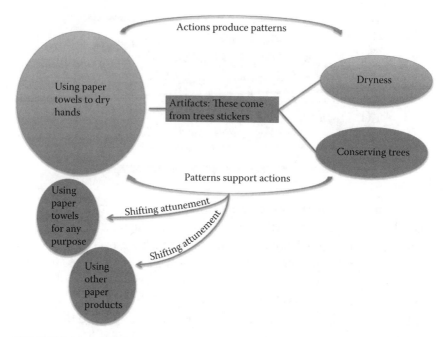

FIGURE 9.2
Resourcing hand drying practices.

is consequential for its development. As a result, practices change not just because the external environment demands change but also because of the internal (or endogenous) dynamics of the practice itself (Feldman, 2000; McIntyre, 2007). McIntyre illustrates this relationship with the example of portrait painting that developed not because patrons demanded changes but because the artists developed new ways of doing portraits as they were painting their patrons' portraits (2007, p. 185).

In the case of the hand drying, the sticker helps to shift one's practical orientation toward being attuned to a different web of connections in which the user of the paper product is connected to the trees used in making the paper product. As a result, the flow of connections related to the practice of hand drying is altered and the web comes to include previously hidden actants. When the trees are included in the web of connections that are enacted through the practice of hand drying, then the trees endogenously influence the practice and the reconstitution of the practice is altered through the inclusion of the trees. The inclusion of the connections between paper products and trees also allows for the connection to other practices involving paper products. It is possible that the flow of connections may extend to other practices involving products made from natural resources.

This ability to tune into the broader web of connections is akin to the analytical move that Suchman refers to as "cutting the network" through which analysts can "expand the frame to metaphorically zoom out to a wider view that at once acknowledges the magic of the effects created while explicating the hidden labors and unruly contingencies that exceed its bounds" (2007, pp. 283–4). The magic of the effect created is the appearance of stability. Analysts need to be able to cut the network as a way of limiting the connections they are considering. In the case of the paper towel use, the effect of the sticker is actually to expand the network we are attuned to so that the hidden labors that produce paper towels are included.

Other Models of Change Agency as They Relate to Hand Drying

Hand drying provides examples of efforts to shift behavior in the direction of greater sustainability and of many different objects that influence the extent to which we conserve trees. These represent different approaches to bringing about change and thus different approaches to change agency. In these other approaches, the objects used in hand drying tend to be experienced as intermediaries rather than mediators and the web of connections tends to be attenuated rather than extended.

Take, for instance, the paper towel dispensers that use a continuous roll of paper but automatically limit the size of the paper that is dispensed. When the size of the pieces of paper is sufficiently small, the clear message is that this *should* be all the paper you need and needing more is perhaps wasteful. The connection or engagement created through this artifact (the size of the towel) is with whomever is deciding that this is a large enough piece of paper. The intent of this change agent is unknown to the user of the towels. Are the small pieces of paper a way of saving money? Are they a way of saving trees? Is there some other motive? My own experience is that I seldom even contemplate the motive. I simply decide that whoever thought 4 inches of paper towel is enough to dry my hands is wrong, and I take two pieces of towel. To the extent that I experience engagement, my engagement connects me to the people behind the small towels rather than to the environmental issues the towels could represent.

Some paper towel dispensers provide a measured amount of towel (often small) when you wave your hand in front of them. Again, these dispensers may provide an opportunity to re-orient to using a smaller amount of towel. The user is certainly engaged with the dispenser. In this case, my own experience is less oriented to the agents behind the dispenser and more to the dispenser itself. Indeed, the process of inducing the dispenser to dispense towels can sometimes be very engaging—either because the dispenser is reluctant or very responsive. The connection, however, is to the dispenser rather than to how my towel use is related to the environment.

Another approach to hand drying is, of course, to do away with paper products altogether. Hand dryers are becoming very effective and efficient. Some research shows that current high speed, energy efficient hand dryers have a lower climate change score than using just one paper towel (Brady, 2010). This research (provided by the manufacturer of one of these dryers) also suggests that the dryers reduce vandalism costs in places where people might be inclined to stuff wads of paper towels down the toilet and also reduces janitorial expenses. Moreover, there is evidence that hand dryers are more hygienic (Ansari et al., 1991) and thus resource other desirable frameworks at the same time that they help to conserve natural resources. So the hand dryers seem to win "hands down" over the "these come from trees" stickers in terms of energy efficiency as well as resourcing several other desirable patterns.

There are two downsides to consider. First, the use of a particular technology locks in a specific contribution to sustainability supported by that technology and the practices associated with it. As technologies and practices change, what is environmentally friendly changes and being locked into expensive technology can make it difficult to update. The Brady research (2010) claims that hand dryers can pay for themselves in a year, suggesting that this technology is not so large that it would constitute locking in. Once the savings have been absorbed into an organizational budget, however, it is not necessarily true that there would be funding available for moving to a more environmentally friendly technology.

The second downside is potentially even more important. Using hand dryers conserves natural resources not because it connects users to the implications of resource use, but because it disconnects users from the implications of their actions. In other words, these blow dryers illustrate an approach to change agency in which resourcing sustainability is not the job of the person drying their hands but is someone else's job. The hand dryers are classic intermediaries, providing little or no opportunity for connecting to a larger web of actants. As a result, hand drying in this way not only inhibits being attuned to the flow of connections that includes the trees, but also does not engage the person drying their hands as a responsible agent in the flow of connections. Consequently, using these hand dryers seems unlikely to have an effect on the practices enacted in other locations or in relation to the use of natural resources in other contexts. Of course, the existence or non-existence of these connections is an empirical question and deserves to be examined as such.

DISCUSSION

My argument about change agency and sustainability, then, can be summarized in the following way:

> Practices endogenously resource different flows of connections. Because of the nature of sustainability as an emergent end, we do not simply want to change behavior but we also want to change attunement. Specifically, we want to become attuned to the connections between our actions and the impact on the environment. This involves orienting to how the environment is implicated in our actions and also to our role as responsible agents in enacting flows of connections. Since practices are entangled with artifacts; situating artifacts as mediators rather than intermediaries either through design or use of the artifact is one way of modifying the particular flows of connections that are resourced or energized.

This approach to change agency, in essence, suggests that we each take the analytical stance of a practice theorist in our everyday lives. This implies that our practical consciousness be attuned to the patterns we create through our actions. When we become attuned to ourselves as integral parts of webs of actants and to our ability to activate or resource connections in those webs, we gain a measure of empowerment as responsible agents. Since the networks connected to our actions are potentially infinite, objects can play an important role in orienting us to particular connections. As we have seen in the example of the ways of influencing hand drying, the connections made may have many different implications for sustainability.

196 • *Martha S. Feldman*

Comparison to Other Views of Change Agency

My approach differs from other approaches to change and the role of objects. Most clearly, it differs from approaches that seek to alter behavior without the active involvement of the people who act (Goldstein, Cialdini, & Griskevicius, 2008). In these approaches objects either prevent us from taking certain actions or impel us to take action. More subtly, my approach differs from approaches that focus on interruption and unavailability as a way of changing practices (Ehrenfeld, 2008; Yanow & Tsoukas, 2009). In these approaches objects or materials inhibit change when they are transparent or available and encourage change when they are unavailable. The approach provides important insights and avenues for action. In the following paragraphs I outline this approach and the subtle, but perhaps important, differences in my argument.

The argument centering on interruption and unavailability is that change occurs when people move from a state of absorbed coping (Yanow & Tsoukas, 2009) to reflection-in-action (Yanow & Tsoukas, 2009) or presencing (Ehrenfeld, 2008). People move from a state of absorbed coping when their patterns of action are interrupted. One source of interruption is "backtalk" or the unavailability of particular objects used to enact patterns of action. Unavailability may involve a change in the object (e.g., a car that does not start [Ehrenfeld, 2008, pp. 147–152]) or a change in the response to the object (e.g., the lecture the audience does not understand [Yanow & Tsoukas, 2009, pp. 17–19][3]). Unavailability of objects or material backtalk makes the pattern of action that involves that material available for reflection and change. The strong version of this argument, made by Ehrenfeld is that interruption is necessary for presencing and that presencing is "a critical step ... in changing habit or routine" (2008, pp. 153–155).

My perspective on change agency highlights a different path. From this perspective, interruption may or may not occur and material unavailability is not always necessary. This perspective brings artifacts or materiality into view not as defining forces, but as significant features of practice. The effect of the sticker described earlier may entail the process of interruption (or backtalk) but the paper towels are no less available. Rather than focusing on what is missing from a currently enacted pattern of action, my argument suggests that the connections currently in place in relation to a

---

[3] Yanow and Tsoukas point out that the audience is part of the material context for the lecture routine.

pattern of action may be unaffected. From this perspective, change may occur from *increased* availability.

The examples of altering driving and hand drying practices I have presented operate through orienting to additional possibilities rather than through making current possibilities unavailable or difficult. In the driving example, the driver continues to resource the speed and safety patterns and adds another pattern to the mix. The addition of the gas conservation pattern may have implications for how speed and safety patterns are enacted, but it does not come about by taking away the ability to enact these patterns. Similarly, the "these come from trees" sticker enables a set of connections in addition to all of the previously available connections. This argument suggests that we have the capacity to orient our actions in the midst of multiple connections and the ability, perhaps even the responsibility, to be attuned to our agental capacity in the network of connections.

Change Agency as Positive and Generative

The approach to change agency I have articulated is positive and generative in a couple of noteworthy ways. First, it suggests that rather than being dependent on an infusion of external resources, we already have significant capacity to bring about change. Second, it suggests that there are many paths to sustainability.

The view I have articulated strongly suggests that bringing about change is a function of already existing potentiality and our ability to change interconnections between people, artifacts, and ideas. It orients us to the importance of attunement toward our position in webs of actants, our ability to activate parts of those webs, and the nature of sustainability as an ever-emergent end in view. These are all currently available potentialities that can be used to resource change.

The view I have articulated is also generative in the sense that it does not rely on one particular path. Theories that rely on altering a particular affective state, such as caring, make that affective state an obligatory passage point. Ehrenfeld, for instance, has argued that design can change caring and in that way promote sustainable practices (2008). While caring and design are surely important, it is also useful to see them as two of the many resources we can draw upon to activate parts of the actant webs that can support sustainable practices. We have many potential resources available that enable us to practice sustainability. Given the enormity of the sustainability challenge, it makes sense to take advantage of our daily practices as a way of contributing.

ACKNOWLEDGMENTS

I am very grateful to many colleagues for helping me develop these ideas. A series of conversations with Alexandra Michel provided the starting point for this chapter and continues to be a source of inspiration. Conversations with Jennifer Howard-Grenville and Monica Worline have been invaluable in helping me develop and articulate the argument. Christine Beckman, Jane Dutton, Karen Golden-Biddle, Wanda Orlikowski, and Leslie Perlow have also provided extremely useful comments.

REFERENCES

Ansari, S. A., Sprinthorpe, V. S., Sattar, S. A., Tostowaryk, W., & Wells, G. A. (1991). Comparison of cloth, paper, and warm air drying in eliminating viruses and bacteria from washed hands. *American Journal of Infection Control, 19*, 243–249.

Bertels, S., Papania, L., & Papania, D. (2010). Embedding sustainability in organizational culture: A Systematic review of the body of knowledge. *Network for Business Sustainability*. Retrieved from http://www.nbs.net/knowledge/culture

Beveridge, R., & Guy, S. (2009). Governing through translations: Intermediaries and the mediation of the EU's urban waste water directive. *Journal of Environmental Policy & Planning, 11*, 69–85.

Bourdieu, P. (1990). *The logic of practice*. Stanford, CA: Stanford University Press.

Brady, R. C. (2010). Throw in the towel: High-speed, energy-efficient hand dryers win hands down. Reprinted from *Architectural Record—Schools of the 21st Century*, January 2010. Retrieved on August 30, 2010, from http://www.exceldryer.com/pdfs/CEUCourse McGrawHill12-09.pdf.

Brickson, S. L., & Lemmon, G. (2009). Organizational identity as a stakeholder resource. In L. M. Roberts & J. E. Dutton (Eds.), *Exploring positive identities and rganizations* (pp. 411–434). New York: Routledge.

Carr, B. (March 27, 2007). Make your car a hybrid simply by turning it off. *Daily Fuel Economy Tip* newsletter. Retrieved from http://www.dailyfueleconomytip.com/driving-habits/turn-your-car-into-a-hybrid-by-simply-turning-it-off/

Czarniawska, B., & Hernes, T. (2005). *Actor network theory and organizing*. Copenhagen: Copenhagen Business School Press.

Czarniawska, B., & Sevon, G. (1996). *Translating organizational change*. New York: Walter de Gruyter Inc.

D'Adderio, L. (2008). The performativity of routines: Theorising the influence of artefacts and distributed agencies on routines dynamics. *Research Policy, 37*, 769–789.

D'Adderio, L. (2010). From Don Quixote to NASA: The role of context in the exact (re)production of a complex capability. Paper presented at AIM capacity building workshop, June 21, 2010.

Dewey, J. (1969). *Democracy and education.* New York: MacMillan.

Ehrenfeld, J. (2008). *Sustainability by design.* New Haven, CT: Yale University Press.

Feldman, M. S. (2000). Organizational routines as a source of continuous change. *Organization Science, 11,* 611–629.

Feldman, M. S. (2004). Resources in emerging structures and processes of change. *Organization Science, 15,* 295–309.

Feldman, M. S., & Orlikowski, W. J. (2011). Theorizing practice and practicing theory. *Organization Science, September/October 22,* 1240–1253; published online before print February 23, 2011, doi:10.1287/orsc.1100.0612.

Feldman, M. S., & Pentland, B. T. (2003). Re-theorizing organizational routines as a source of flexibility and change. *Administrative Science Quarterly, 48,* 94–118.

Feldman, M. S., & Pentland, B. T. (2005). Organizational routines and the macro-actor. In B. Czarniawska & T. Hernes (Eds.), *Actor-network theory and organizing* (pp. 91–111). Stockholm: Liber and CBS Press.

Feldman, M. S., & Quick, K. S. (2009). Generating resources and energizing frameworks through inclusive public management. *International Public Management Journal, 12,* 137–171.

Feldman, M. S., & Worline, M. (2011). Resources, resourcing, and ampliative cycles in organizations. In K. S. Cameron & G. M. Spreitzer (Eds.), *The Oxford handbook of positive organizational scholarship.* (pp. 629–641). New York: Oxford University Press.

Flyvbjerg, B. (1998). *Rationality and power: Democracy in practice.* Chicago: University of Chicago Press.

Gherardi, S. (2006). *Organizational knowledge: The texture of workplace learning.* Oxford, UK: Blackwell Publishing.

Gherardi, S., & Nicolini, D. (2000). To transfer is to transform: The circulation of safety knowledge. *Organization, 7,* 329–348.

Giddens, A. (1984). *The constitution of society.* Cambridge, UK: Polity Press.

Goldstein, N. J., Cialdini, R. B., & Griskevicius, V. (2008). A room with a viewpoint: Using social norms to motivate environmental conservation in hotels. *Journal of Consumer Research, 35,* 472–482.

Howard-Grenville, J. (2005). The persistence of flexible organizational routines: The role of agency and organizational context. *Organization Science, 16,* 618–636.

Howard-Grenville, J. A. (2007). Developing issue-selling effectiveness over time: Issue selling as resourcing. *Organization Science, 18,* 560–577.

Howard-Grenville, J. A., Golden-Biddle, K., Irwin, J., & Mao, G. (2011). Liminality as cultural process for cultural change. *Organization Science, 22,* 522–539.

Howard-Grenville, J. A., Nash, J., & Coglianese, C. (2008). Constructing the license to operate: internal factors and their influence on corporate environmental decisions. *Law & Policy, 30,* 73–107.

Joas, H. (1996). *The creativity of action.* Chicago: University of Chicago Press.

Latour, B. (1996). *Aramis or the love of technology.* Cambridge: Harvard University Press.

Latour, B. (2005). *Reassembling the social: An introduction to actor network theory.* Oxford: Oxford University Press.

Leonardi, P. M., & Barley S. R. (2008). Materiality and change: Challenges to building better theory about technology and organizing. *Information and Organization, 18,* 159–176.

MacIntyre, A. (2007). *After virtue: A study in moral theory* (3rd Ed.). Notre Dame, IN: University of Notre Dame Press.

McNichols, T. (2004). Roads gone wild. *Wired 12* (online magazine),12. Retrieved November 20, 2011, from http://www.wired.com/wired/archive/12.12/traffic.html

Merton, R. (1968). *Social theory and social structure.* New York: The Free Press.

Milne, M., Kearins, K., & Walton, S. (2006). Creating adventures in wonderland: The journey metaphor and environmental sustainability. *Organization, 13,* 801–839.

Orlikowski, W. J. (2009). The sociomateriality of organisational life: Considering technology in management research. *Cambridge Journal of Economics, 34,* 125–141.

Orlikowski, W. J., & Scott, S. V. (2008). Sociomateriality: Challenging the separation of technology, work and organization. *Annals of the Academy of Management, 2,* 433–474.

Pentland, B. T., & Feldman, M. S. (2007). Narrative networks: Patterns of technology and organization. *Organization Science, 18,* 781–795.

Pentland, B. T., & Feldman, M. S. (2008). Designing routines: On the folly of designing artifacts, while hoping for patterns of action. *Information and Organization, 18,* 235–250.

Quinn, R., & Worline, M. (2008). Enabling courageous collective action: Conversations from United Airlines Flight 93. *Organization Science, 19,* 497–516.

Rafaeli, A., & Vilnai-Yavetz, I. (2004). Emotion as a connection of physical artifacts and organizations. *Organization Science, 15,* 671–686.

Sewell, W. H. (1992). A theory of structure: Duality, agency and transformation. *American Journal of Sociology, 98,* 1–29.

Suchman, L. A. (2007). *Human-machine reconfigurations: Plans and situated actions* (2nd ed.). Cambridge, UK: Cambridge University Press.

Vilnai-Yavetz, I., & Rafaeli, A. (2006). Managing artifacts to avoid artifact myopia. In A. Rafaeli & M. Pratt (Eds.), *Artifacts and organizations.* Mahwah, NJ: Lawrence Erlbaum Associates.

Yanow, D., & Tsoukas, H. (2009). What is reflection in action? A phenomenological account. *Journal of Management Studies, 46,* 1339–1364.

10

Connecting Sustainability Movements and Enterprises in Developing Economies: Building Networks and Capabilities

Paola Perez-Aleman
McGill University

INTRODUCTION

During the past two decades, environmental movements have been part of efforts to change production practices to reduce environmental degradation and improve ecological sustainability. Going beyond protests and boycotts, many environmental organizations have formed networks among themselves as well as with major corporations in North America and Europe in an effort to make supply chains environmentally and socially sustainable. With globalization of production and trade, the targeted supply chains in an array of industries (apparel, footwear, flowers, fresh produce, coffee, tea, and cocoa) have significant connections with developing countries. The supply chain often has a significant presence of small producers from developing economies in primary production activities. In the face of many scandals and well-documented problems related to environmental degradation, poor working conditions, and unfair prices, multinational corporations and non-governmental organizations (NGOs) have fostered the adoption of codes of conduct or standards aimed at improving these dimensions. These initiatives have led to the rise of what some refer to as "private regulation" (Vogel, 2008).

The rise of supply chain standards or codes focused on environmental performance means that adoption by the company at one part (retailer, brand owner, processor) influences directly suppliers from developing economies. Primary producers face new pressures to shift to sustainable production. Less is known about how these sustainability standards adopted at the buyer or consumer point of the chain are implemented on the producing side, and how they interact with the strategies of developing country producers for improving their environmental performance.

Most studies tend to focus on the global environmental movement itself, the adoption of codes of conduct in advanced economies, or the interaction between social movements and multinational corporations (in North America and Europe) in making the new regulations. The question of how norms for environmental responsibility affect upstream suppliers has been largely ignored. By contrast, this study addresses the dynamics of implementing new sustainability standards in developing economies, particularly from the perspective of small producers. What process enables small producers connected to global supply chains to shift to sustainable production practices? What is it that indigenous producers do when faced with new global norms focused on greening supply chains? How does the process of changing production practices work? What organizational processes are involved at the level of indigenous developing country enterprises?

This chapter discusses the creation of networks to implement new sustainable production practices as a positive organizational change process. It aims to expand understanding of the processes of change around environmental sustainability. This is positive social change in content as the core of these activities is beneficial to the environment. It is also a positive process as there is building of collective capabilities of enterprises to improve their production practices and to foster local economic development. Finally, it is positive in terms of outcomes as the successful shift to sustainable production entails developing relations that facilitate inclusion, rather than exclusion of poorer producers.

The role of networks in creating resources and knowledge flows has received attention in several publications. For example, the literature on industrial districts (Piore & Sabel, 1984) and the works on regional clusters (McDermott, Corredoira, et al., 2009; Perez-Aleman, 2005) show networks of small, medium, and large firms with important interactions that provide supportive conditions for enterprise development. Similarly, the strategy literature highlights the important role of strategic networks in providing the resources and capabilities that enhance a firm's competitive advantage (Gulati, Nohria, et al., 2000). For some, the relationships are seen as important resources (Eisenhardt & Schoonhoven, 1996). All these publications suggest that networks are important for generating resources that organizations (enterprises) need to survive, compete, and innovate in the face of changing and increasing pressures.

While these publications tend to present the networks as given, this chapter focuses on the creation of new ones in interaction with the emergence of new production norms. The argument is that the activities of environmental movement organizations to create and implement new standards also transform old as well as create new networks to develop the resources to change practices. The active building of interorganizational networks interacts with the creation of standards and their implementation. In this sense, the actor-network theory (Latour, 2007) is helpful for it emphasizes the dynamic nature of associations in time and space, and their constant creation for constituting individual and collective agency. This approach shows that all kinds of actors engage in an ongoing formation of networks along and across multiple levels. In addition, the work on resources and change processes provides a helpful lens by emphasizing that new practices redefine the relevant resources (Feldman, 2004).

The dynamics of creating resources through the building of new networks, locally and internationally, occurs in the process of changing production practices. New norms and changing practices interact with new and expanding local and international networks. This dynamic process underlies the building of collective capabilities among groups of firms, and the shift to improved environmental practices. The case of the movement for sustainability in the coffee supply chain is used to show the connections between the adoption of new norms at a global level and the change in production practices at the level of indigenous coffee producers. In the process of changing practices, new connections form globally and locally.

CREATING NEW GLOBAL NORMS FOR GREENING SUPPLY CHAINS

Diverse value chains have experienced the rise of new private codes, standards, and certification systems that differ from traditional business regulation by focusing on social or environmental impact (Bartley,

2003; Frenkel & Scott, 2002; Fung, O'Rourke, et al., 2001; Gereffi, Garcia-Johnson, et al., 2001; Spar & LaMure, 2003). Since the early 1990s, social movements have organized boycotts and campaigns targeting highly visible firms in North America and Europe, pressuring for corporate social responsibility (den Hond & de Bakker, 2007). There is extensive literature on "transnational activists" (Tarrow, 2005) that have pushed for new transnational institutions that transcend national borders (Bartley, 2003; Djelic & Sahlin-Anderson, 2006; Overdevest, 2010). These norms are defining expectations for more socially and environmentally sustainable production processes. Many of the new standards aim to influence business practices in global supply chains that link multinational companies (MNC) and developing country producers, which grew dramatically in recent decades (Gereffi, Humphrey, et al., 2005).

Existing research explains that usually movements pressure multinationals, often via market campaigns and boycotts, to develop an "ethical sourcing code" for their supply chain practices. This is a growing trend in industries that have "credence" quality standards focusing on production conditions, such as apparel, footwear, food-processing, fisheries, forest products, and mining, among others (Fung, O'Rourke, et al., 2001; Frenkel & Scott, 2002; Locke, Qin, et al., 2007; Spar & LaMure, 2003). One example is the mobilization of the environmental NGO, World Wildlife Fund (WWF), to address forest ecosystem health and biodiversity (Overdevest, 2010). Another example is Oxfam's "Make Trade Fair" campaign that puts pressure on multinationals such as Sara Lee and Nestle to improve international wage and working conditions (Kolk, 2005). Often the pressure is a response to the failure or lack of national or international government regulation (Vogel, 2008).

Subsequently, the goal to achieve broader environmentally green practices frequently leads activists and NGOs to engage in partnerships or alliances with private companies (Argenti, 2004; den Hond & de Bakker, 2007; Doh & Teegen, 2003; Hoffman, 2009; Selksy & Parker, 2005). Typically these collaborations focus on developing new environmental and social standards, and on creating mechanisms for monitoring the company's compliance performance with the new norms (Conroy, 2007; O'Rourke, 2006; Perez-Aleman & Sandilands, 2008; Sethi, 2003). This NGO strategy aims to develop and enforce codes in a global context where multinational firms have grown and expanded; they number more than 60,000 and include more than 800,000 subsidiaries and millions of suppliers (Vogel, 2008).

Though activists target multinationals, a characteristic of the new standards is that the focus is on regulating the entire supply chain (Bartley, 2003). Large buyers and retailers who adopt the code in turn demand their suppliers implement the respective standards to be part of the procurement chain. With globalization, investment and purchasing decisions influence labor and environmental practices beyond the company's home country, and it affects the exporting firms (Vogel, 2008). For example, firms in developing countries, like China, engage in implementing new environmental standards in response to buyer enforcement (Christmann & Taylor, 2001). Typically, these standards are industry or product based; examples can be seen for forestry, apparel, coffee, cocoa, sugar, tea, and flowers, as well as for fishing and tourism. Sustainability standards particularly impact the production practices of upstream suppliers interacting closely with the natural environment.

The coffee industry is an excellent case to address the interactions between global norms for greening supply chains and developing country producers. It has been the focus of social movements advocating corporate social and environmental responsibility. Especially since the mid-1990s, at the height of a major global coffee crisis, NGOs pressured multinationals for a more sustainable supply chain in the coffee trade (Kolk, 2005). The collapse of coffee prices after the end of the International Coffee Organization regime in 1989 led to producer income falling dramatically while the buyer companies in consuming countries in North America and Europe increased incomes and sales. More than 60 developing countries produce coffee involving some 25 million farmers, the majority of which are smallholders with less than 10 hectares of land (Bitzer, Francken, et al., 2008). As prices for farmers declined dramatically, the links between major corporate buyers and poverty in developing countries became the focus of NGOs. Major multinationals such as Nestle, Sara Lee, Starbucks, and Kraft have been the focus of NGO movements (Kolk, 2005), drawing attention both for poor labor conditions as well as for environmentally damaging production methods in their supplying farms.

Coffee production reform is important for the goal of ecological conservation. Coffee farms are located in some of most biologically diverse environments in the world; 19 of the 25 "conservation hotspots" worldwide are major coffee growing regions (Linton, 2005; Zettelmeyer & Maddison, 2004). Research shows that shade-coffee plantations are high in biodiversity in terms of original forests, plant, bird, and insect species.

Many environmental movements promote shade-grown coffee cultivation as the next best thing to a conservation forest. As well, the goal of social sustainability became relevant during the height of the coffee crisis in the mid-1990s, when commodity prices collapsed, which exacerbated bad environmental practices including: cutting more trees, introducing livestock, and polluting water sources in fragile biosphere zones.

Movements to raise awareness and promote "sustainable coffee" raised the bar for what is considered to be "good coffee," focusing attention on the social and environmental conditions for growing the bean and trading through the supply chain (Ponte, 2004; Ponte & Gibbon, 2005; Reardon, Codron, et al., 2001). This gave rise to new products certified as *fair trade, organic, bird-friendly,* and *shade-grown* coffees. Increasing consumer awareness with issues of quality, health, poverty, and environment created a growing demand for specialty coffees.

For example, Conservation International (CI) was part of a network of international NGOs, such as the WWF, to create new standards for sustainable agriculture and certification systems to stop tropical deforestation and improve ecological sustainability (Perez-Aleman & Sandilands, 2008). CI developed the *Conservation Principles for Coffee Production,* published in 2001, with a group of NGOs including the Rainforest Alliance and the Smithsonian Migratory Bird Center. The *Principles* outline general norms that farms and processing facilities must meet to safeguard the environment in coffee-growing regions: conservation of wildlife, soil, water, energy, and ecosystems, waterway protection, and ecological management of pests, disease, and waste. As well, there is a stated goal to create a sustainable supply chain where current and future economic, social, and environmental needs are met for participants at all levels of the chain. Generally, all alliances with conservation NGOs focus on developing standards with environmental sustainability provisions (Bitzer, Francken, et al., 2008).

As important, these NGOs promote that large companies purchase from suppliers of sustainably produced coffee (Bitzer, Francken, et al., 2008). For example, Conservation International established partnerships with Starbucks and Green Mountain Coffee that focused on protecting ecosystems (Linton, 2005). The Rainforest Alliance partnered with Kraft, Green Mountain Coffee, Starbucks, and Neumann Kaffee to protect the environment by encouraging companies to purchase from producers making on-farm improvements toward sustainability (Bitzer, Francken, et al. ,2008).

In its partnership with Starbucks, CI started the Conservation Coffee Project (CCP) in southern Mexico that aimed to spread conservation practices among small-scale producers by promoting a shift to shade-grown coffee cultivation (Perez-Aleman & Sandilands, 2008). CI approached Starbucks in 1997 because as a large buyer, they could purchase their coffee supply from producers using the best environmental practices, which could in turn result in increased earnings for farmers, a stable long-term supply of high quality coffee for the company, and conservation of biodiversity. In 2004, Starbucks began to use the Coffee and Farmer Equity Practices (CAFE) to evaluate its upstream suppliers along four categories: product quality, economic accountability, social responsibility, and environmental leadership (coffee growing and processing) (Perez-Aleman & Sandilands, 2008). Starbucks also played a role in promoting the diffusion of sustainable codes through the Specialty Coffee Association of America (SCAA) (Macdonald, 2007).

The aforementioned experience is just one example of the interaction between NGOs and companies in the creation of new norms. More recently, European multinationals became active in the Common Code for the Coffee Community (4Cs), a multi-stakeholder network to promote sustainability of mainstream coffee, which includes Kraft Foods, Nestle, and Sara Lee/Dowe Egberts (Kolk, 2005). Started in 2002 by the German Agency for Technical Cooperation (GTZ), this network fosters environmental and social sustainability in the production, processing, and trading of mainstream green coffee that led to a 2004 code that involved producer federations, companies, NGOs, unions, and other public and international organizations (Kolk, 2005).

A review of the literature, however, finds that the impact of social movements and new codes on the practices of indigenous firms in developing countries is mostly missing from studies (Vogel, 2008). A focus on developing country producers raises questions on what is actually done at their level, in their local context, to meet new global norms and overcome the challenges they face to change their production practices.

While the global movement for sustainability in coffee has pressured multinational companies to adopt new supply chain norms, the major changes in practices occur at the level of the suppliers. From the buyer company side, the new norms can lead to a procurement system that provides incentives through preferential contracts and payment of price premiums. From the supplier side, many changes must be made to meet the new sustainability norms, and the inability to reach the higher standards can mean exclusion from the supply chain. For example, when Starbucks adopted the Conservation Principles for Coffee Production in 2001, it began a preferred purchasing program, whereby those suppliers that achieved a 60% performance rating were given preferential contracts and purchasing priority (Perez-Aleman & Sandilands, 2008). To achieve a passing grade, coffee producers must demonstrate "environmental leadership" in terms of water, soil, and energy use, as well as biodiversity conservation and waste management during growing and processing, all of which involve substantive changes in their existing production practices, discussed next.

CHANGING PRODUCTION PRACTICES IN DEVELOPING COUNTRIES: BUILDING CAPABILITIES OF LOCAL PRODUCERS

Implementing sustainability standards in developing economies, particularly among small producers, involves multiple changes in local production practices to comply with the higher social and environmental sustainability norms. Table 10.1 illustrates the implications of the new supply chain standards emerging from NGO-company interactions in terms of the differences between "sustainable coffee practices" and "nonsustainable" ones. The conventional norms relied on toxic chemicals for pest management, deforestation, intensive water use, and contamination of waterways with waste products. Sustainable practices involve a shift to ecological pest control, use of shade trees and organic fertilizers, water recycling and treatment, and on-farm pulp waste processing (Table 10.1). This section discusses what local producers do to move from conventional to sustainable production.

Sustainable pest control practice, for example, differs considerably from conventional methods. Restricting the use of agrochemicals is one of the items common to both the 4C code and the Starbucks CAFE norm. These norms are to eliminate or minimize pesticide use because of their negative effects on human health and the environment. At a minimum, this means using the least toxic pesticides, and ideally it involves integrated pest management (IPM) methods that use natural

TABLE 10.1

Comparison of Conventional and Sustainable Coffee Practices

Conventional Practices	Sustainable Practices
Use of toxic pesticides and fungicides for pest control in seedling, planting, and harvesting activities	Manual weed control, traps for pests, no use of toxic pesticides, use of natural enemies, pest monitoring analysis
No shade growing areas, cutting of shade trees to cultivate sun coffee varieties, deforestation	Shade trees, fruit trees, soil terraces, curved to control soil erosion, protection of forest biodiversity
Synthetic fertilizers	Organic fertilizer and composting, earthworms
Use of river water for washing beans and for dumping waste	Water recycling, and water collection in winter, waste management to avoid river water contamination
Environmental contamination from pulp waste and from fermentation process	Use of ecological technology to process waste and treat water

enemies and drastically minimize toxic spraying (Table 10.1). IPM implementation requires that producers become familiar with pest population behaviors, ecological and economic threshold analysis, monitoring via sampling of coffee fields to evaluate pest conditions, and using methods for controlling pests with beneficial insects and manual controls.

The quality of coffee and the trading conditions are also dimensions intertwined with sustainability. Many initiatives to promote sustainable coffee production involve specialty coffee companies (i.e., Starbucks and Green Mountain Coffee). Therefore, efforts to enhance sustainability and the quality of coffee are combined. For many specialty coffee companies, high quality coffee beans are an essential part of their competitive strategy to differentiate themselves from the ordinary or commodity market. For local producers, their ability to improve quality and production practices also opens opportunities to connect directly with the specialty coffee buyers. This is better than selling through intermediaries that offer lower prices at the farm level. For the producer, the market value of coffee and its price differential depend on flavor, direct access to international buyers, and adoption of sustainable practices.

Both the environmental and the quality dimensions require that local entrepreneurs have minimum infrastructure, specialized technical and financial services, knowledge of how to best accomplish the norms for producing and processing coffee from the international buyer's perspective, and trained personnel that know and understand the rationale of the new standards. Studies show evidence that small-scale producers can successfully adopt standards that address social and environmental conditions (Conroy, 2007; Jaffee, 2007); however, shifting to new practices presents significant challenges. Poorer producers benefit from improved agricultural practices as environmental degradation threatens their livelihoods and is linked to poverty (Jaffee, 2007). Depletion of forests, farmlands, watersheds, biodiversity, and soil erosion undermine productive conditions and economic survival. One set of challenges that particularly affects the smallholders in the coffee growing regions of Mexico and Central America is access to financial and technical knowledge resources.

Due to lack of financial services and availability of affordable credit, poorer farmers can rarely afford to make investments for upgrading their production (i.e., new equipment, hiring technical assistants or more workers, infrastructure to treat water and waste) (Muradian & Pelupessy, 2005; Oxfam, 2002). Moreover, farmers generally lack the technical assistance and extension services, which the conversion to sustainable agriculture requires to improve product quality and production efficiency (Ponte, 2002). Sometimes the technical assistance does not reach the marginal zones where smaller producers often cultivate. In other cases, the extension services follow the conventional method of relying on pesticides and they lack training in ecological production and integrated pest management methods. Finally, lack of cupping labs to identify and improve flavors and lack of training for local coffee tasters limit the quality of the coffee produced (Bacon, 2002).

Creating Networks to Build Know-How and Resources

The challenges faced at the production level to produce sustainable coffee mean that greening the supply chain goes beyond setting the norms (Bitzer, Francken, et al., 2008; Perez-Aleman & Sandilands, 2008). While the existing literature emphasizes certification and codes of conduct, the focus on developing country producers reveals that this approach is insufficient and, therefore, an impoverished account of what it takes to "green the supply chain." The know-how and resources required for accomplishing this transformation at the supplier level are substantial and need to be addressed.

A good example is provided by the training courses for local technicians and producers on quality control, organic farming methods, tree planting, pulping, and business management that Mexican producers in Chiapas received as part of the Conservation Coffee Project. CI, along with local Mexican organizations, provided farmers with extensive technical assistance to improve agricultural techniques, thereby increasing crop yields and reducing reliance on synthetic fertilizers and pesticides. As important, the Mexican government, international donors, and Starbucks, provided financial support to several micro-credit organizations to generate affordable credit for local producers. Farmers used these loans to purchase capital equipment or make other investments in their farms to improve product quality and comply with environmental standards.

Other examples show that the new global norms attempting to change the coffee industry do not enter passive local contexts. Indigenous enterprises are themselves engaged in strategizing and organizing endogenous change processes to bring about local development amidst a coffee crisis. As discussed in the previous section, the sustainability movement coincided with a major global coffee crisis in the 1990s, when commodity prices collapsed. Small producers were facing dramatic drops in their income when environmental activists discovered coffee farms as havens for biodiversity, and began to promote sustainable coffee products. Local producers, however, were engaged in their own efforts to develop resources to face their own economic crisis. Therefore, the shift to sustainable production also became linked to local organizing efforts, and sustainable coffee products became one alternative for ensuring the survival and international competitiveness of developing country producers. Moving in the sustainable market direction, however, involved building relationships locally and internationally to generate the resources needed to make the shift to sustainable production practices. Efforts to create and implement new norms in production formed new connections between entrepreneurs and between them and other organizations.

In Mexico, indigenous coffee farmers in the Union of Indigenous Communities of the Isthmus Region (UCIRI) cooperative mobilized to expand the volumes of sustainably produced coffee sold in European markets. As part of local organizing, they created CEPCO in 1989 (see Figure 10.1), as local producers attempted to break their grip from exploitative intermediaries and gain independence along with more stable coffee prices (Jaffee, 2007). They created new resources for processing facilities and negotiated

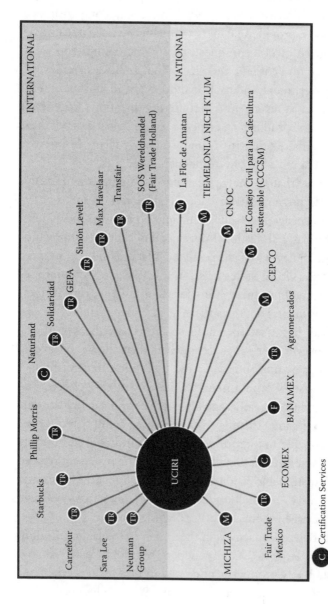

FIGURE 10.1
Mexico: UCIRI's network evolution, 1983–2007.

with the Mexican government for more financial aid programs to help small producers during the coffee crisis. The local producers also expanded their connections with local and international organizations that enabled their shift to sustainable coffee production. Similarly in the Chiapas context, where CI invested efforts in the Conservation Coffee Project, the local small producer organizations also organized training and technical support to shift to organic coffee production (Bray, Sanchez, et al., 2007).

In Nicaragua, for instance, the rise of specialty coffee (including gourmet and green) opened an opportunity during the coffee crisis in the 1990s. The higher price premiums offered by companies such as Green Mountain Coffee, among others, offered an incentive to shift away from conventional to sustainable coffee. Of the 48,000 coffee farms in Nicaragua, 80% are micro-producers with less than 3.5 hectares of coffee and 90% are smallholders with less than 10 hectares (Gomez, 2005; Valkila, 2009). In the early 1990s, these producers faced a collapse of their incomes due to low coffee prices. In addition, they had been affected negatively by Hurricane Mitch. Studies indicate that smallholders dependent on coffee for their primary cash income could not support their households during the coffee crisis (Bacon, 2005).

The Nicaraguan government, for its part, reduced financing and services in the 1990s. There was a weakening of the extension services in the national agricultural system as the government "downsized" and employed few extensionists at the local level (Braun, Herrera, et al., 2004). Many local producers had been organized into co-ops created in the 1980s, when they were promoted by the Sandinista government. By the 1990s, many cooperatives collapsed, while others searched for new organizational strategies.

Paradoxically, the decline in coffee prices coincided with the rise in niche specialty coffee markets, including quality, altitude, gourmet, organic, bird-friendly, sustainable, and fair trade. Many of these were promoted by international NGOs. The idea of using ecologically sound production methods to reach the emerging specialty market generated enthusiasm as coffee smallholders saw this alternative as a way out of their crisis, and thus began to look for ways to enter the organic and other similar markets.

Some began to form cooperative associations to increase their capacity to provide services and financing to their members to fill existing major gaps. Small producers in cooperatives organized associations like PRODECOOP and CECOCAFEN, developing new connections among themselves and with other local and international organizations. Both CECOCAFEN and PRODECOOP are the two largest certified coffee cooperatives in Nicaragua, in fair trade and in organic production. The evolution of CECOCAFEN (Figure 10.2) illustrates how smallholders in a co-op become affiliated with a larger association of cooperatives (union of co-ops) to provide small farmers' co-ops with newly created technical and financial services, as well as processing and commercialization support to its members. Another example is CAFENICA, an association of coffee cooperatives that represents more than 7,000 smallholders (Figure 10.3) (Bacon, 2005).

The cooperative association PRODECOOP, born in 1996, brought together 69 co-ops and 3,000 small coffee producers (Gomez, 2005). PRODECOOP members became aware that quality and environmental degradation were incompatible. The producers organized in PRODECOOP began to develop programs to upgrade their practices and become competitive in the specialty market. These programs received support from local, European, and U.S. foreign aid organizations (both governmental and non-governmental). The next section presents a discussion of two programs that have supported the shift to sustainable coffee production.

Building New Capabilities in Integrated Pest Management

Two programs carried out by PRODECOOP indicate how this organizing effort addressed crucial dimensions related to the sustainability of coffee production: integrated pest management and wastewater management with water conservation. In the first case, PRODECOOP developed an extensive program for alternative pest management. Pesticides and herbicides had become common practice. With the help of the Central American Institute for Tropical Agriculture (CATIE), it began a training program for its members. This program began by establishing experiments in the plots of producers, who then would share their own experience with other producers in their community. The idea was to multiply the knowledge gained. The training programs included producers, agricultural extensionists, and specialists. After initial training sessions with 30 producers in one community, the cooperative would organize meetings and training sessions at what would become demonstration plots to discuss seed selection, disease incidence, plant nutrition, and how to develop seedlings without using chemicals (Hocde & Miranda, 2000). These producers in

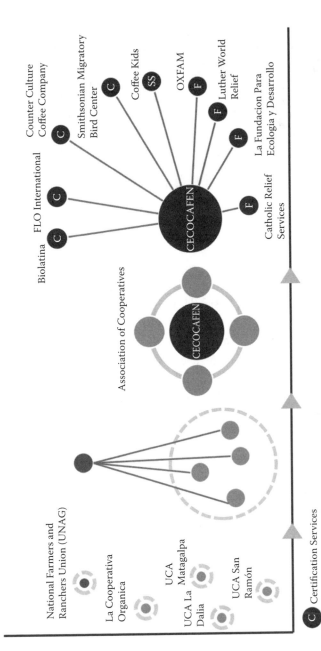

FIGURE 10.2
Nicaragua: CECOCAFEN's network evolution, 1997–2002.

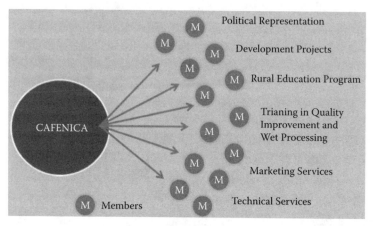

FIGURE 10.3
Nicaragua: CAFENICA—Services provided to member co-ops.

turn would train an equal number of producers, and so forth to spread new approaches at the local level to new groups of farmers through farmer-to-farmer channels. They emphasized building the capacity to manage the local variability created by diverse soils, weather, topography, distance-to-market, and infrastructure (Braun, Herrera, et al., 2004).

In addition to fostering pesticide use reduction, the training promoted the use of natural alternatives for crop pest and disease management, selective manual management of weeds, cover cropping, and green manures. This approach involved increased utilization of local farm resources that otherwise would go to waste, such as the use of manure, litter, and coffee residues in soil conservation and for production of compost and organic fertilizers of various types.

Studies indicate that families receiving training in IPM options were significantly more secure, with a 61% lower probability of suffering total crop loss than those who did not participate in the training programs (Braun, Herrera, et al., 2004). The percentage of coffee farmers using synthetic pesticides has dropped significantly from 90% to 10–20% (Braun, Herrera, et al., 2004). Farmers increased soil and water conservation measures substantially (2–3 times), and the number of trees planted for shade increased by 20–40%. The use of fermented manure has increased from 20–50% (Braun, Herrera, et al., 2004). The vast majority (96%) of farmers has seen quality increases in their crops, and this improvement is reflected in increased prices (Braun, Herra, et al., 2004).

Building New Capabilities in Post-Harvest Water Conservation and Waste Management

The second PRODECOOP program addressed another major problem for Nicaraguan producers: the process used after harvesting the coffee cherries ("beans"). The traditional way of making the cherry ready for consumption involves massive amounts of water, along with large production of solid and liquid waste. In Nicaragua, where the Arabica variety is common, washed post-harvest processing is the most common. The beans are collected in fermentation tanks, which are then washed to remove residues and mucilage. This wet mill process is very water intensive, and typically, this water is not recycled. Even worse, the water used in processing coffee is full of organic pollutants and fermented sugars, which are usually not removed. The usual practice has been to "dump" this "slush" in local rivers and water sources. The high acidity of the water is detrimental to aquatic flora and fauna, reducing biodiversity. Moreover, usually many farms are in the same vicinity, creating further stress on the environment. A secondary negative by-product is the bad odors this waste produces in rivers and waterways.

PRODECOOP has been promoting the reuse of the water as well as the installation of simple filtering and water treatment systems. The idea is to redirect all waste water through the filter treatment system. In 2001, they began to document the situation of wet mills in all the member farms (Gomez, 2005). They then created manuals that described three models for building wet mills of different sizes, and they began to hold training sessions to demonstrate how to make waste water filter systems. Their goal was to have 100% of its members using new wet mills. This effort received support from the Swedish Cooperative Center.

The case of PRODECOOP illustrates how the shift to environmentally friendly production was linked to a local strategy promoting market competitiveness and economic development. The producers built local and international networks to support the process of shifting to sustainable practices, enhancing their local capabilities.

These are just two examples of what local producers are doing to improve their productive practices. The changes are ongoing. For example, there is a new initiative to improve all the wet mills in the cooperatives to further reduce environmental contamination from the coffee pulp. The associations of cooperatives CAFENICA and CECOCAFEN have been working on new engineering designs that will ensure cleaner processing on the farms. Collectively, they have built the capacity to finance and assist in their construction. As well, this initiative will support continuing efforts to expand organic fertilizer production by recycling coffee pulp residues, which were wasted in the past.

The 1990s economic crisis and the quest for higher coffee prices was a clear motivating factor to promote the move into "green" coffee. Nicaraguan producers, however, mention more reasons for changing to sustainable practices: safety for their families without agrochemicals on the farm, lower expenditures for synthetic chemicals, and improvement for the environment, including water protection (Bacon, 2005).

THEORETICAL IMPLICATIONS

The analysis presented in this chapter contributes to our understanding of processes of change around environmental sustainability and greening of supply chains. It highlights the impact of new codes on the practices of indigenous enterprises in developing countries, which has been missing from the existing literature on corporate responsibility, codes of conduct, and social movements. By focusing on developing country producers, this chapter reveals that greening the supply chain goes beyond setting the norms and certification. The know-how and resources required for accomplishing this transformation at the supplier level are significant.

The examples discussed indicate that local producers engage in a capability building process through network creation. Creating new associations is a positive organizational process as indigenous producers build their collective know-how required for accomplishing the shift to new productive practices that are beneficial for the environment. In these cases, capability development depends on expanding knowledge flows and competence-building to produce products or use production methods that meet higher environmental standards. Knowledge means developing new competence to perform novel ways of working (Brown & Duguid, 2001; Tsoukas, 2009). Knowledge circulation depends on the emergence of networks among small producers and of different public and private organizations.

These examples illustrate that the change to green practices does not occur in isolation, but requires the active creation of new associations to support the shift to sustainable production. Resources emerge from creating networks, and the networks themselves can be thought of as resources. The new norms emerging in global supply chains, often created by environmental movements and companies, in turn connect with local development strategies that generate new connections to provide supportive conditions for enabling the shift to a new production system. New ties between local and foreign organizations, including firms, governments, and NGOs, facilitate the flow of knowledge. By being part of these networks, small producers in rural areas can overcome isolation, identify resources, and solve problems, while enabling collective reworking of old and new practices (Perez-Aleman, 2010). All the cases discussed show formation or re-organization of associations, cooperatives, or other networks of organizations to create technical services and training programs and provide financing and infrastructure.

Their focus is on knowledge building to support local product and process innovations using new global sustainability norms as a guide. The ability of small producers to build their knowledge to achieve local environmental innovation depends on increasing the connections among them and different specialized organizations (local and foreign). Services develop as gaps with new norms become explicit. The networks of horizontal relations among producers, as well as links to organizations that can provide knowledge resources help to deal with the pressures of new norms and of producing with improved environmental practices. In this sense, this study supports the view that networks of supporting organizations contribute to provide collective knowledge resources for upgrading products and production processes (Gomes, 2006; Perez-Aleman, 2005; McDermott, Corredoira, et al., 2009).

Importantly, a positive lens highlights how building networks and capabilities helps local producers accomplish the "greening" of their coffee production, and it also brings them benefits. As their production and products improve in terms of environmental sustainability, the poorer producers participate in the global value chain in ways that expand their market channels, diversify customers, and increase income possibilities. This, in turn, has helped small producers to overcome the negative effects of coffee commodity markets and to foster local economic development. By helping to build the capabilities required to transform the production of poorer producers, these networks lead to a positive impact for local producers as sustainability is accomplished in a way that keeps the markets inclusive.

Furthermore, by showing the forming of active associations and the global and local actions required for greening the supply chain, this chapter supports current efforts to bring practice to the center (Latour, 2007). Efforts to make corporations more environmentally responsible depend on the practices of suppliers in developing countries. It takes more than establishing a corporate code of conduct to green a supply chain. At the same time, the efforts of environmental movements to establish new norms for coffee production can constitute a resource for smallholders in developing countries to improve their environmental performance. These changes in the local productive practices can transform the way they commercialize their products so as to increase their incomes, competitiveness, and well-being.

Finally, while this discussion has focused on the specialty coffee chain, the lessons apply to similar agro-industrial chains (milk, tea, cocoa, horticulture), as well as to manufacturing (garments, footwear, furniture, toys) in diverse industries that face increasing demand for supply chain transparency, traceability, and corporate responsibility. Beyond the adoption of corporate codes of conduct and compliance monitoring, this study highlights the process of improving environmental performance in global supply chains that involves building the capabilities of developing country suppliers, particularly poorer producers, through supportive networks that facilitate new know-how and technical and financial resources. Upgrading small-scale and impoverished enterprises in developing countries can be a central aspect of positive organizational change strategies focused on achieving environmental sustainability.

ACKNOWLEDGMENT

I thank Lisa Wanono-Rahman for helpful assistance in creating the figures included in this chapter.

REFERENCES

Argenti, P. A. (2004). Collaborating with activists: How Starbucks works with NGOs. *California Management Review, 47*, 91–116.

Bacon, C. (2002). Knowing what you grow: The story of Nicaragua's Coffee Quality Improvement Project. Evaluation for the Thanksgiving Coffee Company Inc. (preliminary draft).

Bacon, C. (2005). Confronting the coffee crisis: Can fair trade, organic, and specialty coffees reduce small-scale farmer vulnerability in northern Nicaragua? *World Development, 33*, 497–511.

Bartley, T. (2003). Certifying forests and factories: States, social movements, and the rise of private regulation in the apparel and forest products fields. *Politics & Society, 31*, 433–464.

Bitzer, V., Francken, M., et al. (2008). Intersectoral partnerships for a sustainable coffee chain: Really addressing sustainability or just picking (coffee) cherries? *Global Environmental Change, 18*, 271–284.

Braun, A., Herrera, I., et al. (2004). Ecologically-based participatory implementation of integrated pest management and agroforestry in Nicaragua and Central America (Report No. 24). Oslo: Noragric.

Bray, D., Sanchez, L., et al. (2007). Social dimensions of organic coffee production in Mexico. In C. Bacon, E. Mendez, S. Gliessman, D. Goodman, & J. Fox (Eds.), *Confronting the coffee crisis* (pp. 237–260). Cambridge, MA: MIT Press.

Brown, J. S., & Duguid, P. (2001). Knowledge and organization: A social-practice perspective. *Organization Science, 12*, 198–213.

Christmann, P., & Taylor, G. (2001). Globalization and the environment: Determinants of firm self-regulation in China. *Journal of International Business Studies, 32*, 439–458.

Conroy, M. (2007). *Branded! How the certification revolution is transforming global corporations.* Gabriola Island: New Society Publishers.

den Hond, F., & de Bakker, F. G. A. (2007). Ideologically motivated activism: How activist groups influence corporate social change activities. *Academy of Management Review, 32*, 901–924.

Djelic, M.-L., & Sahlin-Anderson, K. (Eds). (2006). *Transnational governance: Institutional dynamics of regulation.* Cambridge, UK: Cambridge University Press.

Doh, J. P., & Teegen, H. (2003). *Globalization and NGOs: Transforming business, government, and society.* Westport, CT: Praeger.

Eisenhardt, K. M., & Schoonhoven, C. B. (1996). Resource-based view of strategic alliance formation: Strategic and social explanations in entrepreneurial firms. *Organization Science, 7*, 136–150.

Feldman, M. (2004). Resources in emerging structures and processes of change. *Organization Science, 15*, 295–309.

Frenkel, S. J., & Scott, D. (2002). Compliance, collaboration, and codes of labor practice: The Adidas connection. *California Management Review, 45*, 29–49.

Fung, A., O'Rourke, D., et al. (2001). *Can we put an end to sweatshops?* Boston: Beacon Press.

Gereffi, G., Garcia-Johnson, R., et al. (2001). The NGO-industrial complex. *Foreign Policy, July/Aug*, 56–65.

Gereffi, G., Humphrey, J., et al. (2005). The governance of global value chains: An analytical framework. *Review of International Political Economy, 12*, 78–104.

Gomes, R. (2006). Upgrading without exclusion: Lessons from SMEs in fresh fruit producing clusters in Brazil. In C. Pietrobelli & R. Rabellotti (Eds.), *Upgrading to compete: Global value chains, clusters, and SMEs in Latin America.* Washington, DC: Inter-American Development Bank and D. Rockefeller Center for Latin American Studies, Harvard University.

Gomez, M. (2005). *Exito empresarial: sistematización de experiencias de pequeños productores de café en Centroamérica.* San Jose: RUTA.

Gulati, R., Nohria, N., et al. (2000). Strategic networks. *Strategic Management Journal, 21,* 203–215.

Hocde, H., & Miranda, B. (2000). *Los intercambios campesinos: Mas alla de las fronteras.* San Jose: IICA.

Hoffman, A. (2009). Shades of green. *Stanford Social Innovation Review, 7,* 40–49.

Jaffee, D. (2007). *Brewing justice: Fair trade coffee, sustainability, and survival.* Berkeley: University of California Press.

Kolk, A. (2005). Corporate social responsibility in the coffee sector: The dynamics of MNC responses and code development. *European Management Journal, 23,* 228–236.

Latour, B. (2007). *Reassembling the social: An introduction to actor-network-theory.* Oxford: Oxford University Press.

Linton, A. (2005). Partnering for sustainability: Business-NGO alliances in the coffee industry. *Development in Practice, 15,* 600–614.

Locke, R., Qin, F., et al. (2007). Does monitoring improve labour standards? Lessons from Nike. *Industrial and Labor Relations Review, 61,* 3–31.

Macdonald, K. (2007). Globalizing justice within coffee supply chains? Fair trade, Starbucks and the transformation of supply chain governance. *Third World Quarterly, 28,* 793–812.

McDermott, G., Corredoira, R., et al. (2009). Public-private institutions as catalysts of upgrading in emerging market societies. *Academy of Management Journal, 52,* 1270–1926.

Muradian, R., & Pelupessy, W. (2005). Governing the coffee chain: The role of voluntary regulatory systems. *World Development, 33,* 2029–2044.

O'Rourke, D. (2006). Multi-stakeholder regulation: Privatizing or socializing global labor standards? *World Development, 34,* 899–918.

Overdevest, C. (2010). Comparing forest certification schemes: The case of ratcheting standards in the forest sector. *Socio-Economic Review, 8,* 47–76.

Oxfam (2002). *Mugged: Poverty in your cup.* Washington, DC: Oxfam International.

Perez-Aleman, P. (2005). Cluster formation, institutions and learning: The emergence of clusters and development in Chile. *Industrial and Corporate Change, 14,* 651–677.

Perez-Aleman, P. (2010). Collective learning in global diffusion: Spreading quality standards in a developing country cluster. *Organization Science,* doi:10.1287/orsc.1090.0514,) 1–18.

Perez-Aleman, P., & Sandilands, M. (2008). Building value at the top and the bottom of the global supply chain: MNC-NGO partnerships. *California Management Review, 51,* 24–49.

Piore, M. J., & Sabel, C. F. (1984). *The second industrial divide: Possibilities for prosperity.* New York: Basic Books.

Ponte, S. (2002). *Standards, Trade and equity: Lessons from the specialty coffee industry.* Copenhagen: Centre for Development Research.

Ponte, S. (2004). Standards and sustainability in the coffee sector: A global value chain approach. International Institute for Sustainable Development.

Ponte, S., & Gibbon, P. (2005). Quality standards, conventions and the governance of global value chains. *Economy and Society, 34,* 1–31.

Reardon, T., Codron, J.-M., et al. (2001). Global change in agrifood grades and standards: Agribusiness strategic responses in developing countries. *International Food and Agribusiness Management Review, 2,* 421–435.

Selksy, J. W., & Parker, B. (2005). Cross-sector partnerships to address social issues: Challenges to theory and practice. *Journal of Management, 31,* 849–873.

Sethi, P. (2003). *Setting global standards: Guidelines for creating codes of conduct in multinational corporations.* Hoboken, NJ: John Wiley & Sons.

Spar, D. L., & LaMure, L. (2003). The power of activism: Assessing the impact of NGOs on global business. *California Management Review, 45,* 78–97.

Starbucks C.A.F.E. Practices Overview (2004). Retrieved August 16, 2006, from http://www.scscertified.com/csrpurchasing/docs/C.A.F.E.PracticesOverview1105.pdf.

Tarrow, S. (2005). *New transnational activism.* Cambridge: Cambridge University Press.

Tsoukas, H. (2009). A dialogical approach to the creation of new knowledge in organizations. *Organization Science, 20,* 941–995.

Valkila, J. (2009). Fair trade organic coffee production in Nicaragua—Sustainable development or a poverty trap? *Ecological Economics,* doi:10.1016/j.ecoleco.2009.07.002.

Vogel, D. (2008). Private global business regulation. *Annual Review of Political Science, 11,* 261–282.

Zettelmeyer, W., & Maddison, A. (2004). *Agroforestry-based enterprise development as a biodiversity conservation intervention in Mexico and Ghana. USAID/PVC matching grant program final evaluation report.* Malaga, Spain & Hereford, UK: USAID.

11

Revealing Themes: Applying a Positive Lens to the Chapters on Environment and Sustainability

Jennifer Howard-Grenville
University of Oregon

In 2000, UN Secretary General Kofi Annan called for an assessment of the consequences of ecosystem change for human well-being. The result, the Millennium Ecosystem Assessment, brought together the input of more than 1,300 experts worldwide and documented the unprecedented changes humans have made in land, water, and ecosystem health (2005). It is amply clear that we are "running down the account" of earth's natural systems, spending natural capital at a far faster rate than it can be replenished (MEA, 2005, p. 5). Consider the following:

- At least one-quarter of the world's marine fish stocks are overharvested; in many sea areas, the weight of fish available to be harvested is less than 10% of that available prior to the onset of industrial fishing.
- The economic value of forests captured through timber and fuel uses represents only about one-third of their total value if their roles in carbon dioxide absorption, watershed protection, and other natural services are included.
- The current rate of species loss is one thousand times higher than that in the historical fossil record; the projected future rate of species loss is more than ten times higher than the current rate.
- Nearly one-quarter of the earth's land surface has been converted to cultivated land. Intensive agriculture has significantly altered nitrogen flows to the atmosphere and water bodies, contributing to climate change and aquatic dead zones.

- Concentrations of carbon dioxide in the atmosphere are now roughly 40% higher than pre-industrial levels, contributing to a 0.7 °C change in global temperature; a further 1 to 6 °C change is predicted during the 21st century (IPCC, 2007).

It is hard to find the positive in these stark facts. Our industrialized society has, through individual patterns of consumption and the operations of businesses and other organizations, drawn down the capital in the earth's account at an alarming rate. As Hoffman, Badiane, and Haigh note in Chapter 7, this has also occurred at the expense of the majority of the world's people; just 20% of the population consumes 86% of goods and services. While this information can provoke gloom, it also suggests that there is no doubt about the immense potential for gains from positive social change in the area of environment and sustainability.

Each chapter in Part III of this book sheds light on positive outcomes that individuals and collectives have attained: businesses that pursue social as well as economic gains (Hoffman, Badiane, & Haigh, Chapter 7), protection of land and livelihood in the vast Great Bear Rainforest (Riddell, Tjörnbo, & Westley, Chapter 8), changes in day-to-day practices that trigger new attention to individual environmental impact (Feldman, Chapter 9), and reduced environmental degradation coupled with greater market access for coffee producers (Perez-Aleman, Chapter 10). Perhaps more importantly, each chapter also illuminates positive change processes that can be applied beyond their specific cases, adding to the repertoires and toolkits of scholars and practitioners of social change agency.

In this commentary, I first aim to position the contributions of these chapters by giving a brief overview of how organizational scholarship has addressed natural environment issues. Next I explore the processes authors identify for social change agency around environmental issues. While each chapter appears to focus on quite different levels of analysis, I found it most intriguing that each takes individual agency as central to instigating or implementing change, and each offers a distinct and complementary perspective on how individuals trigger and shape larger change. In the final section of the commentary, I consider how these processes can inform future scholarly work in an area where fundamental change is so urgently needed.

SCHOLARSHIP ON BUSINESS AND THE ENVIRONMENT

Organizational scholarship on the natural environment has a relatively long history[1] and, from its beginning, has had a concern with positive social change. Some of the earliest works advocated the need for fundamentally new ways of understanding and acting in order to reduce detrimental environmental effects of business (Gladwin, Kennely, & Krause, 1995; Hart, 1995; Jennings & Zandenberg, 1995; Shrivastava, 1995). As the field grew and sought legitimacy within the academy, this vision for fundamental change was tempered in approaches that set out to establish the "business case" for companies going beyond regulatory compliance in their environmental actions (Porter & Van der Linde, 1995; Reinhardt, 1999). Early efforts to seek a relationship between environmental performance and firm financial performance (see, for example, Hart & Ahuja, 1996; Russo & Fouts, 1997; Waddock & Graves, 1997) reflected a desire to demonstrate the potential benefit of environmental actions in economic terms. Over time, attention to the question "does it pay to be green?" gave way to work that called attention to contingencies in this relationship (Aragon-Correa & Sharma, 2003; Sharma, 2000) and positioned it within larger societal and normative conversations (Hoffman, 1999; Lounsbury, 2001; Maguire & Hardy, 2009; Weber, Heinze, & DeSoucey, 2008). Margolis and Walsh called for a more deliberate shift away from the "pays to be green" debate, challenging scholars to take a normative approach and think seriously about how *should* companies act (2003).

The chapters in this volume fit with this normative thrust, yet acknowledge the complexity of specific situations. They reveal and hold tensions between economic and social goals (Chapter 7), between the actions of large multinational corporations and those of activists and producers (Chapters 8 and 10), and between technologies designed to mask or to reveal their environmental impacts (Chapter 9). The authors show that these very tensions generate new, sometimes highly contextual, solutions. Resolving the tensions and answering "does it pay?" is not the goal of these inquiries; rather, the positive outcomes and the processes to arrive at them remain messy, complex, and always "in the making." The questions engaged are "does it matter?" and "how does it work?"

---

[1] Recent review articles capture this history more completely than I can here. See, for example, Bansal & Gao, 2006; Margolis & Walsh, 2003.

Particularly important to advancing scholarship on business and the natural environment is shedding light on the latter question: *how does it work*? Relatively little attention has been paid to date to how individuals actually influence their organizations' environmental actions, or to how organizational cultures can support and sustain their members in attaining positive environmental outcomes (Bertels et al., 2010). Some authors have considered how individual actions such as championing (Andersson & Bateman, 2000) and issue selling (Bansal, 2003; Howard-Grenville, 2007; Sonenshein, this volume) influence the processes by which environmental issues are taken up and acted upon in organizations. What is new about the change processes revealed in these chapters is their emphasis on positive processes, by which I mean those that trigger further positive action and "spillovers," potentially creating virtuous cycles and examples of positive deviance that can fuel further change. Unlike prior work that documents institutional, cultural, technological, and other barriers that change agents must surmount (Howard-Grenville, 2007), these processes highlight how barriers, while present, are transformed or simply approached from a completely different direction so that they become design opportunities (Chapter 9), experiments (Chapter 7), or occasions to undertake transformative personal work (Chapter 8) and build new connections (Chapter 10). In the next section, I elaborate on the main change processes I see in each chapter and explain how others might apply and further develop these in their research.

PROCESSES FOR POSITIVE CHANGE AGENCY

Experimentation and Example Setting

In their chapter exploring the role of hybrid organizations as agents of positive social change, Hoffman, Badiane, and Haigh (Chapter 7) draw our attention to the firm and industry level where organizations with blended social and economic goals act in new ways, offering an example to others. Hoffman and his co-authors portray Maggie's Organics as a positively deviant firm that is an example of a successful, mission-driven company that also reshapes the "rules of the game" within an industry. This example is also one of individual-level, social change agency. Founder Bena Burda undertook an experiment with a new type of product, and new way of doing business (founding and supporting worker-owned cooperatives for organic cotton supply). In some ways, this might be explained simply as the product of an entrepreneurial spirit and perseverance. In other ways, it demonstrates how individuals can lead with their values—a sense of what they "should" do—and discern new potentialities (Steckler & Bartunek, this volume) to create both a successful business and example for others.

I was interested to find that Maggie's Organics' Web site documents Burda's entry into organic cotton apparel as a story of somewhat accidental activism (Maggie's Organics, 2010). Working in the organic foods industry marketing corn chips in the early 1990s, she was approached by a Texas farmer who had planted cotton in a crop rotation to improve his organic corn yield. He had 200 acres of organic cotton, and nothing to do with it. Burda began with socks, and worked with her existing contacts in the natural foods business to distribute the socks. (Reading this story helped me understand why my local grocery store, albeit in progressive-leaning Eugene, Oregon, carries Maggie's Organics socks, and no other apparel items.) The point is that Burda knew what she wanted to do—bring organic cotton to the market—and was not bound by conventions like the need to distribute through conventional channels, the need to scale up and use traditional suppliers, and so forth. Her approach was deliberate and values-driven, yet experimental and cumulative. Her work with cooperatives emerged after spending time working on quality issues that took her to textile plants and exposed her to who worked in these plants and the conditions they worked under. One lesson is that the "master plan" for this type of positive change agency does not exist in advance, but is gradually assembled, perhaps over long time periods (Steckler & Bartunek, this volume) as people like Burda work toward their goals.

Hoffman, Badiane, and Haigh point to other characteristics of this type of change agency. They note that hybrid organizations that lead with values engage differently in competitive dynamics. They share rather than protect valued resources, valuing transparency and even encouraging imitation. The authenticity of such companies creates an advantage in the market place, enabling them to share what might otherwise be considered proprietary, like product formulations (see also Russo, 2010). And larger companies might follow suit in experimenting with ways to share their green innovations. In 2010, Nike launched the GreenXchange as a platform to share technologies developed by one company—like Nike's "green rubber" formulation—with others through licensing. Unlike some other areas of social change, addressing environmental issues often demands new technologies or techniques. Because of this, the experimentation, learning, and sharing that hybrid organizations and their founders engage in is a particularly important mechanism for change agency in this area.

Transformation and Amplification

In a quite different context, Riddell, Tjörnbo, and Westley (Chapter 8) similarly draw attention to how individual experimentation creates an openness to change and new possibilities, in this case for collaboration on a complex, multidimensional issue that confronts environmental protection and its interaction with social and economic stability. Rather than stumbling into an area for experimentation and learning as in the Maggie's Organics case, individuals in this setting began by experiencing the controversy and seeming lack of capacity to make progress that accompanied clashes between environmental activists, aboriginal peoples, government representatives, and forest industry participants. Using complexity theory and the concept of an adaptive cycle, Riddell and co-authors note that this standstill triggered a phase of turbulent change in which "release" first dissolves connections between prior resources and system logics, and produces a process of "creative destruction," enabling eventual reorganization that includes new ways of interacting. Personal transformation led other processes in the release phase, enabling individual activists to see their work for change as part of their unfolding personal story. This in turn helped them to see their opponents differently, and to generate a sense of collective efficacy in face of the challenges of protecting the rainforest.

In some ways, despite very different starting points, the amplification of small change shown in the case of the Great Bear Rainforest mirrors that evident in the examples of hybrid organizations given in Chapter 7. The whole becomes transformed, beginning with individuals acting authentically on their convictions. Complexity theory adds a new dimension for understanding the mechanisms behind this multilevel cascading, however. Experimentation and example setting creates positive spillovers by allowing and encouraging mimicry. Amplification in a complexity theory sense draws attention to how resources produced or reconfigured subsequently enable new forms of action and interaction, some of which may be distinctly different from those that begat the new resources. The image is one of unfolding and unpredictable emergence, rather than replication.

I could not help but think that the processes described in the Great Bear Rainforest case resonate strongly with Feldman's notion of resourcing (2004). Resourcing draws attention to the way that individuals put potential resources to use in order to generate and energize patterns of action (Feldman, 2004; see also Chapter 9). What complexity theory adds is a way of placing resourcing within a cycle that helps to show when and where resources may be most and least available to individuals for new uses. The turbulent "back-loop" of this cycle is chaotic and unsettling, yet also the most ripe for individual change agents to resource new patterns of action. A similar image is offered in Swidler's work when she speaks of cultural transformation being most viable during turbulent "unsettled" times (1986).

We can expect more, not fewer, cases where environmental issues are inseparable from potentially conflicting concerns over social equity and livelihoods. Private organizations alone are unlikely to hold all the solutions, and there is evidence that face-to-face interaction and an experience of a shared fate around the use of resources enables the kind of creative, durable solutions documented in this case (Dietz & Ostrom, 2003). In such cases, the processes of individual-level transformation coupled with resourcing new forms of action at a wider system level may be essential to generating solutions that are likely to be highly contextualized and unavailable through mimicry alone.

Design and Attunement

Feldman's work (Chapter 9) brings forward yet another process for positive social change that is particularly salient to environmental problems. She argues that the "rules of the game" might be changed not just by offering new examples or reconfiguring interpersonal interactions, but also by altering individual day-to-day practices. In our daily lives, we enlist any number of technological (and non-technological) artifacts, many of which mask the connections between our actions and their environmental impacts. Feldman argues that certain artifacts can trigger new behaviors, and, more importantly, create positive spillover by attuning users to previously hidden impacts, perhaps encouraging them to shift their behavior in other settings. Her example of the "these come from trees" label on the paper towel dispenser might compel someone to take fewer towels in that instance, but also cut back on use of paper towels in their own home.

This individual-level focus nonetheless has implications for organizations and larger systems in that it suggests the design of artifacts can significantly alter their patterns of use, either bringing to consciousness or obscuring the role of individual choice in influencing environmental impacts. Feldman argues that electric hand dryers, while more energy efficient than paper towel production, do less to attune people to that fact that they have a role to play and a choice to make in mitigating the environmental impact of their technology-mediated activities. There is a role for both hidden efficiency and attunement in design, however. Drivers of hybrid cars report their fascination with the dashboard display that shows real-time gas mileage and information on whether power is coming from the battery, gas engine, or both. Maximizing the amount of time one can drive "battery only" and seeing an increase in gas mileage becomes almost a game, attuning the driver to the choices she can make even when assisted by a technology that otherwise remains out of reach and "under the hood."

One challenge to designing in attunement and encouraging shifts in everyday practice is the fact that we as humans tend to "tune out" quite easily. The first several times we drive a hybrid, or the first time we encounter a two-button toilet (forcing choice and attunement to water consumption per flush), or a sticker on the towel dispenser, the experience is interesting, engaging, and creates at least momentary reflection. The eighteenth time we do this, it is less likely to have such an effect. We may even revert to doing what is most convenient, ignoring the signals that are meant to mediate our use of the artifact. As a hybrid driver, I admit I now rarely look at the screen that is offering me real-time feedback on my gas consumption. Getting around this challenge is, Feldman argues, partly made possible by considering the abundance of connections between practice and objects and the potential these hold for generating new behavioral patterns and attunements. It is less the "shock value" of a design that disrupts and reorients its user to attend to environmental implications (Ehrenfeld, 2008), but perhaps more the folding of environmental attunement into multiple other considerations (safety, convenience, etc.) that might reorient our day-to-day practices. Where others highlight the importance of turbulent conditions for bringing forward new resources and ways of acting (Riddell, Tjörnbo, & Westley, Chapter 8), this attention to artifacts and design suggests that, for many environmental problems, we need not wait for system disruption but instead already hold the seeds for some change literally in our own hands.

Connecting and Supporting

Finally, Chapter 10 by Perez-Aleman shows how local coffee producers connected to each other and to international organizations and markets in order to learn about new techniques, share this knowledge, and support each other in making transformations in their environmental practices. These changes enabled them to access markets previously unavailable to them, raising the value of their crops and lowering the environmental impact of their production practices. In some ways, the processes described here are somewhat akin to Feldman's notion of attuning. Instead of revealing how daily life in an industrialized country tends to hide our connections to natural resources, attuning in the coffee production case involved raising farmers' awareness of the market opportunities, hidden behind low commodity prices, available to those who changed production practices. The interventions in this case centered on demonstrating new techniques, training farmers and others, and enabling the transfer of knowledge from farmer to farmer. This brought forward new resources—the knowledge and the supportive networks themselves—as well as resourced more traditional financial assistance (e.g., micro-credit and financial aid) to be put to work in supporting new practices. Local efforts also drew on vertical networks that connected small cooperatives to larger ones, and to foreign non-governmental organizations (NGOs) and standards organizations.

The coffee production case comes full circle back to the discussion of hybrid organizations. It shows how the "other" end of supply chains, that which consumers in developed countries rarely see and relatively infrequently consider, respond when firms or NGOs pursue a new social or environmental agenda. It also highlights a critical consideration for scholars and others interested in positive environmental change. Whereas other settings might respond quite rapidly to newly introduced ideas, certain shifts in environmental practice take time because they rely on natural processes, like growing cycles, or ecological interactions. No matter how fervently one advocates or believes in it, it still takes a minimum of three years (per U.S. federal standards) for a field previously planted conventionally to qualify as organic. Similarly, the spread of new practices for coffee production takes a certain amount of time for demonstration plots to be planted, pest management schemes to be implemented, and so forth. Adding these natural processes to our "radar screen," as well as attending to human interactions within the highly dispersed supply chains that bring agricultural and other natural resources to markets, will help us more deeply understand and explain some of the trends observed in the operation of hybrid organizations, like slow growth and long time horizons (Chapter 7).

MANY PATHS AND SOME SUGGESTIONS FOR CONTINUING THE JOURNEY

The processes for positive change agency highlighted in each chapter are different but not mutually exclusive. Despite having been observed in diverse settings, these processes might be leveraged individually or in combination in many other ways, yielding further understanding of "the importance of diverse reference points and perspectives in motivating and sustaining change efforts" (Steckler & Bartunek, Chapter 6). Experimentation by individuals sets examples for others (Hoffman, Badiane, & Haigh, Chapter 7) and, when it invites rather than shuts down mimicry, holds great potential for the development of business models or technologies that can operate more sustainably. Such moves also set up ripple effects through supply chains, perhaps enabling producers to make new connections that bring knowledge, materials resources, and support for undertaking fundamental shifts in their practices (and associated environmental impacts) over time (Perez-Aleman, Chapter 10). In other contextual circumstances (Steckler & Bartunek, Chapter 6), cumulative, emergent change processes are less evident. At times, a shock to the system releases resources and enables individuals and collectives to undertake transformative moves that might amplify (Riddell, Tjörnbo, & Westley, Chapter 8). Simultaneously, many small, disparate "mini-shocks" might be designed into our technological artifacts to attune individuals to the consequences of their use and shift behavior in the day-to-day. Returning to the stark facts presented in the opening of this chapter, and reflecting the sentiment of many natural and social scientists, the solutions to the environmental issues we face will not and cannot come from any one set of actions or interventions alone. The multiple starting points and paths for change agency identified in this chapter—experimentation, amplification, design for attunement, and connection—are all possible, and essential, to enacting positive social change in areas of environmental concern.

Several specific directions for future research are evident. First, future research can consider when and in what contexts these processes yield positive outcomes. For example, when is person-to-person connection (Chapters 8 and 10) needed to reconfigure resources and generate new ways of working, and when is "action at a distance" (by setting examples in a market, Chapter 7, or altering material or symbolic mediators of action, Chapter 9) sufficient? Second, we need to better understand how and under what conditions positive processes undertaken at the individual level create (or fail to create) spillovers and amplification of positive change at a broader level. When do individually driven change efforts cascade through mimicry? How can individuals find or create systems that are ripe for change, given the cycles of complex adaptive systems? Most of the chapters start with the individual, yet others also demonstrate ripple effects in the other direction, showing how changes in a system (of interacting artifacts and people, Chapter 9, or of international standards, Chapter 10) can shift individual practices. When do these changes occur and how can we intervene to keep them occurring, in a way that raises and repeats attunement at the individual level?

A larger question, in the background of many of the chapters, is the degree to which individuals and systems must suffer loss in order to trigger positive change processes; a similar question is raised by Steckler and Bartunek (Chapter 6). Some of the processes uncovered in these chapters suggest that organizational change can be driven by possibility and opportunity, not simply triggered by shocks (Howard-Grenville, Golden-Biddle, Irwin, & Mao, 2010; Weick & Quinn, 1999). For example, Feldman argues that interventions in daily practice need not disrupt, but merely invite new possibilities (Chapter 9). Hoffman, Badiane, and Haigh argue that hybrid organizations seek to draw from the resilience of natural systems rather than insure against their vulnerabilities (Chapter 7). Positive change agency on environmental issues must take seriously the current state of our natural systems, the technologies that have brought us to this point, and the metabolism of earth's restorative systems, but this need not trigger only despair. The processes highlighted in these chapters, of experimentation, amplification, design, and connection offer ways for change agents to move toward new models of interaction with the natural world, while potentially improving the ability of our current models to respond to inevitable shocks that will result from changes already wrought.

REFERENCES

Anderson, L. M., & Bateman, T. S. (2000). Individual environmental initiative: Championing natural environmental issues in U.S. business organizations. *Academy of Management Journal, 43*, 548–570.

Aragon-Correa, J. A., & Sharma, S. (2003). A contingent resource-based view of proactive corporate environmental strategy. *Academy of Management Review, 28*, 71–88.

Bansal, P. (2003). From issues to actions: The importance of individual concerns and organizational values in responding to natural environmental issues. *Organization Science, 14*, 510–527.

Bansal, P., & Gao, J. (2006). Building the future by looking to the past. *Organization & Environment, 19*, 458–478.

Bertels, S., Papania, L., & Papania, D. (2010). *Embedding sustainability in organizational culture: A systematic review of the body of knowledge.* Network for Business Sustainability. Retrieved January 2011 from http://www.nbs.net/knowledge/culture.

Dietz, T., Ostrom, E., et al. (2003). The struggle to govern the commons. *Science, 302*, 1907–1912.

Ehrenfeld, J. (2008). *Sustainability by design.* New Haven, CT: Yale University Press.

Feldman, M. S. (2004). Resources in emerging structures and processes of change. *Organization Science, 15*, 295.

Gladwin, T. N., Kennelly, J. J., et al. (1995). Shifting paradigms for sustainable development: Implications for management theory and research. *Academy of Management Review, 20*, 874–907.

Hart, S. L. (1995). A natural resource-based view of the firm. *Academy of Management Review, 20*, 986–1014.

Hart, S. L., & Ahuja, G. (1996). Does it pay to be green? An empirical examination of the relationship between emission reduction and firm performance. *Business Strategy and the Environment, 5*, 30–37.

Hoffman, A. J. (1999). Institutional evolution and change: Environmentalism and the U.S. chemical industry. *Academy of Management Journal, 42*, 351–371.

Howard-Grenville, J. Golden-Biddle, K., Irwin, J., & Mao, J. (2011). Liminality as a cultural process for cultural change. *Organization Science, 22*, 522–539.

Howard-Grenville, J. A. (2007). Developing issue-selling effectiveness over time: Issue selling as resourcing. *Organization Science, 18*, 560–577.

IPCC (International Panel on Climate Change). (2007). Retrieved December 2011 from http://www.ipcc.ch/.

Jennings, P. D., & Zandbergen, P. A. (1995). Ecologically sustainable organizations: An institutional approach. *Academy of Management Review, 20*, 1015–1052.

Lounsbury, M. (2001). Institutional sources of practice variation: Staffing college and university recycling programs. *Administrative Science Quarterly, 46*, 29–56.

Maggie's Organics. 2010. Retrieved December 2011 from http://www.maggiesorganics.com/2010_history.php.

Maguire, S., & Hardy, C. (2009). Discourse and deinstitutionalization: The decline of DDT. *Academy of Management Journal, 1*, 148–178.

Margolis, J. D., & Walsh, J. P. (2003). Misery loves companies: Rethinking social initiatives by business. *Administrative Science Quarterly, 48*, 268–305.

Millennium Ecosystem Assessment (2005). Retrieved January 2011 from http://www.maweb.org/documents/document.429.aspx.pdf.

Porter, M. E., & van der Linde, C. (1995). Toward a new conception of the environment-competitiveness relationship. *Journal of Economic Perspectives, 9,* 97–118.

Reinhardt, F. (1999). Market failure and the environmental policies of firms: Economic rationales for "beyond compliance" behavior. *Journal of Industrial Ecology, 3,* 9–21.

Russo, M. 2010. *Companies on a mission: Entrepreneurial strategies for growing sustainably, responsibly, and profitably.* Stanford, CA: Stanford University Press.

Russo, M. V., & Fouts, P. A. (1997). A resource-based perspective on corporate environmental performance and profitability. *Academy of Management Journal, 40,* 534–559.

Sharma, S. (2000). Managerial interpretations and organizational context as predictors of corporate choice of environmental strategy. *Academy of Management Journal, 43,* 681–697.

Shrivastava, P. (1995). The role of corporations in achieving ecological sustainability. *Academy of Management Review, 20,* 936–960.

Swidler, A. (1986). Culture in action: Symbols and strategies. *American Sociological Review, 51,* 273–286.

Waddock, S. A., & Graves, S. B. (1997). The corporate social performance-financial performance link. *Strategic Management Journal, 18,* 303–319.

Weber, K., Heinze, K. L., et al. (2008). Forage for thought: Mobilizing codes in the movement for grass-fed meat and dairy products. *Administrative Science Quarterly, 53,* 529–567.

Weick, K. E., & Quinn, R. E. (1999). Organizational change and development. *Annual Review of Psychology, 50,* 36.

Part IV

Health Care

12

Hope as Generative Dynamic in Transformational Change: Creating and Sustaining "Collaborative Care" in the ThedaCare Health System

Karen Golden-Biddle
Boston University

Kathryn Correia
HealthEast Care System

In discussions of U.S. healthcare reform, deep skepticism about the possibility of change prevails, both among those who challenge the desirability of such reform and those who desire it but regard it as impossible to achieve. Yet, in the face of this skepticism, there exist exciting examples of genuine efforts to transform the health care system. For example, Dr. Thomas Frieden, director of the Centers for Disease Control, identified and targeted as priority for the agency's action six "winnable battles" facing our nation today—health care infections, smoking, AIDS, obesity/nutrition, teen pregnancy, and auto injuries—with "proven programs [that] can save lives and reduce harm" (Stobbe, 2010). Similarly, health systems are using innovation to transform the delivery of patient care. Mayo Clinic's Center for Innovation is working to "transform the way health care is delivered and experienced by patients" (Mayo Clinic, 2010). Kaiser Permanente's Health Care Innovation Center uses "elements of human-centered design to improve and innovate physical spaces, technologies and clinical operations" (Kaiser Permanente, 2010). Geisinger Clinic's "care model innovations" (Paulus, Davis, & Steele, 2008) enhance the capacity to redesign models of care and thereby create health care value. These vibrant examples provide important evidence that government and key health systems are innovating to generate high quality and safe care, and that through these efforts are creating value for patients, their families, and their communities.

How do some health organizations become inspiring examples, able to transform care delivery in spite of a context not conducive to change? The literature on organizational and system change does not provide a convincing account. This is a critical oversight in our understanding because new care models such as those illustrated here require the collective and dedicated effort of people to create and to sustain them. How is this effort generated? More particularly, how do people overcome skepticism about the possibility of change in order to be willing to entertain a different and better future?

In this chapter, we ask: *How* do leaders and clinicians collectively undertake change to transform care that makes a positive difference, that is, benefits patients, their families, and society? To address this question, we take a close look inside one specific, vibrant example of creating and implementing an innovative care model that is providing significant value for patients and their families. This case takes place in the ThedaCare health system (http://www.thedacare.org), a horizontally integrated, medium-size community-owned health system in Wisconsin that consists of four hospitals, 130 primary care providers in 22 locations, and more than 5,300 employees. Known as Collaborative Care, the new care model represents a general process of inpatient care delivery across unit and medical condition that enables staff to think about patient stay in a way that emphasizes getting patients well. In contrast to other models that organize care around medical condition (Baggs et al., 2004; Cohen, 2002; Davies et al., 2008; Scott & Cowen, 1997), Collaborative Care is not fundamentally different for medicine or surgery. Rather, the process of care is designed to help pull all patients, regardless of diagnosis, through the system while accommodating each patient's unique needs and fostering a "feeling of safety as well as actual safety." Designed during 2005–2006 and first implemented in February 2007 in a medical-surgical unit in Appleton Medical Center, the second largest hospital in ThedaCare, the care model has subsequently been spread to other medical-surgical and specialty units.

The focus in this chapter is on the origins, development, and early implementation of Collaborative Care. Our account is based on data collected by the first author and comprises three site visits and twenty-five interviews of leadership and clinical staff involved in creating the new model. Analyses disclosed how the generative dynamics of hope enabled people to believe in the possibility of transforming care centrally around patient needs, and to invent a new model of care delivery that, in implementation, realized this possibility. Now multiple years in operation, the model is generating exceptional patient care in terms of its quality and safety, and patient satisfaction. When contrasted with like patients on non-Collaborative Care units, nurse productivity has increased by 11%; length of stay and direct costs have decreased on average 20–25%.

To explain how leaders and front line clinicians transformed inpatient care and achieved these results, we propose a conceptual model of hope as generative dynamic in transformational change consisting of two key processes: *activating* belief that action can make a positive difference about a particular human condition, and *acting on* belief to realize desired change. The first process loosens the hold of prior expectations or assumptions about the human condition, for example, how care is delivered, thereby positioning people to see and to entertain new possibilities. In the second process, people create fresh alternatives, for example, an innovative care model, that cultivate new expectations about care that can be delivered. Together, these processes enable hope as generative dynamic; that is, people looking together at a human condition (Deetz, 2008; Weick, 2007), seeing alternative possibilities, and taking inventive action that creates desired change (Carlsen & Dutton, 2011).

GENERATIVE DYNAMICS IN TRANSFORMATIONAL CHANGE

Our field's predominant understanding of transformational change is represented in the "episodic" model of change (Weick & Quinn, 1999). This model is based on the assumption that change of a fundamental kind requires a significant and disruptive break from the past, originating in the form of exogenous triggers or jolts (Lewin, 1947; Swidler, 1986) that provoke organizations out of inertia. In the absence of jolts, senior leaders become "prime movers" (Weick & Quinn, 1999) who intervene by creating a sense of urgency (Kotter, 1996) designed to motivate change and reduce employee complacency with the status quo.

Recently, a few studies (Howard-Grenville et al., 2011; Plowman et al., 2007; Reay et al., 2006) have illuminated a portrait of transformational change that does not involve the presence of jolts that disrupt inertia. These studies depict the effort of collective insiders in creating change that made a positive difference. In one case, actors used their embedded knowledge to guide their efforts to legitimize a new role that enabled better delivery of health care (Reay et al., 2006). In another case, actors adept at navigating the symbolic world created cultural change in the areas of sustainability and wellness-based healthcare (Howard-Grenville et al., 2011). In a final case, actors collectively created and institutionalized efforts to relieve the suffering of homeless people in their church's community (Plowman et al., 2007).

Our study in this chapter similarly portrays a fundamental change created by the efforts of insiders and that resulted in positive outcomes. Yet, the data challenged us to look beyond the general efforts of clinicians and leaders to their *particular* efforts—of dedication, enthusiasm, patience, exploring, questioning, and persisting expressed as they looked together (Deetz, 2008) at how they delivered care and challenged themselves to invent a desired alternative. These particular efforts represent generative dynamics in change; those experiences that "bring a feeling of energy and aliveness to people and also have the potential to produce more enduring, expansive and transformative consequences" (Carlsen & Dutton, 2011, p. 4). In this chapter, we examine hope as generative dynamic that takes shape in efforts to create and sustain a different and better way of delivering care.

Hope as Generative Dynamic in Change

Hope has emerged only recently in organizational studies as an area of investigation (Carlsen & Pitsis, 2009; Ludema et al., 1997). In using hope we mean a "future-oriented and emotive quality of experience that interacts with other organizational processes" (Carlsen, Hagen, & Mortensen, 2011, p. 298), that is, change. As an emotion, hope is comprised of both cognition and affect. Cognition enters when, in hoping for something, we are "marshaling information and data relevant to a desired future event" (Groopman, 2005, p. 193) in order to envision a different possibility. Affect enters in the "comforting, energizing, elevating feeling that you experience when you project in your mind a positive future" (Groopman, 2005, p. 193).

Hope, then, does not involve just any future. Specifically, it involves a better and desired future generated through reconsidering what is commonly accepted and "entertaining new alternatives for social action" (Gergen, 1978, p. 1346). It is in this respect that we conceive hope as a generative mechanism in change. This conception of hope does not involve embracing a rosy or naïve view; nor does it consist of "simple wishing" (James, 1956). Rather, in hope, we face the human condition clear-eyed, fully recognizing its "unalloyed reality" (Groopman, 2005) while continuing to believe that our efforts can make a positive difference.

Two principle elements of hope are belief and expectation. Belief represents faith in something; it is the readiness to act (James, 1956, pp. 59 & 90). The second element, expectation, represents a relation of something to its future consequences (Groopman, 2005; James, 1956). When we expect the future to be the same as the present, we feel familiarity rather than strangeness in our situation (James, 1956). To expect a different future requires entertaining novelty; we engage strangeness in imagining new possibilities.

Integrating this conception of hope with analyses of how leaders and front line clinicians transformed inpatient care and achieved breakthrough results benefiting patients, families, and staff, we inductively generated a conceptual model of hope as generative dynamic in transformational change, depicted in Figure 12.1. Hope is comprised of two key processes associated with expectations about possibilities for change: activating belief that collective action to create a better care model can make a positive difference to the lives of patients, and acting on belief to realize desired change. In generating hope, the first process results in a loosening of prior expectations about how care delivery happens, thereby positioning people to entertain novel possibilities. Through the creation of an alternative that makes a difference, the second process cultivates new expectations for care delivery and enables trust to develop among clinicians and in the model. Together, these processes enable hope as generative dynamic, altering the change trajectory by helping people prevail in realizing the different and desired future of delivering care.

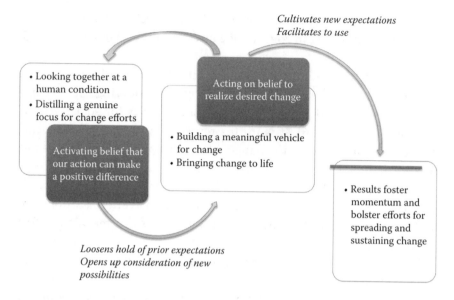

FIGURE 12.1

Hope as generative dynamic in creating transformational change.

CREATING AND SUSTAINING "COLLABORATIVE CARE"

Activating Belief that Action Can Make a Positive Difference

For me, collaborative care started way before the events and the idea of what the actual model is. It started when I went to lead the hospital, and that was at the end of 2003. I saw my job as … bringing out the best of the organization, making sure that the absolute integrity of the hospital is there, and that we would be relevant in 10 to 15 years. And so I was looking around for that. I was searching the hospital to say, what is it that is most important? What is it that has to be right? … So if you look at an integrated system and you look at the continuum of care, what is the most important thing a hospital contributes to that, versus the many things that we do? When I [started searching] the hospital seemed more like a collection of many things, radiology, lab, outpatient surgery, respiratory therapy. And they were each sort of in their own little clusters. I couldn't yet understand what was the essential business. (President)

This quote highlights three central elements in not only the president's early efforts but also in others' efforts to transform inpatient care. First, although the more apparent and visible work of change is designing the actual care model, much of the effort that laid important groundwork occurred "way before." As will be profiled, this also holds true for the efforts of nursing leaders who sought early on to create opportunities for change in patient care. Second, the president's early "looking around" involved closely looking at current reality while imagining future possibilities by asking what "has to be right" as well as what would "bring out the best of the organization," the "absolute integrity of the hospital" and assure its future relevance. Attention to these suggested that only change of a particular kind would suffice. Change needed to be genuine in ThedaCare: strongly connected with and emerging from the people and organizational context. Finally, "looking around" at the reality and possibilities of such change is an embodied as well as cognitive effort; individuals take in and soak up their surroundings by perceiving through senses; hearing, smelling, seeing. It is what is heard, seen, touched, and felt in experience that helps guide the figuring out of possibilities for change.

Looking Together at the Shared World

In addition to the president's efforts, a series of experiences came together during 2004–2005, helping people look together at their world of care, and articulate the need "to do something about" patient care. As one nurse manager described,

> It was the people, it was the dying passion of people like us going, we've got to do something about this, and trying to get the right people's ear. And I give credit to our VP of nursing for saying, "I get it. I see what you're saying." And then she bent the ear of our president who also got it and said "OK, yes".... All this passion is what drove us to open the lights.

Similarly, the VP of nursing to whom the nurse manager referred, shared how "very excited" she was to learn in her conversation with the president that they both "saw it the same way." And the president echoed the VP's enthusiasm:

> Every patient in our hospitals relies on the compassion and clinical expertise of their nurse at the bedside. While other clinicians are critical, it is the nurse who provides ongoing care throughout the patient's stay with us.

One of the earliest experiences of looking together involved a broad group of clinicians and leaders taking part in a "lean event" held to "figure out the hospital" and to get a handle on admission. Through this experience, those involved began to realize that while they wanted to deliver the best care, the current efforts were "vague" at best, chaotic at worst, and most often it was taking nursing "heroics" to get the patients through the system. They vividly saw the need to change care delivery.

> And what we figured sitting through that event, listening to the nurses, and going up on the floor and watching nurses try to get a patient from the beginning to the end—that it was really heroics. That coming in, the plans were very vague about what was going to happen to that patient ... Everyone had their own plan .... We understood how the doctors could decide to admit a patient to the hospital, but we really didn't understand how we actually got patients to leave.... It just seemed very chaotic, and almost by chance. (President)[1]

Multiple conversations ensued between hospital leadership and clinicians. For example, nurses wanted to deliver the best inpatient nursing care with integrity and so that,

> no one would have to ever fear coming to the hospital; would never feel that sort of alone in the middle of the night, when it's dark and you don't know that everyone has your best interest; that you would always feel safe.

Nurses began to share more candidly how chaotic and unsatisfying it was for them in trying to pull all patient care together without a clear sense of a plan. Yet, they also expressed a sense that a real chance for change was emerging. A nurse manager explained that awhile back she and the education manager had created a white paper detailing a different approach to inpatient care. Only now was the white paper being resurrected as experiences came together suggesting that action could make a real and positive difference.

Nursing leadership initiated a series of clinical forums for an even broader range of clinicians—"any clinical person giving care"—to help them look closely at the range of disconnects happening in care, and to see the possibility to do something about the situation. As one nurse commented,

> ...we have all these complaints, we can't solve them. And so we said, OK, to lead this work, we have to make sure that front-line staff is seeing what we're seeing.

---

[1] All quoted material in this section and next was collected from interviews with the authors conducted during the term of the study.

In the forum, nursing leadership read complaint letters from patients and then wondered aloud, "Do you think this happened in our organization?" A nurse leader described the audience response,

> And you could see the audience of different types of clinicians going, mm-hm. There was almost like this fear of speaking up to say, I feel so unsafe practicing here. There are so many things we're doing, that kind of stuff. And we really got the shaking heads. And we got the engagement.

The nurses asked two more questions of the audience: "Does everybody believe that we can do much better in the kind of care we give?" and "Does everybody believe we need to work on this?" The response was a unanimous yes, which made them proclaim, "We've got to do this."

Distilling a Genuine Focus for Change

Two defining events began to move efforts beyond looking together at the current reality to distilling a focus for change efforts, as contextualized in ThedaCare hospitals. First, the president used a hospital leadership retreat in 2004 to propose that inpatient nursing care become the focus of their change efforts. Those present included directors and managers from across the hospital and significantly not only those responsible for inpatient care, but also those who managed outpatient and emergency departments. In preparing for the meeting, the president thought they would consider the proposal and then discuss its rationale in subsequent meetings. However, the response was overwhelmingly enthusiastic, even from those outside of realm of inpatient care. The president explained,

> It's the oddest thing, as a leader, sometimes when you put things out there, you don't know how much it sinks into people. But it was clear that this one they really took it to heart.... It's like a lot of energy. That's the way I'd describe it.... When we talked about the focus at the meeting.... There was a huge amount of energy. It was, OK, let's go.... There was a lot of trust that it would work. Yeah, so we had this intuitive thing that they surprisingly gravitated toward doing, the excitement around it, the idea that this was our focus. I mean, and I remember particular physicians, one is in charge of our cardiac services, which are mostly outpatient, and another who is in radiology and outpatient, say they would help support. They weren't saying, well, I guess I'm not important anymore. They just kind of pitched in.

Leadership collectively embraced the idea that as respected as they were for outpatient services, and as much as it was paying their bills, they needed to focus first on inpatient care. During the rest of the meeting, they discussed the difference a focus on inpatient care would make and how they would know when they achieved optimal care. Reflecting on this meeting later, one hospital leader commented,

> It has been very rewarding being involved from the very beginning. So I was there when we decided collectively to try to shoot for a big breakthrough improvement in inpatient care.

One direct result of the leadership retreat was to hold an "enterprise value stream event" in order to get a better understanding of patient flow in the entire hospital system. Managers from every division and area occupied a large room to literally make a high level map of outpatient, emergency, and inpatient flows. The disconnection in flows across delivery services became clear to all present. As leaders present at this event shared:

> For a week long, we invited volunteers and foundation board members and patients to sit with us ... to get the very highest level flow, and some basics about each care line. What is the flow? And you walk the flow.... You walk each one separately. It was very revealing.... We found out walking the outpatient flow that it was interfering with the inpatient flow. And the outpatient world, it was really not very patient friendly at all. When you walked it as a patient, you understood that if you were bringing elderly people into the hospital, then they were walking way too much for their abilities to get their testing done.

> The separation between inpatient and outpatient was much bigger than we even realized at the time. I mean, that was a big "aha." So it sort of validated our intuition of the separateness between inpatient and outpatient, and that they really, in supporting inpatient and outpatient, we were doing neither very well.

This "aha" further affirmed their focus on inpatient care. Others commented,

> This event affirmed our decision to emphasize inpatient care. So, when we looked at inpatient care, even though other areas had issues, inpatient care was so broken that we agreed that's the first thing we need to fix ... our first "aha" was, if we don't fix inpatient care, we can't do the rest of it.

The leadership retreat, enterprise value stream event, and other conversations helped leaders distill and affirm the focus of change on inpatient care delivery. This focus was perceived as genuine both in its clear sightedness into the reality of care disconnections and potential obstacles, as well as in its promise to make a positive difference in care delivery. Hospital leadership identified compelling reasons for beginning with inpatient services:

- While all patients are exposed to risk, inpatients are at a higher risk due to their compromised health status and extended length of exposure.
- Patients' safety and peace of mind depend largely upon inpatient nurses who render professional care, comfort, and reassurance. Medical staff relies on inpatient nurses to provide assessment and judgment regarding patients' condition and progress.
- As ambulatory care migrates to non-hospital settings, the majority of the hospital's future business will be inpatient care. The value proposition of inpatient care needs to increase in order to remain viable in the future.
- Publicly reported quality indicators focusing on inpatient care. (excerpt from ThedaCare document)

As a hospital leader later commented,

At the time I'm not sure I understood it, but now I would say that the focus on inpatient care was one that was important, not on a bottom line or doctor, not on cardiac, neuro, or other [condition specific] basis. Rather, it was on, What is the right thing to do for all of our patients?

The first process—activating belief that collective action to create a better care model can make a positive difference—generates hope that action is not totally at the mercy of outside forces whether inside the organization or in society. The everyday experiences in which clinicians and leaders in ThedaCare hospitals engaged the reality of disconnects and distilled a genuine focus for change can be seen as hope-generating acts. They helped people begin to see and to take a chance on their efforts making a real and positive difference in care delivery. In generating hope, this process results in a loosening of prior expectations about care delivery, thereby positioning people to open up consideration of new possibilities (Carlsen & Pitsis, 2009). Consider the overwhelming enthusiasm in the retreat when hospital leaders first heard the proposed focus on inpatient care. Here, hope is a future-oriented and emotive quality of experience (Carlsen et al., 2011) that acted in energizing those present.

Acting on Belief to Realize Desired Change

As well as activating belief that action can make a difference, "projects [for change] must be acted on to realize their projective powers" (Carlsen & Pitsis, 2009, p. 91). For Collaborative Care to be realized, clinicians and leaders needed to act on their belief that they could create an alternative model; one that enabled patients to "truly pull care to the bedside."

Building a Meaningful Vehicle for Change

Embracing inpatient care, hospital staff in conversation with leadership undertook the building of a new model. In their first event, a "vertical value stream" mapping of the inpatient care process, clinicians and hospital leadership became aware of the multitude of ways that kept patients in the hospital with little consistency of work directed toward helping them get out. An "aha" moment occurred when they realized that for optimal care, they would need to create a new process that moved the patient through the system. The chief nursing officer described this insight:

> We realized at a different and deeper level that the old process was oriented to justifying patient stay in the hospital. We needed a different process— one that focused on optimal recovery and on pulling the patient through the hospital system.

In the ensuing months they worked without much pause to build the model. Patients were invited to share their ideas and perspectives on what would be their ideal health care experience. Deep conversations ensued among patients, clinicians, and hospital leaders that surfaced issues never before discussed. For example, patients shared the confusion that resulted from not being given even basic information such as what was wrong with them or if they were permitted to see their family. They also shared how uncomfortable it was to lie helplessly in a strange bed with different providers at different times asking them the same question. One patient told clinicians, "I want to feel you are all working together. If I don't feel this, I'm not sure you know what you are doing!"

The shape of a new model of care emerged based in a different patient experience linked with a different form of clinical relationships: collaborating in care at the bedside as enabling the patient to get well. Leadership and clinicians began to consider elements that could become part of the model. A nursing manager described this process:

> It was our pie in the sky kind of stuff. And we made it happen. We got very, very close to what we said was the idealistic there.... We created it right there and said, it's the team together, it's, you know, one electronic medical record together, one plan of care for the patient.

They could have built the model differently, dismissing the idea of patients pulling care to the bedside. But, in the end, they did not. The nursing manager continues,

> I mean, we could have easily said, oh, we'll never get the physicians there, OK, we'll all still admit that way, and then we'll talk to each other later on. But we said no, we're going to be in the room together, we're all going to hear the patient's story together, we're all going to react together, we're all going to put the plan of care together. I mean, it really anchored us ... we never would have gotten pharmacists there if we hadn't held on to the importance of them being there. You know, it was almost like, pinky swear, we're doing this, you guys. And everybody committing to this no matter how hard, we were going to make it happen because we thought this was the anchor to the whole model. So you can see how passionate I am about that!

Figure 12.2 depicts the model built by the team of clinicians and hospital leaders. The care process is represented as a series of horizontal care phases that fit the patient's unique condition and help clinicians to progress care. Upon admission, a coordinated care team of a nurse, pharmacist, and physician—dubbed *TRIO*—meet together in the new patient's room for a bedside conference.

With the patient and family, the TRIO conducts the admitting assessment including education and discharge plans. Together, they create a single plan of care which outlines the sequencing of care to be delivered. It is in essence an agreement among all clinicians that care should progress in the way outlined in the plan and that all clinicians will follow. Updating

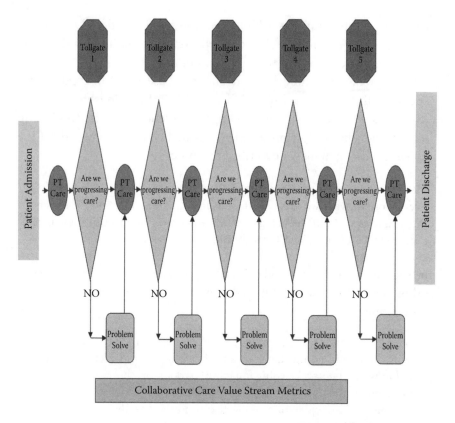

FIGURE 12.2
Collaborative Care patient care progression. (The system and method of Collaborative Care is patented. With permission from ThedaCare.)

of the care plan is triggered by "tollgates," or stopping points marking the end of each phase of a patient's stay.

The idea of using Tollgates™ emerged during the planning meetings. A nurse describes the process,

> In our planning meetings, we asked: How are we going to make sure that what we said should happen to a patient is indeed going to happen?...We learned that there's a tool in lean called the tollgate tool.... You can't pass this tollgate until you make sure all ... is addressed.... So we thought about applying this idea for the first time to patient care. And then what we really did is line up all the things that had to be done for a patient that were usually scattered.... We really lined them up to make sense....We identify what

needs to happen for this patient in this amount of time. Only then can we say we're moving on. And if it's not done, we're pulling the trigger...

Tollgates are built into the care plan and enabled by an electronic medical record that is accessible to all clinicians. The RN is prompted by this record to assess whether or not the specified tollgates have been met. If all is well, the nurse progresses the patient to the next phase. If not, then the nurse determines the reason and works with relevant clinicians to solve the problem and get the appropriate care. Tollgates not only give the nurse authority to call clinicians to the bedside under circumstances specified in the care plan but also represent junctures to reassess the care process.

So the tollgate is, I've got all this stuff that needs to be done, it's not done, I'm pulling the cord, problem solving this and getting it resolved. So CAT scan, tests not done. Why isn't it done? Pull the cord, get all my resources I need to solve the issue before I can move on.

BRINGING CHANGE TO LIFE

Beyond building general elements of the model, all involved undertook substantial effort to bring the model more fully and vibrantly to life. In particular, they distilled differences with Collaborative Care that transformed its potential for desired change into actuality. In this text, we describe particular differences highlighted in the interviews.

Real-Time Enactment of Collaborative Care

In contrast to prevailing care models in which clinicians meet separately with the patient and only later get together to review the case, in Collaborative Care the clinicians meet together in real time with the patient. In this respect, the clinical members of the TRIO vitalize the model each and every time they enter the patient room and work together face-to-face with the patient and family. Enacting the model in real time creates clinician vulnerability and loss of control, especially for physicians, as one describes:

the other big change for us is having input from other clinicians.... I want to say challenged ... having a pharmacist there saying, you know this medication's going to interact, or that dose.... Where we struggle is the loss of control, some loss of autonomy to a degree. You can't just walk in and start seeing patients, you've got to wait for the team to assemble.... Now I've got a team really attached to me, and that has been an adjustment for a number of physicians.... Typically, we're pretty autonomous and we don't like to be told what to do. And now all of a sudden well it's...you can't do it that way, we really need you to do it this way.

Clinicians pointed to this real-time feature as "definitely a role changer." Yet, they also recognized that providing patients understanding to use in promoting their own healing during their stay results in patients paying greater attention to their care progression, as conveyed to the TRIO in this comment: "Oh, you said this would take away my swelling but it didn't—I thought I should ask..."

Continuous Tracking of Delays in Progressing Care

Building the idea of tollgates into Collaborative Care creates a new expectation that progress in care will be monitored according to the single plan of care. Delays are tracked and handled, and Tollgates *trigger* the mindful updating of care progress. "Assessment of care doesn't just happen at the beginning or the end of a patient's stay. It happens every day and virtually at every Tollgate" (President). Further, in the clinician agreement to gather when the nurse pulls the cord based on a care plan deviation, tollgates direct the authority for care toward the patient.

The authority [to pull the cord] is given through that joint understanding of the plan of care created at the bedside. It's, we all agree on this plan of care, and if it's not going to go right, call me. I need to know what's not happening here. (Nurse Manager)

Defects still exist in the Collaborative Care model, but through the tollgate mechanism, each is now recognized, recorded, prioritized, and solved. They are considered beneficial as they draw attention to areas in need of adjustment for optimal care delivery. Some nurses shared:

It still wasn't perfect, I mean, we still did work-arounds and we still have a lot of missed toll gates, but it's given us a ton of information to go back ... and say ... it was a missed tollgate.... If we couldn't make that happen, what could we do to at least get to the best possible point that we needed to get to for the patient?

Physicians ordered this lab test, but we can't get it. Now, instead of nurses trying to manage the situation and make the things happen, we examine what the department is going to do to meet what was expected for that patient.... So care's not driven by what the therapy can deliver, but it's driven by what the patient needs. That's a whole different paradigm shift.

Thus, the tollgates make a positive difference in care by moving the authority of care to the bedside and by assuring continuous tracking of care plan deviations. Together, the TRIO and tollgate generate continuing hope in Collaborative Care as desired change.

Space redesign

I had just visited a friend who was in a semiprivate room, and I was appalled. I was just appalled. How could you get well when your neighbor next to you was moaning and groaning and all that?... Up until that point, we had been sort of going unit by unit refreshing our inpatient units, but not doing anything significant.... Then as we started going through Collaborative Care, we said, well, we don't need to just refresh them. We need to totally change them. (President)

Redesigning the physical space of the unit and patient rooms also vividly differentiated Collaborative Care from the prior way of delivering care. As expressed in this quote, the hospital president began to wonder how someone could get well "when your neighbor next to you was moaning and groaning...." Concurrently, people creating the model recognized that current patient rooms provided neither the privacy nor space for the TRIO to talk comfortably with the patient and patient's family.

A subgroup was formed to link with a hospital-wide renovation initiative to address the redesign of space for Collaborative Care. They visited newer hospitals and picked up ways to incorporate safety into space design such as needing to put gases on the same side of the bed in the same order, or installing showers stalls without lips. Senior leadership secured a substantial donation from a board member to cover the additional costs of redesigning the space.

Patient rooms were enlarged to accommodate the patient, family, and TRIO. A white grease board, used to post test results and next steps in the care plan, was placed on the wall in full view of the patient. Telephones were attached to the bed rail for easy accessibility. The bathrooms had a new type of rubber flooring that provided better grounding for patients in their socks. There were sinks in each room located to be accessible to clinicians providing care.

The unit was redesigned so that clinicians could more readily and visually identify any problems. In the place of a nursing station was a central area visible from all rooms. Open alcoves were designed into the unit for the TRIO and other clinicians to "huddle" and discuss patient care. Instead of the old laundry hampers in the hallways, newly designed supply servers were installed in the walls of each patient room. Containing over 80% of needed supplies, these servers are stocked outside the room and are accessible inside the room. Nurses describe how the open space and servers allow them to focus more attention on patients. Whereas in the past, they had to "hunt," "gather," and even "hoard" necessary supplies, now those supplies are automatically stocked. A study conducted after the first unit opened found that nurses saved three to four hours of time per shift by not having to hunt for supplies. A clinical nurse assistant described how this happens:

> In my experience it's nice because for us we don't run like we used to run. I'm a nursing assistant, and all our supplies are in the [server] so whatever we need we just get them out of there.... We used to run for everything, and it was a waste of time because you're running looking for things constantly. This way we have more time for patient. I can now help patients with all their cares, I walk them, and help them do simple things ... teach them things.

Thus, space redesign vitalized the new idea of "collaborating" in care.

Trialing

> Each (of us) needs to see it, feel it, touch it, give input on it. Come to consensus ... you can't just walk in one day having had someone else develop it for you. (Physician)

> Until you actually go and do it, you don't know what you don't know. (Pharmacist)

As expressed in these quotes, trialing the model before "going live" on the first unit was an important and different experience in creating Collaborative Care. Experiencing the model, feeling and seeing it in action, enabled clinicians to get more familiar with its novelty. And through their experiencing of it, they developed new understanding of what they would expect of each other, and began to concretely see the difference their actions would make in patient care.

Although there were small trials undertaken of model sub-processes using existing or mocked up patient rooms, the most significant trialing comprised a six-week offsite session that took place just prior to the "go live" date of the new model. A first in ThedaCare, nurses (all shifts) who would staff the initial Collaborative Care unit were taken offline to participate in trialing the model and team building. Physicians and pharmacists joined the offsite for intensive periods of time equaling two of the six weeks. Senior leadership support and nursing leadership's commitment to the trialing effort were so strong that the expense of the time out was not debated in the larger system.

Going offsite and using vacant space, a mocked up "Collaborative Care" unit was created that included patient rooms, servers, and central space. Using volunteers as patients, the clinicians together trained on and practiced the new processes. In addition, the new unit's nursing staff engaged in team building exercises designed by internal organizational development experts. With an organizational development (OD) specialist, nursing staff explored how their roles and responsibilities would be different in the Collaborative Care model. In particular, they re-envisioned the nursing role as partner with pharmacists and physicians. As the OD specialist shared,

> This is a different challenge for nursing staff who may have perceived themselves in a more dependent role, as opposed to a partner role with a pharmacist and physician ... to be able to give and receive feedback to other members of that professional team, especially if something is not going well.

By contrast, Collaborative Care challenged pharmacists and physicians to let go of tasks that other clinicians could perform, trusting them to do the tasks correctly. Pharmacists shared,

> We were holding onto a lot of things that nurses were already double-checking and that the doctors were double-checking, so we needed to build more trust that it's being covered.

> Yes, it's tough to let go of because you want to make sure you're doing the right thing for the patient and the ball is not getting dropped somewhere.

And I think having the face-to-face contact with the nurses and doctors makes that easier. You can see it being done versus assuming that it's being done correctly.

A physician shared:

I was somewhat skeptical of the nurse being in the room with me, the pharmacist being in the room with me, and why.... Trialing was incredibly important to say, OK, how does the flow work, do we do this first, do we do this second. Are all the pieces of information right? So, really to run through with a few mock patients to make sure that you're ... practiced so it'll go smoother when you get real patients. And secondly, I think just to make sure that it worked the way you thought it was going to work. So we did that ... before we even opened ... that's pretty critical.

Indeed, the manager who worked in the area of physician engagement noted that trialing made "the biggest difference" in helping them accept being in a team with nurses and pharmacists in the patient's room. She explained:

I saw this big "aha" ... that they truly were in a team and that the pharmacist and nurse had something to add and contribute and challenge them. And that this is really different from rounds because on rounds you're kind of on show and this is more, you are thinking differently. And on rounds you're thinking differently about your peers because it's more like you are doing your thing and you might be speaking out loud or whatever. On rounds it's not even really like you're collaborating.

Similarly, the OD specialist observed:

The physicians now speak about the learning that they've had from a pharmacist being there and the nurses as well. They see themselves as teachers, to help the team learn. Those are different relationships than the telling and doing and sending off orders.

In assembling clinicians to experiment together with the new model, trialing activated belief among those clinicians still sitting on the fence. It also fostered trust among clinicians in creating the new model. As one physician noted, "It works. It really works."

In the second process—acting on belief to realize desired change—clinicians and leaders invented an alternative model to make a positive difference in care delivery. By building a meaningful vehicle in the form of Collaborative Care, and bringing it to life, they created a different and better future in which care would be pulled to the bedside by the patient, assembling people and resources needed to get the patient well. In the process, clinicians would become members of a TRIO who shared a single care plan and trusted each other to fulfill their responsibilities. Clinicians described the most salient differences in their early "live" experiences with the new model:

> So I've seen both sides of the world. And the difference is, with Collaborative Care … there's better communication. The patient has a better experience. You have all the supplies that you need.… There is a decrease in infection rate, decrease in cost, a decrease in just about every aspect of nursing that we want a decrease in. And, you know, the whole mentality, teamwork, and mindset of other staff toward each other is different as well. I think it's, you know, the mindset basically is we all have a goal and it's to get the patient the best care that they need. (Clinical Nurse Assistant)

> Working on Collaborative Care, there's dramatically less family conflict and confusion.… What typically happens in the real world doesn't happen on the Collaborative Care Unit.… We're there and we're visible.… It's just that communication piece with family and patient, it's much better. (Physician)

> I noticed pretty immediately … a lot of the little things that, well, I wouldn't call them little things.… Just the level of respect when I was shadowing that the nurses were given by the physicians, and how they all worked together … there were times when the doctor would pause, and get input from them, like it was expected. Like they valued what nurses had to say. I thought immediately of the times I had to try and hunt down physicians, and finding them trying to get two seconds to say what you had to say about a patient. A big difference. (Registered Nurse)

DISCUSSION

In this chapter, we explored how leaders, together with front line clinicians, undertook change to transform care so that it is more beneficial for patients, their families, and society. In ThedaCare hospitals, clinicians and leaders dedicated substantial, committed, and enthusiastic effort to designing and realizing Collaborative Care, an innovative care delivery process that is creating patient care outcomes and satisfaction demonstrably better than with like patients on non-Collaborative Care units. The differences in Collaborative Care are readily noticeable and felt, and this palpable difference continues to generate hope in all those who visit, become patients, and/or work there.

Our inductive conceptual model proposes hope as an important generative dynamic in creating transformational change consisting of two main processes—activating belief that action can make a positive difference and acting on belief to realize desired change—and the associated loosening of prior expectations to make room for and cultivate new expectations. As the case and the feedback loops in Figure 12.1 suggest, these processes are interdependent rather than sequential in nature because efforts to activate belief unfold continuously in experience as individuals begin to see how their action could make a positive difference.

Accessing and Theorizing Generative Dynamics in Change

Generative dynamics and transformational change are deeply related. We cannot "enlarge our understanding of [a] human condition" (Weick, 2007, p. 18), "produce something of value to society" (Carlsen & Dutton, 2011, p. 16), or challenge prevailing expectations and create "fresh alternatives" (Gergen, 1978, p. 1356) in the absence of generative dynamics. Yet, our theories about change are curiously silent on the matter. Our field has begun to develop a process view of change that brings forward the fluidity and open-endedness of people's efforts, and this view has improved theorizing about what goes on in-between the more traditionally examined steps along a trajectory of change (Langley, 1999; 2000; Tsoukas & Chia, 2002). But as scholars in this field, we have not yet undertaken a similar development in our change theories to examine generative dynamics as a particular form of process that illuminates the centrally human endeavor of people in a community engaging pressing social issues with inventive and creative responses.

This chapter takes a first step by developing hope as generative dynamic in transformational change. Leaders and clinicians in ThedaCare hospitals looked collectively and with clear sight (Groopman, 2005) at their care delivery during meetings, offsite trialing of the model, clinical forums, conversations, and other experiences. They not only interacted with each other, but interacted with each other about a genuine human condition in their shared world (Deetz, 2008) of inpatient care. This was not easy; many clinicians spoke about being vulnerable in front of the patient, for example, or not knowing what to expect from each other. Yet, these efforts enabled them to challenge prevailing expectations about how care is and could be delivered, and to consider new and fresh alternatives. In creating Collaborative Care, they had imagined and realized a different and better future. Hope helped leaders and clinicians "grab [the] will to believe" (Carlsen & Dutton, 2011, p. 5; James, 1956) in themselves and in their future—in spite of a skeptical environment in healthcare.

Proposing hope as generative mechanism also provokes researcher reflection on how we "think and talk about the worlds" we study (Deetz, 2008; Gergen, 1978; Ludema et al., 1997) and write about in our work. Hope enriches our theorizing by providing expansive language that helps us notice, access, and explain what is significant and meaningful enough to people that they dedicate amazing effort, open themselves to vulnerability, and fully engage in an inventive endeavor to create a better future. In this respect, hope as generative mechanism is not an isolated event experienced in the efforts of leaders and clinicians profiled in this chapter. Hope is potentially present more generally in all efforts to create a better and desired future. Its promise can be accessed in organizations as shown in this study, when people come to believe through experience that their actions can and do make a positive difference.

Incorporating Generative Dynamics in Leading Transformational Change

What are the implications of generative dynamics such as hope for leading transformational change? We saw in the present case how hospital leaders established a context that enabled people to activate belief that their action would make a difference through encouraging new ideas and experiences that prompted reflection on prevailing assumptions and expectations. We also saw how leaders cultivated conditions for people to act on belief in designing the new model of care that included offsite trialing, space redesign, and incorporating the innovative elements of TRIO and tollgates. The portrait of leader work in this case is quite different from those prevailing in the business press and implied in episodic theories of change. We develop two insights for leading transformational change based in this different portrait.

Incorporating generative mechanisms requires a different style of leading; one that shifts focus away from the leader and toward creating interactions with each other that bring visibility to human conditions people experience as significant and needing attention. These are human conditions that matter in the shared world, as with inpatient care delivery in the present case. In this scenario, change comes about by humans creating something new to resolve the human condition, rather than about leaders moving people through defined steps. This scenario is riskier for leaders because in not knowing exactly how the change effort will turn out, they become vulnerable much as the clinicians did when enacting the TRIO. To enact generative mechanisms in change, then, requires leaders to become comfortable with uncertainty, trusting people to create something of more value.

Incorporating generative mechanisms illuminates that transformational change, even in its subsequent spread to other units or organizations, cannot just be about implementing a given solution; that is taking change "A" and putting it into a different setting. If we take seriously that generative dynamics are constitutive of transformational change efforts, then everyone needs to engage the human condition in their shared world, and be afforded the opportunity to "grab their will to believe" that action can make a positive difference. This means that people need time to interact with each other around the condition as they realize desired change for a new context. It recognizes that generative dynamics can and do transform relationships and meanings as people create change. And it illuminates trialing as central to spreading change because it enables people to get to know what to expect of each other, and to grow in trust with each other and in the solution being created.

CONCLUSION

In the face of societal problems, it can be a daunting endeavor to see possibilities for achieving a different and better future. We feel hopeless in our ability to effect change. Although a desire for a better future is a vital part of our human society, we often disbelieve that our action can make a difference. Vibrant examples such as Collaborative Care show us the importance of cultivating generative dynamics in change in reconnecting our desire for a better future with believing that action can make a positive difference. Seen from this vantage point, generative mechanisms such as hope are the heart of transformational change.

ACKNOWLEDGMENTS

A conversation with Bill Kahn helped to illuminate the significance of "hope" for understanding people's efforts in creating Collaborative Care. We also greatly appreciate the multiple readings and feedback on earlier drafts by Jane Dutton and Elana Feldman. And finally, we are indebted to all the participants who created and implemented Collaborative Care for sharing their insights and helping us learn about how they made a positive difference in transforming care.

REFERENCES

Baggs, J. G., Norton, S. A., Schmitt, M. H., & Sellers, C. R. (2004). The dying patient in the ICU: Role of the interdisciplinary team. *Critical Care Clinics, 20*, 525–540.

Carlsen, A., & Dutton, J. E. (2011). Research alive: The call for generativity. In A. Carlsen & J. E. Dutton (Eds.), *Research alive: Exploring generative moments in doing qualitative research* (pp. 12–24). Copenhagen: Business School Press.

Carlsen, A., Hagen, A. L., & Mortensen, T. F. (2011). Imagining hope in organizations: From individual goal-attainment to horizons of relational possibility. In K. S. Cameron & G. Spreitzer (Eds.), *Handbook of positive organizational scholarship* (p. 298). New York: Oxford University Press.

Carlsen, A., & Pitsis, T. (2009). Experiencing hope in organizational lives. In L. M. Roberts & J. E. Dutton (Eds.). *Exploring positive identities* (pp. 77–98). New York: Taylor-Francis Group.

Cohen, J. J. (2000). Collaborative care: A new model for a new century. *Academic Medicine, 75*, 107–112.

Davies, M. A., McBride, L., & Sajatovic, M. (2008). The collaborative care practice model in the long-term care of individuals with bipolar disorder: A case study. *Journal of Psychiatric and Mental Health Nursing, 15*, 649–653.

Deetz, S. (2008). Engagement as co-generative theorizing. *Journal of Applied Communication Research, 36*, 289–297.

Gergen, K. J. (1978). Toward generative theory. *Journal of Personality and Social Psychology, 36*, 1344–1360.

Groopman, J. (2005). *The anatomy of hope: How people prevail in the face of illness.* New York: Random House.

Howard-Grenville, J., Golden-Biddle, K., Irwin, J., & Mao, J. (2011). Liminality as cultural process for cultural change. *Organization Science, 22*, 522–539.

James, W. (1956). *The will to believe*. New York: Dover Publications.

Kaiser Permanente (2010). *Innovation*. Retrieved October 2010 from http://www.kaiserper manentejobs.org/innovation.aspx.

Kotter, J. (1996). *The Heart of change: Real-life stories of how people change their organizations*. Boston: Harvard Business School Press.

Langley, A. (1999). Strategies for theorizing from process data. *Academy of Management Review, 24*, 691.

Langley, A. (2009). Studying processes in and around organizations. In D. A. Buchanan & A. Bryman (Eds.), *Sage handbook of organizational research methods* (pp. 409–429). London: SAGE Publications.

Lewin, K. (1947). *Field theory in social science: Selected theoretical papers*. New York: Harper & Row.

Ludema, J. D., Wilmot, T. B., & Srivastva, S. (1997). Organizational hope: Reaffirming the constructive task of social and organizational inquiry. *Human Relations, 50*, 1015–1052.

Mayo Clinic. (2010). *Center for innovation*. Retrieved October 2010 from http://centerfor innovation.mayo.edu/.

Paulus, R. A., Davis, K., & Steele, G. D. (2008). Continuous innovation in health care: Implications of the Geisinger experience. *Health Affairs, 27*, 1235–1245.

Plowman, D. A., Baker, L. T., Beck, T. E., Kulkarni, M., Solansky, S. T., & Travis, D. V. (2007). Radical change accidentally: The emergence and amplification of small change. *Academy of Management Journal, 50*, 515.

Reay, T., Golden-Biddle, K., & GermAnn, K. (2006). Legitimizing a new role: Small wins and micro-processes of change. *Academy of Management Journal, 49*, 977–998.

Scott, E., & Cowen, B. (1997). Multidisciplinary collaborative care planning. *Nursing Standard, 12*, 39–42.

Stobbe, M. (2010, September 30). CDC chief picks 6 winnable battles in health. *Washington Times*. Retrieved from http://www.washingtontimes.com/news/2010/sep/30/ cdc-chief-picks-6-winnable-battles-in-health/

Swidler, A. (1986). Culture in action: Symbols and strategies. *American Sociological Review, 51*, 273–286.

Tsoukas, H., & Chia, R. (2002). On organizational becoming: Rethinking organizational change. *Organization Science, 13*, 567–582.

Weick, K. E. (2007). The generative properties of richness. *Academy of Management Journal, 50*, 14–19.

Weick, K. E., & Quinn, R. E. (1999). Organizational change and development. *Annual Review of Psychology, 50*, 361.

13

Promoting Positive Change in Physician–Administrator Relationships: The Importance of Identity Security in Managing Intractable Identity Conflicts

Michael G. Pratt
Boston College

C. Marlene Fiol and Edward J. O'Connor
University of Colorado Denver

Paul Panico
Cheyenne Regional Medical Center

While debates have ensued regarding the best solutions for improving health care in the United States, everyone seems to agree that the United States spends more per capita on health care than any other industrialized nation but ranks among the lowest on health-care effectiveness. Essentially, we pay more but receive poorer results than our peers. Certainly change is needed. But rather than focusing on institutional-level changes, our focus here is on *intergroup dynamics*. Specifically, we hone in on one primary reason for the current health-care woes in the United States: the quality of intergroup physician–administrator relationships.

Examining documented conflicts in this relationship seems logical from a resource-based perspective. First, administrators are often charged with the economic viability of hospitals and health-care systems, and physician-controlled expenditures account for the majority of medical costs in hospitals (Fiol & O'Connor, 2009). Second, economic pressures experienced by both physicians (declining volumes, professional fee cuts, rise in practice costs, etc.) and hospitals (continued cost pressures, declining reimbursement, payer mix shifts, and looming physician shortages) will continue to create a greater urgency for enhanced cooperation between physicians and administrators. Third, with the reform-based development of new accountable care models and payment systems, the risks for cost utilization and quality performance will shift to providers. This places a premium on hospital-physician alignment as a means to achieving better coordination and efficient and ultimately higher quality care. Even modest shifts in the traditional fee-for-service payment paradigm toward pay-for-performance and clinical outcomes will require significant engagement of physicians by hospitals to improve the overall cost effectiveness and quality of care. Simply put, only those health systems that are able to overcome the poor quality of intergroup physician–administrator relationships will survive and thrive in the uncertain environment of health-care reform.

We further believe that to improve physician–administrator relationships, you have to focus squarely on identity. Conflicts among physicians and administrators are not tied exclusively to resource usage. Rather, they are often linked to issues of "who we are" and "who we aren't." The negative identity linkages between physicians and administrators make these conflicts seemingly intractable, and make traditional solutions for their resolution untenable (Fiol, Pratt, & O'Connor, 2009). *Intractable identity conflicts* are ongoing and pervasive conflicts that exist when two or more groups are bound together in a state of mutual disidentification. That is, each group defines itself, at least in part, as <u>not</u> being part of the other group (see Fiol et al., 2009, for a review). A classic example on the world scene might be Northern Ireland, where being Irish Catholic means not being Irish Protestant. In the sports world, being a Red Sox fan means that one must never cheer for the New York Yankees and vice versa. One of the implications of mutual disidentification is that the parties are locked together in an ongoing cycle of mistrust and zero-sum thinking whereby a gain for one party is seen as a loss for the other.

Many physicians and administrators are locked in intractable identity conflicts. From the decades of combined experience of our authors, we have learned that physicians see themselves as not being administrators, whom physicians view as financially motivated, profit-oriented, non-clinical experts who make medical decisions and waste time on non-essential activities (e.g., paperwork). Administrators, in turn, do not see themselves as physicians, whom they view as egotistical, narcissistic, financially self-interested individuals with a strong need to always "win." These negative identity dynamics are bolstered by deep differences in the values and beliefs held by each group. Physicians, for example, view themselves as members of an "expert culture" of autonomous, fast-paced decision makers (Atchison & Bujak, 2001). Administrators, in turn, are more team-oriented and collective (Atchison & Bujak, 2001), and work more by consensus (Cohn et al., 2005). Physicians' primary loyalties are to their profession and their patients; whereas administrators' primary loyalties are to the health-care system, yet they have to answer to a broader range of stakeholders, including patients, physicians, hospital employees, and boards of directors (Cohn et al., 2005; Shortell, 1991). These and other differences (see Table 13.1) accentuate the disparities between the groups, and provide "ammunition" for negative identity stereotyping. These negative identity dynamics get played out in the conflicts between these groups which are characterized by prolonged tension with occasional outbursts, multiple chronically salient issues, and the fulfillment of each group's desires seeming to depend on the failure of the other group (Fiol & O'Connor, 2009).

The purpose of this chapter is to motivate research on positive social change in healthcare by focusing attention on the management of intractable identity conflicts between physicians and administrators. We take as a starting point the notion that "positive" change refers, at least in part, to the outcomes of change. That is, positive change here means moving toward ongoing intergroup harmony between physicians and administrators. As we will discuss, however, our notion of "positive change" evolved over the course of our writing. Thus, we end this chapter by examining positivity in terms of types, concepts, and processes.

We begin by briefly reviewing our phase model of intractable identity conflict resolution (IICR). However, like all phase models, ours is abstract and illustrates general dynamics; but "its descriptions of people and processes are not particularly accurate or generalizable" (Littell & Girvin, 2002, p. 253). To better theorize about social change in healthcare, we take advantage of the multiple hats worn by our authors—academic, consultant, and practitioner—and apply our ideas and our model in the field. Specifically, we summarize our experiences in a "synthetic case." This synthetic case compiles our experiences with physician–administrator (P-A) intractable identity conflicts into a coherent narrative in order to raise new theoretical issues with our model. The net result of this exercise is that we now theorize intractable identity conflict resolution differently

TABLE 13.1

Different Group Orientations of Physicians and Administrators

Orientation	Physicians (P)	Administrators (A)	Major Barriers to Managing IICs
Decision Making	• Autonomous (expert culture) • Fast-paced experience based • More outcome than process oriented	• Team oriented (collective culture)[1] • Slower/consensus based[2] • More process oriented[3]	• Lack of entitativity (P) • Relevance (P)
Focus of Attention/ Responsiveness	• Individual patients/ own practice • Inward in response to complexities • Responsive to individual patients/ colleagues	• Hospital/health system[4] • External[5] • Patients, physicians, employees, community, board[6]	• Relevance (P)
Time Horizon	• 24-48 hours	• Months/years[7]	• Perseverance (P, possibly A)
Knowledge Basis/Rules of Evidence	• Biomedical sciences • Prefer hard facts	• Social/management sciences[8] • Can act on "soft" information[9]	• Relevance (P)
Dominant Identity/ Allegiance	• Professional identity • Allegiance to subject matter/profession	• Organizational[10] • Allegiance to organization	• Relevance (P)
Control	• Manage people and processes related to own productivity	• Manage assets[11]	• Relevance (P, A)
Income Sources	• Office visits/ procedures	• Salary/incentives[12]	• Relevance (P, A)

[1] Atchison & Bujak (2001)
[2] Cohn et al. (2005)
[3] Cohn (2009)
[4] Cohn et al. (2005)
[5] Billiar (2001)
[6] Cohn et al. (2005)
[7] Cohn et al. (2005)
[8] Shortell (1991)
[9] Shortell (1991)
[10] Shortell (1991)
[11] Cohn (2009)
[12] Cohn et al. (2005)

by (a) focusing much more on identity security, which is at the heart of our IICR model; (b) disentangling different forms of "positivity"; and (c) revisiting the entire notion of viewing intractable identity conflicts as "resolvable."

INTRACTABLE IDENTITY CONFLICTS IN ORGANIZATIONS: A BRIEF REVIEW

Drawing in research on intergroup conflict (Sherif, Harvey, White, Hood, & Sherif, 1961), international conflict management (Crocker, Hampson, & Aall, 2004, 2005; Kelman, 2006), and theories of social identity (Gaertner & Dovidio, 2000; Tajfel & Turner, 1979), Fiol et al. (2009) initially conceptualized the resolution of IICs as a series of phases or states that groups need to pass through to move from readiness to enduring intergroup harmony. As illustrated in Figure 13.1, we argued that the process begins with a state of readiness or conflict ripeness whereby the conflicting groups are motivated to change how they relate to each other. To illustrate, unions and managers trapped within IICs may become motivated to change their patterns of relating if the organization they both work for is going bankrupt. Once motivated to change, groups must be encouraged to decouple their intergroup identities. That is, they must begin to separate their sense of who they are from how they view the other party or parties in the conflict, that is, managers discontinue viewing themselves as anti-union and union workers as anti-management. This process of decoupling is facilitated by a specific intervention: promoting mindfulness. When mindful, individuals in conflicting groups become aware of and open to multiple perspectives and meanings (Fiol & O'Connor, 2003; Langer, 1989; Weick, Sutcliffe, & Obstefeld, 1999).

Once separated, these now-fragile group identities must become more secure and defined by their positive ingroup distinctiveness (i.e., by each group's own merits) rather than their mutual disidentification. For example, unions may emphasize their role in keeping the organization going on a day-to-day basis; and managers can highlight their roles as providing strategic guidance for the organization's future. Once group identities are secure, it becomes possible for groups to hold dual identities, especially when both parties are encouraged to simultaneously consider how their

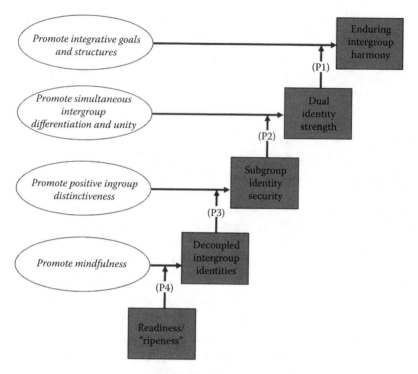

FIGURE 13.1
The intractable identity resolution model. (Fiol, Pratt, & O'Connor, 2009)

group (e.g., physicians) is alike and different from the other group (e.g., administrators). A dual identity exists when individuals can identify both with their own group as well as with a superordinate group that incorporates each of the conflicting parties. For example, an overarching organizational identity "we are all Company Y" may come to incorporate both union workers and managers. Only when these dual identities exist, can integrative structures such as superordinate goals and common visions be useful for bringing together fundamentally different identity groups.

The last point is particularly salient in healthcare. To date, attempts to manage the physician–administrator relationship have often been structural. For example, attempts at structural integration, such as vertical integration (Budetti et al., 2002) and alliances (e.g., physician-hospital organizations) have largely failed to produce their intended results (Holm, 2004; Medical Group Management Association, 2008). Similarly, attempts to "fuse" roles into a "physician-manager" are also not often effective. Intractable identity conflicts set up strong "either/or" dynamics that make it difficult for physician-managers to bridge the conflicting groups. That is, one can be part of one camp, but not both (Pratt & Doucet, 2000). To illustrate:

> I would not count someone who's given up clinical work for management anymore as a physician.... I mean, they're administrators. I'm sure they have memories of what it's like to be a provider, but that's not their role. (Physician, as cited in Hoff, 1999, p. 336)

To help rectify this tendency to begin interventions with structural changes, we instead engaged the conflicting parties to do the requisite "identity work" needed to move from conflict readiness to enduring intergroup harmony (see Figure 13.1). We now discuss our initial attempts.

Synthetic Case: Our Interventions at Paul Revere General Hospital

Paul Revere General Hospital was facing several external crises. Patient complaints were high, President Obama was making health-care reform a top priority of his administration, and the hospital had lost money for three consecutive years. Both physicians and administrators were feeling a lot of pain. Both parties knew they must work together, but something needed to change. In the past, when crises like this arose, there were no real alternatives available to change things for the better, and if there were, new initiatives were often short-lived and the relationships quickly regressed back into their comfortable, but negative, patterns of interaction. However, this time, the CEO approached a consultant from our team who offered both groups a new alternative for resolving intractable conflicts.

An overall multiphase plan was proposed and embraced by the participants. Initial survey data indicated a high level of intractable conflict between the two groups and insufficient cohesion or trust within each of the groups to be able to confidently address the problems. The data further indicated only a moderate level of motivation to change. The first phase of the intervention enhanced the motivation of both groups to engage in the change process by highlighting the costs of remaining stuck in the conflicts and the benefits of changing, as well as clarifying the realistic risks of working together. The conflicts were then addressed through a series of interventions. For example, small groups of physicians and administrators independently conducted an analysis of an intractable conflict between labor and management in another industry. As unbiased outside observers, each group identified behaviors that kept that conflict in place and made recommendations for resolving the distrust. Lights began to come on as both physicians and administrators recognized that their recommendations for ending that labor-management dispute could be relevant to actions they needed to resolve of their own.

Initial Success and Subsequent Failure

Consistent with the first phases of our model of promoting readiness and decoupling, the interventions described here were successful, while many prior attempts to resolve similar conflicts using traditional conflict resolution approaches have failed (Fiol & O'Connor, 2009). Pre- and post-intervention surveys and anecdotal evidence revealed great progress toward overall success. There were reports from administrators, physicians, and even nurses that physician–administrator relationships were improving. Each group further reported expanded optimism about future possibilities for healthcare in the community. With some confidence, we moved forward with our interventions, only to have them come to a screeching halt.

Despite improved intergroup relations, the cohesion within each group was limited, with numerous subgroup agendas on both sides; in fact, removing the "other" as the enemy made room for a focus on internal differences. To begin to build collaboration within each of the groups, the consultant engaged people in positive processes of assessing their own value. For example, he asked both physicians and administrators to answer questions like, "What is our (physician or administrator) dream?" "What do we value most, no matter what?" "What do we really want to accomplish?" and "What are we best at and/or proudest of?" These questions were meant to help each group stand on their own, to create an identity that was not based on the negation of the other (i.e., groups that were both decoupled and secure).

Unfortunately, at this point, small subgroups of powerful physicians decided to push their own agendas forward. Dreams of physicians, as an entire group, were set aside and replaced with demands from warring tribes within the physician community. Issues of what "we" value most were appropriated to mean what various physician subgroups valued. Conflicts among physicians erupted. At the same time, administrators— who had their own internal divisions—did not take the opportunity to push the process forward. The end result is that progress in resolving the IICs was stalled.

As the synthetic case suggests, efforts to move P-A groups out of intractable conflicts and toward intergroup harmony may stall at the identity securing phase. While we had hoped that the momentum gained from successfully decoupling the intergroup identities would carry participants forward to the next phase of our model, securing the identities of each group, something quite different took place. As noted in our case, both groups described the relationship between physicians and administrators as improved. Both sides reported feeling more positive about the other party, and both reported being significantly less motivated by pain. As a result, some believed that the problem of P-A conflicts was solved and that further work was no longer needed. Energy was drained from the entire process. This appears to have led to a balkanizing sub-process in which physician subgroups, in particular, turned on each other. Finally, old ways of thinking re-emerged because although pictures of positive futures existed, they were not pursued to continue to motivate the process.

Building Theory from Failure

In an attempt to theoretically account for the failure of our process, we began to look more closely into the phase where our progress stopped: identity security. In doing so, we developed a richer understanding and conceptualization of identity security, especially in comparison to the more common notion of identity strength. We also began to understand how the experience of both identity strength and security has different potentials for the experience of "positivity" in our positive social change process. Finally, we began to see the phases in our model less as "endpoints" and more as sign posts on an ongoing cyclical process. The aforementioned experiences of positivity, in turn, can signal "off ramps" in this cyclical process.

Identity Security

In implementing our IICR model, intergroup relationships were generally improving. As such, we felt that the groups were becoming more secure. However, after reviewing concepts such as "outgroup tolerance" (Mummendey & Wenzel, 1999), subgroup identity acknowledgement/ "subgroup respect" (Huo & Molina, 2006; Huo, Molina, Sawahata,

TABLE 13.2

Identity Strength versus Security

	Identity Strength	Identity Security
Experience	One's group is seen as self-defining and members feel pride	One's group is seen as self-defining and comfortable/safe to be a member
Antecedents	Positive or negative distinctiveness	Positive distinctiveness *and* perceived outgroup validation
Individual Outcomes	Attention and investment narrowing	Attention and investment broadening
Group Outcomes	Ingroup cohesion, but high potential for intergroup conflict if negative distinctiveness	Ingroup cohesion and high potential for dual or multiple identifications

& Deang, 2005), and Berry's (1991) "multicultural assumption," we came up with a clearer distinction between the characteristics of identity security and identity strength. These characteristics are listed in Table 13.2.

Following Berry (1991, p. 34), we distinguish identity strength from identity security by noting that the former refers to ingroup "glorification" or a "strongly positive ingroup attitude." As Berry (1991) notes, identity strength is not positively related to intergroup harmony; rather when one group is focused inward on its own virtues, the resulting pride may blind individuals to the commonalities one has with outgroup members, thus diminishing chances for cooperation. Identity security, by contrast, occurs when one feels safe and confident in one's group membership such that one recognizes, "the positive qualities but also the limitations" of one's group, and "the group's uniqueness and distinctiveness as well as the commonalities with others" (Berry, 1991, p. 35). This notion of security is similar to Allport's "warmer grade of tolerance" (1954, p. 425), which he distinguishes from tolerance based on simply enduring the existence of the other party:

> [There is] a type of tolerance that involves enduring something we dislike or find aversive and a "warmer grade of tolerance" (p. 425) which means a feeling of friendliness toward all kinds of people and, thus, not only enduring but accepting them (Allport, 1954, as cited in Mummendy & Wenzel, 1999, p. 167).

In our interventions, we believe we achieved the former type of tolerance, not the warmer kind.

In defining these terms, several differences between identity strength and security become clear. First, with regard to antecedents, identity security involves not only perceptions of positive distinctiveness when compared with an outgroup, but also perceptions that this outgroup validates them (Huo & Molina, 2006). By including positive perceptions of what other groups think, identity security expands the sphere of attention of group members beyond their own group. Consequently, we believe that this increases the chances for broadening one's investment beyond one's own group as well. At the group level, both identity strength and security involve feelings of ingroup cohesion. And in this regard, our interventions clearly did not even lead to identity strength for physicians—as this group fell into infighting. However, we argue that identity security additionally involves higher potential for dual or multiple identifications—that is, for claiming multiple group memberships. Indeed, research on pluralism suggests that to the degree that a group experiences identity security, they are more likely to claim a superordinate identity as well. Thus, Huo and Molina (2006) found that in an ethnically diverse population of Californians, minority groups (e.g., African Americans and Latinos) that experienced identity security were more likely to also claim an American identity.

The Experience of Positivity

Common to both identity security and identity strength is an experience of positivity. Indeed, we could argue that groups may feel some degree of positivity throughout the process of reconciling intractable conflicts. As we have noted earlier, when groups are engaged in intractable identity conflicts, they feel quite good about their group memberships—though this good feeling is at the expense of tearing down the other group (Fiol et al., 2009). We refer to this type of positivity as "exclusionary," in that it comes from mutual disidentification. Moreover, during this initial phase of intractability, both groups likely have high identity strength built on negative distinctiveness (i.e., we are better than you). Hence, exclusionary positivity may be conceptualized as a "double negative" (−,−) whereby two negatives make a positive.

The type of positivity that physicians and administrators experienced after we attempted to decouple their identities, however, was of a different sort. Here, each group felt better about the other. But as noted earlier, these good feelings did not go as far as outright acceptance of the other group. We refer to this type of positivity as "satisficed" positivity. Borrowing from work on "satisficing" where one takes the first minimally acceptable solution to a problem, satisficed positivity occurs when the pain is diminished enough that positive feelings exist between the groups. Here, intergroup relationships appear to be "good enough" that further work seems unnecessary; but in this state, deep conflicts have not been solved. As in our synthetic case, physicians and administrators had not resolved their identity conflicts yet, nor had individuals within each group resolved lingering ingroup issues. However, there were improvements and good feelings all around. We can thus conceptualize this type of positivity as "double positive" (+,+). But as with exclusionary positivity, there remained an absence of respect and validation of each party by the other. Thus, while the potential for identity strength existed to some degree, identity security was not yet possible.

This realization made us start to think about the type of positivity that could result from a true sense of identity security, and which kind could be used to move the process of intractable conflict resolution forward. Exclusionary positivity keeps groups locked in a cycle of mutual disidentification and impedes forward momentum toward change. Similarly, satisficed positivity appears to sap energy from the process. If these types of positivity lead to stagnation, what might a generative form of positivity look like?

In our search for this type of positivity we came across two concepts that seem to hold promise. One is "ambivalence as wisdom" (see Pratt & Pradies, 2011). Weick (1998), building from Campbell's path breaking work, argues that wisdom involves the retention of oppositional forces:

> In multiple-contingency environments, the joint presence of opposing tendencies has a functional survival value. Where each of two opposing tendencies has survival relevance, the biological solution seems to be an ambivalent alternation of expressions of each rather than the consistent expression of an intermediate motivational state. Ambivalence rather than averaging, seems the "optimal compromise." (Campbell, 1965, as quoted in Weick, 1998, p. 61).

Similarly, Plambeck and Weber (2009) suggest that CEOs who can retain their ambivalence are more likely to be creative and adaptive. Healthcare is definitely a multiple-contingency environment, characterized by a high degree of decision-making complexity, and in need of both creative and adaptable leadership.

Unlike ambivalent CEOs, however, ambivalent wisdom in healthcare needs to become an attribute of a collective, not an individual. In fact, such a movement from individuals to collectives may be integral to deal with complex, systemic changes, such as those characterizing healthcare. Building from theoretical work by Pradies and Pratt (2010), we argue that wisdom may stem from a type of "ideographic group ambivalence," where distinct points of view are held by members of different subgroups—or here, held by members of different health-care groups: physicians and administrators. As noted, these groups hold very different perspectives (see Table 13.1), and when the entire collective is comfortable with holding these competing thoughts (e.g., due to a culture of psychological safety or trust), this may allow for collective flexibility in solving problems and acting upon them.

A similar logic is at the heart of creative abrasion. "Creative abrasion" is a term coined by Gerald Hirshberg at Nissan Design International (Hagel & Brown, 2005). In his role as founding director, Hirshberg would deliberately pair designers with very different work styles so as to stimulate creativity via the introduction of diverse perspectives. However, these individuals would also serve as "checks and balances" for each other—keeping the creative process from being derailed (Hagel & Brown, 2005). Building on this, a similar process could work in healthcare. For this process to work, however, there also needs to be strong time pressures (akin to "readiness" in our model), parties who are experts in their various domains (such as physicians and administrators), as well as shared meanings and trust (which are essential for integrative structures to work—see Figure 13.1).

Whether referred to as creative abrasion or ambivalent wisdom, both concepts point to acknowledging differences (central to exclusionary positivity) and commonalities (a state that was approached, but not achieved, in satisficed positivity). This is essentially the state we would predict in the final phase of our model—where parties would find themselves secure in their subgroups, allowing them to acknowledge differences, while also sharing a common, overarching, or superordinate identity that both competing groups could identify with (e.g., patient advocates). Framed in terms of positivity, it would appear that a generative positivity would involve identity security that would allow competing groups to share information in a safe environment, and clear distinctiveness in terms of what each could add to common problems.

This type of generative positivity creates the unique form of intergroup harmony that we suggest, but do not fully elaborate upon, in our original model. It is harmony based on a balance of different and sometimes opposing elements (i.e., a +/–, +/– positivity) rather than on the cessation of conflict. This is because in our model, our goal is not simply to bring both parties together, but to also retain, secure, and celebrate the unique attributes of each party in the conflict. To achieve the latter, the different worldviews and perspectives are not integrated into a new whole, but are retained in service of a greater whole.

Beyond Phases to Cycles

In addition to compelling us to define more clearly what we mean by identity security, and to better delineate the right kind of "positive" needed in "positive social change" in healthcare, our experiences and our theorizing also led us to rethink our phase model as one ending in "resolution." Several issues cause us to doubt casting intractable identity conflicts in terms of "resolution." First, our experiences reminded us that physicians and administrators are not necessarily cohesive groups. Taking physicians as examples, it is clear that physicians, as a group, have very little entitativity. That is, they do not view each other as members of a single, cohesive group. Moreover, there are long and bitter historical divisions between groups, such as between internal medicine and surgeons (Pratt, Rockmann, & Kaufmann, 2006). This is not to say that administrators are always homogeneous groups—far from it. We have seen administrator groups divided by culture (e.g., new guard versus established caretakers) and by disciplinary background. What made the physician conflict so potent, however, is that, like the conflict between physicians and administrators, it is ongoing and pervasive. Such conflicts may experience a temporary reprieve, such as when physicians are united in opposition to administrators, or when both physicians and administrators are facing extreme external pressures. When the pain of P-A conflicts subsides a bit, however, as it did when we made progress in decoupling the negative entanglements, old fights may re-erupt.

During this time of relative peace, a few powerful physician leaders began to stir up old conflicts. While these conflicts were packaged as being about resources, they were often interpreted in light of "who we are" as different physician groups. Because administrative leaders did not push to keep the resolution process going, the physicians got wrapped up in their own conflicts, and the IIC resolution process ground to a halt.

In the language of recent theory on intractable identity conflicts (Coleman, Vallacher, Nowak, & Bui-Wrzosinska, 2007), it became clear to us that in complex social systems, such as health-care systems, patterns of social relationships may be comprised of more than one form of IIC. In our case, while we were attempting to promote identity security, some physician leaders took this as an opportunity to revisit enduring intragroup conflicts and agendas. This is not that different from what sometimes happens in ethno-national conflicts or even in politics. One need look no further than the recent balkanization of the Democratic Party when they gained control of both the executive and legislative branches of the U.S. government in 2008: with the Republican enemy defeated, old conflicts re-awakened and the new majority turned on each other. Unfortunately, as with all IICs, these old conflicts serve to collapse cognitive complexity and serve to attract other issues in their wake (Coleman et al., 2007).

Because of the persistent danger of "slipping into old habits" or the emergence of other intractable identity conflicts within the health-care system, experience reminds us of the importance of promoting readiness throughout the process, not just at the beginning. If we view the entire process as having its own energy, then ironically, some success may actually serve to sap that energy, making conflicting parties too comfortable (i.e., by promoting a satisficed positivity). Some see these small wins and newfound comfort as excuses to rush into integrative solutions, even though much-needed identity work is still required. One needs to feel safe within one's group, and one must feel validated by the party with whom one's group is in conflict.

Building on these points, the potential for other intractable identity conflicts to inhibit progress and the importance of constantly supplying "readiness" in the process, we believe that the phases in our model may be momentary accomplishments rather than end states. This shift in thinking leads us away from more variance-based phase models and more toward process models (Mohr, 1982), in particular, an ongoing cyclical model. That is, dealing with identity intractability is not like a race to be won and a goal to be achieved. Rather, like total quality management, it involves an entirely different way of approaching how one sees the world: where it is the ongoing pursuit of an ideal that is both enacted and celebrated.

One consequence of viewing identity intractability in this way is that it necessitates a movement from "thinking/feeling" to "thinking/feeling and doing" throughout our model. Returning to identity security which has been a focus of our writing here, it (as well as identity strength) has traditionally been conceptualized as an attitude—that is involving the thoughts and feelings of individuals. However, if the process by which one handles intractable identity conflicts is ongoing, then one must not simply feel secure, one must also act. These actions should, at minimum, take the form of validating the "other" party (i.e., administrators for physicians and vice versa) and ideally involve advocacy of each others' needs. Otherwise the process falls apart. This distinction between "thinking/feeling" and "thinking/feeling and doing" has been noted in other change-related literatures, such as conversion theory. Conversion theory distinguishes between "verbal" conversion—or the extent to which members profess belief in an organization's ideology and are believed to be sincere by others—from "total" conversion which is verbal conversion accompanied by ideologically appropriate behaviors (cf. Lofland, 1966; Lofland & Stark, 1965). In our failed implementation attempts, we found that physicians and administrators "felt good" about themselves (i.e., were verbal converts), but neither group took the next step and actually enacted validating behaviors.

Bringing our discussion full circle, our reasoning for viewing the handling of IICs in this way is two-fold. First, because these conflicts represent a well-worn groove in the fabric of social relationships, groups must be vigilant not to fall back into that groove (Coleman et al., 2007). In addition, groups must be aware of other IICs in the social system as well—though we hope that knowing how to deal with one form of IIC (e.g., P-A) may help groups better approach other forms (e.g., P-P conflicts). Thus, vigilance in addressing IICs is ongoing. Consequently, we may need to rename our model from the intractable identity conflict *resolution* model to the *managing* intractable identity conflicts (MIIC) model. The switch from resolution to managing suggests that we are not fixed on an end-point, but on a continuing management process. Even if new more positive grooves in the social fabric are created, it is possible that some event may serve to push physicians and administrators back into old ways of inter-relating. This new model is featured in Figure 13.2.

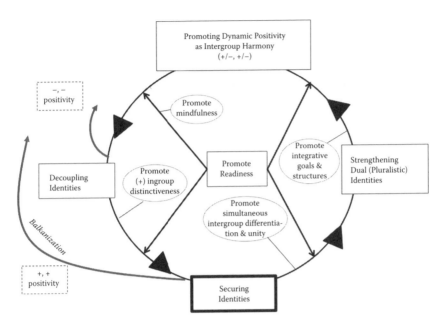

FIGURE 13.2
A modified managing intractable identity conflict model.

A MANAGING INTRACTABLE IDENTITY CONFLICTS (MIIC) MODEL

Our revised MIIC model is similar to our IICR model in several respects—they both contain the same identity phases and same interventions. However, several key differences exist. First, building from our insight that managing intractable conflicts are ongoing, we now represent the model as cyclical. Thus, even when groups achieve enduring intergroup harmony, there is the potential for intractability to re-emerge, and additional identity decoupling, identity securing, and dual identity strengthening to occur. This possibility is made more apparent by a second change: reconceptualizing how we talk about enduring intergroup harmony. In our original conceptualization, we viewed harmony in terms of peacefulness (Fiol et al., 2009, p. 37). We more explicitly flesh out our conceptualization here by noting that peacefulness does not necessarily mean the cessation of all conflict—just destructive conflict. However, the presence of "negative charges" in the relationship (+/−, +/−) suggests that it may be possible, perhaps through a scandal or crisis, that the positive elements get stripped away, leaving double negative positivity (−,−). Alternatively, as we have noted, it is also possible for other intractable identity conflicts in the health-care system to impose themselves upon the physician–administrator relationship. Thus, we use the term "generative positivity" to remind us that this type of positivity is volatile and changeable.

Third, in line with process theorizing (Langley, 1999), we view each of these phases in more dynamic oriented terms (verbs, rather than nouns) and place "promoting readiness" as being critical throughout the process—not just at the beginning. The process of managing intractable identity conflicts has its own "energy." We felt momentum when we started our intervention, but that momentum stalled. As a result, it may be necessary to continue providing motivation for continuing in the process throughout the process. The ongoing promotion of readiness is especially critical since there is no static end-state for our model. However, it is important to recognize that the nature of readiness may change as the process unfolds. While in our experience initial readiness is often brought about by pain, research on intractable conflicts suggests that positive sources of readiness, such as opportunities for mutual gain, are likely to be more successful than negative sources as they do not add additional stress to an otherwise stressed system (Fiol et al., 2009). Thus, positive sources of readiness (e.g., opportunities for mutual gain) may become more helpful as the process moves along.

Fourth, our model more clearly distinguishes "off-ramps," especially prior to the identity securing phase. Ironically, these off-ramps may be signaled by the presence of positive affect. At the start of the conflict, there may be positivity of an exclusionary nature (−,−). Research in intractable conflicts also suggests that these conflicts become perceived as "normal"; thus there may even be some positivity associated with the existence of the conflict itself (Crocker et al., 2005). Another off-ramp may occur as one attempts to move from decoupling identities to securing them. Here, the reduction of pain to tolerable level makes both parties feel that their progress has been "good enough" (even if not optimal) and thus that the hard work is over. This satisficed positivity may also be associated with positive feelings (+,+), especially between parties. Both exclusionary and satisficed positivity may not only signal off-ramps, however; they may also highlight the importance of looking at patterns of positivity within and across groups. For exclusionary positivity, created by intractable conflicts, there was positivity within groups, but not between. Satisficed creativity, by contrast, led to increasing positivity between groups, but decreasing positivity within groups.

During the promotion of identity security, in particular, satisficed positivity can be deadly to the MIIC process. To begin, it may create inertia; unless these positive feelings are accompanied by actions, it is possible for other intractable conflicts and/or negative political forces to derail the process. For example, balkanization of groups may be possible here, especially in large and complex groups that are unified primarily in their opposition to others. Groups that are fundamentally low in entitativity may be especially at risk during identity securing. This suggests that scholars of intractable identity conflict need to be aware of the characteristics and history of the groups in process, in addition to familiarizing themselves with the characteristics and history of the conflict itself. Historically fragmented groups, such as physicians, may not only be vulnerable to "off-ramps," but they may also need additional time and other resources in cycling through the MIIC as both ingroup and intergroup conflicts need attention.

CONCLUDING THOUGHTS: LESSONS FOR POSITIVE SOCIAL CHANGE IN HEALTHCARE

At a general level, we hope that this chapter encourages scholars of social change in healthcare to look at change more from the bottom-up. If our arguments are valid, broad structural changes, which have historically been applied in this context, may not be effective until work is done at a much more micro-level: in relationships between groups. Moreover, we encourage change scholars to look closely at issues of identity. While we do not deny that resource-based issues are critical in health-care contexts, we also argue that such resource-based conflicts may come to take on identity dynamics, which make traditional sources of conflict management either ineffective or harmful. Finally, we encourage anyone who wants to theorize about social change to refine their theorizing by applying their ideas and concepts in the field, and reaching out to a broad set of stakeholders. Our efforts to theorize were greatly enriched by our failures in the field, and in our ability to draw upon our roles as academics, consultants, and practitioners.

With regard to theorizing about "positivity" in positive social change, we leave you with three insights around concepts, processes, and types. First, the positive organizational studies (POS) movement has made tremendous contributions by creating new theoretical constructs, or enriching old ones. For example, noting how spirals can be virtuous as well as destructive has changed how we view cyclical processes in organizations. Our contribution to this effort is in more fully theorizing the concept of "identity security," which we believe is a POS analog to the more common concept of identity strength. We not only believe that fostering identity security will be fruitful as we attempt to change healthcare, we also believe that its origins in theorizing about pluralism may make it useful in understanding and improving diversity in organizations.

Second, we began our work by viewing positive social change as referring largely to outcomes. However, the mutual validation inherent in forming identity security also suggests that positivity relates to processes as well. Our advocacy of finding mutual opportunities for gain as the engine for the ongoing promotion of readiness reflects positive process as well.

Third, while opportunities for mutual gain and respectful interactions are one aspect of positivity, we should not equate positivity with simply "feeling good." Indeed, the POS movement has been criticized for focusing too much on positive states—and even for being too "Pollyannaish,"—even if that is not the intent of all or even most POS scholars. We hope to further clarify that "positivity" is not always about holding hands and singing "Kumbaya." Generative positivity, as conceptualized here, brings to the forefront the importance of keeping a type of "creative abrasion" alive in a social system—just as a sand irritant is essential for the formation of a pearl (Hagel & Brown, 2005). If our theorizing can help keep these productive tensions alive in the transformation of physician–administrator relationships, it could truly create a pearl of great price.

ACKNOWLEDGMENTS

We wish to thank Doug Lepisto, Jane Dutton, Karen Golden-Biddle, and the participants of the Exploring Positive Social Change and Organizations Conference for their input on earlier drafts of this chapter.

REFERENCES

Allport, G. W. (1954). *The nature of prejudice.* Cambridge, MA: Addison-Wesley.

Atchison, T., & Bujak. J. S. (2001). *Leading transformational change: The physician-executive partnership.* Chicago: Health Administration Press.

Berry, J. W. (1991). Understanding and managing multiculturalism: Some possible implications of research in Canada. *Psychology and Developing Societies, 3,* 17–49.

Billiar, T. R. (2001). Presidential address: Routine complexity. *Surgery, 130,* 123–132.

Budetti, P. P., Shortell, S. M., Waters, T. M., Alexander, J. A., Burns, L. R., Gillies, R. R., & Zuckerman, H. (2002). Physician and health system integration. *Health Affairs, 21,* 203–210.

Crocker, C., Hampson, F., & Aall, P. (2005). *Taming intractable conflicts.* Washington, DC: United States Institute of Peace Press.

Cohn, K. H. (2009). A practicing surgeon dissects issues in physician-hospital relations. *Journal of Healthcare Management, 54,* 5–10.

Cohn, K. H, Gill, S. L., & Schwartz, R. W. (2005). Gaining hospital administrators' attention: Ways to improve physician-hospital management dialogue. *Surgery, 137,* 132–140.

Coleman, P. T., Vallacher, R., Nowak, A., & Bui-Wrzosinska, L. (2007). Intractable conflict as an attractor: A dynamical systems approach to conflict escalation and intractability. *American Behavioral Scientist, 50,* 1454–1475.

Crocker, C., Hampson. F., & Aall, P. (2004). *Grasping the nettle.* Washington, DC: United States Institute of Peace Press.

Fiol, C. M., & O'Connor, E. J. (2003). Waking up! Mindfulness in the face of bandwagons. *Academy of Management Review, 28,* 54–70.

Fiol, C. M., & O'Connor, E. J. (2009). *Separately together: A new path to healthy hospital-physician relations.* Chicago: Heath Administration Press.

Fiol, C. M., Pratt, M. G., & O'Connor, E. J. (2009). Managing intractable identity conflicts. *Academy of Management Review, 34,* 32–55.

Gaertner, S. L., & Dovidio, J. F. (2000). *Reducing intergroup bias: The common ingroup identity model.* Ann Arbor, MI: Sheridan Books.

Hagel, J., & Brown, J. S. (2005). Productive friction. *Harvard Business Review, 83,* 82–91.

Hoff, T. (1999). The social organization of physician-managers in a changing HMO. *Work and Occupations, 26,* 324.

Holm, C. E. (2004). *Allies or adversaries: Revitalizing the medical staff organization.* Chicago: Health Administration Press.

Huo, Y. J., & Molina, L. E. (2006). Is pluralism a viable model of diversity? The benefits and limits of subgroup respect. *Group Processes & Intergroup Relations, 9,* 359–376.

Huo, Y. J., Molina, L. E., Sawahata, R., & Deang, J. M. (2005). Leadership and the management of conflicts in diverse groups: Why acknowledging versus neglecting subgroup identity matters. *European Journal of Social Psychology, 35,* 237–254.

Kelman, H. C. (2006). Interests, relationships, identities: Three central issues for individuals and groups in negotiating their social environment. *Annual Review of Psychology, 57,* 1–26.

Langer, E. J. (1989). Minding matters: The consequences of mindlessness-mindfulness. In L. Berkowitz (Ed.), *Advances in experimental social psychology* (pp. 137–173). San Diego: Academic Press.

Langley, A. (1999). Strategies for theorizing from process data. *Academy of Management Review, 24,* 691–710.

Littell, J. H., & Girvin, H. (2002). Stages of change: A critique. *Behavior Modification, 26,* 223–273.

Lofland, J. (1966). *Doomsday cult: A study of conversion, proselytization, and maintenance of faith.* Englewood Cliffs, NJ: Prentice-Hall, Inc.

Lofland, J., & Stark, R., (1965). Becoming a world-saver: A theory of conversion to a deviant perspective. *American Sociological Review, 30,* 862–874.

Medical Group Management Association. (2008). MGMA cost survey reports: 2000–2006. *MGMA Connexion.* February 14, 2008.

Mohr, L. B. (1982). *Explaining organizational behavior.* San Francisco: Jossey-Bass.

Mummendey, A., & Wenzel, M. (1999). Social discrimination and tolerance in intergroup relations: Reactions to intergroup difference. *Personality and Social Psychology Review, 3,* 158–174.

Plambeck, N., & Weber, K. (2009). CEO ambivalence and responses to strategic issues. *Organization Science, 20,* 993–1010.

Pradies, C., & Pratt, M. G. (2010). Ex uno plures: Toward a conceptualization of group ambivalence. *Academy of Management Annual Meeting Proceedings.*

Pratt, M. G., & Doucet, L. (2000). Ambivalent feelings in organizational relationships. In S. Fineman (Ed.), *Emotions in organizations, Volume II* (pp. 204–226). Thousand Oaks, CA: Sage.

Pratt, M. G., & Pradies, C. (2011). Just a good place to visit? Exploring positive responses to ambivalence. In K. Cameron & G. Spreitzer (Eds.), *The Oxford handbook of positive organizational scholarship* (pp. 924–937). New York: Oxford University Press.

Pratt, M. G., Rockmann, K., & Kaufmann, J. (2006). Constructing professional identity: The role of work and identity learning cycles in the customization of identity among medical residents. *Academy of Management Journal, 49,* 235–262.

Sherif, M., Harvey, O. J., White, B. J., Hood, W. R., & Sherif, C. W. (1961). *Intergroup conflict and cooperation: The robber's cave experiment.* Norman, OK: University of Oklahoma Book Exchange.

Shortell, S. (1991). *Effective hospital-physician relationships.* Ann Arbor, MI: Health Administration Press Perspectives.

Tajfel, H., & Turner, J. C. (1979). An integrative theory of intergroup conflict. In W. G. Austin & S. Worchel (Eds.), *The social psychology of intergroup relations* (pp. 33–47). Monterey, CA: Brooks/Cole.

Weick, K. E. (1998). The attitude of wisdom: Ambivalence as the optimal compromise. In S. Srivastva & D. L. Cooperrider (Eds.), *Organizational wisdom and executive courage* (pp. 40–64). San Fransisco, CA: The New Lexington Press.

Weick, K. E., Sutcliffe, K. M., & Obstfeld, D. (2005). Organizing and the process of sense-making. *Organization Science, 16,* 409–421.

14

Amplifying Resources and Buffering Demands: How Managers Can Support Front Line Staff in Loving Action for Each Child

Rebecca Wells
University of North Carolina

> As (the child) and I started to build a rapport in our relationship and started to get that therapeutic bond, he started to talk more about the father and the relationships and family dynamics. The family got back together, and then they started to work on things ... and (the child) really settled down.
>
> **Counselor, mental health agency, 2010 interview**

> They ended up closing the case because she didn't follow through—again. So that was that.
>
> **Counselor, mental health agency, 2010 interview**

When children experience mental illness, a number of organizations may become involved. Schools are often the first places where behavioral problems become apparent and children begin to receive counseling and other services (Burns et al., 1995). Mental health agencies provide counseling and medication management. Child protective services may refer children to mental health services to recover from maltreatment and improve family dynamics. Juvenile justice systems provide and refer to mental health services (Farmer, Burns, Phillips, Angold, & Costello, 2003).

This chapter includes all of these organizations because they all work to help children with mental illness recover to the extent possible and maximize functioning when illnesses cannot be cured. Moreover, the fundamental management challenge in all of these contexts is to support the teachers, clinicians, caseworkers, and other front line staff who facilitate access to mental health care, provide care, or both. Although the number of hierarchical layers varies across these organizations, this chapter refers collectively to all levels above those directly interacting with children as management. In keeping with the theme of social change in transforming healthcare, this chapter theorizes about how managers at all levels can best support front line staff in their work for children with mental illness.

MOVING TOWARD A POSITIVE LENS ON BOTH CHILDREN AND THE ORGANIZATIONS THAT SERVE THEM

In the last two decades, families and professionals have advocated for "Systems of Care" for children with serious emotional disturbance (Bickman, Noser, & Summerfelt, 1999), and more recently for all children with complex needs. The Systems of Care paradigm emphasizes shifting control from organizations to children and their caregivers and moving from a "deficit" to an "asset" based perspective on children, families, and communities (Benson, 2006; Lawson, Claiborne, Hardiman, Austin, & Surko, 2007, p. 4). In recent years, policy makers and agency leadership have sought to re-frame outcomes in positive terms, from preventing dropout to school completion (Lehr, Hansen, Sinclair, & Christenson, 2003); from violence and pathology to "physical and psychological safety and security" (Eccles & Gootman, 2002, p. 7); and from out-of-home placements to placement stability (Golden, 2009).

The shift toward strengths-based approaches to children has affected leaders' views of their organizations as well. I learned this when I was helping to evaluate an initiative that places nurse-social worker teams in high need schools throughout North Carolina (Gifford et al., 2010). When the project leader circulated a draft of our survey, representatives of three out of four state agencies independently objected to the negative focus. Relying largely on previously validated items, we had not realized the survey had a negative focus! As Rick Zechman, Special Projects Coordinator for North Carolina's Division of Social Services, observed in an e-mail,

"It's certainly been a learning journey and continues to be through our own evaluations to try to strive toward re-framing in more strengths-based approaches" (R. Zechman, 2009, personal communication).

That e-mail exchange inspired this chapter. Substantial scholarship on health and human service organizations documents the causes and consequences of burnout, a condition characterized by emotional exhaustion and "depersonalization," or a tendency to treat people in rote, mechanistic ways (Maslach, 1998, p. 69; Smith & Mogro-Wilson, 2007). However, studying dysfunction does not necessarily yield insights into how to foster individual or organizational health. Recently, Hakanen and colleagues have demonstrated that the positive analogues to burnout's core components of exhaustion and depersonalization are not simply ends of the same continua, but are instead distinct phenomena they refer to collectively as "engagement" (Hakanen, Bakker, & Schaufeli, 2006; Schaufeli & Bakker, 2004, p. 248). This chapter builds on their *job demands-resources model* to include how engagement affects front line outcomes, as well as focuses on positive staff behaviors rather than negative outcomes.

To explicate the causal pathways through which managers can affect engagement as well as burnout, this chapter also incorporates a second framework. Cameron et al. describe *organizational virtuousness* as entailing both amplifying positive effects on employees and buffering them from negative forces (Cameron, 2003; Cameron, Bright, & Caza, 2004). Although previous work on job stress had incorporated buffers from stressors (Blau, 1981; Cordes & Dougherty, 1993; Parkes, Mendham, & von Rabenau, 1994), Cameron et al. noted the potential for positive moderation as well. Drawing on both Hakanen et al. and Cameron et al., Figure 14.1 shows how managerial actions can increase staff engagement by amplifying resources and reduce staff burnout by buffering them from demands. The result is posited to be loving action on behalf of each child.

HOW MANAGERS CAN SUPPORT LOVING ACTION FOR EACH CHILD

This chapter's theory begins with two key assumptions. The first is that front line staff members generally begin their careers with an intrinsic love of children that provides a powerful source of energy (Hobfoll & Shirom,

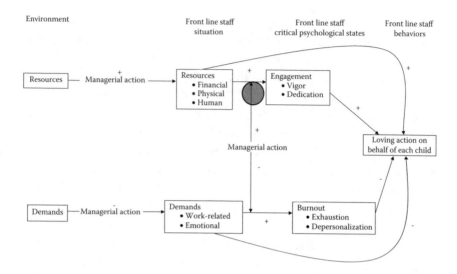

FIGURE 14.1
How managerial amplifying and buffering actions can support loving action for each child.

2001; Ryan & Deci, 2000) and motivation (see Schaufeli & Bakker, 2004). The challenge for managers is not to create staff engagement, but instead to feed and protect it (Hobfoll, 1989). This assumption is not universally valid: Some people begin working with children as the path of least resistance. The theory that follows would not apply well to them.

This theory's second key assumption is that children will engage more actively in mental health services and benefit more from them when front line staff brings *loving action* into their work with *each child*. The "loving" part entails connection, awareness, appreciation, concern, and unconditionality (Fromm, 2000). The "action" part may involve talking to a child, caregivers, and other staff to discern needs; watching and listening to the child attentively; mulling cues that an initial appraisal may not be complete ("Why is she suddenly quiet?"); scheduling meetings when everyone involved can attend; re-scheduling those meetings when someone cancels; and questioning policies that do not address a child's needs.

The "each child" part is equally important because mentally ill children may behave in ways that disrupt and even endanger others, can threaten schools' federal performance ratings, and often come with caregivers who are overwhelmed and angry. Loving children in general is not enough. Staff within the organizations that serve these children need to love *them*.

This focus on the tone of interactions with children is not meant to diminish the importance of technical competence or evidence-based practices. However, this chapter's model is premised on the assumption that, all else being equal, children will become healthier when the staff they encounter take loving action on their behalf. Thus, unlike other work on front line staff examining more collective outcomes such as organizational commitment (Hakanen et al., 2006) or even prosocial behavior, which also emphasizes giving to other people (Cameron et al., 2004), the framework depicted in Figure 14.1 culminates in efforts on behalf of individual children. This focus is dyadic, although the action taken on behalf of a child may entail interactions with caregivers, other family and community members, and other organizations.

The theory then entails ten testable propositions (Figure 14.1). The first two, drawing on the *job demands-resources* model (Hakanen et al., 2006), are that front line staff members' *engagement* and *burnout* have separate effects on their loving action on behalf of each child. Specifically, staff members' sense of *vigor*, or positive energy, resilience, and willingness to invest effort, as well as *dedication*, or belief in the significance of their work, will lead to more loving effort. Conversely, but potentially true in combination with the positive dynamics of engagement, staff who experience *exhaustion* and *depersonalization* will take fewer loving actions on each child's behalf. Using language from the job design literature, engagement and burnout are referred to as critical psychological states (Hackman & Oldham, 1976), posited here to mediate between the situations front line staff face and the actions they take.

Next, this theory hypothesizes that *resources* affect engagement and *demands* affect burnout. Here resources are categorized as financial (e.g., ability to pay for services), physical (e.g., cars for transporting children to appointments), and human (e.g., staff member expertise). In keeping with previous work, demands are categorized as those relating to workload and emotions (Hakanen et al., 2006). Both workload and emotional demands such as witnessing children's suffering as well as staff's own exposure to abusive behavior are expected to lead to burnout.

The theory depicted in Figure 14.1 further posits that managers can increase loving actions undertaken for children both by *amplifying* resources and *buffering* staff from demands. The vertical bidirectional arrow in the middle of Figure 14.1 depicts moderation, in keeping with previous conceptualizations of amplifying and buffering (Bakker,

Hakanen, Demerouti, & Xanthopoulou, 2007; Cameron et al., 2004). Here, managerial action is shown increasing the effect of given levels of resources on staff engagement and decreasing the effect of demands on staff burnout.

In addition, the framework depicted in Figure 14.1 includes managerial potential to mediate between resources and demands in the environment and the situations experienced by front line staff. Turning to the lay definitions of these terms, amplifying means "to make larger or more powerful"; one way to "make larger" is to make more resources from the environment available to front line staff. Similarly, buffering can entail either intercepting environmental demands to lessen or absorb their shock or moderating their impact.

Finally, the direct lines from resources and demands respectively to loving efforts reflect the expectation that front line staff members' critical psychological states will not fully mediate the associations between situations and actions. In other words, to some extent, the situation determines what people can do, regardless of how engaged or burned out they feel. For instance, having more flexible funding will increase the range of options a staff member can take. Conversely, even highly engaged staff members would still be constrained in the actions they could take if their caseloads doubled.

AMPLIFYING RESOURCES TO ENHANCE STAFF MEMBER ENGAGEMENT

Whether managers can amplify resource levels, amplify their effects, or both is expected to depend on the nature of the resource. Higher level managers in particular may be able to increase the financial, physical, and other human resources available to front line staff. For instance, some child welfare agencies allow staff to use early periodic screening, detection, and treatment funds to supplement standard reimbursements from Medicaid, the primary public insurance program in the United States for the poor (Chuang, 2010). Such funds make it possible to secure mental health services that would otherwise be unavailable and thus may have a direct effect on actions taken by staff. In addition, staff who can do more for a child may experience greater engagement as a result. Thus resources may both directly and indirectly contribute to the loving actions taken on each child's behalf.

Managers may also increase physical resource inputs that directly and indirectly increase loving actions taken on children's behalf. A school-based counselor noted that the lack of private space in schools limited the types of sessions she could hold: "Sometimes we had to meet in the hall-way. Sometimes we had to meet in the social worker's office, so we couldn't always talk about really personal issues" (personal communication, 2010 interview). The direct path from resources to the counselor's ability to engage with children is obvious. Less obvious is the potential for resource constraints to decrease the vigor and dedication with which staff experience their work, and thus indirectly undermine loving action as well.

Managers may also increase front line staff access to existing human resources such as staff at other agencies. For instance, in our recent field-work, two counselors worked with a very vulnerable child for several weeks, one in the context of family therapy and one in individual ther-apy. However, the counselors never talked to each other. Leadership in North Carolina child serving systems are promoting "child and family" teams that include representatives of all involved organizations in addi-tion to caregivers and, where developmentally appropriate, the children. Management support for such teams can range from mundane (e.g., allow-ing staff to travel off site) to the more complex (e.g., rewarding staff for effectively participating in these meetings). Thus, managers may enhance staff engagement in part through supporting access to the human capital available at other agencies and among families. One social worker noted that staff sometimes realized in those meetings that a family could not do everything the agencies were telling them to do because their require-ments contradicted each other. Conversely, when agencies work together with families, they may both directly improve actions for children and indirectly support such actions through increased staff engagement.

In addition to increasing the levels of resources available to front line staff, managers may also increase the impact of resources on engagement. Potential moderators include managerial interventions that give staff more discretion over their work, reason for optimism, positive individual and collective identity, and time to see their efforts affect children. Each will be discussed in turn here.

Unlocking children's potential to thrive often hinges on the flexibility to do "whatever it takes" to mobilize family and community supports

(Harlem Children's Zone, 2010). Another agency that unfortunately often encounters children in traumatic situations is the police. In Durham, NC, a police officer responding to a traumatic incident changed out of her uniform, brought blankets, and spent the rest of her work day comforting the family (NC Collaborative for Children Youth and Families, 2010). Such *professional discretion* may also increase the effects of resources on staff engagement as they experience greater power to do good. Research on how professional discretion affects staff engagement and actions for children would diverge from previous scholarship in this area, which has focused largely on potential for misuse (e.g., Scott, 1997). Such effects would be most likely in contexts in which leadership at higher levels, within organizations, as well as funders and federal auditors, agree to allow staff greater discretion (Schorr, 1997).

In many mental health agencies, supervisors now only have time to ensure that front line staff bill for their services. However, according to the framework outlined here, more supportive supervision could both increase the human resources available through staff capacity and moderate the effects of these and other resources on staff engagement. This may entail skill development, as well as cultivation of the *psychological safety* (Edmondson, 1999) that may each in turn foster staff members' engagement with their work (Grant, 2007). Specifically, staff may be more willing to invest in children (i.e., have more "vigor") as well as believe more in the work they are doing (i.e., have more "dedication") when they develop skills that increase their effectiveness. To return to the previous example of child and family teams, supportive supervision may increase their impact on staff engagement as staff learn how to interact with representatives of other organizations who use different terminology and have different priorities, as well as feel safe admitting their own uncertainty in these meetings.

The *expectancy-value* model may also help explain how supportive supervisors can increase the engagement payoff of given levels of resources. This model views motivation as a product of anticipated likelihood of an outcome and how much someone values that outcome (Bandura, 1996; Carver & Scheier, 2002). This chapter's framework shows how a focus on more proximal child outcomes and more positive valuation of those outcomes may each increase the effects of resources on staff engagement. Supervisors may also enhance staff engagement by helping staff visualize children's thriving futures as if in the present and thus making these outcomes feel more attainable (Cameron, Dutton, & Quinn, 2003; Weick, 1979). Such mentoring techniques might help staff engage with children based on hope for their healthy potential (Bandura, 1996) without glossing over the reality of often substantial obstacles.

In addition to discretion and supportive supervision, when front line staff feel personally validated for the actions they undertake for children they may respond to given levels of resources with greater engagement. Reflecting on successful programs for children, Schorr comments in *Common Purpose* that "It is striking how often effective practice is characterized precisely by how it departs from traditional norms about what is considered 'professional'" (Schorr, 1997, p. 14). Managers may improve the engagement benefits of a range of resources by helping front line staff maintain their *positive identities* as advocates for children in the face of such conflicting professional norms (Dutton, Roberts, & Bednar, 2010; Ibarra, 1999).

Similarly, managers' use of *superordinate goals* or a compelling common mission may increase the impact of resources on staff engagement (Schorr, 1997). In child-serving organizations, this may serve as a form of collective identity reinforcement as members are reminded of their shared devotion to children. Cooperrider and Sekerka argue that the most important thing any organization can do is to "...make the positive core the common and explicit property of all" (2003, p. 234). This statement implies that agency managers may help staff better translate resources into engaged work experiences through a shared emphasis on actualizing child potential rather than agency routines or professional status.

Finally, *job design* may affect the engagement yield of available resources. Some child welfare agencies are restructuring case management so that the same person manages intake and subsequent coordination for each child, a job design innovation reminiscent of patient-centered nursing (Dreachslin, Hunt, & Sprainer, 1999). These and other initiatives that increase continuity with individual children may build staff engagement by allowing more time to build mutual understanding with everyone involved and to see the results of their efforts (Bandura, 1996; Hackman & Oldham, 1976). For instance, one could imagine that any given level of funds available will be more useful, and thus encourage more staff engagement, when the staff can see those funds translate into services and improved mental health over time.

BUFFERING STAFF FROM DEMANDS TO ENHANCE STAFF MEMBER ENGAGEMENT

In addition to amplifying resources for sustaining the loving action of staff for each child, the current section explores the possibility that managers may also sustain loving action for each child by buffering staff from the forces that threaten to deplete them. Staff in child-serving organizations must often contend with overwhelming amounts of paperwork. Paradoxically, efforts at system improvement may also contribute to burnout by adding to high workloads in disjointed and even contradictory ways. Exposure to children's suffering can cause "secondary trauma" among front line staff. Children and families can also be abusive toward staff. The result is often staff experiences of emotional exhaustion and depersonalization, reduced efforts for children, and even leaving organizations entirely (Golden, 2009; Schorr, 1997).

The single greatest workload-related demand on staff across all child-serving organizations is arguably documentation. School teachers and clinicians must record compliance with state and federal regulations as they address students' academic and health needs; clinicians in mental health agencies bill in 15-minute increments for services by diagnosis; and child welfare and juvenile justice staff are subject to random audits of case files. These monitoring mechanisms can identify deficiencies but are unlikely to surface opportunities for actualizing children's potential. They also divert up to 90% of staff time from direct service provision (Schorr, 1997, p. 83) and foster atmospheres of fear. A manager in a large child welfare agency told me that when caseworkers were asked to share their case files for internal discussion about process improvement, not a single person volunteered.

The framework outlined in Figure 14.1 implies two potential options for buffering front line staff from the burden of documentation and thus supporting loving action for each child. First, and likely the most powerful, managers may reduce the amount of paperwork front line staff must complete. For instance, recent advances in agency level performance measurement may offer opportunities to reduce documentation of day-to-day activities (Schorr, 1997). Perhaps the most notable change in the last ten years in the United States has been the implementation of No Child Left Behind testing in all public schools, measuring school-level performance in children's academic skill development. School principals might use such outcomes measures to justify reducing documentation of some work for individual children (Meyer & Rowan, 1977), although it is also possible that No Child Left Behind documentation will simply add to pre-existing requirements.

The second option reflected in Figure 14.1 is to reduce the impact of existing paperwork requirements on staff burnout, for instance through enhanced electronic information systems, internal guidance about procedures, or more sufficient administrative support. Such approaches would have low political cost because they would not challenge external stakeholders or fundamentally alter internal routines. Previous research suggests that such managerial interventions might reduce the effects of paperwork on front line staff burnout by increasing their control over these demands (Fox, Dwyer, & Ganster, 1993).

Sustaining front line staff energy to act for children may also entail both active prioritization and passive resistance in the face of efforts at system improvement. Making systems truly work for children often entails fundamental changes in practice, instead of "graft[ing] new approaches on top of existing practices without altering ... norms or routines" (Coburn, 2003, p. 4). Agency leaders must therefore be selective about the changes they seek to implement. Of course, such choices may sometimes be made openly and explicitly. However, given all the competing demands on child-serving organizations and limited budgets, managers may sometimes use covert strategies to reduce the impact of potentially overwhelming dictates on front line staff (Pfeffer & Salancik, 1978). Both overt and covert managerial actions to reduce the amount of innovation front line staff experience may paradoxically reduce workload and burnout and thus preserve energy for loving action on behalf of each child.

As with documentation, in addition to reducing the magnitude of innovation-related demands, managers may also reduce the effect of given levels of such demands on staff burnout. Here the actions hypothesized to moderate the impact of innovation are similar to those for reducing the impact of paperwork requirements, and would essentially take the form of providing support. For instance, one would expect that a given innovation would produce less staff burnout when managers gave staff more control over implementation, and provided hands-on training with follow-up personal coaching to staff, as well as information system and administrative support.

Another potential way to support loving action for each child is to buffer front line staff from emotionally draining aspects of their work. The lives of children with serious mental illness can be heartbreaking. Verbal abuse of staff by families can also be traumatic (Walsh & Clarke, 2003). The result can be emotional exhaustion as well as a tendency to depersonalize children—that is, burnout (Schaufeli & Bakker, 2004).

Several managerial actions may buffer front line staff from emotional demands. The previously outlined job design change of giving staff start-to-finish case responsibility may reduce the emotional demands staff face by allowing more time to see children's health improve. In this sense, managers may be able to reduce this "input" into burnout. However, it may be more feasible for managers to moderate the effects of trauma on staff burnout than to reduce its occurrence, as organizations continue to see greater numbers of more disturbed children. For instance, staff whose coworkers and supervisors are emotionally available may experience less burnout after helping children recover from traumatic events. Again, this moderating mechanism may be one of enhancing the staff member's sense of control (Fox et al., 1993), as he or she has a chance to process the experience in a supportive context.

The potential mechanisms to buffer front line staff from abusive child and parent behavior generally parallel those for exposure to trauma, with one difference. This is the potential for managers to reduce abuse experienced by staff by supporting staff in engendering more positive interactions with children and caregivers. Positive Behavior Intervention and Support provides an illustration of this dynamic. This is an approach to discipline in schools that shifts the focus to positive child behaviors. For instance, teachers write notes and call caregivers when children are behaving especially well as well as when there are problems. Teachers employing Positive Behavior Intervention and Support have reported better interactions with children and caregivers. As one middle school teacher commented, "I feel I am teaching instead of disciplining in my class" (Bartelt, 2006).

The previous section described how managers might amplify the potential of financial, physical, and human resources to support loving action for each child. This section outlined how managers might also sustain such staff behaviors by buffering them from negative forces, using paperwork, secondary trauma, and abusive child and parent behavior as three illustrative stressors. These hypotheses built on the premise that managers may support loving front line staff behaviors both by amplifying the positive potential of the environment and by buffering staff from negative forces.

WHAT A POSITIVE LENS ON ORGANIZATIONS SERVING CHILDREN WITH MENTAL ILLNESS IMPLIES FOR SOCIAL CHANGE

The theory outlined in this chapter uses a positive approach to organizational scholarship in two ways. First, the dependent variable of loving action enriches the humanity of organizations for their staff and the people they serve. The loving part of this construct might be measured through coding observational data for affective tone (e.g., spoken and body language), staff self-report of how they experience interactions with children and caregivers, or child and caregiver reports of the tone of interactions with staff. Action might be measured through persistence within any one type of activity, such as the number of phone calls a counselor makes to reschedule appointments when a child does not come as scheduled. Another way to measure action could be the variety of approaches taken to achieve a goal such as connecting a child with the right counselor, e.g., calling the family, calling the provider, participating in meetings at schools or other settings, and visiting the family at home. By focusing on what enables front line staff to act on their innate love of children instead of negative outcomes such as turnover, positive organizational scholarship may yield new insights that ultimately support more effective services.

The second way this chapter exemplifies positive organizational scholarship is by theorizing about the positive causal mechanisms of change. Specifically, building on the *job demands-resources* model (Hakanen et al., 2006, 2004) and the framework of *virtuous organizations* (Cameron, 2003; Cameron et al., 2004), this chapter has outlined testable propositions about how agency managers may sustain and even reignite staff engagement and thus their loving action on behalf of each child. At the same time, the bottom causal path focuses on reducing dysfunction. The model thus examines how managers may engage with both positive and negative dynamics to achieve outcomes that benefit children, staff, and the organizations as a whole.

302 • *Rebecca Wells*

By shifting focus from visible dysfunction to often hidden potential, a positive lens may ultimately yield more accurate insights into organizations that serve children with mental illness. A colleague of the system dynamics pioneer Jay Forrester quotes him as reflecting that "People know intuitively where leverage points are. Time after time I've done an analysis of a company, and I've figured out a leverage point—in inventory policy, maybe, or in the relationship between sales force and productive force, or in personnel policy. Then I've gone to the company and discovered that there's already a lot of attention to that point. Everyone is trying very hard to push it *in the wrong direction*" (Meadows, 1999, p. 1).

The intrinsic love front line staff bring for children and those children's own potential for growth are arguably the greatest leverage points for organizations that serve those with mental illness. It is in the day-to-day interactions with and for children that staff have the chance to identify and act on each one's needs and strengths. Aware of these children's vulnerability, policy makers have developed many protective layers of accountability. In so doing, they may have been pushing in the wrong direction, toward mechanized processing and risk minimization instead of doing "whatever it takes" to liberate each child's remarkable potential.

The theory outlined in this chapter builds on the premise that a range of organizations share the common managerial challenge of supporting front line staff in work with children. At the same time, differences across and within organizations may affect the ranges of factors present and how they affect interactions with children. For instance, some agencies may be so small or understaffed that managers cannot provide coaching to front line staff. Similarly, start-to-finish case responsibility may entail a broader range of skills than staff in some contexts can develop. In child protective services, families may fare better when they can start again with a new person after an initial period often characterized by anger and denial. The effects of staff engagement and burnout on action may be attenuated in juvenile justice by the particularly short and unpredictable amounts of time adolescents tend to spend in this system. These caveats indicate that, despite the commonalities of the organizations described in this chapter, differences in roles and resources may affect the validity of specific hypotheses.

Future research may identify additional pathways between factors depicted within Figure 14.1 (Hakanen et al., 2006), including reinforcing loops. One potential "virtuous loop" may be that from loving staff actions to positive child outcomes that may in turn foster greater engagement and/

or reduce burnout (Cameron et al., 2004). The mental health director in a juvenile detention facility writes of: "success stories [such as] the youth who will ask for ongoing therapy after release and show concrete signs of positive growth…" and notes that "These occasional opportunities for optimism help us keep our chins up as we strive to provide necessary and optimal mental health services to a population that, on the surface, can appear to be beyond repair" (Lewis, 2010). A positive lens on organizations that serve children with mental illness may discover more ways of supporting such devoted staff in this critically important endeavor.

REFERENCES

Bakker, A., Hakanen, J., Demerouti, E., & Xanthopoulou, D. (2007). Job resources boost work engagement, particularly when job demands are high. *Journal of Educational Psychology, 99*, 274.

Bandura, A. (1998). Personal and collective efficacy in human adaption and change. In J. G. Adair, D. Belanger, & K. L. Dion (Eds.), *Advances in psychological science: Social, personal and cultural aspects*, Vol. 1 (pp. 51–71). Hove, England: Psychology Press/ Erlbaum Taylor & Francis.

Bartelt, G. (2006, April 5). Wake County Schools adopting new behavior system. *News 14 Carolina.* Retrieved September 29, 2010 from http://charlotte.news14.com/ content/82868/wake-county-schools-adopting-new-behavior-system.

Benson, P. L. (2006). *All kids are our kids: What communities must do to raise caring and responsible children and adolescents* (2nd ed.). San Francisco: Jossey-Bass.

Bickman, L., Noser, K., & Summerfelt, W. T. (1999). Long-term effects of a system of care on children and adolescents. *The Journal of Behavioral Health Services & Research, 26*, 185–202.

Blau, G. (1981). An empirical investigation of job stress, social support, service length, and job strain. *Organizational Behavior and Human Performance, 27*, 279–302.

Burns, B. J., Costello, E. J., Angold, A., Tweed, D., Stangl, D., Farmer, E. M., et al. (1995). Children's mental health service use across service sectors. *Health Affairs, 14*, 147–159.

Cameron, K. S. (2003). Organizational virtuousness and performance. In K. S. Cameron, J. E. Dutton, & R. E. Quinn (Eds.), *Positive organizational scholarship: Foundations of a new discipline* (pp. 48–65). San Francisco: Berrett-Koehler Publishers.

Cameron, K. S., Bright, D., & Caza, A. (2004). Exploring the relationships between organizational virtuousness and performance. *American Behavioral Scientist, 47*, 766.

Cameron, K. S., Dutton, J. E., & Quinn, R. E. (2003). *Positive organizational scholarship: Foundations of a new discipline.* San Francisco: Berrett-Koehler Publishers.

Carver, C. S., & Scheier, M. E. (2002). Optimism, pessimism, and self-regulation. In E. C. Chang (Ed.), *Optimism & pessimism: Implications for theory, research, and practice* (pp. 31–51). Washington, DC: American Psychological Association.

Chuang, E. (2010). Facilitating service access for children and families in child welfare: An ecological perspective. ProQuest Dissertations & Theses. The University of North Carolina-Chapel Hill. 2010.

Coburn, C. E. (2003). Rethinking scale: Moving beyond numbers to deep and lasting change. *Educational Researcher, 32,* 3–12.

Cooperrider, D. L., & Sekerka, L. E. (2003). Toward a theory of positive organizational change. In J. E. Dutton, R. E. Quinn, & K. S. Cameron (Eds.), *Positive organizational scholarship: Foundations of a new discipline* (pp. 225–240). San Francisco: Berrett-Koehler Publishers.

Cordes, C., & Dougherty, T. (1993). A review and an integration of research on job burnout. *Academy of Management Review, 18,* 621–656.

Dreachslin, J. L., Hunt, P. L., & Sprainer, E. (1999). Communication patterns and group composition: Implications for patient-centered care team. *Journal of Healthcare Management, 44,* 252–268.

Dutton, J., Roberts, L., & Bednar, J. (2010). Pathways for positive identity construction at work: Four types of positive identity and the building of social resources. *The Academy of Management Review (AMR), 35,* 265–293.

Eccles, J. S., & Gootman, J. A. (2002). *Community programs to promote youth development.* Washington, DC: National Academy Press.

Edmondson, A. (1999). Psychological safety and learning behavior in work teams. *Administrative Science Quarterly, 44,* 350–383.

Farmer, E., Burns, B., Phillips, S., Angold, A., & Costello, E. (2003). Pathways into and through mental health services for children and adolescents. *Psychiatric Services, 54,* 60.

Fox, M. L., Dwyer, D. J., & Ganster, D. C. (1993). Effects of stressful job demands and control on physiological and attitudinal outcomes in a hospital setting. *Academy of Management Journal, 36,* 289–318.

Fromm, E. (2000). *The art of loving.* London: Continuum International Publishing Group.

Gifford, E. J., Wells, R., Bai, Y., Troop, T. O., Miller, S., & Babinski, L. M. (2010). Pairing nurses and social workers in schools: North Carolina's school-based child and family support teams. *Journal of School Health, 80,* 104–107.

Golden, O. (2009). *Reforming child welfare.* Washington, DC: The Urban Institute.

Grant, A. M. (2007). Relational job design and the motivation to make a prosocial difference. *Academy of Management Review, 32,* 393.

Hackman, J. R., & Oldham, G. R. (1976). Motivation through the design of work: Test of a theory. *Organizational Behavior and Human Performance, 16,* 250–279.

Hakanen, J., Bakker, A., & Schaufeli, W. (2006). Burnout and work engagement among teachers. *Journal of School Psychology, 43,* 495–513.

Harlem Children's Zone. (2010). From cradle through college: Using evidence-based programs to inform a comprehensive pipeline. Retrieved November 21, 2011, from http://www.hcz.org/images/stories/From%20Cradle%20through%20College_11.6.09.final.pdf

Hobfoll, S. (1989). Conservation of resources. *American Psychologist, 44,* 513–524.

Hobfoll, S., & Shirom, A. (2001). Conservation of resources theory: Applications to stress and management in the workplace. In R. T. Golembiewski (Ed.), *Handbook of organization behavior,* 2nd ed. (pp. 57–81). New York: Marcel Dekker.

Ibarra, H. (1999). Provisional selves: Experimenting with image and identity in professional adaptation. *Administrative Science Quarterly, 44,* 764–791.

Lawson, H. A., Claiborne, N., Hardiman, E., Austin, S., & Surko, M. (2007). Deriving theories of change from successful community development partnerships for youths: Implications for school improvement. *American Journal of Education, 114,* 1–40.

Lehr, C. A., Hansen, A., Sinclair, M. F., & Christenson, S. L. (2003). Moving beyond dropout towards school completion: An integrative review of data-based interventions. *School Psychology Review, 32,* 342–365.

Lewis, R. Mental health services in San Francisco's juvenile justice system. Retrieved November 21, 2011, from http://www.sfms.org/AM/Template.cfm?Section=Home &SECTION=Article_Archives&TEMPLATE=/CM/HTMLDisplay.cfm& CONTENTID=1845

Maslach, C. (1998). A multidimensional theory of burnout. In C. Cooper (Ed.), *Theories of organizational stress* (pp. 68–85). New York: Oxford University Press.

Meadows, D. (1999). *Leverage points: Places to intervene in a system.* Hartland, VT: The Sustainability Institute.

Meyer, J., & Rowan, B. (1977). Institutionalized organizations: Formal structure as myth and ceremony. *American Journal of Sociology, 83,* 340–363.

NC Collaborative for Children Youth and Families. (2010). October 8 meeting minutes. Retrieved November 21, 2011, from http://www.nccollaborative.org/content/meetin g+minutes+%26amp%3B+archive+of+announcements/9656

Parkes, K., Mendham, C., & von Rabenau, C. (1994). Social support and the demand-discretion model of job stress: Tests of additive and interactive effects in two samples. *Journal of Vocational Behavior, 44,* 91–113.

Pfeffer, J., & Salancik, G. R. (1978). *The external control of organizations: A resource dependence perspective.* New York: Harper & Row.

Ryan, R., & Deci, E. (2000). Self-determination theory and the facilitation of intrinsic motivation, social development, and well-being. *American Psychologist, 55,* 68–78.

Schaufeli, W., & Bakker, A. (2004). Job demands, job resources, and their relationship with burnout and engagement: A multi-sample study. *Journal of Organizational Behavior, 25,* 293–315.

Schorr, L. B. (1997). *Common purpose: Strengthening families and neighborhoods to rebuild America.* New York: Anchor Books, Doubleday.

Scott, P. G. (1997). Assessing determinants of bureaucratic discretion: An experiment in street-level decision making. *Journal of Public Administration Research and Theory, 7,* 35.

Smith, B. D., & Mogro-Wilson, C. (2007). Multilevel influences on the practice of interagency collaboration in child welfare and substance abuse treatment. *Children and Youth Services Review, 29,* 545–556.

Walsh, B. R., & Clarke, E. (2003). Post-trauma syniptoms in health workers following physical and verbal aggression. *Work & Stress, 17,* 170–181.

Weick, K. (1979). *The social psychology of organizing.* Reading, MA: Addison-Wesley.

15

Generative Change in Health Care Organizations: Co-Creating Health to Reduce Health Disparities

Valerie Myers and Lynn Perry Wooten
University of Michigan

The popular media has celebrated dramatic improvements in Americans' overall health during the last century. Healthcare research, however, shows that subsets of the population disproportionately experience poor health outcomes and problems accessing high-quality healthcare services. People of lower socioeconomic status, racial and ethnic minorities, or people that live in underserved geographic areas have poorer health outcomes than the national average. Studies also show differences in the quality of health care provided to women, children, the elderly, and people with chronic illness, which results in disparities in health outcomes (Institute of Medicine [IOM], 2003). These differences are labeled health disparities and are considered inequitable differences in health, health care, and health outcomes that are potentially systematic and avoidable (Carter-Pokras & Baquet, 2002).

Health disparities have individual and national consequences. More specifically, health disparities are burdensome personally, making it difficult for individuals to participate fully in their community's social, cultural, and economic life. When health disparities are clustered among identifiable subsets of the population, the adverse effects can result in exclusion, stigmatization, hopelessness, and higher mortality rates (Health Disparities Task Group, 2005).

At a macro level, health disparities have persisted in the United States since the nation's founding and are perceived as a never-ending problem that pervades the American health system (Mullins, 2006). Although the type of health disparity varies in magnitude by clinical condition and population, disparities are observed in almost all aspects of health care

(Agency for Healthcare Research and Quality [AHRQ], 2005). Perhaps most importantly, disparities in health care are preventable and unnecessarily increase healthcare costs. These financial costs are then transferred to insurance companies, consumer premiums, healthcare organizations, and taxpayers (AHRQ, 2005). Untenable personal and national costs priority for some government agencies, medical researchers, healthcare organizations, and community groups. Specific clinical areas are being targeted to alleviate health disparities, including the prevalence of pre-term births among women of color.

In 2005, the annual economic cost of preterm births in the United States was estimated at $26.2 billion, with an average cost of $51,600 per preterm infant born (Behrman & Butler, 2007). These costs are due to greater risks of adverse health and developmental outcomes including cerebral palsy, mental retardation, hearing loss, impaired vision, behavioral problems, academic difficulties, emotional problems, and other disabling adult-onset diseases (Behrman & Butler, 2007). The cost of preterm births increases longitudinally with expenditures on special education. These financial costs however, pale compared to human costs; indeed, preterm births are a leading cause of infant mortality and are highest among women of color.

African-American babies have the highest infant mortality rate in the developed world. Twice as many African-American babies as Caucasian babies die in infancy or have low birth weights. Further, African-American women are three times more likely than Caucasian women to die during pregnancy (David & Collins, 1997). Historically, this gap in birth outcomes between whites and people of color has not only persisted, but worsened in recent years, despite federal and state government funding to organizations working to eliminate the difference (United States Department of Health and Human Services, 2000). This costly and long-standing problem is somewhat of a medical mystery because it is not easily explained by the mother's age, access to prenatal care, or socioeconomic status (Kashif, 2003). Research does show, however, that certain stressors (neighborhood environment, discrimination, economic adversity, marginalization) create a "hostile" physiological environment for African-American mothers (Lu & Chen, 2004; Mullins, 2006), which can result in preterm births.

Little is known about successful strategies to eliminate these and other health disparities, yet effective solutions do exist. Some organizations possess knowledge and capabilities to alleviate health disparities that can be transferred across clinical conditions and organizations (Bradley, Curry,

Ramanadhan, Rowe, Nembhard, & Krumholz, 2009). In instances where organizations have developed effective solutions, however, we know little about the mechanisms that propelled them from inertia, to action, to reducing health disparities, including preterm births.

The goal of this chapter is to elucidate the processes by which organizations can successfully alleviate health disparities for African-American women and their babies. Toward that end, we present two case studies to illustrate generative changes and mechanisms in the process of "co-creating health." The World Health Organization (1948, p. 100) defines health as: "the state of complete physical, mental, and social well-being and not merely the absence of disease or infirmity." Our case studies show how individuals and organizations partner to co-create health in ways that align with the Institute of Medicine's aims for safe, efficient, effective, timely, patient-centered, and accessible care. Through the lens of Positive Organizational Scholarship, we examine mechanisms of the generative change process used to improve maternal-child health. We focus on the dominant mechanism of relationships, which is supported by cognitive, behavioral, and affective mechanisms. We conclude by discussing the theoretical and practical implications of these findings for positive social change in health care.

BACKGROUND

Generative Change in Health Care

Positive organizational scholarship (POS) provides a lens to examine how organizations work with constituents to solve complex problems, such as alleviating health disparities, by organizing for generative change (Glynn & Dutton, 2007). Generative change entails the ability to acquire, create, expand, reconfigure, diffuse, and transform resources to achieve organizational goals. Resources are the specific physical, human, and organizational assets that can be used to implement strategies (Eisenhardt & Martin, 2000). In this instance, the goal is to promote health—not merely treat diseases—which ultimately eliminates birth outcome disparities. This goal necessitates acquiring resources, expanding capabilities, reconfiguring the clinical encounter, and diffusing practices throughout the healthcare system and beyond.

Some contend that generative change in health care requires system reforms and structural reorganization to foster a culture of excellence (Davies, Nutley, & Mannion, 2000; Donaldson, Muir, & Gray, 1998). System change must be implemented at multiple levels including the macro-environment that establishes and enacts healthcare policies; the organizational infrastructure for delivering health care; and work units that are responsible for the patient care experience (IOM, 2003). Systems for seeding this excellence already exist throughout the healthcare delivery process, but need to be redesigned for comprehensive and coordinated patient-centered care (Berwick, 2002).

Generative change also requires mental and tactical shifts toward a healthcare delivery model that creates and uses resources to anticipate patients' needs and provides customized services aligned with patients' values and cultural norms. The resulting generative changes will shift the focus of primary health care from "visits" to patient-centered, continuous healing relationships. The question is: *How do we begin the process toward such a generative change?*

Mechanisms of Generative Change to Reduce Health Disparities

Research suggests that organizational change intended to improve health-care practices and outcomes can be understood through the interaction of context process and content of change (Pettigrew, Ferlie, & McKee, 1992). Internal and external contexts explain the *why* of change; stakeholders' actions constitute the process of *how* change is achieved; and content is *what* is changed (Heward, Hutchins, & Keleher, 2007). This model of change recognizes that interventions to improve healthcare practices and outcomes are embedded in a pre-existing set of social, political, and structural contexts that must be considered when planning the change process (Green & Kreuter, 1999). Here, we are interested in *why* organizations have seized the challenge to eliminate disparities in maternal-child health (antecedents); *what* specific variables organizations modified to produce the desired result; and *how* the change process unfolded (mechanisms).

Mechanisms are of particular interest because they represent the "cogs and wheels" in theorizing that describe a set of interacting parts. When assembled, these parts produce an effect not inherent in one of them (Davis & Marquis, 2005; McAdam, Tarrow, & Tilly, 2001). Mechanisms describe implicit cognitive, affective, behavioral, and relational components of a theory (Weber, 2006). The focus of our inquiry is to understand the invisible mechanisms, and their generative properties, that were instrumental in closing the health disparity gaps. We found that the relational mechanism of co-creation was central to solving this vexing problem.

Co-Creating Health: A Type of Generative Change

Co-creating health is one of many generative change processes that can promote health and reduce disparities. Although the term co-create might be considered analogous to collaboration, we use co-create because we believe it is inherently more positive and generative and is linked to processes and outcomes. The prefix *co-* suggests an egalitarian, inclusive partnership process that requires mutuality or comparable investment. The word *creation* is outcome focused, indicating a new or unique invention that is constructive and beneficial. Egalitarian and inclusive processes are not normative in health care, nor have different collaborations resulted in the beneficial outcome of reducing disparities. We thus use the term co-create to describe relational mechanisms and processes that resulted in radically improved maternal-child health.

Toward that end, we present case studies of two organizations that deployed generative change processes to reduce poor health outcomes for African-American women and their babies. These cases are remarkable because while other healthcare organizations have made incremental to nonexistent progress to reduce birth outcome disparities in the past decade, these organizations have succeeded (U.S. Department of Health & Human Services, 2005). In analyzing these case studies, we make ambiguous and implicit processes explicit and accessible. We hope that these processes can then be replicated to alleviate health disparities more broadly and promote positive individual, organizational, and societal changes.

RESEARCH METHODOLOGY

Sample

The results presented here were drawn from a larger interdisciplinary study funded by the National Institutes of Health. This study examined health disparities from the perspective of leadership, healthcare providers, and patients. For this segment of the study, we collected a purposive sample of data from approximately 75 organizations, including hospitals, health clinics, government agencies, and other nonprofit organizations. Purposive sampling allowed us to select organizations that use an array of practices to reduce birth outcome disparities (Strauss & Corbin, 1998).

For each organization, we coded leadership practices, approaches used to address birth outcome disparities, knowledge management strategies, partnerships, funding sources, and program outcome measures. As we coded data, it became clear that birth outcomes varied across organizations, and we had not fully captured the mechanisms that contributed to success strategies that reduce birth outcome disparities for African Americans. To gain additional insights, we analyzed case study data from a subsample of organizations that achieved positive outcomes such as reduced infant mortality and low birth weight. In this chapter, we focus on two organizations from this subsample in which the generative change processes for alleviating health disparities are "transparently observable" (Eisenhardt, 1989).

Case Studies

We present two case studies that examine organizational sets, comprised of partnerships with a focal agency that use a particular model of maternal-child health. These sets represent new organizations that formed specifically in response to the complex problem of birth outcome disparities. Each case illustrates generative change processes at different levels of analysis, which all provide insights that will enhance theory and practice. The first organizational set, Focusing on Pregnancy, illustrates generative changes in the process of delivering health care services (e.g., patients and healthcare providers) to improve patient health. The second organizational set, the County Health Coalition, illustrates macro-level systemic changes designed to improve population health in a vulnerable community.

Case Study 1: The Focusing on Pregnancy Institute Model of Care

Focusing on Pregnancy (FOP) is a nonprofit healthcare institute founded by a nurse-midwife. Its mission is to change the paradigm of health services to a group care model in order to improve the overall health outcomes of mothers, babies, and new families. FOP's staff of five develops training materials, certifies sites, conducts workshops, and assures the organization's financial stability. In addition to the staff, a network of 30 certified trainer affiliates teach healthcare providers to use the FOP model of care. More than 300 organizations have adopted the model as a means to reduce birth outcome disparities for African Americans, including public health clinics, hospitals, healthcare systems, and private physician practices.

The FOP model of care entails groups of 8–12 women whose pregnancies are at a similar gestational stage who attend 10, two-hour visits together. Organizations choose the Focusing on Pregnancy model for its health promotion component, comprehensive services, and its ability to address both psychosocial and medical needs of women (Klima, Norr, Vonderheid, & Handler, 2009; Rising, 1998). This model of group prenatal care differs from individual prenatal care in four key practices, which are interconnected and mutually reinforcing (Rising, Kennedy, & Klima, 2004):

1. Health promotion group discussions are substantially longer than patient-provider discussions during a traditional obstetrics appointment.
2. Repeated interactions foster peer support and information sharing among the participating women.
3. A feminist approach to health care emphasizes symmetry in the patient-provider relationship and shared decision-making (Andrist, 1997).
4. Patient education enhances mothers' skills by teaching self-management, maintaining health records, and how to observe and monitor changes in mothers' health over time.

The model has resulted in numerous positive outcomes for participating organizations and their patients, including lower infant mortality rates; reduced risk factors of infant mortality such as low birth weights and premature births; and higher rates of breastfeeding, which has protective health benefits (Ickovics, 2003; Ickovics, Kershaw, Westdahl, Magriples, Massey, & Reynolds, 2007; Klima et al., 2009). Interestingly, preterm infants born to Focusing on Pregnancy patients actually had higher birth weights than those born to mothers receiving traditional patient care (Klima et al., 2009). For this analysis, we collected data from the Focusing on Pregnancy Institute, which developed the model, and three healthcare organizations:

a county health department and two university-affiliated hospitals that had implemented the model with their patients and healthcare providers.

Case Study 2: County Health Coalition's Community Care Model

The County Health Coalition (CHC) was created in 1992 in the aftermath of local manufacturing plant closures; it's mission was to improve the health status of area residents by improving the quality and cost effectiveness of the health care system. It is a nonprofit partnership between healthcare providers and purchasers, health service consumers, county citizens, government agencies, insurers, and educators. The Coalition has a staff of nine and partners with 26 organizations to execute its goals of better access to care, improved quality of care, reduced costs, and improved patient health outcomes. It advances both policy and practice agendas that improve the culture of health care; increases the use of evidence-based practices; promotes preventive health, health literacy, and effective management practices; and encourages healthy lifestyle choices through advocacy, education, and other community initiatives.

To achieve their goal of system-wide generative change, including reduced birth outcome disparities, CHC implemented a grassroots effort called "Community Care." For our analysis, we collected data from CHC board members, staff, and representatives from seven partnering organizations. As a result of CHC's work over seven years, the county's infant mortality disparity gap narrowed by 33%, and the death of African-American infants was reduced by 57%.

Although both of these case studies feature organizational partnerships, we use the term "organization" as shorthand to describe new organizations that emerged as a result of collective efforts to co-create health using either the Focusing on Pregnancy model or the Community Care models. This shorthand is consistent with Mintzberg's (1979) definition of an organization; that is, people working together to achieve a goal that could not be accomplished alone, using purposeful partnerships, divisions of labor, and a structure for coordinating work.

Data Analysis

Data were collected from archival sources and professionally transcribed field notes from interviews and directly observed meetings.

Data was entered into Microsoft Word and content analyzed using NVivo qualitative software. To understand the organizational practices and mechanisms involved in alleviating birth outcome disparities, the research team analyzed and categorized data by deploying approaches that integrated deductive (theory-based) and partly inductive (data-driven) procedures to guide our process of analyzing case data (Strauss & Corbin, 1998).

We conducted an open-ended coding process that used theoretical frameworks from the organizational change and learning literatures. We examined the data for similar themes and then organized them into coding nodes related to overarching theoretical concepts and categories. Then, we analyzed cases using both a within-case and cross-case analysis strategy (Miles & Huberman, 1994). Within-case studies allowed us to place a particular organization's actions in context, whereas the cross-case analysis permitted us to compare experiences across two organizations. The combination of deductive and inductive analysis of cross-case data provided a foundation for our theoretical inferences (Eisenhardt, 1989; Yin, 1999).

Results

Both organizations achieved significant improvements in the birth outcome disparities gap. But how did they do it? Our data show similar antecedents of the generative change process, as well as similar relational, cognitive, and behavioral mechanisms at work, albeit in very different ways.

Antecedents of Generative Change to Improve Birth Outcomes

Why did organizations embark on the challenge to reduce birth outcome disparities? We found the common antecedents of change for both organizations were leaders' use of empirical, experiential, and ideological phenomena. While empirical and experiential data focused on the problem and prevalence of health disparities, ideological phenomena were particularly generative because of their positive focus on health. The combination of all phenomena heightened leaders' awareness of and sensitivity to the disparities issue and provided the impetus for action.

Empirical and Experiential Data: Practical Reasons to Change

Empirically, epidemiological data about birth outcome disparities is accessible and publicized to national and local healthcare organizations. Not all leaders scan the environment for such data, however, or integrate those data with experiential knowledge. The leaders of Focusing on Pregnancy and the County Health Coalition gathered epidemiological data from the Centers for Disease Control and Prevention (CDC), healthcare systems, state public health departments, and university research centers. As one County Health Coalition member noted:

> So in the initial years of the County Health Coalition, we looked at quality, cost, and access data to understand how to reduce the county's healthcare costs. Our thoughts were you have to reduce the number of folks that are experiencing challenges in the healthcare system. So you look across the board and identify the fact that in this county, more African Americans are suffering disproportionately from these things. You've got to—you have to really take a good look at that.[1]

In addition, leaders of the County Health Coalition read published articles that showed that disparities existed despite income. This was an eye-opener:

> ...and we're suddenly at the point where we're realizing it's not just poor African-American women who are having babies who die in the first year, okay. It's really across the spectrum socio-economically, which means that we may have been looking at this wrong.

These observations were the impetus for County Health Coalition leaders to collaborate with human service and faith-based agencies to frame and coordinate a consumer-driven, interagency referral and case management service, which would be available to all pregnant women. One person remarked,

> Okay, and we looked at the information from, from all sides. That's why the Coalition came up with this concept that it's come up with. We are trying to literally just turn everything upside down and look at it from all sides and come up with something new.

---

[1] All quoted material in this section comes from interviews and communications the authors conducted during the study.

Coalition leaders also collected experiential data by observing and listening to community concerns. They learned that community members attributed disparities in infant mortality to the government, parents, poverty, lack of insurance, and discrimination within the healthcare systems and among its practitioners. These empirical and experiential data led the County Health Coalition to develop the "Community Care" model, which was designed to reduce racism, foster community mobilization, and enhance the prenatal healthcare system. The leaders' awareness of and sensitivity to birth outcomes disparities data, combined with ideological shifts, propelled the organization from inertia to action.

The founder for Focusing on Pregnancy reflected upon her experiences from 27 years as a nurse-midwife. She recognized that patient group meetings were not only efficient, but could also help empower patients to engage in the process of improving birth outcomes. She believed that groups were a better way to engage patients and providers in the prenatal care process and that mutuality offered both great potential for the personal growth and reduced birth outcome disparities (Rising et al., 2004). Further, she thought that the group care model would enhance patients' learning, promote high-quality connections among patients, and create an atmosphere of learning and sharing with physicians that could not be replicated in a one-on-one encounter (Rising & Jolivet, 2009).

Professional Ideology: The Ethical Imperative for Change

Both Focusing on Pregnancy and County Health Coalition relied upon existing professional work ideologies to establish their goals. A work ideology is a set of shared, logically integrated beliefs and practices binding individuals to their occupation that is developed over time from professional training and work experiences (Trice & Beyer, 1993). It provides members of a profession with an explicit mode for reasoning solutions and serves as a schema for interacting with stakeholders. A work ideology gives occupational members a sense that they possess unique values and abilities. Ideologies are enacted through standard practices for achieving excellence in professional work and a propensity to serve the community and benefit society with their expertise (Bunderson, 2001; Van Mannen & Barley, 1984). The ideologies of nurse-midwifery and public health are integrative in that they identify disease and problematic health outcomes, yet are inherently generative in their focus on health and the potential for partnerships to promote it.

Focusing on Pregnancy's Nurse-Midwifery Ideology

Nurse-midwife professionals are trained in both nursing and midwifery. Their professional practices focus on managing women's health, particularly through a non-interventional, individualized approach to normal pregnancy that involves patient education (Rooks, 1997). The work ideology of nurse-midwives emphasizes a partnership model of care, which entails collaborating with the communities they serve to promote health, implement health interventions, and reduce health problems (Goeppinger & Shuster, 1987). Nurse-midwives often serve vulnerable populations such as low-income patients, immigrants, ethnic minorities, and women who lack access to health care (Rooks, 1997).

The founder of Focusing on Pregnancy drew upon her nurse-midwife ideology of group care to promote generative changes among patients and healthcare providers. Foremost, she considered patients and healthcare equal partners that could co-create goals and seek appropriate means to achieve them. Further, the Focusing on Pregnancy staff trained healthcare providers to draw upon the nurse-midwifery work ideology as they diffused this model of group prenatal care.

County Health Coalition's Public Health Ideology

County Health Coalition members used a public health work ideology to frame their mission to reduce birth outcome disparities for African Americans. Public health workers perceive their professional role as agents who prevent diseases, promote health, and prolong life in communities through organized and informed efforts (Winslow, 1920). Public health practitioners accomplish their goals through collaborative actions that result in sustainable and supportive systems for community health (Beaglehole, Bonita, Horton, Adams, & McKee, 2004). Partnerships are a central tenet of the public health ideology because of the underlying assumptions that: (1) complex community health goals cannot be achieved by working alone; (2) participants in public health partnerships should include a diversity of individuals or groups to represent the population's concerns; and (3) a shared interest facilitates consensus among partners (Roussos & Fawcett, 2000).

The County Health Coalition framed health disparities as a public health issue after hearing a former surgeon general's speech. Subsequently, coalition board members determined that health disparities were an underlying factor in many of their local health issues. They subsequently decided that infant mortality should be a priority because: (1) their county had the highest infant mortality rates in its state, and (2) the greatest disparity gap in infant mortality rates was between the African-American and Caucasian populations. Coalition partners reasoned that the rate of infant deaths signaled inadequate community commitment to its most vulnerable members. Thus, by tackling this problem, the coalition could not only improve poor outcomes for infants, but also focus attention on the health and lifestyles of adults as a byproduct. Ideally, this would manifest in better community health practices and health outcomes in other areas.

To summarize, the cognitive mechanisms of empiricism, awareness, and ideology, coupled with experience, explain why organizations embraced the challenge to reduce birth outcome disparities. The ideologies of both organizations extol the need for partners and help those partners identify useful professional practices that can serve as a foundation for future work in the generative change process (Ganz, 2002). Next, we examine *what* changed (content) and *how* (process).

Initiating the Change Process: Transitioning to New Models of Maternal-Child Health

Building upon data and ideology, both case studies relied upon a theory of change to guide the transition to their chosen model. A theory of change describes the process of planned social change and why certain programs are expected to enable that change (Mackinnon & Amott, 2006). It is a cognitive mechanism that explains the cause-and-effect logic of programming that will use resources (dollars and people) as inputs to achieve desired outcomes (Bradach, Tierney, & Stone, 2008). A theory of change shapes operating principles and program design by making implicit assumptions explicit. It is informed by the organization's values, best practices within a sector, and data that indicates the needs of beneficiaries (Colby, Stone, & Carttar, 2004). Thus, theories of change are cognitive mechanisms that integrate tacit and formal knowledge to guide future actions.

Focusing on Pregnancy embraced a theory of change that promoted a paradigm shift in prenatal care delivery—from individual care to group care. To achieve this shift, they recognized the need to acquire resources and develop talent in the form of training "evangelists" to use their approach at various healthcare organizations. Training included workshops for healthcare professionals, consultation services, developing educational materials, certifying trainers, and site approvals. They also thought it was important to train patients.

The County Health Coalition's theory of change was based on the need to transform the culture of the maternal-child healthcare system through better customer service and ameliorating institutionalized racism. They hypothesized that better customer service would break down barriers between patients and the healthcare system, improve patient access to care, and increase use of healthcare services before, during, and after prenatal care (Indiana Perinatal Network, 2003).

The County Health Coalition (CHC) was also concerned with the cumulative, negative effects of institutionalized racism, which result in adverse life experiences, increased stress, poor access to care, poor quality of care, and the lack of services to address the needs of specific ethnic groups (Barnes-Josiah, 2004). To accomplish their goals, CHC recognized the need to acquire resources and develop talent. CHC pursued a two-pronged approach to talent development. To accomplish their goals, CHC recognized the need to acquire resources and develop talent. Pursued a two-pronged approach to developing talent. First, they invited the Disney Institute to conduct service excellence training for healthcare providers. They also worked with a national organization to conduct seminars that "educate, challenge, and empower people to 'undo' the racist structure that hinders effective social change" (Pestronk & Franks, 2003, p. 330). In these seminars, participants considered various ways that racism is manifest in healthcare settings and how to move from reticence and complacency to acceptance and actively engaging in reducing racism.

Both organizations used theories of change that made previously implicit goals and assumptions explicit. They focused attention on impediments to alleviating health disparities and factors that enabled the process of co-creating health. The agencies' professional ideologies and theories of change provided the platform for concrete actions to acquire resources, develop talent, and empower patients. We next examine the generative ways in which those actions unfolded, given practical constraints.

Mechanisms for Co-Creating Health

Relational mechanisms dominated the change process of both organizations. The generative nature of relational mechanisms led us to use the term "co-creation,"—as opposed to collaboration—to define the change processes. In addition to our previous definition of health, we expand on the World Health Organization's definition to suggest that co-creating health to reduce health disparities encompasses the collective resourcefulness of relevant stakeholders, including healthcare providers, patients, payors, and legislators who leverage high-quality connections to foster "the state of complete health" for all. This implies not only access to health care, but incorporates learning and applying the "best" evidenced-based practices to support physical, mental, and social well-being, in addition to meeting basic needs (e.g., food, housing, safety, and dignity).

We found that relational mechanisms were supported by cognitive, behavioral, and affective mechanisms, all of which align with the mechanisms of health promotion (Green & Kreuter, 1999). These mechanisms became evident as organizations pooled their resources, acquired new resources, developed talent, and empowered patients. We describe the generative properties of each mechanism, although boundaries between mechanisms are sometimes porous.

Relational Mechanisms: Partnerships, High-Quality Connections, and Collective Resourcefulness

Partnerships were a central mechanism of the generative change process for both FOP and CHC. Partners varied however, depending on the organization and model-in-use that we observed (Figures 15.1 and 15.2). The County Health Coalition fostered partnerships across sectors between healthcare providers and purchasers, health services consumers, county citizens, government agencies, and educators. In contrast, Focusing on Pregnancy promoted within-sector partnerships among health professionals, scholars, and patients to enhance interpersonal dynamics of the clinical encounter and to encourage peer support. Both models deployed an egalitarian approach to promoting health that valued all stakeholders, particularly the most vulnerable. The Community Care model focused on the health of an entire population, situating patients in a broader community. In contrast, Focusing on Pregnancy targeted individual patients,

FIGURE 15.1
County Health Coalition Community Care Model.

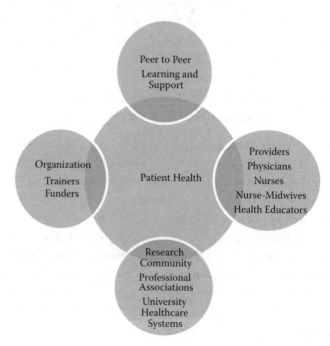

FIGURE 15.2
Focusing on Pregnancy Model.

within their relevant relationships, and sought to enlarge the patient's role with education and empowerment. With a leader's guidance, these partnerships emerged organically from professional ideologies about the "correct way" to treat and prevent health problems.

Interviews with County Health Coalition members convey the value of partnerships and their importance for coalescing different people to address infant mortality rates for African Americans in their county:

> Solving our area's healthcare problems is a big challenge. The issues are complicated and the answers are complex. By working together, we can do so much more than any of us could ever accomplish alone.

> There was a great interest for the partnership to be inclusive. It's like if we could work on the recipients, but if you don't work on the other side you're going to have this one-sided effort. So, it was all the work that we are doing, I think that let us know that they [referring to a diversity of stakeholders] needed to be at the table as a partner.

The County Health Coalition's public health work ideology explicitly values diverse individuals working together to solve problems because each brings different perspectives, epistemological styles, information, and contacts to the table (O'Neill, Lemieux, Groleau, Fortin, & Lamarche, 1997; Page, 2007). CHC believes that public health partnerships with diverse members create resources that help diffuse evidence-based medical models and wellness-based practices that address the social, economic, cultural, and environmental determinants of health (Weiner, 1996). As one County Health Coalition member suggested, their work ideology resulted in systems thinking about why diverse perspectives were needed to address the problem of health disparities in their community:

> To address health disparities in this county, we need a coalition not just looking at one piece of the system. We need to look at and do work on multiple layers of the system, and the social system that continues to maintain a system that lends itself to these racial disparities whether it is from an access perspective or even from an individual person's perspective. So, it is a way of thinking we adopt.

Similarly, another member of the County Health Coalition discussed the importance of a public health work ideology. He framed the coalition's task as establishing partnerships to develop resources for to alleviate health care and links community organizations to the health delivery systems (Witmer, 1995):

> To address birth outcome disparities, you have to go beyond dealing with health-care issues because all you're talking about is health professionals and buildings and facilities and programs. All you're talking about are the more proximal causes of a problem. And sooner or later, you have to deal with the things that are in the environment in which the proximal causes exist. Like you have a community where two out of five houses on a block are missing, schools are closing, police and fire protection is being withdrawn. That increases stress levels of people who don't have choices about where they're going to live. We have to consider if that contributes to disease and health.

Both the nurse-midwifery and public health ideologies fostered partnerships that were perceived as vital for co-creating community health by reducing disparities. The partnerships were effective in achieving their goals because of core generative properties—high-quality connections and collective resourcefulness.

High-quality connections between people are characterized by mutuality, positive regard, and vitality (Dutton & Heaphy, 2003). They are fueled by growth and learning that occurs during interactions; hence, high-quality connections are life-giving and endow individuals with useful and valuable resources, such as trust and psychological safety. Consequently, high-quality connections facilitate co-constructing roles and outcomes. With FOP and CHC, "high quality" enhanced the nature of existing collaborative relationships between community organizations, between patients and healthcare providers, and among patient peers in a group setting. High quality connections also created a climate in which collective resourcefulness could flourish.

Collective resourcefulness is an organizational phenomenon that expands members' capabilities (Glynn & Dutton, 2007). Collective resourcefulness is an organizational phenomenon that expands members' capabilities in ways that promote thriving, extraordinary work practices; superior organizational learning; and heightened adaptability. Collective resourcefulness enhances the likelihood that organizations will achieve positive outcomes and optimal performance.

High-quality connections and collective resourcefulness were central and evident in both case studies and were supported by other generative mechanisms.

Relational and Behavioral Mechanisms:
Partnerships for Resource Acquisition

To realize their envisioned changes, the organizations using both prenatal health models needed to fortify their infrastructure with additional funding, program changes, and training (Joffres, Health, Farquharson, Barkhouse, Latter, & MacLean, 2004). In the case of Focusing on Pregnancy, leaders sought external grant funding to finance program costs and evaluation. External funders included state health departments, local chapters of The March of Dimes, university medical centers, and foundations. Obtaining funding to conduct program evaluation was generative because evaluation results conferred legitimacy and helped the founder promote the model. Focusing on Pregnancy further enhanced its financial resources by creating a donor movement that was committed to advocating for health care improvements. They sought donors through direct mail and the Internet. The donor campaign produced financial, relational, and intangible resources. Donors' gifts symbolized their commitment to the organization's mission and helped cultivate a network of evangelists (Crutchfield & Grant, 2007). As a result of their development efforts, Focusing on Pregnancy tripled the number of organizations that used its group prenatal care model and earned awards for innovation and it effectiveness.

In contrast, not all of the County Health Coalition's fund-raising attempts were fruitful, but they did lead to new and surprising partnerships. The County Health Coalition's application ranked fourth for a national grant to fund high-quality and culturally appropriate maternal and child health services. Funding was only disbursed to three communities, however, which eliminated CHC. Still CHC believed that applying for the grant "was the right thing to do and would provide the conceptual glue needed to link the many maternal and child health interventions already being implemented in the community."

The County Health Coalition persisted with a unique fundraising approach: they invited three local foundations to the same luncheon, where they asked for financial support for the Community Care model. This approach is remarkable because potential funders of healthcare projects are not usually hosted simultaneously. Yet, representatives from all three foundations attended and agreed to fund parts of the program during the first year. Later, the national grant-maker was so astonished by the commitment of those local foundations that they invited County Health Coalition to be the fourth demonstration site and awarded the organization $181,500 in funding. Continuing their fundraising persistence, CHC also received support from foundations, federal government agencies, local corporations, and public health departments.

In both instances, fundraising was contingent upon, and a catalyst for, building relationships. FOP cultivated new organizational partners by publicizing outcome data, which attracted new organizations to implement their model. CHC cultivated new relationships among funders and salvaged a funding relationship that was almost lost. With necessary revenue, both organizations began the process of developing constituents that could implement their new models to co-create maternal-child health and reduce health disparities.

Developing Talent to Co-Create Health

Our data suggest that developing talent is essential to co-creating maternal-child health. When developing talent, the case study organizations emphasized the importance of relationships based on shared goals, shared knowledge, and mutual respect for the various partners (Gittell, 2002; Wooten & Crane, 2004).

Focusing on Pregnancy developed talent by training nurses and midwives to facilitate a "discovery learning" process rather than using a traditional lecture style of patient education (Vonderheid, Kilma, & Norr, 2008). In a discovery learning environment, practitioners provide in-depth prenatal care information to a group of patients and create a safe space for patients to share their problems and resources. In addition, as a certified nurse-midwife noted, "facilitative leadership demands listening skills and the ability to be tuned in to the educational needs of the patients." Another nurse midwife explained that discovery learning also requires the ability to co-create relevant knowledge within the group experience:

> In truth, I continue to be awed by the power of the group. We are having such a good time and have such laughs. I am learning that it doesn't matter what we don't talk about, because we are talking about what matters to the group.

Interestingly, healthcare providers using Focusing on Pregnancy's discovery learning methodology found that group visits were more efficient, effective, and professionally rewarding (Rising, 2010). As a result, nurses valued the increased time with patients and the high-quality connection that formed, which contributed to improved patient compliance (Rising et al., 2004).

A nurse-midwife affiliated with Focusing on Pregnancy reflected on her experience with high-risk, African-American women:

> I learned from my past experiences that the group prenatal care is a very powerful bonding community. It became a cornerstone of what we were doing here because I could not get hospital privileges. I felt that I needed to do something to keep a community of prenatal patients going instead of turning into a robot like the private office care, when perhaps you see eight patients in a row and push out the same spiel.

The County Health Coalition took a different approach, focusing on developing staff and coalition members to mobilize evidence-based health care from the "benches to the trenches" (Pestronk & Franks, 2003). "Benches" is analogous to clinical healthcare research, which the County Health Coalition used to educate key stakeholders about disparities; assess epidemiological trends in specific geographical areas within the county; and inform programming decisions to reduce birth outcome disparities. "Trenches" refers to community mobilization to enhance the healthcare system through education, advocacy, mentoring, and support beyond the healthcare provider's office. For instance, the County Health Coalition employed staff to help patients acquire basic needs such as housing, utilities, and food. Staff also helped coordinate transportation to prenatal visits. The County Health Coalition also felt that it was important to train people that had relevant life experiences, personal styles, or backgrounds to provide this extended care. They believed that those providers might be more acceptable to patients than formally degreed professionals.

In sum, Focusing on Pregnancy Institute leveraged professional norms and ideology to train new practitioners to facilitate a highly generative, "discovery learning" group process that was culturally competent, fostered high-quality connections, and enhanced patient knowledge and efficacy. In the process, relational and affective mechanisms improved interpersonal dynamics during the clinical encounter, while cognitive mechanisms helped increase provider knowledge and skill. In contrast, the County Health Coalition's training focused primarily on building the capacity of coalition members so that they could collaborate with health-care providers and organizations more effectively. CHC's approach relied primarily on cognitive mechanisms in training and relational mechanisms to facilitate new ways to collaborate with diverse partners (e.g., physicians and community members). The next step was to train patients.

Empowering Patients to Co-Create Health

Patient empowerment was developed in the 1990s after health educators became frustrated with ineffective practices designed to help patients self-manage chronic diseases (Funnell, Anderson, Arnold, Barr, Donnelly, Johnson, Taylor-Moon, & White, 1991). Patient empowerment entails a shift in beliefs and behaviors—from provider-centered care to patient-centered collaborative care, which is a goal of the Institute of Medicine (IOM, 2003). Traditional provider-centered care emphasizes the professional's expert role in modifying patient behavior. In contrast, patient empowerment incorporates interactive teaching strategies that involve the patient in solving problems and addressing their cultural and psychological needs.

Patient empowerment assumes that positive health behaviors are both learned and strengthened through a participatory experience and gaining greater control over health encounters with medical professionals (Ouschan, Sweeney, & Johnson, 2000). The empowerment process equips patients to discover and develop their inherent capacity to be responsible for their life. Thus, patients are empowered when they have knowledge to make rational decisions, adequate resources and sufficient control over them to implement decisions, and expertise to evaluate the effectiveness of their choices (Funnell & Anderson, 2003).

To empower patients, the Focusing on Pregnancy model redefined relational dynamics in the clinical encounter. For example, a patient assessed her own health statistics (e.g., weight and blood pressure) and recorded the data in her own medical record. Much like Rising et al.'s (2004) findings, a certified midwife opined that:

> This enhances her understanding of the physiological measures and their implications for her total health, moving her from being a passive to an active participant in her care. This also contributes to her sense of control in the care process.

The County Health Coalition empowered its clients with education and advocacy that linked patients to maternal and infant health resources. For example, patient advocacy services helped clients navigate the prenatal healthcare system and reduce stressors associated with barriers to health care (Hunte et al., 2004). Advocates were flexible in their work and changed their approach based on the client's situation. CHC deeply believed that their greatest strength was empowering mothers with essential resources.

Patient empowerment efforts in both models resulted in pregnant women gaining a greater sense of self-efficacy. However, differences were evident in the approach each organization took. CHC trained organizational members to support one another and patients in acquiring resources (behavioral), whereas FOP's training increased patients' mastery by teaching them new skills to manage their health and the clinical encounter (cognitive and behavioral). In addition, through the group model, FOP trained patients to help and support one another (affective).

Focusing on Pregnancy's group model of prenatal care fostered high-quality connections among gestating mothers by drawing upon the nurse-midwifery philosophy of relational patient care (Andrist, 1997; Green & Kreuter, 1999; Rising et al., 2004). Group members talked and shared feelings in a safe environment. They also exchanged tacit knowledge with peers and gained explicit knowledge from professionals about prenatal care. These interactions resulted in teachable moments as group members reflected upon and strategized about actions associated with their well-being (Walker & Worrell, 2008). In Focusing on Pregnancy, group interactions instilled hope, affirmed their common experiences, and provided emotional and tangible support as they shared stories about their pregnancy journey (Novick, 2004). As one group leader recounted:

> They really bonded with each other and developed a community. It's like another group of friends. They reach out to each other with offers to help with childcare. I hear from group members, "I'll come help you in labor."

Their bonds also resulted in group norms that encouraged healthy decisions and increased accountability among group members:

> I have no clue why, but on the third session when the group came together they had dramatically decreased smoking. They had almost stopped their soda intake. They were eating healthier food. It was the most astounding

330 · Valerie Myers & Lynn Perry Wooten

thing, and I do not know what really happened. But this is what we see in our groups. There is sort of a group norm that develops and enables women to move toward a norm that tends to be healthier... I mean that is really universal, but they struggle of figure out how to get there. So within the group, women look to each other and a woman says to another woman, "I was a three-pack-a-day smoker, too, and I stopped. If I can stop you stop too. Why would you continue doing something that is so harmful to your baby?"

Both Focusing on Pregnancy and Community Care models of co-creating health resulted in numerous benefits. They both improved access to care, provided better quality of healthcare, and increased patient knowledge. They also allowed healthcare providers to detect problems earlier and take preventive actions. Finally, both models integrated health and human services and ameliorated racial disparities in maternal-child health.

DISCUSSION

We began this research with the goal of exploring processes that organizations use to reduce birth outcome disparities for African-American women and their babies. We noted that this is important because of its cost to society and its implications for the health and well-being of a large segment of America's population. POS is an ideal lens through which to examine this topic because it focuses on positive outcomes, as well as the processes and attributes of organizations and its members (Cameron, Dutton, & Quinn, 2003). The POS lens elucidates novel strategies, resources and capabilities that reflect the best of human behavior and organizing processes.

By applying a POS lens to the study of generative change in healthcare, we discovered that certain mechanisms were instrumental for co-creating health and reducing health disparities. We were able to identify and explain the *why* of generative change, the *what* of generative change, and *how* generative changes emerged (Dutton & Sonenshein, 2009). Cognitive mechanisms initiated the generative change process generative change. For instance, acquiring and analyzing empirical and experiential data heightened leaders' awareness of health disparities for the populations they served and helped them make sense of the issues. Professional ideologies were sense-giving, in that they provided a vision, a way of communicating, and a roadmap for developing solutions and actions (Gioia & Chittipeddi, 1991). Further, leaders recognized the potential to transfer existing ideologies to a new healthcare problem (Wooten & Crane, 2004). In doing so, organizational members were prompted to look for solutions within their existing repertoire of professional values, skills, beliefs and practices (Trice & Beyer, 1993). Professional ideologies thus helped frame the health disparities problem as an issue that is within the normal scope of professional work and for which relevant competencies exist.

Each organization used a professional ideology to craft a theory of change and a logic for what needed to change and requisite processes to facilitate program implementation (Bradach et al., 2008). Each theory of change guided organizational learning and the process of integrating tacit and explicit knowledge. In addition, the theories of change spurred innovation by bringing non-traditional practices to reduce disparities to the forefront, such as the group model of prenatal care, excellence in customer service, and undoing racism. The synthesis of information and ideology were the impetus for generative change.

Ideologies matter. Although positive organizational scholarship focuses on positive and generative phenomena, we found that embracing the paradox of co-creating health and reducing health disparities was essential for this generative change process (Table 15.1). Further, our case studies showed that both the nurse-midwife and public health ideologies articulated the need for partnerships. We discovered that those partnerships were highly generative, characterized by high-quality connections and collective resourcefulness. Further, those partnerships were forged and sustained by underlying mechanisms that varied depending upon the partners and their purposes.

We observed relational mechanisms at the core of how each organization changed its practices to co-create health and reduce health disparities. Generative relational mechanisms were evident in high quality connections and collective resourcefulness among partners and stakeholders. Partners were educated and trained so that they could actively engage in the process of co-creating health at every level—community to provider, among coalition members, provider to patient, and patient to patient. Consequently, each organization expanded their behavioral capabilities in ways that influenced maternal child health (e.g., fundraising, emotional

TABLE 15.1

The Generative Process of Co-Creating Health to Reduce Birth Outcome Health Disparities

	Focusing on Pregnancy Model (FOP)	County Health Coalition (CHC)	Generative Outcomes
Background	A nonprofit health institute. Mission: Use group care model to improve overall health outcomes of mothers, babies, and new families.	A nonprofit healthcare coalition of healthcare providers, purchasers, consumers of health services, county citizens, government agencies, insurers, and educators. Mission: Improve access and quality, reduce cost, and improve healthcare and outcomes for the community.	Synthesis of tactic and formal knowledge increased sensitivity to health disparity issues
Antecedents: Why Change (Cognitive mechanisms that defined and framed critical issues)	Empirical data from CDC	Local epidemiological data about birth outcome disparities.	Sense-making
	Professional experience of nurse-midwife with group model.	Community experiences	Sense-giving
	A nurse-midwife ideology of partnerships to achieve health goals through health intervention, promotion, and education.	A public health ideology to prevent diseases, prolong life, and promote community health through collaboration.	

Content: What Changed (Cognitive and behavioral mechanisms to foster transition)	Theory of change promotes a paradigm shift from individual to group prenatal care. Trained evangelists (other healthcare providers) in its approach. Planned capacity building to acquire resources, develop talent, and improve patient skills.	Theory of change promotes transforming the culture of the maternal-child healthcare system through better customer service and ameliorating institutionalized racism. Trained staff in service excellence and undoing racism. Planned capacity building to acquire resources, develop talent, and improve patient skills.	Mobilization of stakeholders for action Change the clinical encounter Change structural impediments to care Customer service/patient-centered orientation Heightened value of diversity A model of culturally competent healthcare
Mechanisms: How Change Was Achieved (Dominated by relational mechanisms that were supported by cognitive, behavioral, and affective mechanisms)	Forming within-sector partnerships among health professionals, scholars, and patients to acquire resources and diffuse the model of group prenatal care. Created a donor movement to raise money and informally advertise Trained healthcare providers in the "discovery learning" and egalitarian approach to group prenatal care. Patient empowerment to redefine relational dynamics in the clinical encounter. Patient-to-patient support within prenatal health groups to facilitate knowledge exchange and emotional support.	Forming cross-sector partnerships between healthcare providers and purchasers, consumers of health services, county citizens, government agencies, and educators to develop resources to alleviate disparities. Interorganizational partnerships and build relationships with grantors to acquire financial resources. Train staff and coalition members to work across differences and to mobilize evidence-based healthcare. Empower patients to navigate the healthcare system with education, advocacy, and links to resources.	High-quality connections Collective resourcefulness Professional engagement and satisfaction Organizational learning Patient empowerment and self-efficacy

334 • *Valerie Myers & Lynn Perry Wooten*

support, clinical encounter, etc.) Most importantly, partnerships among patients and between patients and healthcare provider transformed the prenatal clinical encounter.

CONCLUSION

Health disparities and disparities in infant mortality are not easily explained or eliminated; they are like a mysterious "Gordian Knot"—a metaphor for complex and vexing problems that seem impossible to untangle because the ends are not apparent. According to ancient legend, whoever untied the Gordian Knot would rule Asia. Many struggled to untie it, but Alexander had an epiphany: why struggle? With a bold stroke of his sword, he cut through the knot. His revolutionary approach was a step toward becoming Alexander the Great!

Health disparities and disparities in infant mortality are complex, intractable problems that originate from multiple causes. Reasons to attempt to cut through them are obvious—health disparities are a costly and preventable societal problem. Quality data show that there is no end in sight, even though many healthcare organizations have tried unsuccessfully to unravel this knotty problem (AHRQ, 2007). Like Alexander, however, the results from our study show that co-creating health is a bold stroke that can cut through the problem of birth outcome disparities.

We found that to be effective, co-creative partnerships must cut through the problem at various levels including policy, community, organization, clinical unit, and patients. Relevant interventions need to address structural barriers and causes, the organization's climate, build upon professionals' standards and ideologies, and educate patients to take an active role in their own health and support the health of their peers. But organizations need not attempt to do everything at once to be effective. Our case studies of maternal-child health interventions had very different targets for generative change, from the top down and from the bottom up. Focusing on Pregnancy primarily engaged health providers and patients, and secondarily the community, as co-creators of maternal-child health. Conversely, the County Health Coalition engaged community leaders, government, and healthcare organizations that could be instrumental in changing the healthcare environment and social root causes of health disparities. Yet the impetus for moving from inertia to effectiveness was similar in both instances: the leaders, awareness of and sensitivity to empirical and experiential data and their ability to leverage existing professional ideologies to serve their goals were vital.

The POS lens helped us cut through this knotty problem by identifying cognitive, behavioral and relational mechanisms in the generative change process. Although this chapter focuses on the process of reducing disparities in birth outcomes, we are hopeful that lessons learned about the generative process of co-creating health will transfer to other clinical areas. By co-creating health, we can save lives, improve the quality of life, and save dollars resulting in a healthcare system and societal outcomes that are truly great.

REFERENCES

Agency for Healthcare Research and Quality. (2005). *2004 national healthcare disparities report* (2nd ed.). Retrieved May 2010 from http://www.qualitytools.ahrq.gov/ disparities report/documents/nhdr2004.pdf.

Agency for Healthcare Research and Quality. (2007). *2007 national healthcare disparities report*.

Andrist, L. (1997). A feminist model for women's health care. *Nursing Inquiry, 4,* 268–274.

Barnes-Josiah, D. L. (2004). *Undoing racism in public health: A blueprint for action in urban MCH.* Omaha, NE: CityMatch at the University of Nebraska Medical Center.

Beaglehole, R., Bonita, R., Horton, R., Adams, O., & McKee, M. (2004). Public health in the new era: Improving health through collective action, *Lancet. 363,* 2084–2086.

Behrman R. E., & Butler, A. (2007). *Preterm birth: Causes, consequences, and prevention.* Washington, DC: National Academies Press.

Berwick, D. M. (2002). A user's manual for the IOM's "QualityChasm" report: Patients' experiences should be the fundamental source of the definition of "quality." *Health Affairs, 21,* 80–90.

Bradach, J., Tierney, T., & Stone, N. (2008). Delivering on the promise of nonprofits. *Harvard Business Review, December,* 88–97.

Bradley, E., Curry, L., Ramanadhan, S., Rowe, L., Nembhard, I., & Krumholz, H. (2009). Research in action: Using positive deviance to improve quality of health care. *Implementation Science, 4,* 1–11.

Bunderson, J. S. (2003). Recognizing and utilizing expertise in-work groups: A status characteristics perspective. *Administrative Science Quarterly, 48,* 557–591.

Cameron, K. S., Dutton, J. E., & Quinn, R. E. (2003). Foundations of positive organizational scholarship. In K. S. Cameron, J. E. Dutton, & R. E. Quinn (Eds.), *Positive organizational scholarship: Foundations of a new discipline* (pp. 3–13). San Francisco: Berrett-Koehler.

Carter-Pokras, O., & Baquet, C. (2002). What is a health disparity? *Public Health Reports,* *117,* 426–432.

Colby, S., Stone, N., & Carttar, P. (2004). Zeroing in on impact. *Stanford Social Innovation Review, 2,* 24–33.

David, R., & Collins, J. (1997). Differing birth weight among infants of U.S.-born blacks, African-born blacks, and U.S.-born whites. *New England Journal of Medicine, 337,* 1209–1214.

Davies, H. T. O., Nutley, S. M., & Mannion, R. (2000). Organizational culture and quality of health care. *Quality in Health Care, 9,* 111–119.

Davis, G. F., & Marquis, C. (2005) Prospects for organization theory in the early twenty-first century: Institutional fields and mechanisms. *Organization Science, 16,* 332–343.

Donaldson, L. J., & Muir-Gray, J. A. (1998). Clinical governance: A quality duty for health organizations. *Quality of Health Care, 7,* 37–44

Dutton, J. E., & Heaphy, E. (2003). The power of high quality connections. In K. Cameron, J. E. Dutton, & R. E. Quinn (Eds.), *Positive organizational scholarship* (pp. 263–278). San Francisco: Berrett-Koehler.

Dutton, J. E., & Sonenshein, S. (2009) Positive organizational scholarship. In S. Lopez (Ed.), *Encyclopaedia of positive psychology* (pp. 737–742). Oxford: Wiley-Blackwell Publishing.

Eisenhardt, K. (1989). Making fast strategic decisions in high-velocity environments. *Academy of Management Journal, 32,* 543–576.

Eisenhardt, K., & Martin J. (2000) Dynamic capabilities: What are they? *Strategic Management Journal, 21,* 1105–1121.

Funnell, M., & Anderson, R. (2003). Patient empowerment: A look back, a look ahead. *Diabetes Education, 29,* 454–458.

Funnell, M., Anderson, R., Arnold, M., Barr, P., Donnelly, M., Johnson, P., Taylor-Moon, D., & White, N. (1991). Empowerment: An idea whose time has come in diabetes education. *Diabetes Educator, 17,* 37–41.

Ganz, M. (2009). *Why David sometimes wins: Leadership, organization, and strategy in the California farm worker movement.* New York: Oxford University Press.

Gioia, D. A. & Chittipeddi, K. (1991). Sensemaking and sensegiving in strategic change initiation. Strategic Management Journal, *12,* 433–448.

Gittell, J. H. (2002). Coordinating mechanisms in care provider groups: Relational coordination as a mediator and input uncertainty as a moderator of performance effects. *Management Science, 48,* 1408–1426.

Glynn, M. A., & Dutton, J. E. (2007). *The generative dynamics of positive organizing.* Ross School of Business (unpublished working paper).

Goeppinger J., & Shuster, G. (1988). Community as client: Using the nursing process to promote health. In M. Stanhope, & J. Lancaster (Eds.), *Community health nursing* (pp. 253–270). St Louis, MO: Mosby/Year Book.

Grant, H. M., & Crutchfield, L. R. (2007). Creating high-impact nonprofits. Retrieved July 21, 2011, from http://www.ssireview.org/articles/entry/735/.

Green, L. W., & Kreuter, M. W. (1999). *Health promotion planning: An educational and ecological approach* (3rd ed.). Mountain View, CA: Mayfield.

Health Disparities Task Group of the Federal/Provincial/Territorial Advisory Committee on Population Health and Health Security (2005). Reducing health disparities–Roles of the health sector: Discussion paper. Canadian Ministry of Health.

Heward, S., Hutchins, C., & Keleher, H. (2007). Organizational change: Key to capacity building and effective health promotion. *Health Promotion International, 22,* 170–178.

Hunte, H. E., Turner T. M., Pollack H. A., & Lewis E. Y. (2004). A birth records analysis of the Maternal Infant Health Advocate Service program: A paraprofessional intervention aimed at addressing infant mortality in African Americans. *Ethnic Disparities, 14,* S102–S110.

Ickovics, J., Kershaw, T., Westdahl, C., Magriples, U., Massey, Z., & Reynolds, H. (2007). Prenatal care and perinatal outcomes. *Obstetrics Gynecology, 110,* 330–339.

Ickovics, J., Kershaw T., Westdahl, C., Rising S. S., Klima, C., & Reynolds H. (2003). Group prenatal care improves preterm birth weight: Results from a matched cohort study at public clinics. *Obstetrics Gynecology, 102,* 1051–1058.

Indiana Perinatal Network (2003). Indiana symposium examines strategic directions for improving maternal and child health services. *Perinatal Perspectives, 9,* 9.

Joffres, C., Health, S., Farquharson, J., Barkhouse, K., Latter, C., & MacLean, D. (2004). Facilitators and challenges to organizational capacity building in heart health promotion. *Qualitative Health, 14,* 39–60.

Kashif, Z. (2003). Why African-American babies have the highest infant mortality rate in the developed world. *Race Wires-Color Lines,* Retrieved December 2009 from http://www.arc.org/racewire/030210z_kashef.html.

Klima, C., Norr, K., Vonderheid, S., & Handler, A. (2009). Introduction of centering pregnancy in a public health clinic. *Journal of Midwifery & Women's Health, 54,* 27–34.

Lu, M. C., & Chen, B. M. (2004). Racial-ethnic disparities in preterm birth: The role of stressful life events. *American Journal of Obstetrics and Gynecology, 191,* 691–699.

Mackinnon, A., & Amott, N. (2006). *Mapping change: Using a theory of change to guide planning and evaluation.* New York: GrantCraft.

McAdam, D., Tarrow, S., & Tilly, C. (2001). *Dynamics of contention.* New York: Cambridge University Press.

Miles, M., & Huberman, M. (1994). *Qualitative data analysis: An expanded sourcebook.* Newbury Park, CA: Sage.

Mintzberg, H. (1979). *The structuring of organizations.* Upper Saddle River, NJ: Prentice Hall.

Mullins, L. (2006). *Stress and resilience: The social context of reproduction in central Harlem.* New York: Kluwer Academic/Plenum Publishers.

Novick, G. (2004). Centering pregnancy and the current state of prenatal care. *Journal of Midwifery & Women's Health, 49,* 405–411.

O'Neil, M., Lemieux, V., Groleau, J., Fortin, J., & Lamarche, P. A. (1997). Coalition theory as a framework for understanding and implementing intersectoral health-related interventions. *Health Promotion International, 12,* 79–87.

Ouschan, R., Sweeney, J., & Johnson, L. (2000). Patient empowerment: Implications for professional services marketing. *Health Marketing Quarterly, 18,* 99–114.

Page, S. (2007). *The difference: How the power of diversity creates better groups, firms, schools, and societies.* Princeton, NJ: Princeton University Press.

Pestronk, R., & Frank, M. (2003). A partnership to reduce African American infant mortality in Genesee County, Michigan. *Public Health Reports, 118,* 324–335.

Pettigrew, A. M., Ferlie, E. B., & McKee, L. (1992). *Shaping strategic change.* London: Sage.

Rising, S. S. (1998). Centering pregnancy: An interdisciplinary model of empowerment. *Journal of Nurse Midwifery, 43,* 46–54.

Rising, S. S. (2010). Centering pregnancy: From exam room to group space for prenatal care. Webcast for Clinical Directors Network hosted by the United States Department of Health Resources & Service Administration. Retrieved February 2010 from webcast.hrsa.gov/conferences/mchb/amchp2005/ppt/g3a.ppt

Rising, S. S., & Jolivet R. (2009). Circles of community: The CenteringPregnancy© group prenatal care model. In R. Davis-Floyd, L. Barclay, B. A. Daviss, & J. Tritten (Eds.), *Birth models that work* (pp. 365–384). Berkley: University of California Press.

Rising, S. S., Kennedy, H., & Klima, C. (2004). Redesigning prenatal care through centering pregnancy. *Journal of Midwifery & Women's Health, 49,* 398–404.

Rooks J. P. (1999). The midwifery model of care. *Journal of Nurse-Midwifery, 44,* 370–374.

Roussos, S. T., & Fawcett, S. B. (2000). A review of collaborative partnerships as a strategy for improving community health. *Annual Review of Public Health, 21,* 369–402.

Smedley, B. D., Stith, A. Y., & Nelson, A. R. (Eds.). (2003). *Unequal treatment: Confronting racial and ethnic disparities in health.* Washington, DC: The National Academy Press.

Strauss, A., & Corbin, J. (1998). *Basics of qualitative research: Techniques for developing grounded theory* (2nd ed.). Thousand Oaks, CA: Sage.

Trice, H. M., & Beyer, J. M. (1993). *The cultures of work organizations.* Englewood Cliffs, NJ: Prentice-Hall.

U.S. Department of Health and Human Services (2000). *Healthy people 2010: Understanding and improving health* (2nd ed.). Washington, DC: U.S. Government Printing Office.

U.S. Department of Health and Human Services (2005). *National Healthcare Disparities Report.* Rockville, MD: AHRQ Publication No. 06–0017.

Van Mannen, J., & Barley, S. (1984). Occupational communities: Control in culture in organizations. In B. M. Staw & L. L. Cummings (Eds.), *Research in organizational behavior* (pp. 287–365). Greenwich, CT: JAI Press.

Vonderheid, S., Kilma, C., & Norr, K. (2010). Centering pregnancy: A group model of prenatal care holds promise for improving access to the quality of prenatal care. *Child Research Network.* Retrieved February 2010 from http://www.childresearch.net/RESOURCE/RESEARCH/2008/VONDERHEID.HTM.

Walker, D., & Worrell, R. (2008). Promoting health pregnancies through perinatal groups: A comparison of centering pregnancy group prenatal care and childbirth education classes. *Perinatal Education, 17,* 27–34.

Weber, K. (2006). From nuts & bolts to toolkits: Theorizing with mechanisms. *Journal of Management Inquiry, 15,* 119–123.

Weiner, B. J., Alexander, J., & Shortell, S. (1996). Leadership for quality improvement in health care: Empirical evidence on hospital boards, managers, and physicians. *Medical Care Research and Review, 53,* 397–416.

Winslow, C. (1920). The untilled field of public health. *Modern Medicine, 2,* 183.

Witmer, A. (1995). Community health workers: Integral members of the health care work force. *American Journal of Public Health, 85,* 1055–1058.

Wooten, L. P., & Crane, P. (2003). Nurses as implementers of organizational culture. *Nursing Economics, 21,* 275–279.

Wooten, L., & Crane, P. (2004). Generating dynamic capabilities through a humanistic work ideology: The case of a certified nurse midwife practice in a professional bureaucracy. *American Behavioral Scientist, 47,* 848–866.

World Health Organization (1948). *Constitution of the World Health Organization.* Geneva, Switzerland.

Yin, R. (1999). Enhancing the quality of case studies in health services. *Health Services Research, 24,* 1209–1224.

16

Revealing Themes: Applying a Positive Lens to the Chapters on Health Care

Trish Reay
University of Alberta School of Business

What can we do about health care? Nations around the world are searching for effective solutions to ensure that people can access high quality services and that these services can be somehow affordable. This is proving to be a difficult task. Many change initiatives have been designed, but it is during implementation that our lack of knowledge about organizational change in health-care settings becomes obvious. So far, organization theory has not been particularly helpful. However, as a recent editorial in *Health Affairs* clearly points out, when you take time to look, there are important examples of innovation taking place and there is much to learn from them (Dentzer, 2011). The preceding Chapters 12–15, in Part IV, contribute valuable insights into how change initiatives can help improve health-care. The authors of these chapters do so by purposely taking a positive lens to focus on the ways in which meaningful changes can occur. In this commentary, I first summarize the ways in which each of the four previous chapters employ a positive lens to improve our understanding of effective change in health-care, and then I provide my overall views of their collective insights.

CHAPTER HIGHLIGHTS

Golden-Biddle and Correia (Chapter 12) investigate how leaders and clinicians in a community-owned health system brought in a new model of care (Collaborative Care) that effectively turned providers' focus onto getting patients well instead of treating medical conditions. To readers outside the world of health-care, this may sound like a minor change. To those inside health-care, the significance of this new focus will not be lost. What Golden-Biddle and Correia found is that the creation of hope—hope that the system could, in fact, be changed—was a critical precursor to change. Furthermore, they propose that as a generative dynamic of change, the development of hope relies upon: (1) *activating belief* that action can make a difference, and (2) *acting on belief* to realize the desired change. In other words, belief is at the heart of the matter, but it must be ignited or activated before change initiatives can be effective.

In Chapter 13, Pratt, Fiol, O'Connor, and Panico draw attention to a common sticking point in health-care systems, the potential for ongoing (and possibly intractable) conflict within physician–administrator relationships. They explain that both physicians and administrators draw clear lines around their own identity, and commonly express strong views that they are definitely not part of the other group. Such an obvious divide between two important actors in all health-care systems is clearly a potential barrier to the effective delivery of services. However, instead of focusing on the barrier, these authors adopted a positive lens to revisit their previously developed resolution model (Fiol, Pratt, & O'Connor, 2009). They developed new insights by theorizing the concept of *identity security* and incorporated it into their model to show how opportunities for mutual gain could facilitate collaboration between physicians and administrators.

Focusing at the service delivery level of analysis, Wells (Chapter 14) builds a new conceptual model of managerial approaches to support front line staff. She employs a positive view of front line professionals by focusing on their inherent motivation to engage in loving action for each child within their client base. This positive stance allows her to incorporate a current approach already established in the mental health field, that of specific attention to consistently re-frame desired outcomes for children in positive terms. Wells suggests that change can occur by amplifying small positive actions of front line workers, and also by buffering them from constraints or demands that prevent them from fulfilling their desired actions to fully support children in need.

In the final chapter of this part, Myers and Wooten (Chapter 15) present their findings from an in-depth empirical study of how health-care professionals in two different settings partnered to co-create improved maternal child health outcomes. They were driven by the relatively depressing statistics that American women of lower socio-economic status, those who are members of racial and ethnic minorities, or those living in underserviced geographic areas have poorer health outcomes in terms of both their own pregnancy and the health status of their babies. In addressing this challenging problem, Myers and Wooten employ a positive lens by drawing on literature concerning generative change. As a result, they were able to focus their research attention on understanding how patient-centered, continuous healing relationships could be developed. They show that high-quality connections and collective resourcefulness were critical in developing partnerships between patients and health-care providers, and in turn, it was these partnerships that led to the co-creation of healthy moms and babies.

TAKING A POSITIVE RESEARCHER STANCE

In looking across the four chapters, it is interesting to note how the authors have carefully adopted a positive stance. They purposely focused their research attention to understand how meaningful change can occur. This approach was not necessarily easy for the authors. It revealed the strength of taken-for-granted research perspectives as so clearly explained by Wells (Chapter 14) in her story about proposing a commonly used (and thus highly reliable) survey instrument, and her surprise on being informed by participants that it was not suitable because the survey questions were worded so negatively—asking people to evaluate their level of dissatisfaction or frustration. Similarly, Pratt et al. (Chapter 13) explained how purposefully focusing on positivity pushed them to reconsider their own previously drawn conclusions about ways to resolve ongoing identity conflict. These examples show how a purposefully positive stance can give researchers the opportunity to re-examine their own preconceived beliefs about change. In taking this new perspective, researchers open up avenues of insight that may previously have been overlooked.

POSITIVE OUTCOMES FOR PATIENTS

Most change initiatives are focused on achieving positive outcomes. What is interesting and different about the accounts of change in these four chapters is that the ultimate positive outcomes of interest are those experienced, not by the organization, but by the patients or clients. This is a big difference. Wells focused on "loving care for each child," Golden-Biddle and Correia identified the desired outcome as significantly improved quality of patient care, safety, and satisfaction. In Myers and Wooten's study, the goal was improving health outcomes for mothers and babies. And for Pratt et al., the objective was to promote harmony between physicians and administrators so that the health system could deliver higher quality care. This is an interesting characteristic of health-care settings in that although organizations must balance finances in accordance with their underlying financial model (for-profit or not-for-profit), the ultimate evaluation of performance must be viewed from the patient or client perspective. By adopting a positive lens, the authors were able to maintain their research attention on the underlying purpose of health-care organizations—to improve the health of people. Although this sounds like an obviously important outcome of change initiatives, all too often we see that other factors such as cost or conflict get more attention than people's health. I commend the authors of these chapters for so clearly staying grounded in their attention to improving health.

INSIGHTS ON THE POSITIVE PROCESS OF CHANGE

In addition to the importance of working toward a positive and meaningful outcome, the chapters in this part also reveal insights through their positive lens on the process of change. For me, this contribution to our understanding of change in health-care is particularly enlightening. I see four key ways in which these studies collectively advance our knowledge.

Relationships as a Source of Energy

First, all the studies show that relationships among actors can be a source of energy in achieving desired change. This observation provides an interesting way to re-conceptualize resistance to change initiatives. Instead of looking to established relationships as a source of resistance (e.g., Kotter & Schlesinger, 2008), the chapters in this part show how relationships can generate positivity. Similar to previous work on high quality connections (e.g., Dutton & Ragins, 2007), we can see that positive relationships at work do exist and can be critical resources for change. For example, Golden-Biddle and Correia (Chapter 12) showed how the strength of relationships across organization levels allowed people to recognize the importance of hope in generating change. Similarly, Myers and Wooten (Chapter 15) showed how relationships among partners could form the foundation for co-creating healthy moms and babies. Interestingly, even though their study was about conflict, Pratt et al. (Chapter 13) showed how the (conflict-based) relationship between physicians and administrators could serve as a platform for promoting positive change initiatives. And Wells (Chapter 14) proposed that the manager–care provider relationship could serve to support front line professionals' attention to "loving action for each child." In each case, relationships that would normally be classified as potential sources of resistance in many models of organizational change were instead turned into foundations for positive action. By giving attention to relationships as positive sources of change, these authors have shown us how connections among people can bring energy to fuel a change initiative—to get it started and keep the momentum going.

Professional Conviction as Catalyst

Second, the chapters in Part IV show how health-care professionals' deeply held conviction to do the right thing for patients can be the spark that ignites a positive process of change. Myers and Wooten (Chapter 15) show that by purposefully integrating patients and healthcare workers as part of the change initiative, the process of change became guided by a philosophy of patient empowerment that facilitated an ongoing learning process for mothers. It was this integration of patients that reminded healthcare providers of their overall goal—healthy moms and babies. Also focused on professionals' convictions and beliefs, Wells (Chapter 14) proposed that removing workplace constraints would release pent up professional desire to improve patients' quality of life. It is this common interest in high quality patient care that can unite various healthcare professionals—even when they are engaged in established patterns of conflict (Pratt et al., Chapter 13). Golden-Biddle and Correia's study (Chapter 12) illustrates the power of professional conviction in describing the key motivator for change—the need to focus on getting patients well. Most studies of change in healthcare settings acknowledge the fact that providers are usually united on an overarching focus on patients. However, the studies in this part are among the few that actually draw on the importance of such deeply held conviction and the potential for releasing the power that it holds. Rather than change leaders trying to create a sense of urgency—as is commonly advised by Kotter (1996) and others—the authors here show us that when people providing services are given the opportunity, their knowledge and understanding of what really matters (patients and clients) can serve as the catalyst for change. In these examples, managerial pressure was not the trigger for change. Instead, health professionals themselves identified the need for better patient services—providing a rationale for change that was deeply felt and could withstand the tests of time.

Blurring the Boundary Between Top-Down and Bottom-Up

Another way these chapters provide new insights into the process of change is the lack of distinction between top-down or bottom-up change. The chapters in this part show how change can happen when the boundaries between bottom-up and top-down models are blurred and even erased. Many models of change are based on a top-down approach where executive leaders identify strategic problems, develop what they consider to be appropriate organizational solutions, and then implement them by convincing workers to follow the new plan (e.g., Burke & Litwin, 1992; Kotter, 1996). There are many relevant concepts within such models that can (and have been) effectively applied to change in healthcare settings. However, there are also many notable failures, which led scholars to consider the impact of bottom-up change (unplanned) on top-down (planned) change (Burke, 2011). Healthcare is characterized by a highly professionalized workforce that holds the ability to determine the appropriate type and level of services required. As a result, bottom-up change is a critical consideration. Instead of either top or bottom, these chapters show change leadership occurring at all organizational levels. For example, although the CEO was prominent in highlighting the need for change, Golden-Biddle and Correia's (Chapter 12) empirical story was one of joint (all organizational levels) evaluation of the problem, joint decision-making, and joint efforts to make Collaborative Care a reality. In Chapter 15 by Myers and Wooten, we see tremendous energy for change emanating from professionals who are near the organizational front line. However, we also see support and energy from higher levels—and most important of all, we see the engagement of patients, who are not even organizational members. Similarly, Wells' (Chapter 14) and Pratt et al.'s (Chapter 13) models are based on change leadership from both managers and professionals.

By bringing a positive lens to understand the process of the change, and particularly by focusing on the generativity of the process, we lose a sense of whether the top or the bottom of the organization is leading. I believe this is an important insight because it shows that change must be co-created. Instead of designing change initiatives with one person in charge, these studies suggest that distributed leadership can be more effective in healthcare settings. It is the heartfelt involvement of people throughout the organization that is needed to support and nourish change. This focus on the importance of shared leadership across all organizational levels could improve current models of change. Traditional theory suggests that the change leader must find ways to get others to "buy-in" and join him in achieving the pre-determined goals. The chapters suggest a process that is almost the reverse. These authors have shown how multilevel leadership generates the goals of change, thereby reducing the need to get "buy-in." Neither the top nor the bottom of the organization is pushing for change independently of the other. We need new models of change (such as those provided in the previous four chapters) that incorporate the importance of joint problem recognition, joint decision-making, and joint efforts to make change happen.

Incorporating Power Dynamics into the Process of Change

The fourth key contribution of these chapters is their inherent attention to the importance of power dynamics in organizational change. Healthcare is organized with many hierarchical relationships, but in addition, there are a myriad of other important power dynamics that influence processes of change (Buchanan & Badham, 2008). Because of the positive lens employed by authors of these four chapters, they have been able to draw attention to sources of power other than authority. They show us how people (in particular, those at mid-levels and lower) involved in change initiatives can push "barriers" to the background, and move "facilitators" and "work-arounds" to the foreground. In doing so, they reinforce ideas that middle-managers and front line workers can make a big difference (e.g., Meyerson, 2001).

Myers and Wooten (Chapter 15) show how professionals and clients combine their different sources of knowledge to co-create improved delivery of services. Similarly, Golden-Biddle and Correia (Chapter 12) explain how the CEO shared power with others in developing a new model of care. This attention to "shared power" as an effective strategy for encouraging change is a potentially revolutionary revision to traditional models of change based on authority and chain-of-command. Instead of crediting the executive team as the key source of knowledge and power, giving recognition and encouragement to the power and knowledge of those at the middle or front line could lead to more robust models of change. Consistent with this line of thinking, Pratt et al. (Chapter 13) propose that encouraging the strong identities of both physicians and managers could promote integrative goals of change even though it facilitates conflict between them. In this model of change, power sharing can happen, largely because each group views itself as holding a high level of power. Without that security, change cannot occur. Wells (Chapter 14) also views power dynamics in an unusual way. She suggests that managers use their hierarchical power to protect those at the front line. This idea of buffering service providers recognizes that people closest to the work hold important knowledge (and therefore power). Overall, the chapters open up the role of power dynamics for consideration. But what we see is the use of power not for personal advantage, but as a way to achieve desired change.

IMPLICATIONS FOR PRACTICE: STAYING FOCUSED ON THE FUTURE PERFECT

Although all of these contributions have important implications for practice, each of the chapters highlights the practical value of attending to a future desired state (future perfect) rather than being distracted by barriers that stand in the way (Pitsis et al., 2003). When people involved in processes of change keep themselves grounded in the future, they open up possibilities for action in the present that might otherwise not exist. This is particularly evident in Chapter 12 by Golden-Biddle and Correia, where the focus is on how to achieve a new model of care that values patient experience above all. In Wells' model, focus on the future perfect means directing managerial resources to amplify small actions that are in line with the desired goal and also buffering front line workers from every-thing except doing the work that inherently aligns with the desired goal. In Chapter 15 by Myers and Wooten, we see that by encouraging people to find ways to reach the future perfect, they are able to engage with each other in the dynamic and even enjoyable work of co-creating healthy out-comes. And Pratt et al. (Chapter 13) focus on harmony between physicians and administrators as the future desired state. Overall, we can see that by focusing on the future perfect, people engaging in change initiatives can be freed from their usual institutionalized patterns of thinking and thus find new ways of achieving their goals.

I recently saw this in action at a meeting of health managers and research-ers. The purpose of the meeting was to share knowledge and generate dis-cussion about a proposed research project regarding primary health care. To start off the event, the chairperson (an executive manager) displayed a visual image representing the desired future where primary health care was inextricably linked into the fabric of the community. "There it is," she said. "Now we just have to *act as if* we are already there. So, what is the compelling work to be done?" She and others maintained this framing throughout the meeting, and in spite of recognizing a number of difficul-ties in proceeding with the proposed research, the day was characterized by positivity and energy. For me, this meeting and the four chapters in this part of the book provide stellar examples of how the power of the future perfect can energize individuals and help them see new routes to desired goals.

IN CONCLUSION

To conclude, I return to the editorial by Dentzer (2011) discussed at the outset. As she points out, positive examples of change are going on right under our noses, but we have to have the desire to look for them. The four chapters in this part of the book strongly reinforce the same message. Important innovations are happening in health-care, and we can learn critical information about change by studying them. With the adoption of a positive lens, the authors have highlighted the importance of pro-cesses such as: (1) relationship building as a source of energy for change, (2) employing professional conviction as a catalyst, (3) making top-down and bottom-up distinctions irrelevant, and (4) engaging in alternate power dynamics to facilitate change. In addition, these studies point to the power of adopting a "future perfect" stance. That is, in practice, when people in an organization can envision themselves to have already achieved the desired future state, they seem to be more able to enact the underlying processes of change that will help them move forward. When people find ways to generate hope for better models of healthcare, or when they develop ways of truly engaging patients in co-creating health, they are tapping into energy for change that we are only beginning to understand. The authors of these four chapters are pointing the way toward improving healthcare—we just need to follow their lead.

REFERENCES

Buchanan, D., & Badham, R. (2000). *Power, politics and organizational change.* Thousand Oaks, CA: Sage.

Burke, W. W. (2011). *Organization change: Theory and practice* (3rd ed.). Thousand Oaks, CA: Sage.

Burke, W. W., & Litwin, G. H. (1992). A causal model of organizational performance and change. *Journal of Management, 18,* 532–545.

Dentzer, S. (2011). Memo to innovation center: "We're so glad you're here." *Health Affairs, 30,* 6–7.

Dutton, J. E., & Ragins, B. R. (2007). *Exploring positive relationships at work.* Mahwah, NJ: Lawrence Erlbaum.

Fiol, C. M., Pratt, M. G., & O'Connor, E. J. (2009). Managing intractable identity conflicts. *Academy of Management Review, 34,* 32–55.

Kotter, J. P. (1996). *Leading change.* Boston, MA: Harvard Business School Press.

Kotter, J. P., & Schleisinger, L. A. (1979). Choosing strategies for change. *Harvard Business Review, 57,* 106–114.

Meyerson, D. E. (2001). *Tempered radicals: How people use difference to inspire change at work.* Boston, MA: Harvard Business School Publishing.

Pitsis, T. S., Clegg, S. R., Marosszeky, M., & Rura-Polley, T. (2003). Constructing the olympic dream: A future perfect strategy of project management. *Organization Science, 14,* 574–590.

Part V

Poverty and Low-Wage Work

17

Positive Organizational Change by and for the Working Poor

Carrie R. Leana
University of Pittsburgh

Ellen Ernst Kossek
Michigan State University

In this chapter, we focus on positive organizational change by and for the working poor. Such change may be initiated informally by employees and/or their managers; it may be enacted through formal organizational policy or informal norms; or it may be the result of organizational reactions to larger societal forces. Regardless of its source we consider organizational change to be positive to the extent that it is both beneficial to employees and sustainable by employers. Positive organizational change thus results in increased well-being for lower wage employees, involving workplace practice or policy that can be supported and embedded over the long term.

Over the past decade, we have conducted research projects focused on opportunities (or lack thereof) as well as positive interventions for structuring organizational policies and workplace practices to address the needs of the working poor (e.g., Hammer, Kossek, Bodner, & Zimmerman, 2011; Kossek & Hammer, 2008; Leana, Appelbaum, & Shevchuk, 2009; Mittal, Rosen, & Leana, 2009). Each project has addressed somewhat different research questions but all conclude that a multilevel approach is needed to better understand how the condition of poverty can affect career progression, job attachment, and in-role and extra-role performance at work (Leana, Mittal, & Stiehl, 2010), as well as work-family relationships and the need for workplace flexibility (Kossek et al., 2008). For example, Kossek and Hammer's recent research with grocery store clerks shows that training *supervisors* to increase support to manage work-life conflict can have beneficial effects on low-wage *workers'* job attitudes, job attachment, and overall health (Hammer et al., 2011; Kossek & Hammer, 2008). Leana's research with low-wage childcare workers similarly shows the effects of *group-level* factors such as teamwork and collaboration on *individual-level* work attachment and performance (Leana, Appelbaum, & Shevchuk, 2009). Thus, our central argument is that change efforts designed to target only one level of change to foster organizational integration (often "correcting" individual-level deficiencies in human capital or performance) will not produce lasting change.

As we will illustrate in later descriptions of this research, organizational change that is both positive and sustainable is a complex undertaking requiring cooperation across organizational levels and often presenting challenges to existing organizational norms. Our goals in this chapter are threefold. First, we describe why managing the working poor has become an increasingly important issue, and one that is not addressed adequately in existing organizational theory or management practice. Here we profile the working poor in the United States, describe their employment, and discuss why they are often managed so poorly at work. Second, using data and examples from our own ongoing research projects, we examine "top-down" and "bottom-up" approaches to positive organizational change that can benefit the working poor. We contrast these with more traditional "stepping-stone" models of change. Third, we offer foundational principles for future positive organizational change theory development, research, and practice. Our main tenet is that to benefit the working poor, positive organizational change must be undertaken using multilevel (i.e., targeting both individual and workplace contextual social systems) and multipronged (i.e., avoiding oversimplified uni-dimensional change tactics) approaches. Moreover, such change often entails proactive efforts to make visible the assumptions, preferences, and ongoing practices of various stakeholders that are typically invisible and often deliberately so.

BEGINNING CAVEATS

At the outset, we wish to make explicit two boundary conditions in our discussion. First, our focus is on internal organizational dynamics and, thus, we do not address relevant public policy ameliorations such as raising the minimum wage. At the same time, raising wages and benefits for workers—whether done voluntarily by employers or driven by collective action or public mandates—are the most direct and efficient means of benefiting the working poor. Our focus on alternative policies and practices is not meant to usurp or serve as a substitute for these necessary changes. Second, we limit our discussion to the working poor in the United States. In doing so, we do not discount poverty's significance in other areas of the world, nor impose geographic limitations on practices to remediate its detrimental effects. Instead, we confine our discussion to U.S. workers because our research has been conducted primarily with samples in the United States. We recognize that employment practices are influenced by the cultural context in which they are embedded (Heyman, 2009; Romero-Stone & Stone, 2009) and, thus, confine our discussion to those contexts to which we can generalize with some confidence. With this in mind, we begin with a description of the working poor and the kinds of employing organizations that hire them.

WHO ARE THE WORKING POOR IN THE UNITED STATES?

The Organization for Economic Cooperation and Development defines the working poor as the proportion of employed persons living below or close to the economic poverty levels for their country (OECD, 2002). The federal poverty threshold is the most common measure for counting the poor in the United States. This is a tiered scale that determines a household's poverty status based on income and family size (U.S. Census Bureau, 2009).[1] Households whose income falls below 100%

---

[1] The federal poverty level in the United States is based on an estimate first used in the mid-1960s which is based on the cost of food and family size based on the assumption that a household uses about one-third of its income for food consumption. The poverty threshold listed by the U.S. Census Bureau for a household of four with two dependent children was $21,834 in 2008, which translates to an hourly wage of about $10.50 for one full-time employee (U.S. Census Bureau, 2008). Households with one adult employed full-time earning the federal minimum wage ($6.55 per hour) would fall below this poverty threshold, and even if two adults are working full-time, year-round at the 2008 federal minimum wage, their combined income would still fall within 125% of the poverty threshold.

of the poverty threshold are considered poor by all assessors and U.S. government agencies (e.g., Social Security Administration) although others (e.g., National Research Council) count those earning less than 200% of the poverty threshold (Ackerman, 2006; Neumark, 2004). In the United States, the working poor are disproportionately female, racial minorities, and recent immigrants (DeNavas-Walt, Proctor, & Smith, 2007).

In a recent paper about the working poor, Leana, Mittal, & Stiehl (2010) distinguish full-time U.S. workers along two dimensions: (1) Does the individual have a history of economic deprivation (i.e., did he grow up in poverty)? and (2) Are his current wages sufficiently low that he is now economically deprived? According to Leana et al. (2010), members of the working poor would answer both of these questions in the affirmative. They argue that a history of economic deprivation is what distinguishes workers who are currently earning low wages from those who are categorized as the working poor. Thus, the "working poor" are a subset of "low-wage workers" since both groups are characterized by their small earnings and continuing employment. The working poor, however, are further bounded by a past history of poverty, leading to dampened expectations of ameliorating their situation. Even those who escape poverty and are currently earning middle to high wages (those Leana et al., 2010, label "aspirants") can still see their current identity in terms of past poverty. Sennett (1998) and others vividly describe how such individuals find it difficult to be comfortable in their current advantaged positions because of their experience with past economic hardship. As we will discuss, building the ranks of "aspirants" is an explicit goal of "stepping-stone" models—an approach to positive change for the working poor favored by many economists.

LIVING IN POVERTY

Leana et al. (2010) describe poverty as a "strong situation," or a context in which situational attributes tend to overpower individual differences, minimizing the effects of factors like personality on behavior, and narrowing the set of behaviors the individual deems appropriate in a given environment. The evidence supporting poverty as a strong situation can be found in its effects on several aspects of life, including health, family, and individual development.

People living in low-income households have higher rates of morbidity and mortality and report poorer overall health than those in non-poverty households (Adler & Ostrove, 1993; Taylor & Repetti, 1997; Williams & Collins, 1995). Indeed, recent studies have found a widening gap in longevity between the highest and lowest income brackets in the United States (Singh & Siahpush, 2006). Those living in poverty have a higher incidence of mental health problems as well, and report lower levels of emotional well-being. Hudson's (2005) seven-year study of linkages between socioeconomic status and mental illness found that economic stressors related to unemployment and lack of affordable housing are more predictive of mental illness than the reverse.

There are several explanations for these disparities in health and longevity. First, residents of low income areas have more limited access to health services (Macintyre et al., 1993; Williams, 1990; Wyke et al., 1992), making them less likely to receive preventative health care. Second, the working poor may lack the resources (i.e., time, money) to access and pursue superior medical treatments or technologies (Singh & Siahpush, 2006). Third, a number of studies have shown that low socioeconomic status (SES) is associated with a decreased level of physical activity, an increased propensity to consume a high fat diet, and a decreased knowledge about healthy behaviors (Adler & Ostrove, 1993; Williams & Collins, 1995). The lack of resources (e.g., money to purchase healthy food or a gym membership, or the time to exercise or cook meals at home) limits healthy behavior. Fourth, since there are fewer residential options available to them, the poor may live in unsafe neighborhoods (Anderson & Armstead, 1995; Durden, Hill, & Angel, 2007). Taylor and Repetti (1997) argue that impoverished neighborhoods are characterized by a number of factors that are detrimental to health, including higher crime rates, sub-standard transportation and recreation facilities, greater exposure to physical hazards such as air and water pollutants, more crowding, and exposure to constant noise.

For many of the same reasons cited earlier, poverty has a strong effect on the development and function of children and families. Research has shown that marriage rates are lower, out-of-wedlock birthrates are higher, and teen pregnancy is more prevalent among the poor (Devine et al., 2006; Furstenberg et al., 1999; Small & Newman, 2001; Wilson,

1987). Growing up in poverty is associated with a higher incidence of mental health problems and trouble at school (Barrett & Turner, 2005; Farah, Noble, & Hurt, 2005; Jackson et al., 2000). Young children in low SES households are less likely to receive cognitive stimulation (e.g., they may have less access to zoos and museums and own fewer toys and books), sometimes leading to dampened cognitive development (Farah, Noble, & Hurt, 2005).

In summary, the working poor make up a sizable and growing portion of the U.S. workforce. Research from a variety of disciplines provides compelling evidence that poverty is a strong situation that can affect important aspects of an individual's life, including physical and mental health, family structure, and individual development. At the same time, the jobs in which the working poor tend to be employed are typically constraining and may exacerbate the hardships of poverty and pose obstacles to individuals attempting to escape it.

Employers of the Working Poor

Many of the working poor are employed in organizations that use low wages as a basic component of their business model. Payroll is a major portion of total costs and reductions in payroll expenses can be a significant source of competitive advantage in industries such as retail sales, fast food, hospitality, and carework. The working poor tend to cluster into jobs that are structured around short-term monetary incentive systems (albeit substandard ones) while higher-paying jobs tend to offer a broader array of both intrinsic (e.g., job autonomy, interesting work) and extrinsic (e.g., promotion opportunities, flexible hours) rewards. Moreover, many higher-paying jobs offer incentives with both short-term and long-term payoffs (e.g., training and development, pension plans, career tracks), whereas incentives in low-wage jobs tend to be short-term and immediate (e.g., hourly pay).

A sizable number of working poor are former or current welfare recipients who join organizations that offer low-skilled jobs as a way to enter the labor force. The U.S. policy on poverty eradication has been redesigned over the past 15 years to emphasize a philosophy of "welfare to work." Burtless (2001) notes that U.S. public policy uses a supply side approach to encourage employers to hire difficult-to-employ workers. That is, policies are designed so as *not* to impose economic market constraints on employers that might make it unattractive to hire the working poor. For example, U.S. payroll taxes, and employer regulations on working hours, benefits, and the minimum wage remain very low by OECD standards. The consequence of this trend is that growing numbers of U.S. employers are hiring low-wage workers for jobs at the bottom of the organization and income hierarchy. Thus, the U.S. government's support for the working poor is to encourage labor market "equality" by removing barriers to working for the unemployed, such as focusing on child care or training and then providing time-limited public supports, educational training, or food stamps. Once an individual is able to gain access to the labor market and get a job, even a low paying one, her earned income often disqualifies her for key supports for housing or education. This laser focus of labor market participation ultimately works against the individual's ability to escape poverty, even while working full time.

Management Practices and Roles

There are several indicators suggesting that the working poor are not being managed well by the organizations that employ them. Turnover rates tend to be high, although low-wage workers often leave one poorly paid job to go to another that pays similar wages. The working poor also are likely to have higher stress rates, poorer health, and depressive symptoms in part due to having to manage more stressful working conditions than the general population (Iverson & Armstrong, 2007). Studies indicate that low-paid workers are more likely to experience job insecurity, job bullying, sexual harassment, irregular hours, long or insecure hours, burnout, fatigue, and negative work-life spillover (Broom et al., 2006; Masterman-Smith & Pocock, 2008). They are also much less likely to have control over work schedules and working time and how their jobs are done (Presser & Cox, 1997), creating challenges of either not getting enough hours of work to meet basic family financial needs and qualify for healthcare and other benefits, or having too many hours such as being forced to work overtime, being "on call," or having unpredictable hours such as in retail where management can call them in or send them home on short notice depending on how busy the store is at the moment (Lambert, 2008). This instability makes it difficult to plan for child care or meet other social and family needs that higher-paid employees have less difficulty juggling.

Further, many of the working poor have little or no paid sick leave or vacation time. Discipline policies are sometimes written to penalize workers for absenteeism even if the reason is legitimate (e.g., family illness). Because of this many work even when they are sick or they do not take any vacation time (Masterman-Smith & Popcock, 2008). Even if they have vacation time (typically unpaid), they may have little control over when they can take it. For example, they may be forced to take an unpaid holiday during the off-season or get very limited time off at holidays, as that is typically the busy season in retail, hospitality, and food service industries.

Front-line managers of the working poor also are often quite different in terms of the nature of their work than the managers typically described in the management literature. Overall, these managers are more like higher-level employees than traditional managers. Many, especially retail managers, may actually still be hourly workers themselves, earning only slightly more per hour than the people they supervise. Another unique aspect of management work in retail and food services is that the manager is often expected to "roll up his sleeves" and perform the jobs of the low-wage workers they supervise, especially during busy periods or if a worker is absent. This may make interpersonal relations and job interdependence between workers and managers even more important as a work context feature, and lead to crossover of stress.

Evidence backs this up. A study of hotel managers found that if a worker's manager had high work-family conflict, the worker was more likely to experience higher work-family conflict as well (O'Neill, Harrison, Cleveland, Almeida, Stawski, & Crouter, 2009; National Work-Family and Health Network, 2010). Worse, poor management may literally be making some workers sick. In one recent study of employees in long-term care settings, workers who had inflexible bosses were significantly more likely to be at risk for cardiovascular disease (Berkman, Buxton, Ertel, & Okechukwu, 2010). Often management is also under-resourced in terms of staffing and penalized if workers are paid overtime, which means workers either subtly or forcibly work "off the clock" (which is illegal) or experience extreme pressure to get their work done within the regular schedule, even if workloads rise. Not only is employee churn higher in such jobs, but management churn is high as well, leading to unstable systems at all levels, making it simply more difficult to sustain change or improve working conditions because there is little institutional memory.

SUMMARY

The preceding review has a number of implications for theorizing about the working poor. First, while employers in the United States may hire the working poor, there is limited incentive for employers to move them out of poverty. Second, while the organizations' literature often assumes that work is inherently motivating, beneficial, and leads to career opportunities, many of the working poor cannot expect that the act of working itself—even if full-time—will lead to a better life. Third, it is not typical for U.S. employers to invest in the working poor in terms of training, career development, or other human resource initiatives to foster a long-term employment relationship, and in fact the working poor often serve as an economic buffer for fluctuations in demand for services. Fourth, most traditional human resource systems such as training, rewards, and scheduling as currently enacted may have limited relevance or linkages to help the working poor, as the assumption is that the employees will not stay, or if they do they will have limited opportunities for advancement.

Approaches to Organizational Change By and For the Working Poor

Having discussed the challenges of the working poor, we now discuss three approaches to address these challenges, each grounded in a distinct theory of change and human dynamics at work: (1) "stepping-stone" approaches to change focused on human capital development and the use of internal labor markets; (2) management-led "top-down" relational approaches grounded in theories of the benefits of increasing positive social and organizational support to reduce work-family conflicts; and (3) "bottom-up" job crafting initiated informally by workers either alone or in collaboration to make the job a better fit for their skills, preferences, and perceptions regarding how to do their work most effectively.

"Stepping-Stone" Approaches to Strengthen Human Capital

The goal of "stepping-stone" models is to offer opportunities for individual workers in low-wage, low-skill jobs to work their way into better-paying higher-skill jobs, often within the same organization and almost always within the same industry. Such models draw on labor economics theories of human capital development whereby workers are encouraged to invest in their own skill development both for themselves and for the benefit of their employer, who can utilize such skills and thus justify paying higher wages to the worker. Examples of "stepping-stone" models can be found in care work, where lower-skilled nursing assistants (certified nursing assistants, or CNAs) are encouraged to take classes (often on their own time and at their own expense) to qualify to be licensed practical nurses (LPNs) so that they can earn higher wages and in return take on more of the healthcare (rather than personal care) responsibilities of caring for patients.

While appealing on their face, particularly to economists and some policymakers, there are several potential problems with "stepping-stone" models for the working poor. First, to be a worthwhile investment for organizations, they require that the employer maintain a significant internal labor market system so that employees who acquire more human capital can move to higher-level positions within the organization. Such internal labor markets were the hallmark of the post-World War II corporation, and assume long-term commitments by both employers and employees, and a system of training and advancement up an internal job ladder. But as Osterman (1999) and others have demonstrated, over the past 40 years such internal career systems have been abandoned by most organizations in favor of more open markets where neither employee nor employer expect to have long-term employment with the same organization. At the same time, the costs of any investments in human capital development are increasingly being shifted from the employer to the employee (Lambert, 2008)—a particularly high hurdle for the working poor.

A second fundamental problem with "stepping-stone" approaches is that even if internal career ladders are available and individuals can thus benefit from investing in developing their human capital, such approaches do nothing to address the fundamental deficiencies in the job being abandoned. Instead, the job is seen as something to escape, only to be filled by the next person at the bottom rung of the economic ladder. Thus, there is little real organizational change and certainly no improvement in work conditions, supervision, etc. Instead, there is only a rotation of the individuals sufficiently unfortunate to have to take the jobs as a starting point or, worse, be stuck in them over time because they do not have the resources (e.g., time, tuition money) to move to something better.

Finally, and related to the last point, many workers do not want to "move up" into other jobs but would be happy staying with their current jobs if only they paid better and the conditions were more tolerable. Mittal et al. (2009) found that most of the direct care workers they interviewed in nursing homes did not want to become nurses because they enjoyed the hands-on care they provided to patients and did not want to lose the personal connection they found so fulfilling in their work. At the same time, they realized that the only way to make a living wage was to move into a job they saw as far less motivating and engaging. For many, the trade-off was not worth it—particularly when combined with the expense of extra education—so they stayed in their current job, resigning themselves to its low wages, lack of respect, and challenging work. Thus, the "stepping-stone" approach does not entail real organizational change, and for many workers there is little positive about the opportunities it creates.

"Management-Led" Relational Approaches

The second approach is management-led, top-down change that crosses levels and is aimed at improving relations between supervisors and workers through relational change. This approach draws on theories of organizational support, which maintain that employees form positive social exchanges with organizations that are supportive of them (Eisenberger, Armeli, Rexwinkel, Lynch, & Rhoades, 2001), which can be content general (e.g., my workplace or my supervisor supports me on the job) or content specific social support (e.g., my workplace or my supervisor supports my work-family needs [e.g., Allen, 2001; Kossek, Pichler, Bodner, & Hammer, 2011]). When employees develop positive perceptions of supervisor and organizational support they feel cared for and appreciate, and/or are able to get direct (e.g., HR policies, schedule changes) or indirect (e.g., emotional help, such as listening) help with problems from their direct manager and the organization in general (Kossek et al., 2011). Such support is a critical job that can reduce negative psychological effects such as burnout from poor working conditions (Kossek et al., 2011). The goal is to change management culture and enactment of HR to be more supportive and adaptive to workers' needs on and off the job.

An example of this approach comes from a recent study conducted by the National Work-Family and Health Network, which implements work interventions to improve worker health and productivity, while reducing work-family conflict. This study developed, implemented, and evaluated a training program designed to increase supervisor support for work-family issues in twelve stores with several hundred grocery store workers and managers in Michigan (Hammer et al., 2011; Kossek & Hammer, 2008).

Retail Work

The retail industry is a very prevalent organizational context in the United States as about two-thirds of the gross domestic product (GDP) in the United States is from retail consumption (BLS, 2011). According to Bureau of Labor Statistics (BLS, 2010) estimates, retail employees held about 4.5 million jobs in 2008, spanning industries from clothing to warehouse clubs to grocery. Nearly one-third (30%) of retail employees work part-time and thus do not qualify for health care benefits, or if they can be purchased, the benefits are very expensive and often have costly co-payments. The average workweek for non-managerial retail employees is 29.4 hours, compared with 33.6 hours for workers in all industries, and the median hourly wages of wage-and-salary retail sales-persons, including commissions, were $9.86 in 2008 (BLS, 2010). Retail jobs typically involve more dispersed and variable work schedule patterns than other occupations. Stores can and often are open or being stocked 24-7, and employees are needed to cover many shifts from early morning to evenings, nights, weekends, and holidays. Schedules also are highly unpredictable, largely because employers can transfer the risk of fluctuations in demand for products and services onto the low-wage workers (Lambert, 2008).

Although many retail employees work inside with air conditioning and clean environments, work can often be very hectic, especially during peak retail hours. Interacting with customers can be stressful, involve emotional labor, and even subject the worker to bullying and aggression from customers. Some loss of personal identity is also an aspect of being a retail worker, particularly when working for larger brands. The BLS (2010) notes that most retail employees are required to wear some form of uniform or clothing with store branding that identifies them as a store employee. Retail workers often have to follow de-individualizing scripts ranging from how to interact with the public to how to clock in and out of work. Not surprisingly, turnover in retail is quite high, sometimes up to 100 to 200 percent a year.

"Top-Down" Intervention

To develop a change intervention aimed at improving conditions for low-wage retail workers, the researchers first developed a measure of positive supervisor support for work and family. The work-family literature for professionals and managers often focuses on formal corporate work-family policies such as flextime or telework. Yet many retail organizations such as grocery stores do not have a lot of formal work-family policies like flextime, let alone a work-life manager. In addition, some of the most popular work-life programs like telework are not applicable to hourly retail workers who have to do face-to-face work most of their time. So much of the work-life support research needed to be customized to be more informal and relational between employees and their supervisors, who are the key linking pin in enacting positive work-family policy. If a manager is viewed as work-family supportive, then workers are more likely to view the employer as work-family supportive which in turn leads to lower work-family conflict (Kossek et al., 2011).

The researchers conducted focus groups in an East Coast grocery chain to identify what supervisory behaviors would be considered family supportive (Hammer, Kossek, Zimmerman, & Daniels, 2007). The research team wanted to design a positive intervention to identify how to increase social support for work and family, and identified four behaviors that created a global scale of family supportive supervisory behaviors (FSSB) (Hammer, Kossek, Yragui, Bodner, & Hansen, 2009). The first behavior identified was emotional support, such as being available to ask about or listen to workers' personal work-family needs. The researchers found that many managers were not viewed as approachable to the low-wage workers they supervised, making it difficult for interpersonal issues to be positively discussed. The second behavior was positive work-family role modeling. The managers themselves worked long hours and if they did not model positive work-family self care, it was likely to create a culture where workers felt they could not ask for personal help. The third behavior was instrumental support for schedule conflicts. Schedule conflicts are inevitable for all workers, and especially low-income workers with precarious child care and more life problems such as cars that break down, domestic violence, and other issues (Kossek, Huber-Yoder, Castellino, & Lerner, 1997). Supervisors who helped employees solve problems were viewed as more supportive. The fourth behavior was creative work-family management where supervisors were open to trying new ways of working that helped meet business needs at the same time that employees' work-life needs were met.

To evaluate the intervention longitudinally, baseline data on worker health, work attitudes such as job satisfaction and work-family conflict, and background data on demographics were collected from over 300 workers and managers in 12 stores. Biodata on blood pressure and sleep using actigraphy watches were collected on a subsample of employees. A small group of spouses and children were also surveyed. Nine months later the research team went to six randomly assigned stores to implement the intervention, which consisted of one-on-one laptop training on FSSB with the managers participating in role plays and a debriefing session, and asking managers to volunteer to self-monitor their behavior on the job for several weeks to support transfer of FSSB (Hammer et al., 2011; Kossek & Hammer, 1998). The research team went back 1-2 months later to all 12 stores to measure health and work attitudinal change.

The results showed that for workers who were high in work-family conflict at time 1, if their supervisor was trained they had lower depressive symptoms, higher job satisfaction, lower work-family conflict, and were more likely to follow safety procedures at time 2. The study did have one unintended consequence. While the researchers found that this approach had strong, positive health and productivity effects for workers who had high work-family conflict, having one's supervisor trained had the unintended consequences of reducing job satisfaction for individuals who had initially had lower work-family conflict (Hammer et al., 2011). This finding suggests that managing positive organizational change is complex and may have unintended consequences, and that recursive and cross group relational dynamics must be managed. Improving one part of the system for low-wage workers high in work-family conflict as in this example can have mixed consequences for other low-wage groups such as workers who did not need work-family support at this time.

The intervention to increase FSSB was largely a relational cultural change. It improved social interaction between workers and managers but did not result in structural change to the overall scheduling system, which was controlled by corporate headquarters. Each store was tightly scrutinized on how labor costs were allocated, and keeping overtime to a minimum was the goal. This computer scheduling system was developed at a centralized location and allocated labor cost hours to each store based on store trends and availability. The centralized scheduling system was not affected by FSSB relational training. Thus, it was perhaps a constraint to implementing structural change to support the working poor. So even though relations between managers and workers needing support were enhanced, the larger scheduling systems were not adaptive enough to accommodate all workers, resulting in some workers having their work hours increased to allow more flexibility for others. It may be that both cultural (relational change) and structural (i.e., the automated schedule system) support to reinforce cross-level change are needed to ensure positive change (Kossek, Hammer, & Lewis, 2010).

"Bottom-Up" Job Crafting Approaches

Organizational change that is bottom-up originates with the employees themselves rather than with their managers or through organization-wide policies. Such change is best captured in Wrzesniewski and Dutton's (2001) description of "job crafting"—the active role that workers play in altering the boundaries of their jobs and shaping ongoing work practice in order to make the job a better fit to their own preferences, competencies, and perceptions of how the job ought to be done. Such change comprises actions to alter work processes and the boundaries of the job that are developed and sustained *by* workers rather than *for* them. Job crafting is initiated by employees rather than managers, and such activities are not found in the written job description or necessarily condoned by management. Instead, the change is informal, idiosyncratic, and often deliberately kept invisible in terms of documented practice.

Employees engage in job crafting for a variety of reasons, but Wrzesniewski and Dutton (2001) focus on its cognitive benefits. By changing job tasks, relationships, and boundaries, job crafters can enhance the meaning of the work they do and the sense of positive identity from work in terms of their association with an organization and/or occupation. Thus, hospital janitors can expand their self-initiated job responsibilities to include not just keeping patients' rooms clean, but also soothing patients who are lonely or in pain, and welcoming visiting family members. In these ways, the boundaries of the job are expanded to make the work more personally meaningful to the individual worker, as well as contributing to the larger organizational mission of healing (Wrzesniewski & Dutton, 2001).

As indicated previously, low-wage work is often highly regimented and closely monitored. In these regards, there appears to be little room for job crafting. Yet recent work by Leana et al. (2009) shows how low-wage workers who provide care to others (in this case, childcare workers) proactively craft their jobs to expand their scope, meaning, and interpersonal relationships. In the process, the workers gain benefits for themselves in terms of their own attachment to, and satisfaction with the work, as well as for the organization in the form of enhanced job performance. Thus, such job crafting is a form of "bottom-up" change that is positive and potentially self-reinforcing in carework.

Carework

England, Budig, and Folbre (2002, p. 445) and England (2010) define carework as occupations in which workers provide face-to-face services which are meant to develop the capabilities of the recipient, or meet physical or emotional needs that care receivers cannot meet themselves. Examples of low-wage carework include childcare workers, home health aides, nursing assistants, and personal care aides. Approximately five million workers in the United States were employed in these occupations in 2008 according to BLS estimates.[2] By 2018, the direct care workforce is expected to grow by 40% and become the second largest occupational grouping in the United States (BLS Employment Projections Program, 2008-2018). Nearly all care workers are female (90% in personal and health care; 97% in childcare), roughly half are minorities, and approximately 20% are non-native born (BLS, 2008; Smith & Baughman, 2007).

Care workers comprise a significant portion of the working poor in the United States. Among personal and health care aides, the median hourly wage was $10.42 in 2008 (vs. $15.57 for all U.S. workers) and only about half of such workers receive employer-based healthcare coverage. Among childcare workers, median hourly wages are lower ($9.12) and only about a quarter receive employer-based healthcare. Forty-four percent of care workers live in households earning below 200% of the poverty threshold, and 40% receive public assistance such as food stamps or Medicaid payments (PHI Facts 3, 2010).

---

[2] Although this number is probably low because of underreporting of income by independent contractors and/or those employed directly by families.

Like retail sales, carework is demanding. Emotional labor is an inherent part of the job and providing care for pay is what Ashforth and Kreiner (1999) label "dirty work"—jobs that involve physical and/or social taint. Some parts of carework are closely monitored and regulated (e.g., the frequency with which a patient is bathed in a nursing home), while other aspects of the job involve a great deal of discretion (e.g., the extent to which bathing is done in a manner that respects a patient's privacy and personal dignity). Scheduling changes are frequent, and rotating shift work and mandatory overtime are common.

"Bottom-Up" Change Initiated by Workers

Leana et al. (2009) argue that job crafting is an inherent part of carework and recently reported on job crafting among childcare workers. Childcare work is improvisational as classroom staff work to meet the often unpredictable needs of young children. It is also inherently collaborative in most childcare centers due to state licensing requirements which mandate staff-child ratios that require more than one teacher and teacher aide in a classroom. Thus, work in center-based childcare programs is performed interdependently with teams of teachers and teacher aides jointly attending to the education and needs of children in their care. Consequently, there are ample opportunities for childcare workers to collaboratively define their tasks and carry out their work in a way that addresses children's changing needs. Achieving high quality is complex in this situation, and attention to improvisational work process and collaboration is at the heart of high quality care.

To better understand worker-initiated social change, we studied 62 childcare centers in New Jersey and Pennsylvania to examine the potential benefits of teacher job crafting in preschool classrooms. We interviewed childcare center directors, surveyed 232 classroom teachers and aides, and commissioned independent performance assessments in all centers to examine the factors that contribute to high quality care. Like other recent studies of childcare workers, we found that teacher education and experience—that is, the "human capital" of the workforce—did not explain differences among classrooms in the quality of care. Instead, something more was at work. We found that interaction and improvisation among childcare staff (what Leana & Van Buren, 1999, and others have labeled "social capital") are far more important elements in affecting classroom quality. Moreover, the effects of such collaboration on quality were greatest for those teachers and aides with less experience on the job.

While the effects of collaborative job crafting were quite positive for children, as well as the center as a whole, such behavior was not rewarded by center directors, nor did workers necessarily bring it to the attention of their managers. Instead, job crafting was initiated and sustained by the workers themselves without the encouragement or, in most cases, the awareness of management. A reasonable question, then, is why workers would do this. Here our findings are illuminating in that childcare workers who reported engaging in the most job crafting with their peers also reported higher levels of job satisfaction and organizational commitment (Leana et al., 2009). Further analysis of the data also indicated that job crafters reported lower levels of emotional distress and higher levels of attachment to the children in their care (Rawat, 2010). Thus, "bottom-up" change initiated by workers was beneficial to themselves, the children, and families that received care, and the center as a whole.

These findings have implications for positive social change in organizations and for managers. The aspects of quality that tend to receive the most attention from managers and policy makers are teacher education and qualifications, teacher-child ratios, and class size. Our research suggests that other—usually unobserved—job process characteristics also have important effects on the quality of childcare, and are amenable to action by management and policy makers. For example, professional development of childcare workers could be expanded to include training in teamwork and joint improvisation in order to promote effective collaboration among staff in childcare classrooms. Further, center managers could support such activities through promoting strong ties among workers and rewarding job crafting overtly rather than making it an "underground" activity that workers tend to hide from management.

UNDERLYING PRINCIPLES OF POSITIVE ORGANIZATIONAL CHANGE

Regardless of whether change in organizations is initiated for ("top-down") or by ("bottom-up") the working poor, as these examples suggest, increased systemic disconnects and paradoxes may occur across levels and between visible/formal and invisible/informal systems. As Kossek's study of grocery store workers demonstrates, organizational stratification gaps that exist between existing formal policies and rules made at the *organizational* level that are enacted at a *supervisory level* and hinder an *individual* worker's ability to manage non-work needs may be increasingly exposed. Kossek (2006) also argues that the work-life benefits offered by many organizations (e.g., dependent care spending accounts that allow one to set aside pretax dollars for work-life expenses) are far more useful to high- or middle-income than low-income workers.

Tensions are also created among practices that are highly visible—even touted by management—and those that operate far less visibly when they are initiated by low-income workers. Because a low-income worker also tends to be low in the organization hierarchy, he may be socialized to expect management to formally initiate change from the top, and be wary of implicitly challenging the hierarchy by publicly deviating from formal practice. Instead, less visible accommodations may be made either by the individual worker (Wrzesniewski & Dutton, 2001), the work group (Leana et al., 2009), or through "off the books" collaboration between the worker and his supervisor (Kossek & Hammer, 2008).

Yet in order for positive social change to be systematized and sustained, such "under the radar" practices must become visibly incorporated into the organization's accepted systems of norms, policies, and rewards. This may require a re-socialization of managers and workers to give greater voice in how organizational policies and practices are initiated and enacted. Such shifts may challenge the hegemony of existing organizational assumptions and, at least in the short term, create social tensions and mixed messages. In our own research, we are continually reminded of such paradoxes. Management may express a desire for low-income workers to take more responsibility and initiative for job-related duties, but when workers in turn require more discretion and flexibility to do so, management is reluctant to make such changes as these could mean a redistribution of decision-making power and resources across levels as well. Similarly, when workers seek flexibility for family needs, managers offer sympathy but little support for systemic changes that could reduce ongoing work-family conflict.

In addition to the need for positive organizational change to be approached from multiple levels, programs and interventions aimed at the working poor are further complicated by the tendency of some workers to hide their own innovations, or at least not draw attention to them, because of fear of being judged as deviant (Leana et al., 2009). Hazel Markus and her colleagues show that working-class and middle-class workers hold different beliefs about what constitutes "good" or appropriate action by individuals (e.g., Snibbe & Markus, 2005; Stephens et al., 2007). In their research, middle-class students and adults were more likely to value independence and uniqueness in the choices they make while those from less advantaged backgrounds were likely to make choices based on a desire to be similar to others and not "stand out from the crowd" (Snibbe & Markus, 2005). Similarly, managers who make informal accommodations to help low-income workers address issues such as work-family conflicts (which may be more frequent and severe for low-wage workers due to a lack of back-up resources) may not wish to draw attention to such exceptions. And a worker may be reluctant to call attention to herself by requesting individual accommodations to attend classes or care for children if she believes she can be labeled as a "troublemaker" for requesting flexible hours. As a consequence, workplace systems such as scheduling may be automated in ways that do not account for such needs and instead allocate sufficient work hours to earn a living and health benefits only to workers who *do not* ask for exceptions.

In addition to multilevel change that is visible, we offer two other observations regarding over-arching change principals that we found from our work in this area. First, change must be contextualized, and is adaptive change as opposed to technical change. Lasting positive organizational change is a process that must be customized to the occupation, industry context, and labor markets. What worked in childcare centers, for example on job crafting, would look different in retail where the work is less inherently improvisational. Indeed, Leana et al. (2009) argue for the importance of context even within educational settings. Many practitioners seek to improve early childhood education by incorporating the K-5 model into childcare classrooms. But our study of childcare suggests that this may not be appropriate because of the inherently improvisational and collaborative nature of childcare work—factors that do not necessarily characterize K-5 settings which typically have only one teacher per classroom. In K-5 classrooms, job crafting may be beneficial for the teacher and her students, but this is likely to be individual rather than collaborative crafting. In childcare classrooms, conversely, Leana et al. (2009) report that while collaborative crafting is associated with enhanced job satisfaction, they found that teachers who reported more individual job crafting reported *lower* levels of satisfaction. Thus, contextual effects may be quite pronounced even within settings (e.g., preschool classrooms vs. first-grade classrooms) that appear to have much in common.

A final principle is that small changes or interventions can move and "unstick" a seemingly intransigent system for large positive effects for those most in need of change, although sometimes not without facing some system resistance from other employee groups. Referring again to the NIH National Work-Family and Health Network grocery example, the researchers found that simply training managers on basic work-life issues for a few hours, identifying what it meant to be supportive, asking them to set a goal, and try to enact supportive behaviors resulted in improved job satisfaction, job attachment, and physical health for working poor individuals who had higher work-family conflict. Simple things like coaching managers to ask about family needs and be a little flexible had huge payoffs in terms of work-family conflict reduction over time. Yet attempts to "unstick" the system to improve the well-being of the workforce segment higher in work-family conflict did face some short-term backlash from employees who were also among the working poor but were not experiencing high work-family stress. This suggests a short-term negative repercussion for longer-term gain in family support.

IMPLICATIONS FOR RESEARCH ON POSITIVE SOCIAL CHANGE

Future research is needed that compares the effectiveness of stepping-stone, top-down, and bottom-up approaches to workplace change strategies by and for the working poor. Studies might be done to replicate the ideas in this chapter and demonstrate across contexts whether multilevel strategies truly are more effective than others. It also would be important to understand whether some segments, occupations, and organizational contexts require certain kinds of change strategies to be sustainable. For example, perhaps in an over-bounded bureaucratic system (e.g., one that is that is highly regulated such as nursing homes), it may be that top-down change is needed to increase management support for individuals lower in the hierarchy in order for "invisible" job crafting to be legitimated and visibly incorporated into the work.

Research might also be conducted to see how the effectiveness of these strategies is moderated by the specific needs of the working poor. Younger individuals might need targeted support focusing on childcare, education, and language skills. Older workers might require help with health maintenance or updating skills such as learning how to use a computer. Recent immigrants might need language training with on the job skills such as how to read instructions (Kossek et al., 1997). We hope this chapter spurs future research to identify comparative effectiveness studies of organizational change, as well as delve into how to customize organizational change strategies for the needs of different segments of the working poor.

CONCLUSION

Organizations can change in ways that offer sustainable assistance to the working poor. Here we provide two examples of such change—one initiated by managers and the other by employees. As we have noted throughout, for such changes to be effective they must take into account multiple levels of the organization, as well as endeavor to make visible the often-covert behavior of employees who take it upon themselves to improve their jobs and their ability to perform well in them. In addition, for any change to be sustainable, it must be contextualized, taking into account both the nature of the work and the nature of the workers. Finally, we observe that small changes can have large effects and can become the impetus for broader system changes that are both beneficial and sustainable over time.

REFERENCES

Adams, J. (2010). Family reform through welfare reform: How TANF violates constitutional rights to volitional family formation. Retrieved July 2011 from http://www.law.berkeley.edu/faculty/sugarmans/Family%20seminar%20Jill%20for%20website.doc.
Adler, N. E., & Ostrove, J. M. (1993). Socioeconomic status and health: What we know and what we don't. *Annals of the New York Academy of Sciences, 896*, 3–16.

Allen, T. D. (2001). Family-supportive work environments: The role of organizational perceptions. *Journal of Vocational Behavior, 58*, 414–435.

Anderson, N. B., & Armstead, C. A. (1995). Toward understanding the association of socioeconomic status and health: A new challenge for the biopsychosocial approach. *Psychosomatic Medicine, 57*, 213–255.

Baker, M., & Tippin, D. (2002). Health, beneficiaries and welfare to work: Competing visions of employability. In T. Eardley & B. Bradbury (Eds.), *Competing visions: Refereed proceedings of the national social policy conference 2001*, SPRC Report 1/02 (pp. 45–63). Sydney: Social Policy Research Centre, University of New South Wales.

Barrett, A. E., & Turner, R. J. (2005). Family structure and mental health: The mediating effects of socioeconomic status, family processes, and social stress. *Journal of Health and Social Behavior, 46*, 156–169.

Berg, P., & Frost, A. C. (2005). Dignity at work for low wage, low skill service workers. *Industrial Relations, 60*, 657–682.

Berkman, L., Buxton, O., Ertel, K., & Okechukwu, C. (2010). Managers' practices related to work-family balance predict employee cardiovascular risk and sleep duration in extended care settings. *Journal of Occupational Health Psychology, 15*, 316–329.

Berry, J., & Sam, D. (1997). Acculturation and adaption. In H. Berry, M. Segall, & C. Kagitcibasi (Eds.), *Handbook of cross-cultural psychology: Social behaviour and applications*, Vol. 8 (pp. 291–326). Boston: Allyn and Bacon.

Bradley, R. H., Corwyn R. F., McAdoo, H. P., & Garcia Coll, C. (2001). The home environments of children in the United States. Part 1: Variations by age, ethnicity, and poverty-status. *Child Development, 72*, 1844–1867.

Broom, D., D'Souza, R., Strazdins, L., Butterworth, P., Parslow, R., & Rodgers, B. (2006). The lesser evil: Bad jobs or unemployment? A survey of middle aged Australians. *Social Science and Medicine, 63*, 575–586.

Bureau of Labor Statistics (BLS) (2008). Washington, DC: U.S. Department of Labor. Retrieved July 8, 2010, from http://www.bls.gov/oco/ocos170.htm and http://www.bls.gov/oco/cg/cgs024.htm.

Bureau of Labor Statistics (BSL) 2011. Occupational outlook handbook, 2010–11 edition. Washington, DC: U.S. Department of Labor. Retrieved November 16, 2011, from http://www.bls.gov/oco

Bureau of Labor Statistics (BLS) (2010). Washington, DC: U.S. Department of Labor. Retrieved July 8, 2010, from http://www.bls.gov/emp/empiols.htm.

Burtless, G. (2001). Can supply side policies reduce unemployment: Lessons from North America. Centre for Economic Policy research. (Discussion paper 440.) National Australian University.

Devine, C. M., Jastran, M., Jabs, J., Wethington, E., Farell, T. J., & Bisogni, C. A. (2006). "A lot of sacrifices": Work-family spillover and the food choice coping strategies of low-wage employed parents. *Social Science & Medicine, 63*, 2591–2603.

Durden, E.D., Hill, T. D., & Angel, R. J. (2007). Social demands, social supports, and psychological distress among low-income women. *Journal of Social & Personal Relationships, 24*, 343–361.

Eisenberger, R., Armeli, S., Rexwinkel, B., Lynch, P. D., & Rhoades, L. (2001). Reciprocation of perceived organizational support. *Journal of Applied Psychology, 86*, 42–51.

Eisenberger, R., Huntington, R., Hutchison, S., & Sowa, D. (1986) Perceived organizational support. *Journal of Applied Psychology, 71*, 500–507.

England, P. (personal correspondence, March 14, 2010).

England, P., Budig, M., & Folbre, N. (2002) Wages of virtue: The relative pay of care work. *Social Problems, 49*, 455–473.

Farah, M. J., Noble, K. G., & Hurt, H. (2005). Poverty, privilege and brain development: Empirical findings and ethical implications. In J. Illes (Ed.), *Neuroethics in the 21st century* (pp. 277–288). New York: Oxford University Press.

Furstenberg, F. F., Cook, T. D., Eccles, J., Elder, G. H., & Sameroff, A. (1999). *Managing to make it: Urban families and adolescent success.* Chicago: University of Chicago Press.

Griffin, M., Neal, A., & Parker, S. (2007). A new model of work role performance: Positive behavior in uncertain and interdependent contexts. *Academy of Management Journal, 50*, 327–347.

Hammer, L. B., Kossek, E. E., Bodner, T., Anger, K., & Zimmerman, K. (2011). Clarifying work-family intervention processes: The roles of work-family conflict and family supportive supervisor behaviors. *Journal of Applied Psychology, 96*, 134–150.

Hammer, L., Kossek, E., Yragui, N., Bodner, T., & Hansen, G. (2009). Development and validation of a multidimensional scale of family supportive supervisor behaviors (FSSB). *Journal of Management, 35*, 837–856.

Hammer, L. B., Kossek, E. E., Zimmerman, K., & Daniels, R. (2007). Clarifying the construct of family supportive supervisory behaviors (FSSB): A multilevel perspective. In P. L. Perrewe & D. C. Ganster (Eds.), *Research in occupational stress and well-being* (Vol. 6, pp. 171–211). Amsterdam: Elsevier Ltd.

Henly, J., & Lambert, S. (2009). *Precarious work schedules in low-level jobs: Implications for work-life interferences and stress* (working paper). The University of Chicago. Presented at IESE International Work and Family Conference. Barcelona, July 6–8.

Heyman, J., & Earle, A. (2009). *Raising the Global Floor: Dismantling the myth that we can't afford good working conditions for everyone.* Palo Alto: Stanford University Press.

Hudson, C. (2005). Socioeconomic status and mental illness: Tests of social causation and selection hypothesis. *Journal of Orthopsychiatry, 75*, 3–18.

Iverson, R., & Armstrong, A. (2007). Parents' work, depressive symptoms, children, and family economic mobility: What can ethnography tell us? *Families in Society, 88*, 339–350.

Jackson, A. P., Brooks-Gunn, J., Huang, C., & Glassman, M. (2000). Single mothers in low-wage jobs: Financial strain, parenting and preschoolers' outcomes. *Child Development, 71*, 1409–1423.

Karasek, R. A. (1979). Job demands, job decision latitude, and mental strain: Implications for job redesign. *Administrative Science Quarterly, 24*, 285–308.

Kossek, E. E. (2006). Work and family in America: Growing tensions between employment policy and a changing workforce. A thirty year perspective. Commissioned chapter by SHRM Foundation and University of California Center for Organizational Effectiveness for the 30th anniversary of the State of Work in America. In E. Lawler & J. O'Toole (Eds.), *America at work: Choices and challenges* (pp. 53–72). New York: Palgrave MacMillan.

Kossek, E., & Hammer, L. (2008). Supervisor work/life training gets results. *Harvard Business Review, November*, p. 36.

Kossek, E., Pichler, S., Bodner, T., & Hammer, L, (2011). Workplace social support and work-family conflict: A meta-analysis clarifying the influence of general and work-family specific supervisor and organizational support. *Personnel Psychology, 64*, 289–313.

Kossek, E., Pichler, S., Meece, D., & Barratt, M. (2008). Family, friend and neighbor child care providers and maternal well-being in low income systems: An ecological social perspective. *Journal of Organizational and Occupational Psychology,* 369–391.

Kossek, E. E., Huber, M., & Lerner, J. (2003). Sustaining economic and psychological well-being of mothers on public assistance: Individual deficit and social structural accounts. *Journal of Vocational Behavior, 62,* 155–175.

Kossek, E. E., Huber-Yoder, M., Castellino, D., & Lerner, J. (1997). The working poor: Locked out of careers and the organizational mainstream? *Academy of Management Executive.* Issue on careers in the twenty-first century, *Winter,* 76–92.

Kossek, E. E., Lewis, S., & Hammer, L. (2010). Work-life initiatives and organizational change: Overcoming mixed messages to move from the margin to the mainstream, *Human Relations, 63,* 1–17.

Lambert, S. (2008). Passing the buck: Labor flexibility practices that transfer risk onto hourly workers. *Human Relations, 61,* 1203–1227.

Leana, C., Appelbaum, E., & Shevchuk, I. (2009). Work process and quality of care in early childhood education: The role of job crafting. *Academy of Management Journal, 52,* 1–24.

Leana, C., Mittal, V., & Stiehl, E. (2009). *Organizational behavior and the working poor* (working paper). Center for Health and Care Work, University of Pittsburgh.

Lepak, D., & Snell, S. (1999). The human resource architecture: Toward a theory of human capital allocation and development. *Academy of Management Review, 24,* 31–48.

Macintyre, S., Maciver, S., & Sooman, A. (1993). Area, class and health: Should we be focusing on places or people? *Journal of Social Policy, 22,* 213–234.

Masterman-Smith, H., & Pocock, B. (2008). *Living low paid: The dark side of prosperous Australia.* Crows Nest, Australia: Allen and Unwin.

Mittal, V., Rosen, J. R., & Leana, C. (2009). A dual-driver model of retention and turnover in the direct care workforce. *The Gerontologist, 49,* 623–634.

National Work-Family and Health Network. Retrieved July 19, 2010, from http://www.kpchr.org/workfamilyhealthnetwork/public/default.aspx.

OECD (Organization for Economic Cooperation and Development). Retrieved July 10, 2010, from http://stats.oecd.org/glossary/detail.asap?ID=4841.

O'Neill, J. W., Harrison, M. M., Cleveland, J., Almeida, D., Stawski, R., & Crouter, A. C. (2009). Work-family climate, organizational commitment, and turnover: Multilevel contagion effects of leaders. *Journal of Vocational Behavior, 74,* 18–29.

Osterman, P. (1999). *Securing prosperity.* Princeton, NJ: Princeton University Press.

PHI Facts. (2010). *Who are direct care workers?* Para Professional Health Care Institute. Retrieved July 10, 2011 from http://phinational.org/.

Pocock, B., Elton, J., Preston, A., Charlesworth, S., MacDonald, F., & Baird, M. (2008). The impact of work-choices on women in low paid employment in Australia: A qualitative analysis. *Journal of Industrial Relations, 50,* 475–488.

Presser, H. B., & Cox, A. G. (1997). The work schedules of low-educated American women and welfare reform. *Monthly Labor Review, April,* 25–34.

Rawat, A. (2010). Examining work as calling (unpublished doctoral dissertation). University of Pittsburgh.

Rousseau, D. (2005). *I-deals: Idiosyncratic deals employees bargain for themselves.* New York: Sharpe.

Singh, G. K., & Siahpush, M. (2006). Widening socioeconomic inequalities in US life expectancy, 1980–2000. *International Journal of Epidemiology, 35,* 969–979.

Smith, K., & Baughman, R. (2007). *Low wages prevalent in direct care and child care workforce.* Carsey Institute Policy Brief #7, University of New Hampshire.

Snibbe, A. C., & Markus, H. R. (2005). You can't always get what you want: Educational attainment, agency and choice. *Journal of Personality and Social Psychology, 88,* 703–720.

Stephens, N., Hamedani M., Markus, H., Bergsieker, H., & Eloul, L. (2009). Why did they "choose" to stay? Perspectives of Hurricane Katrina observers and survivors. *Psychological Science, 20,* 878–886.

Stone, D., & Romero-Stone, E. (2008). *The influence of culture on human resource management processes and practices.* New York: LEA Press.

Taylor, S. E., & Repetti, R. L. (1997). Health psychology: What is an unhealthy environment and how does it get under the skin? *Annual Review of Psychology, 48,* 411–447.

Tigges, L. M., Browne, I., & Green, G. P. (1998). Social isolation of the urban poor: Race, class, and neighborhood effects on social resources. *Sociological Quarterly, 39,* 53–77.

Tolman, R. M., & Raphael, J. (2000). A review of research on welfare and domestic violence. *Journal of Social Issues, 56,* 655–682.

Williams, D. R. (1990). Socioeconomic differentials in health: A review and redirection. *Social Psychology Quarterly, 53,* 81–99.

Williams, D. R., & Collins, C. (1995). US Socioeconomic and racial differences in health: Patterns and explanations. *Annual Review of Sociology, 21,* 349–386.

Wilson, W. J. (1987). *The truly disadvantaged: The inner city, the underclass, and public policy.* Chicago: University of Chicago Press.

Wrzesniewski, A., & Dutton, J. E. (2001). Crafting a job: Revisioning employees as active crafters of their work. *Academy of Management Review, 26,* 179–201.

18

Building Organizations to Change Communities: Educational Entrepreneurs in Poor Urban Areas

Christine M. Beckman and Brooking Gatewood
University of California, Irvine

We pay our taxes. We do what you ask. Do what we want now. We want our kids to get an education. It's so hard to get a school built here, but as soon as she gets to be an adult, they'll build a jail so easy to put her in.

A parent's plea to the Oakland Unified School District (OUSD) to accept the community's proposal for a new charter school, circa 1998 (Schorr 2002)

I was bor i california and im mexican america. My old shcool name was Lockwod wassan ril good.

Oakland 4th-grader's response to his first homework assignment as a charter school student, circa 2000 (Schorr 2002)

Our school will be founded on the belief that all children can learn at a high level. ... Race, culture, income, and ethnicity will not be predictors of achievement. Instead, our school will hold uncompromisingly high standards for all of its students, while providing active and flexible support to ensure that they meet those expectations.

North Oakland Community Charter School Petition (OUSD 2010)

INTRODUCTION

Despite being one of the wealthiest nations in the world, the United States is one of the highest-ranking OECD countries in relative poverty[1] (Foerster & d'Ercole, 2005). More than one in five children in the United States lives below the federal poverty line ($21,756 for a family of four),[2] and families in poverty tend to live in neighborhoods lacking social resources such as good public schools and jobs. They also have increased risks for disease, substance abuse, social isolation, and criminal victimization (Jargowsky, 1997; Pebbly & Sastry, 2004).

Although many factors contribute to poverty, in this chapter we focus on access to quality education as an important component of the perpetuation of poverty. Beginning with James Coleman's famous 1966 report, "The Equality of Educational Opportunity," scholars have understood that family background and socioeconomic status are key contributors to poor educational outcomes (Coleman, 1966). Poor children are less likely to complete basic schooling and are more likely to perform at lower levels; together these factors depress potential future earnings and perpetuate the cycle of poverty (Rouse & Barrow, 2006).

Despite this daunting history, attempts to improve the educational experience of poor children have continued over a long span of time. In fact, many organizations are founded in an effort to enact social change in this challenging environment. The organizational solutions are varied: non-profit organizations offering supplemental educational opportunities and social services, private school scholarship programs, new curriculum offerings or teacher training and development, and public school experiments like magnet and charter schools. Some of these efforts remove children from their local environment (e.g., the SEED School of Washington, DC, a boarding school for 320 urban children); others are more minor tweaks on the existing model (e.g., charter schools that innovate at the local school level by providing an extended school day or extended school year). Some reformers are visionaries with specific ideas for how to change

---

[1] Relative poverty is an internationally used poverty metric that penalizes for large income distributions. Even with the locally preferred poverty threshold metric that does not account for the poverty gap, the United States consistently has a poverty rate around 15%.

[2] Income, earnings, and poverty data from the 2008 American Community Survey, U.S. Census Bureau, 2009, available at http://www.census.gov/acs.

the system. Others, like the father quoted at the beginning of this article, are parents who want their kids to get a good, safe education in their own neighborhood.

This chapter focuses on charter schools in poor urban areas. Charter schools are an organizational form that emerged in the early 1990s as one potential solution to failing public schools. Rather than address the performance of charter schools relative to district schools (see Hanushek et al., 2007; Hoxby et al., 2009), we seek to understand differences among urban charter schools. There is much heterogeneity among charter schools by design, and we examine the various human, financial, and organizational resources that a charter school utilizes. For example, we measure the involvement of non-educators in the school, the extent to which charters rely on outside funding, and the formalization of the school model. We examine how these resources contribute to the survival of the school and to the academic success of charter students. We introduce a method useful for examining the *combinations* of resources and factors that are important to these two outcomes: fuzzy set qualitative comparative analysis (fsQCA). FsQCA is a method that highlights multiple pathways to an outcome, rather than a single solution. It is a useful method for looking at an organizational form that has spawned a great diversity of models. Our results tell a story of two pathways—one driven by the power of community partnerships, and the other by the power of formalization.

CHARTER CONTEXT AND THEORETICAL ORIENTATION

The charter school movement began as a response to calls for public education reform in the late 1980s, with Wisconsin and California passing the first state charter laws in 1991 and 1992. As of June 2009, 41 states had adopted charter laws (Meyerson et al., 2009a). Petitioners submit a charter school application to their district—or in some cases county or state—in which they provide a blueprint of their educational model and proposed school. If a charter petition is approved, charters receive state funding on a per student basis. The school continues to operate with state funding as long as it adheres to the goals set forth in the charter (Meyerson et al., 2009a; Wells et al., 1999b). Although state laws differ from state to state (Wells et al., 1999a), support for charter schools has come from all sides of the political spectrum (Loveless & Jasin, 1998; Wells et al., 1999b). The end result is that charter schools are now central in the national dialogue about education reform.

Leaving aside the question of whether charter schools provide advantages over district schools, we seek to examine diversity among charter schools in urban areas. Given the rhetoric of decentralization, autonomy, and choice, it is perhaps not surprising that charter schools themselves are remarkably heterogeneous (Henig et al., 2005; King, Clemens, Fry & Konty, 2011; Wells et al., 1999a). Yet it means that when we talk about "charter schools," we are talking about schools that adhere to vastly different curricula and philosophies, with different levels of financial and community support. We seek to unpack those differences and examine variety within charter schools. This is an important task because it allows us to uncover the multiple pathways by which charter schools attempt to reach their goals.

Using fsQCA, we examine the different paths by which charter schools survive and succeed. We differentiate between organizational success and survival as judged by the institutional logics of legitimacy and accountability. Schools, although traditionally judged by the logic of legitimacy, are increasingly subject to the accountability pressures as a result of standards-based reform (Elmore, 2000). These logics are more intense for charter schools because a charter school is generally founded with the agreement that it will demonstrate its effectiveness or be closed; while a more traditional school is seen to be legitimate by their "incorporation of institutionalized elements... that protects the organization from having its conduct questioned" (Meyer & Rowan, 1977, p. 349). The end result is that charters are both legitimate because they have been approved in a highly institutionalized setting and accountable because they are measured by student scores on standardized tests (the state accepted measure of performance that demonstrates accountability). Thus, theoretically, charter schools are an interesting case where pressures for legitimacy and accountability are both present. As a result of these dual logics of legitimacy and accountability, we have an opportunity to explore whether the factors that lead an organization to survive as a legitimate organization are the same as the factors that lead an organization to be successful according to accepted standards of performance.

Although the context for this study is charter schools in an urban area, the larger question raised by this book revolves around positive social change. Whether charters succeed in accomplishing social change, and whether this change is, in fact, positive, is a matter of some debate. From an entrepreneurial lens, however, spurring positive social change is the entrepreneurial intent for many of these charter operators (e.g., see the third introductory quote). Although most charters are focused on change within the local context, charter management organizations (CMOs) expressly talk in terms of high impact and scalability (Meyerson et al., 2009b). The fact that at least some of these entrepreneurs are interested in large-scale social change makes legitimacy both more important and more contested. Social change goals by definition threaten the status quo, and thus goal attainment implies some disruption of the existing system—positive from the perspective of the social change agent, but not necessarily from that of the institutional actors. In a delicate balancing act, social change organizations must obtain enough legitimacy to be seen as an entity worthy of support—which the organizational form in and of itself can provide (McCarthy & Zald, 1977; Snow & Soule, 2010)—but also create enough waves to allow the organization to effect the change it seeks.

To summarize, we seek to understand the different combinations of human, financial, and organizational resources that help charter schools succeed and survive. More broadly, in the context of this book, where understanding large-scale social change is the object, we examine the factors that shape the success of small-scale deviations of form. We discuss the multiple pathways by which organizations accomplish dual goals (legitimacy and accountability), and we introduce qualitative comparative analysis as a useful method for examining these larger questions.

DATA AND METHODS

Sample and Data Sources

The context for this study is the population of charter schools in Oakland, CA. We focus on this urban city because of the high rates of poverty in Oakland and the stated intention of many charters to focus on helping this underserved population. As one informant put it, all schools in the area movement are "aiming for equity and giving poverty kids the same chance as others." The key measure of socioeconomic status among schools is the percentage of students in the National School Lunch Program (NSLP), which offers free and/or reduced price meals to students in low-income families.[3] The state average NSLP participation among public school students in California is 54%, the average for all Oakland Unified School District (OUSD) schools is 70%, and is 80% for OUSD charter schools. Thus, Oakland charter schools as a group have a higher proportion of poor children than all Oakland schools and than the average California school. Thus, this narrow scope of OUSD allows us to look at the factors that help these charter organizations survive within a high poverty, urban education context where the goal of helping children in poverty is widely shared. That said, even within this narrow population, there is variation in what a charter looks like and the resources on which it draws, and it is this variation that we seek to examine.

Although charters are prevalent in many urban cities, we focus on Oakland because it was an early adopter of the charter form. Oakland's charter movement was catalyzed by early investment in new schools by "philanthropic elites" involved in the technology boom of the 1990s with an interest in education reform (Meyerson et al., 2009b). The first charter in Oakland was authorized in 1992, and as of June 2010, 51 OUSD charter schools had been founded, with 35 still open in the district.[4]

Our primary data source is archival and includes the approved founding charter petition documents and state-level historic data. All charter schools in California must submit a petition to be considered by their school districts for charter school status. We chose these initial documents because we know the early resource endowments and decisions made about the structure of the organization shape future decisions and outcomes (e.g., Aldrich & Zimmer, 1986; Baum et al., 2000; Beckman & Burton, 2008; Hannan et al., 1996). Although these documents are aspirational rather than measures of actual practices, they reflect the entrepreneurial intentions and initial resources of the organization. One interviewee suggested these documents contain "the kernel" of the mission but may be vague because of the subsequent accountability to the charter document. To the extent this is widely true, our measures may not capture the full diversity

---

[3] Free meals are offered to students whose families are from 0–130% of the national poverty line; for example, a child in a family of four making less than $28,665 in 2009 qualifies for free lunch (USDA, 2010).

[4] Data from OUSD Charter School Office (OUSD, 2010).

of charter models. The content of the petitions varies, but all contain sections on the school's mission, goals, curriculum, board and governance structure, human resources, admission and discipline policies, and financial planning information. Many of the charter petitions contain supplemental materials including letters of support and board bylaws. We also collected 16 additional variables from state sources including test scores, demographics, teacher credentials, and poverty rates. Unfortunately, we are limited in these additional variables. For example, charters are often (although not always) established with non-unionized teachers and with lotteries to manage excessive demand. We cannot examine any potential variation in our population with regard to unionization and student demand. This is an important limitation. We combined the archival and state sources of data. In addition to collecting the archival data, we compiled field notes from three site visits and two telephone interviews with charter school staff members. Additional qualitative depth came from a book on the early charter school movement in Oakland and conversations with the book's author (Schorr, 2002).

The majority of these petitions, which range between 15 and 430 pages, are available online through Oakland Unified School District's Legislative Information Center. Of the 51 schools whose petitions were approved, we were able to locate 39 of the original documents (information for an additional 5 charters were obtained from Schorr's 2002 book). For 48 of the 51 schools on this list, we were able to gather supplemental historic data from state sources. The three schools without historic data were approved but never opened. Our final sample includes 41 schools. These schools are largely representative of charters in Oakland, although they are larger, have more Hispanic/Latino students, and have fewer African-American students than the 7 charters for which we have no petition information. The missing schools are not significantly different in age, API scores, levels of poverty, or teacher credentials.

Variables and Coding Procedures

Our coding procedures began with a theoretically guided list of 30 preliminary coding categories. Using ATLAS.ti qualitative analysis software, we broadly coded for information on vision and mission, educational philosophy, parental involvement, partnership types, curriculum and program structure, funding sources, teacher salaries and student to teacher ratios, board and decision-making, admissions, demographics, goals and metrics of success, facilities, key personnel, disciplinary and human relations information, level and size of the schools, and length of the petition document. From these categories, we created 65 codes in 9 categories that we used to code the documents. Of particular importance for this analysis, we coded for whether the school is part of a charter management organization (CMO), board composition, external funding, partnerships, and parental involvement.[5] We use these as measures of formalization and governance, financial resources, and community and local level social capital, respectively.

Table 18.1 reports descriptive statistics for some key variables.

Our outcome variables warrant particular attention. As with any social change endeavor, defining and measuring success is a challenging task.[6] School closure may happen for multiple reasons (e.g., financial problems, poor performance, or loss of leadership), and there is no clear district guideline for when a school should be closed. Charters must be renewed every five years but a school can close outside of this schedule as well. Broadly speaking, school closure is an indication that the school is no longer legitimate. In terms of accountability, we focus on the school's performance on the state recognized metrics for student performance— standardized tests. Measuring education quality is a contentious issue, and Oakland's charter schools certainly differ in their philosophies about how to measure student achievement. However, regardless of how objectively valid the metrics are, a school's ability to achieve success by these criteria is a sound measure of accountability within the institutional context of public education. These are the measures on which they have agreed to be judged.

In California, a primary standard metric—institutionalized with the *Public Schools Accountability Act of 1999*—is the Academic Performance Index (API). The API is a composite on a scale of 200–1,000 of scores from the Standardized Testing and Reporting (STAR) Program and the California High School Exit Examination (CAHSEE) tests. These tests generally cover (as applicable by grade) language arts and mathematics for elementary students, in addition to science, life science, and history/social

---

[5] We thank Debra Meyerson for sharing her coding of CMO status as a means of verifying our coding.

[6] For a review of measurement challenges across fields, see for example Geoff Mulgan's article in the *Stanford Social Innovation Review* (Mulgan, 2010).

TABLE 18.1

Descriptive Statistics

Variable	Mean Value	Range (non-binary)	Sample Size for This Variable*
Expected school size	305.8	12–700	48
Number of elementary schools in sample**	18	–	51
Middle schools	25	–	51
High schools	23	–	51
CMOs, %	45	–	48
Schools still open (as of 2010), %	69	–	51
School age (as of 2010)	7	0–17	51
Board of director size	7.0	2–13	41
Actual partner orgs. mentioned in charter, no.	4.5	0–25	44
Intended partner orgs. mentioned in charter, no.	1.7	0–21	38
Level of parental involvement, scale 0–4	2.2	0–4	44
Schools with parents on board, %	38	–	42
Schools with staff on board, %	24	–	42
Schools with both parents and staff on board, %	16	–	42
Schools with extended day program, %	41	–	42
Schools with extended year program, %	39	–	42
Schools with private funding of some sort, %	74	–	43
API scores***	727.5	468–977	37
Students per teacher	23.7	16.5–50	36
Years of teacher experience	6.2	1–24	38
Schools in program improvement, % ****	33	–	42
Students in national school lunch program, %	80	34–100	38
State credentialed teachers in a school, %	69	0–100	45
Student ethnicity breakdown:			46
Hispanic or Latino, %	44	0–95	46
African American, %	42	2–100	46
Asian, %	6	0–55	46
Pacific Islander/Filipino, %	1	0–7	46
White, %	3	0–48	46
American Indian/Alaskan, %	0.4	0–11	46

* The sample size varies and is often lower than the total 51 charters for two reasons: first, only 39 original charters were available and not all charters reported information on each variable, leading to some sample sizes smaller than 39. Second, we were able to find supplemental information on some variables from state data archives and ethnographic studies of the schools during founding (see, in particular Schorr, 2002).

continued

TABLE 18.1 CONTINUED

Descriptive Statistics

** Some schools serve multiple ages (e.g., K-8 or K-12), so the total number by type of school is larger than 48. Schools that intended to expand to include additional grade levels were also included in this count, whether or not those proposed expansions actually happened.

*** Note that student-level data for closed schools comes from the most recent year the school was open, but otherwise this data is reported from 2010.

****Program improvement is a probation system for California public schools, implemented by the California Department of Education as part of the national Elementary and Secondary Education Act, which demands statewide accountability systems for reading and mathematics test scores.

studies for older students. School-wide API scores for the most recent year reported are the metric of accountability we use in this analysis.

Analysis Technique

We are interested in the combination of resources that charter schools rely on to survive and to perform well on standardized tests. Analyzing causal complexity is a strength of fuzzy set qualitative comparative analysis (fsQCA) (Fiss, 2007), our method of choice. This technique uses Boolean algebra, set logic, and calibrated variables for comparative case study or small "n" analyses (Ragin, 1987). By focusing on the presence or absence of causal conditions contributing to an outcome, it offers a means to reveal and reduce causal complexity to a parsimonious set of causal combinations, or "recipes" (Ragin, 1987, 2008).

Before presenting the results of our analysis, we must briefly explain two central fsQCA concepts. First is the set-theoretic *consistency* with which the existing examples of a causal combination display the outcome in question (Ragin, 2008). For example, if having funding and having many partnerships lead to high API scores in every school that exhibits that combination, the consistency would be 100%, or 1.0. Ragin suggests a minimum consistency score of 0.8 to draw any causal conclusions (2008), so this is the cut-off we use in our analysis. The second concept is set-theoretic *coverage* which assesses the degree to which a single causal recipe or pathway accounts for instances of an outcome (Ragin, 2008). The *total coverage* score is similar to an R^2 value in regression analyses. The best scores with theoretical merit in our dataset have total coverage scores ranging from .50-.60. This means the recipes we report account for over 50% of the possible pathways to the given outcome. The fsQCA method requires theory driven exploration to find recipes with both theoretical merit and good consistency and coverage scores (Ragin, 2006, 2008; Rihoux, 2006), and the recipes reported here are the result of that process.

RESULTS AND DISCUSSION

The five variables that emerge as important causal conditions for our two outcomes are detailed in Table 18.2. As noted earlier, API scores and whether the school remains open are the two outcomes of interest. We consider schools with average API scores of 800 or higher to be high performing schools; school with scores of 600 or lower are considered low performing. The cut-off for high performance is based on state metrics that allow for more flexibility for schools with greater than an 800 API score. This cut-off is much higher than the 2009 average API score in OUSD of 695. The five independent variables include measures of financial and social resources (external partnerships, parental involvement, and funding), as well as measures of structure and governance (board composition and CMO structure). We examined other variables of human capital, such as teacher experience and credentials, as well as extended class time, the level of poverty in the schools, and the ethnicity of the students, but these variables did not appear in causal recipes that had a significant amount of coverage. Thus we do not include them in any of the models that follow.

Survival Pathways

Table 18.3 presents the results of our analysis. For the legitimacy outcome, school survival, three pathways exist. Two of these pathways (1 and 2) suggest that schools meeting accountability metrics (i.e., high test scores) are likely to survive. We see attention to test scores by many of the charter schools. For example, at KIPP Bridge Charter School (Oakland, CA), a school that is part of a successful national charter network, a "rock the test" campaign with banners listing goals such as "at least 90% advanced or proficient" was in progress during our visit. More surprising, a *lack* of funding appears in two paths. The American Indian Model (AIM) Public Charter School (Oakland, CA), for example, is a thriving charter school with high test scores despite a very lean staff and budget. In our tour of

TABLE 18.2

Analysis Variables

Code	Variable	Explanation	Approximates
TEST	API Scores	0 to 1 calibrated scale of high API. API scale is 200–1000. 1=score of 800 or above, 0=600 or below, and the cross-over point is 700.	Accountability: Test Scores
OPEN	Open school	Binary. 1=charter school still open; 0=school abandoned, or closed (charter revoked).	Legitimacy: Survival
CMO	Multiple Charters	Binary. 1=Charter management organization with central office (CMO) or networked schools (e.g., elementary and high school); 0=single school.	Structure and Formalization
FUND	Money, or Supplemental Funding	0 to 1 calibrated scale of the degree of certainty and security of funding outside of the standard state-level public school funds. 1=presence of individual, corporate, and foundation funding; 0=no funders listed.	Financial Resources
PARENT	Parental Involvement	0 to 1 calibrated scale of the degree to which parental involvement is mentioned and elaborated on as important in founding charter petition. 1=highest coding rating ("parent handbook included"); 0=parents not mentioned.	Internal Social Resources
PARTNERS	Network, or Partnerships	0 to 1 calibrated scale of network connectedness as measured by the number of intended and actual partners mentioned in charter petition. 1=more than 5 confirmed partners mentioned; 0=no partners listed.	External Social Resources
BOARD	Locals on Board	0 to 1 calibrated scale of board membership. 1=presence of parents and staff members on board. 0=absence of both.	Structure and Governance

TABLE 18.3

fsQCA Results

Recipe	Raw Coverage	Solution Consistency	Cases	Age (av.)
OUTCOME=OPEN: SURVIVAL PATHWAYS *(total coverage: .59)*				
1. TEST*fund	.32	.98	E. Oakland Leadership Academy, N. Oakland Community, World Academy, American Indian (2)	6
2. TEST*PARENT	.29	.98	Lighthouse (2), Aspire (2), COVA, KIPP, E.C. Reems Academy	6.7
3. fund*parent* PARTNERS	.21	.98	Oakland Unity, World Academy, Oasis, Arise, American Indian	4.8
OUTCOME=TEST: PERFORMANCE PATHWAYS *(total coverage: .53)*				
4. CMO*FUND* partners*board	.14	.99	Lighthouse (2)	4.9
5. FUND*parent* PARTNERS*BOARD	.17	.98	Oakland Charter Academy and High	10
6. CMO*parent	.36	.99	LPS, World Academy, Achieve, American Indian (2), Aspire	5.6

Causal factors that are *present* for a recipe are represented in *CAPITALS*. Factors that are *absent* in a recipe are represented in *lowercase*. The asterisks between variables indicate that these variables together contribute to an outcome. The first recipe, for example, can be read as follows: high test scores combined with a lack of private funding and low parental involvement are a pathway by which the charters in our sample remained open. The (2) in parentheses after some of the school names indicates that multiple levels of that school (e.g., middle and high school) showed up in a recipe.

the school grounds, as we passed through a tiny blacktop where children ran laps on our way from one surprisingly small classroom building to another, our guide simply commented: "Humble facilities, but it works." Consistent with other research on mobilization in low-resource contexts, strategic use of available resources can offset a lack of traditional resources (Cress & Snow, 2000).

We also see one pathway to survival that does not rely on high test scores (3). This pathway combines low levels of both funding and parental involvement with high numbers of partnerships. Again referencing one of the AIM schools, we were told quite candidly during one of our campus visits that the basic view of the AIM schools is that parents are part of the problem: unlike parent contracts of many schools where the contract includes commitment to volunteering and other means of parental engagement, this contract entails agreeing to school "the way it used to be done in the old days where the school decides what's best for the students" (personal interview). Without significant financial support or parental involvement, often key resources for schools, these charters rely on external partnerships for legitimacy and support. At ARISE, for example, the operations manager talked about the high level of collaboration among charter schools and the importance of respecting and restoring the community. This is also reflected in ARISE's 11 partnerships described in the founding document.

In sum, these schools maintain their legitimacy through demonstrated performance on tests or through partnerships. That is, they either rely on their success on performance metrics or they develop organizational partnerships that embed them in the community. Interestingly, it is organizational partnerships and not parents that seem to provide that legitimacy. The coverage for these three pathways ranges from .21 to .39,[7] and the total coverage for the combination of variables is .59.

Performance Pathways

Again referencing Table 18.3, three pathways exist for the accountability outcome (high API test scores), with a total coverage of .53. Most notably, two of these pathways require being a Charter Management Organization (4 & 6). A CMO is a charter model that involves centralized support and multiple schools, and these results suggest that high test scores are well supported by this type of formalization (being a CMO). The two CMO pathways include one with high funding but low partnership and local board representation (4), and one with low

---

[7] Solution consistency scores for both outcomes were very high, above .98, for all the reported causal combinations and so are only reported individually in Tables 18.2 and 18.3. Unique coverage scores are not reported as they were all around .10, with the exception of recipe 3, which was at .27.

parental involvement (6). The shortest pathway (6) has about double the coverage of the other two pathways and relies on formalization rather than funding to support performance. The third pathway, which does not include CMO formalization, combines funding, high partnership and local board representation, and low parental involvement to achieve high test scores (5).

Contrary to conventional wisdom, two of the pathways to high test scores include low parental involvement. How can we make sense of these findings? First of all, deciding to send a student to a charter school rather than the neighborhood school requires awareness of the options and an explicit decision of the parent to apply to the charter school (see Hanushek et al., 2007). We are not capturing this parental involvement because all charter parents have selected their school, but rather we are measuring parental involvement in the daily operations of the school like input on school curriculum and classroom volunteering. This is the kind of involvement that seems less helpful to high performance, though there does seem to be a benefit to parental involvement at the board level (5). We hesitate to offer an interpretation of this finding without further research (see also Hoxby et al., 2009), but we do know from our qualitative data that low parental involvement sometimes reflects a philosophical choice on the part of the school. As noted earlier, one high performance CMO, the American Indian School (AIM), is explicit about keeping parents out of the day-to-day school functioning.

We also see that parental involvement and partnerships never co-occur in a recipe. They seem to act as substitutes for each other, with schools being deeply involved with the parent community or with a larger community of organizations. In terms of social change, this suggests that the micro-involvement of parents creates a local embeddedness that may hinder change, whereas the macro-support of broader community embeddedness can contribute to both legitimacy and performance and, thus, support social change. Further, board composition with parent membership does seem beneficial and may be more akin to community embeddedness. Consistent with that, we see organizational partnerships and local representation on the board co-occurring (5). Other research on community engagement in social change has recently begun to point to similar trends (e.g., Lee & Lounsbury, 2010; Lounsbury, 2001).

For the dual logics of accountability and legitimacy, our results make several contributions. First, it appears that these new organizations rely on high student performance to maintain legitimacy in the majority of instances. Rather than legitimacy coming from the approval process alone, student performance acts as an important determinant of survival. Meeting the accountability metrics becomes a predictor of legitimacy. Second, the formalization of the CMO model predicts student performance (success according to accountability metrics) but not survival itself. In the case of this new organizational form, the structure itself does not provide legitimacy. This is surprising inasmuch as the institutionalized elements of a school might be expected to protect it from having the context questioned (as noted earlier, these charters are incremental tweaks on what it means to be a school and are often not dramatically different in their daily operations). This speaks perhaps to the contested nature of the CMO model in particular within the traditional education community. CMOs are often the organizations that most directly speak to large-scale transformation of the education system. Finally, other resources can substitute and contribute to outcomes as well.

In fact, organizational partnerships create an alternative pathway for both legitimacy (survival) and accountability (high test scores). This is consistent with theory that network forms offer a viable alternative to formal hierarchy (Powell, 1990). The presence of partnerships as a key alternative pathway for both outcomes speaks to the importance of cross-sectoral networks for charter school success (Wohlstetter et al., 2004), and more broadly to their relevance for scaling positive social impact (Wei-Skillern & Marciano, 2008) and legitimizing change (Greenwood et al., 1999). This community embeddedness may, in fact, be a potential benefit of being a CMO in addition to (or instead of) the structure it provides: CMOs are part of a professional community of other CMOs and charter schools. Our findings speak to the interrelationship between the legitimacy and accountability logics, and highlight potential contestation about the legitimacy of the new organizational form itself.

CONCLUSION

Our results indicate that there are a number of ways that urban charter schools serving children from low socioeconomic backgrounds use resources and build organizations. Given the diversity of charter school models that exist, it is useful to examine the combination of resources that seem to be most beneficial. Formalization and funding stand out as main positive contributors to meeting the accountability standards. Rather than formalization and funding being tools that allow organizations to decouple from the core of the organization and obtain surface legitimacy, in this instance they appear to help in achieving positive outcomes (e.g., high test scores and accountability).

For organizations that are attempting to create positive social change, these are important findings. The importance of formalization is mirrored in research on the role of organizational infrastructure in supporting political outcomes (Andrews, 2001; McCammon et al., 2001) and even enabling more radical action within a legitimated organizational form (Rucht, 1999). The CMOs are both legitimate within the larger system of organizations as a recognizable "school" *and* they are able to operate differently (and with more freedom) than other non-charter schools. They are in a sense embedded and legitimate in two worlds—that of education reform and that of traditional education, and thus their position is in many ways ideal (Hillman, 2008). Interestingly, the formalization and structure that a CMO provides has some similarity to the structure of a district in the arguably failing district of Oakland. But the structure is used to support a different set of practices (e.g., low parental involvement in the classroom in the case of AIM, an extended school day or year in the case of Aspire and others, or a strong discipline focus in the case of KIPP).

There are other important implications of these results. The results indicate multiple kinds of legitimacy at play in this context since performance and community embeddedness both offer pathways to survival. The fact that high test scores are not necessary for survival has a few interesting implications. It suggests that other "success" factors may be important in this urban context. This warrants further research. Perhaps obtaining petition approval protects the charter school from some accountability pressures. Or perhaps simply having a small, safe, community space where children get attention and learn moral and life skills may be valued. Though improved educational outcomes remain essential for improving the lives of impoverished youth in the United States, a myriad of outcomes may contribute to positive social change in this context. In addition, financial resources are not required for legitimacy, which is a very hopeful finding for those interested in mobilization in a high poverty context. That said, funding is related to two of the pathways to high performance, so financial resources clearly have measurable benefits and provide accountability. Finally, partnership, or community embeddedness, emerges as a key mechanism for social change in contexts where more traditional resources—money or formal organizational structure—are lacking. The importance of this finding for understanding social change in high poverty environments cannot be underestimated.

Taken in total, our results speak to a common debate among those trying to enact positive social change—does change best happen from the top down or from the bottom up? The formalized charters in our sample represent a "top-down" approach, and a few of these schools are CMOs from other states that have expanded their system into this context. Is this the effective scaling of impact that so many social change agents and funders aim for (e.g., Bradach, 2010; Dees et al., 2004)? Is it more effective than the homegrown Oakland schools that represent more grassroots efforts to educate locally? Our results do suggest a benefit to this "top-down" approach in terms of accountability. Of course, there may also be a self-fulfilling prophecy in this context in that funders support those efforts that match corporate solutions to scaling. We know that external resources often demand rationalization and professionalization of an organization (Hwang & Powell, 2009). That said, we do see a CMO recipe that occurs without the condition of funding.

Yet, our findings also point to cases of "bottom-up" success. Each outcome also has a path that involves using networks to offset the lack of the more traditional assets of structure and high performance. In addition, many other idiosyncratic paths not involving formalization showed up in our data, though they were not reported because they had low unique coverage as they usually existed in only a few schools. This is the very nature of the grassroots approach. Thus both top-down and bottom-up strategies are alive and well in the Oakland charter school movement, and the diversity may well be a healthy element of this movement (Clemens & Minkoff, 2004). Although the range of charter options that we do see may be driven by the initial legitimacy screening necessary to be approved as a charter (and to receive funding), thus making our findings more conservative with regard to the potential success factors for charters, it suggests that the possibilities for successful models are undoubtedly more diverse than currently exist in the population.

The charter schools that we examine are trying to create opportunities for poor, urban children. Our study examines the factors that help them achieve their goals. The structure of a CMO seems to provide an important tool for the schools to achieve their goals. The support of the community also seems to be helpful. Although the goal of many of these charter school operators is systemic change, they are attacking the problem one school at a time with a variety of financial, organizational, and social resources. These small successes require maintaining legitimacy in a system while simultaneously challenging the system and creating a new model that demonstrates results. Although achievement of the larger goal often seems out of reach, we see positive social change occurring through multiple pathways in local communities. The eventual goal of reforming the entire education system and eliminating the achievement gap between white and colored and between rich and poor is not one that will be achieved by one solution. The very fact that multiple pathways exist for successful charter schools—at least in one urban education experiment— is ground for hope for charters and for other educational experiments.

REFERENCES

Aldrich, H., & Zimmer, C. (1986). Entrepreneurship through social networks. In D. L. Sexton & R. W. Smilor (Eds.), *The art and science of entrepreneurship* (pp. 3–23). Cambridge, MA: Ballinger.

Andrews, K. (2001). Social movements and policy implementation: The Mississippi civil rights movement and the war on poverty, 1965 to 1971. *American Sociological Review, 66,* 71–95.

Baum, J. A. C., Calabrese, T., & Silverman, B. S. (2000). Don't go it alone: Alliance networks and startups' performance in Canadian biotechnology, 1991–97. *Strategic Management Journal, 21,* 267–294.

Beckman, C. M., & Burton, M. D. (2008). Founding the future: The evolution of top management teams from founding to IPO. *Organization Science, 19,* 3–24.

Bradach, J. (2010). Scaling impact: How to get 100x the results with 2x the organization. *Stanford Social Innovation Review, 6,* 27–28.

Clemens, E. S., & Minkoff, D. C. (2004). Beyond the iron law: Rethinking the place of organizations in social movement research. In D. Snow, S. Soule, & H. Kriesi (Eds.), *The Blackwell companion to social movements* (pp. 155–170). Boston: Prentice Hall.

Coleman, J. S., et al. (1966). *Equality of educational opportunity.* Washington, DC: U.S. Office of Education.

Cress, D. M., & Snow, D. A. (2000). The outcomes of homeless mobilization: The influence of organization, disruption, political mediation, and framing. *American Journal of Sociology, 105,* 1063–1104.

Dees, G., Anderson, B. B., & Wei-Skillern, J. (2004). Scaling social impact: Strategies for spreading social innovation. *Stanford Social Innovation Review, 2,* 24–32.

Elmore, R. F. (2000). *Building a new structure for school leadership.* Washington, DC: Albert Shanker Institute.

Fiss, P. (2007). A set-theoretic approach to organizational configurations. *Academy of Management Review, 32,* 1180–1198.

Foerster, M., & Mira d'Ercole, M. (2005). Income distribution and poverty in OECD countries in the second half of the 1990s. In *OECD Social, Employment and Migration Working Papers: No. 22,* (p. 22, figure 6). Paris.

Greenwood, R., Suddaby, R., & Hinings, C. R. (2002). Theorizing change: The role of professional associations in the transformation of institutionalized fields. *The Academy of Management Journal, 45,* 58–80.

Hannan, M. T., Burton, M. D., & Baron, J. N. (1996). Inertia and change in the early years: Employment relations in young, high technology firms. *Industrial and Corporate Change, 5,* 503–536.

Hanushek, E. A., Kain, J. F., Rivkin, S. G., & Branch, G. F. (2007). Charter school quality and parental decision making with school choice. *Journal of Public Economics, 91,* 823–848.

Henig, J. R., Holyoke, T. T., Brown, H., & Lacireno-Paquet, N. (2005). The influence of founder type on charter school structures and operations. *American Journal of Education, 111,* 487–588.

Hillmann, H. (2008). Mediation in multiple networks: Elite mobilization before the English civil war. *American Sociological Review, 73,* 426–454.

Hoxby, C. M., Murarka, S., & Kang, J. (2009). How New York City's charter schools affect achievement, August 2009 report (second report in series). Cambridge, MA: New York City Charter Schools Evaluation Project.

Hwang, H., & Powell, W. W. (2009). The rationalization of charity: The influences of professionalism in the nonprofit sector. *Administrative Science Quarterly, 54,* 268–298.

Jargowsky, P. A. (1997). *Poverty and place: Ghettos, barios, and the American city.* New York: Russell Sage Foundation.

King, B. G., Clemens, E. S., & Konty, M. F. (2011). Identity realization and organizational forms: Differentiation and consolidation of identities among Arizona's charter schools. *Organization Science, 22,* 554–572.

Lee, M. P., & Lounsbury, M. (2010). Under pressure: Community amplification of protest and corporate response. Paper presented at the Annual Meeting of the Academy of Management, August 6–10, Montreal, Canada.

Loveless, T., & Jasin, C. (1998). Starting from scratch: Political and organizational challenges facing charter schools. *Educational Administration Quarterly, 34,* 9–30.

Lounsbury, M. (2001). Institutional sources of practice variation: Staffing college and university recycling programs. *Administrative Science Quarterly, 46,* 29–56.

McCammon, H., Campbell, K., Granberg, E., & Mowery, C. (2001). How movements win: Gendered opportunity structures and U.S. women's suffrage movements, 1866 to 1919. *American Sociological Review, 66,* 49–70.

McCarthy, J. D., & Zald, M. N. (1977). Resource mobilization and social movements: A partial theory. *The American Journal of Sociology, 82,* 1212–1241.

Meyer, J. W., & Rowan, B. (1977). Institutionalized oganizations: Formal structure as myth and ceremony. *The American Journal of Sociology, 83,* 340–363.

Meyerson, D., Quinn, R., & Oelberger, C. (2009a). The emergence of the CMO: A social movement account (working paper).

Meyerson, D., Quinn, R., & Tompkins-Stange, M. (2009b). Elites as agents of institutional change: Philanthropic elites in the California charter school movement (working paper).

Mulgan, G. (2010). Measuring social value. *Stanford Social Innovation Review*. Summer, August.

Oakland Unified School District. (2010). Retrieved from Office of Charter Schools website: http://www.ousdcharters.net

Pebbley, A. R., & Sastry, N. (2004). Neighborhoods, poverty, and children's well-being. In K. M. Neckerman (Ed.), *Social Inequality* (pp. 119–146). New York: Russell Sage Foundation.

Powell, W. W. (1990). Neither market nor hierarchy: Network forms of organization. In B. Shaw & L. L. Cummings (Eds.), *Research in organizational behavior* (vol. 12, pp. 295–336). Greenwich, CT: JAI

Ragin, C. C. (1987). *The comparative method: Moving beyond qualitative and quantitative strategies*. Berkeley: University of California Press.

Ragin, C. C. (2008). *Redesigning social inquiry: Fuzzy sets and beyond*. Chicago: University of Chicago Press.

Ragin, C. C. (2006). *User's guide to fuzzy-set/Qualitative comparative analysis 2.0*. Tucson, AZ: Department of Sociology, University of Arizona.

Rihoux, B. (2006). Qualitative comparative analysis (QCA) and related systematic comparative methods: Recent advances and remaining challenges for social science research. *International Sociology, 21,* 679–706.

Rouse, C. E., & Barrow, L. (2006). U.S. elementary and secondary schools: Equalizing opportunity or replicating the status quo? *The Future of Children, 16,* 99–123.

Rucht, D. (1999). Linking organization and mobilization: Michel's "iron law of oligarchy" reconsidered. *Mobilization, 4,* 151–70.

Schorr, J. (2002). *Hard lessons: The promise of an inner city charter school*. New York: The Ballantine Publishing Group.

Snow, D. A., & Soule, S. A. (2010). *A primer on social movements*. New York: W.W. Norton & Company.

United States Department of Agriculture, Food and Nutrition Service. Income eligibility guidelines. http://www.fns.usda.gov/cnd/governance/notices/iegs/iegs.htm.

Wei-Skillern, J., & Marciano, S. (2008). The networked nonprofit. *Stanford Social Innovation Review, 6,* 38–43.

Wells, A., Grutzik, C., Carnochan, S., Slayton, J., & Vasudeva, A. (1999a). Underlying policy assumptions of charter school reform: The multiple meanings of a movement. *The Teachers College Record, 100,* 513–535.

Wells, A., Lopez, A., Scott, J., & Holme, J. J. (1999b). Charter schools as postmodern paradox: Rethinking social stratification in an age of deregulated school choice. *Harvard Educational Review, 69,* 172–204.

Wohlstetter, P., Malloy, C. L., Hentschke, G. C., & Smith, J. (2004). Improving service delivery in education through collaboration: An exploratory study of the role of cross-sectoral alliances in the development and support of charter schools. *Social Science Quarterly, 85,* 1078–1096.

19

Navigating Change in the Company of (Dissimilar) Others: Co-Developing Relational Capabilities with Microcredit Clients

Lisa Jones Christensen
University of North Carolina at Chapel Hill

INTRODUCTION

Pictures and stories of poverty and environmental degradation increasingly populate our televisions, e-mail inboxes, and the Internet—a consequence of our growing global connectedness. Concurrently, several calls for social change argue that poverty alleviation is both a social imperative and a business opportunity (Cortese, 2003; Pearce, 2005; Prahalad & Hart, 2002; UNDP, 2004; WBCSD, 2004). Management scientists suggest that businesses and business schools can lead the charge on social issues—in part because business schools are well-positioned to shape leaders focused on both environmentally and socially sustainable behaviors (Bennis & O'Toole, 2005; Dudley, Dudley, Clark, & Payne, 1995; Gordon, 2008). Addressing such large-scale problems from *any* institution requires the creation of new knowledge and capabilities—as current capabilities may not be sufficient to change the status quo (Sen, 1999). Thus, even as business leaders recognize the need for new knowledge in order to work effectively in low-income and developing country contexts, most are left to navigate social issues with few "signposts"—for an exception, see BoP Protocol (2010). In an attempt to address this need, this chapter outlines a theory-driven process model for knowledge creation in developing country contexts. Herein, I use evidence from a field engagement to suggest how actionable new knowledge for subsistence contexts can be co-created with stakeholders—while improving all parties' ability to relate and innovate. I argue for careful project and partner selection as well as for a deliberate sequencing of four elements of the engagement process.

To illustrate the process, this chapter focuses on a particular business school response to the issue of poverty alleviation via microcredit. Specifically, the case involves co-creating entrepreneurship training for (and with) microfinance clients living in the slums of Nairobi, Kenya. This chapter unfolds as follows: First, I briefly define microcredit and microfinance. (Please see Canales, Chapter 20, for an in-depth explanation of microcredit, microfinance, and the evolution of the industry.) I follow the explanation with a rich description and theoretical accounts of how business school students and a microcredit provider co-created new tactics for delivering entrepreneurship education. Next, I illustrate the different outcomes enjoyed by the individuals, groups, and organizations involved in this case. Finally, I close with a discussion of how to extrapolate lessons from the case, including implications for theory-building and practice.

MICROFINANCE BASICS

Microcredit is a poverty-alleviation tool that focuses on self-reliance, initiative, and accountability in relation to the taking and repayment of small loans. It typically involves income-poor micro-business owners who take out small uncollateralized loans from a microfinance institution to enhance their businesses. These borrowers then repay the loans with interest (and sometimes build savings) ostensibly by using the profits from the business. Loans are disbursed primarily to groups who are jointly accountable for each member (the communal model of lending), but individual relationships with lending institutions also exist.

Evidence on the impact of microcredit on client poverty reduction is mixed (Khandker, 2001), but since its inception over thirty years ago, microcredit remains a major force in international development and finance, particularly because most microfinance institutions report repayment rates of over 97% (Hatch, 2004) and offer consistent anecdotal evidence of quality of life improvements for clients (Morduch, 1998). As another signal of the ascendancy of microcredit, the founder of one early microfinance organization, Muhammad Yunus of the Grameen Bank, was awarded the Nobel Peace Prize in 2007 for his work in poverty alleviation. The term "microfinance" refers to a broader suite of pro-poor financial products such as microinsurance, housing or other custom loans, and/or health insurance in addition to microcredit loans. Thousands of microfinance institutions, many of them Grameen replications, now advance the practice of microcredit and microfinance throughout the world (MixMarket, 2010). In addition, it has become the focus of numerous elective courses at business and policy schools around the world (Beyond Grey Pinstripes, 2010; Jones Christensen, Peirce, & Hartman, 2007) in part because microfinance marries a pro-market and business-focused orientation with development objectives. The significant press allocated to microfinance, to the Grameen Bank, and to the positive effects of the loans has increased the number of individuals interested in microfinance.

Building on this type of interest, and in reaction to an invitation from a major microfinance institution in Africa, a team of business school students had the opportunity to travel to Kenya to act as educators (and learners) to create an entrepreneurship training program for microcredit clients.

The Case: A Multifaceted University— Microfinance Institution Partnership

In summer of 2008, Ingrid Munro, the feisty and dynamic founder of the Kenyan microfinance organization Jamii Bora, contentiously challenged more than 100 MBA professors to stop focusing on elite students and to start helping the working poor in Africa and around the world. She did this in Kenya at an annual gathering of educators from top-rated universities located around the world. Munro, as a guest speaker, explained that it was frustrating to see international educators focused only on the elite in her country. In private conversation she admitted that it was particularly frustrating as she had organizational problems related to her educational offerings with which she needed assistance. Ingrid had already worked with a Kenyan university partner to develop a general business curriculum for her 200,000 clients, but she was experiencing a high drop-out rate from the classes—even when clients had paid hard-earned money for the instruction. Ingrid knew that part of the reason for the attrition was that the content itself needed adjustment.

I learned of this problem when I pressed her to consider an unorthodox idea—that of using U.S. and Kenyan business students as master teachers.

Ingrid reluctantly agreed that graduate students (instead of business school professors) could, with the right preparation, *potentially* be participants in the educational revolution that she envisioned for the poor around the world. We agreed to attempt a pilot engagement using graduate students and star clients. Ingrid asked us for help in making her eight-module entrepreneurship curriculum into something that was more educational, more relevant, and more authentic to client realities. From that basis, I proposed that University of North Carolina (UNC) students would work with her organization and with a nearby private university, African Nazarene University (ANU), in a three-way partnership to evolve and sustainably deploy the business curriculum. The project began with a handshake and the promise to return with a team in approximately six months.

Project Implementation—Pre-launch Preparation

The enabling conditions for this project began with top management support in the United States and with sufficient funding to allow for travel. The dean of the Kenan-Flagler Business School at the University of North Carolina (KFBS) supported the idea of working in Africa with a microfinance institution and created funding for six students and a faculty advisor to participate.

Another enabling condition was that I was free as a faculty member to structure the course for optimal results. Thus, we instituted an adjusted schedule and a rigorous screening process that involved an essay application and an interview. We found the interview critical in screening applicants because there was not enough variance in the quality or content of the majority of the essays to allow meaningful differentiation or ranking. However, the very unusual interview questions and the students' responses to them proved a powerful screening mechanism.

Specifically, we asked applicants three questions: (1) Tell us about a time where you were extremely physically uncomfortable—what was the situation and how did you handle it? (2) Name one particular life experience that required you to act with great compassion or empathy—what was the experience and how did you respond? (3) What experience, whether on your résumé or not, are you most proud of and why? A final question was: If you are not selected for the travel, would you still be interested in participating in the preparatory class? An important element at this juncture was the inclusion of four judges at the interviews. The judges' varied responses to the applicants and the vigorous debates about what did or did not occur in the interviews were critical to the selection process, as we chose people who would not have been chosen without those debates. Ultimately, we selected twelve people to participate in the class and six who would be guaranteed travel. After the selection process was complete, students and faculty jointly created a seven-week plan to (1) learn about Jamii Bora, microfinance education, and the organization's current program offerings; (2) investigate current best practices in entrepreneurship education; (3) identify teaching techniques that work when people cannot read or write; and (4) find or create action-learning and role-playing activities that were culturally appropriate to Kenya and/or Africa. We also formed teams to communicate with Jamii Bora and with ANU, and to plan and coordinate our travel and cultural inauguration.

Project Implementation—Travel to Africa

A critical structural element of the engagement involved meeting the "clients" and partners in their day-to-day context and intentionally sharing the reality of local conditions. This requirement was equally important to our partners. Thus, after an entire quarter of formal classroom-based preparation where students painstakingly researched, revised, and role-played a modified Jamii Bora entrepreneurship education program (in relative isolation from partners), a team of five students[1] traveled to Nairobi. The first few days were intense cultural immersions. For example, the UNC students went with the ANU and Jamii Bora hosts to two different church services on the first full day—one a tribal meeting of the Maasai, and another an evangelical service in town. As one participant explained:

> We basically met Jamii Bora on their terms and encouraged them to show off their successes. [X Kenyan] and [Y Kenyan] showed us their workshop, [Z Kenyan] showed us her house, [Q Kenyan] allowed us to meet her daughter. The trust began in the first couple of days when the Jamii Bora members opened up their lives to us.[2]

Over a period of two and half weeks, the UNC team and several Jamii Bora members lived and worked with seven students from ANU to listen

---

[1] Our sixth was not allowed to travel due to his military affiliation and travel warnings that came too late for a substitute to replace him. Ultimately we traveled with two men and three women, and one of the men was an undergraduate rising senior. All others were MBA students.

[2] All quoted material was collected by the author in interviews and informal conversations during the term of the study (2009–2010).

to stories from successful Jamii Bora members, to hear suggestions from current clients, to visit local branch locations, and to revise (again) the business training program late at night on student laptops. The new team lived in the ANU facilities and shared all waking hours. As one student reports:

> We also shared a curfew—the dogs were released at a certain time (I think 11 p.m.), so we had to make sure we were back in our housing by that time. This kept us focused and we had to make good use of our time. Also, the location made it difficult for us to get around on our own because it was very isolated.

In the first week, the students listened to individual stories and analyzed the lives of microfinance clients to determine what made them succeed in their business ventures. They analyzed the small details—family history, upbringing, influences, and so forth. In essence, they conducted multiple case studies of Kenyan people who had risen from street begging and sometimes criminal backgrounds to become extremely successful business owners. By learning about their backgrounds, key skills, and the people who had impacted their lives, the students gained incredible insight from what Ingrid called these "professors" of life. They also worked with these "professors" to co-create a better process experience for all. As the team lead describes:

> The 1st day I arrived [X from Jamii Bora] handed me a schedule for the first workshop week. As we began the workshop we realized that having each Jamii Bora member take one-plus hour to "tell their story" was probably not an effective use of time. After visiting the main banking hall and casually interviewing people there we are also realized that we could gain a tremendous amount of information. Yes, we should study the successful Jamii Bora members, but what about the ones just starting to form their accountability group or the ones just picking up an application form to join Jamii Bora? We went back to the table multiple times with [Y and Z] and the Jamii Bora members. We decided that a better use of time would be to break out in small groups and have Jamii Bora members tell their story to an ANU and an UNC student...

> These small groups allowed the members to open up beyond their "generic" stories. As [Member 1 and Member 2] from Jamii Bora told us—they know "Jamii Bora English." In this small group setting, members could speak in Kiswahili or the mother tongue and the ANU student or [X] from Jamii Bora could help translate. We tried to make the workshop more an informal

discussion. Also, we quickly realized that we needed more time in the field. We adjusted the schedule so we could visit some of the Jamii Bora branches near ANU and ask a list of questions of these members. We listened to the people Ingrid assigned to help with the project, but we also expanded the scope (this was decided on by both ANU and UNC).

As a result of these kinds of exchanges, the teams had extensive meetings with the borrowers and the ANU students where everyone gathered the necessary information to *radically* revise (in real time) the business curriculum. One example of a radical rewrite using such localized knowledge was the decision to blend the teaching of life skills, and to highlight certain life skills, with the teaching of business principles. Examples of the life skills included: self-awareness, critical thinking, honesty, and discipline. Each business skill taught in a day's lesson was matched with one or more appropriate life skills (see Table 19.1 for the business subjects and the corresponding life skill).

During the last part of the three-week stay, the U.S. students and the ANU students traveled to the slums to teach the revised business curriculum. They taught over 70 Jamii Bora clients during that time.

Project Design Details

The general outline of the three-way partnership included three important structural design elements—it was designed for specificity, sustainability,

TABLE 19.1

Co-produced learning: Life skills matched with entrepreneurship training.

Life Skills	Business Skills
• Hope	• Being an entrepreneur
• Self-awareness	• Being an entrepreneur
• Receiving mentoring	• Being an entrepreneur/team building
• Problem solving	• Identifying viable businesses
• Perseverance	• Business planning
• Conflict management	• Team management/customer care
• Honesty	• Team management/customer care
• Critical thinking	• Product differentiation
• Creative thinking	• Product differentiation/diversification
• Discipline	• Budgeting
• Decision making	• Budgeting/record keeping

and possible expansion. Regarding specificity, Ingrid convened her team of staff who were focused on education to explain just one of their current and most vexing problems: taking their current entrepreneurship and general business training, refining it, making it compelling, and taking it to scale. Ultimately, she wanted the program to go to every one of the 200,000 members, but language issues necessitated a compromise to deliver the training to the English-speaking branch managers and organizational leaders—a "train the trainers" intervention. This level of specificity (the decision to work on one major aspect of the education problem and to work in one language) was key to minimizing the level of ambiguity in this nebulous arrangement.

Regarding sustainability, we agreed that the intervention should be designed such that the U.S. partners design themselves out of a job. Ultimately, the goal is for Kenyans to train other Kenyans in a sustainable and long-term arrangement. From this shared belief, the three-way partnership between UNC Kenan-Flagler Business School (KFBS), Jamii Bora, and the nearby African Nazarene University (ANU) ensued. The selection of the third partner was simple, as Ingrid and the vice chancellor of ANU (Professor Leah Marangu) were already collaborating.

Lastly, regarding expansion, we created the first year as a non-binding pilot year, while at the same time remaining open to considering the first year as part of a longer-term relationship.

Post-Implementation: Follow-Up and Analysis

In one sense, the engagement lasted fifteen weeks—eight in team-based U.S. preparation, almost four co-located on site in Africa, and three additional weeks of report writing and e-mail follow-up. In another sense, the engagement is ongoing, as we have continued the partnership. We created simple surveys to use at the end of classes, and a workplan for how to track results for the entrepreneurs, and for ANU and Jamii Bora.

Case Lessons: Sequencing and Simultaneity in the Process of Co-Creating Knowledge

The case illustrates several topics, in particular how practicing reflective thinking, care, contextual embeddedness, and humility in the engagement enhanced the bidirectional and simultaneous nature of the learning.

The case also illustrates the importance of appropriately sequencing the preparation, the actual immersion, and the real-time adjustments in order to optimally co-create an improved product. All of these elements combine as depicted in Figure 19.1. The figure offers a theoretically-grounded process model that may enable replication in other settings. Here, I utilize Kozlowski and colleagues' (Kozlowski et al., 1999) theory of compilation and performance by describing the inputs, processes, and outputs that developed over time in the team interactions. The three elements combine to enable relational capabilities and co-created knowledge and other outcomes depicted in the figure.

Project Inputs

The project inputs consisted of human *and* non-human resources. From the perspective of those of us in the United States, we originally saw ourselves as a human resource put in the position of "teacher." Assigning ourselves this title in the retelling is not hubris, as our partners had either enthusiastically (ANU) or reluctantly (Jamii Bora) asked us to act as experts on entrepreneurship and business education principles. We saw our role as one that required acknowledging the reluctance and the concomitant suspicions about our motives and capabilities. I felt our role was to rise to the occasion by creating valuable deliverables, where "valuable" was a moving target ultimately to be defined by Ingrid. Part of the tension involved in such an assignment was the need to arrive in Kenya with something useful, complicated by the lack of communication with anyone in Kenya about what constituted "useful" or "valuable." During our preparation phase we never obtained direct input from partner institutions about their actual characteristics and needs—despite our many attempts. However, we kept them mentally present by constantly trying to imagine the different possible needs and reactions they might have.

The other human resources in the project were the "students"—primarily the entrepreneurs from the microfinance institution. Without having occasion to meet them beforehand or during the pre-departure phase, we conceptualized them as "typical" microcredit clients of Jamii Bora. We acted on the assumption that the clients were primarily illiterate or marginally literate women who were market- and street-savvy, and who were interested in profits.

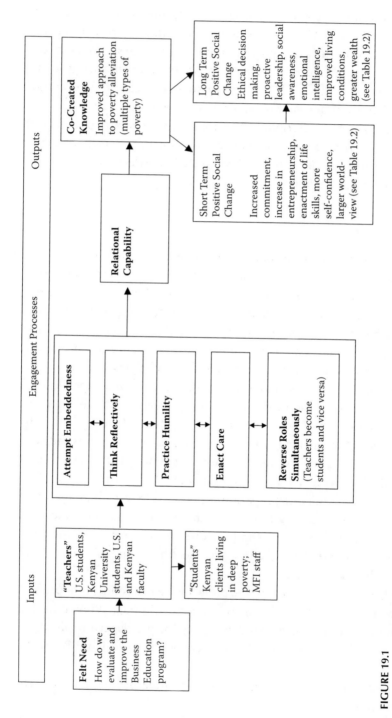

FIGURE 19.1

Case-based process map for developing relational capability, knowledge, and social change.

The final input element was not a human resource. Rather, it was the need or opportunity itself. Without the felt need, we would not have had reason to meet with ANU or with Jamii Bora—nor would we have obtained such deep organizational entrée. By the same token, without the need, neither ANU nor Jamii Bora would have had access to the resources that we assembled and deployed over the length of the project. Thus, finding and properly scoping the problem (or opportunity) statement remains one key to replicating the quality of the engagement.

PROCESSES OF ENGAGEMENT: BECOMING EMBEDDED, THINKING REFLECTIVELY, ENACTING CARE, AND CULTIVATING HUMILITY

Even before we left home, everything we attempted in the project had one goal in mind—to prepare ourselves to co-create something better than any party could create alone. This goal was built into our structure and it dominated every process that we enacted because we were aware of our limitations as "experts." As one student stated:

> We needed our partners immediately because we had no way of relating to Kenyans (no true source of commonality—different backgrounds, education, upbringing, exposure, etc.). Jamii Bora members were the source for knowing what would work and what would not. We had to test the curriculum on them and learn from them, while supporting them with our knowledge.

The model in Table 19.2 depicts four major subprocesses that together constitute the engagement process and that mediate between the inputs and the joint creation of the final products. More specifically, the deliberate processes of becoming (or attempting to become) *embedded*, of practicing *reflective thinking*, and of practicing *humility* and enacting *care* in knowledge creation all contributed to the co-created end-product. Incorporating these processes allowed us to subvert traditional status lines and avoid common cross-cultural consulting pitfalls. Such incorporation also kept us thinking about the men and women in Jamii Bora rather than our peers or a class grade. While each particular process must be presented in some

412 • *Lisa Jones Christensen*

sort of sequence in order to communicate it, it is important to reiterate that many of these processes occurred simultaneously. Also, each process reinforced and accelerated the others. For example, while it was important to become embedded outsiders as quickly as was authentically possible, accomplishing such a goal would have been impossible without invoking a humble attitude and great care and reflection in all exchanges between parties.

Becoming Embedded Through Co-Location

Embeddedness (Granovetter, 1985, 1992) refers to the network of relations that affect economic and social outcomes for some or all of the actors involved. Social relations and embeddedness often have constraining effects (Uzzi, 1996) but embeddedness can enable individuals to access desired outcomes such as increased social support (Pescosolido, 1992). In our case, it describes becoming more connected to others via social relations in order to affect an outcome (such as the new training material or more mutual respect and understanding). It is meant to describe the process of improving social relations by immersing ourselves in the reality of the lives of seemingly dissimilar others. Our attempts at embeddedness were informed by at least three different sources. First, we were informed by the work of Robert Chambers, whose explications of the methods of participatory rural appraisal (PRA) invoke a call to be as participative as possible—in part to be aware of any social actors being inadvertently excluded (Chambers, 1994; Chambers, 1995). Chambers also encourages practitioners to be aware of the items, behaviors, and artifacts that create distance even in the attempts to lessen distance (consider the difference between arriving on a bus versus in a car; the signaling effects of cell phones and video equipment, or in the favoring of wealthy informants over poor ones, etc.). Further, the BoP Protocol (BoP Protocol, 2010) offers a template for multinational corporate engagement with income-poor communities, which also outlines principles of co-discovery and co-creation based on local context. At the center of both is the premise that one cannot genuinely co-discover or co-create without building high-quality relationships and increasing connectedness among participants. Essentially, both argue that such geographically and culturally diverse partners in engagements must do all they can to "walk miles in the moccasins" of the other.

The third source that informed our quest for embeddedness was Ingrid herself. She fully supported the concept as evidenced by her instructions to the UNC team when they arrived. The UNC project lead describes Ingrid's frame of mind at the outset:

> In my meeting with Ingrid and [others] the first day, Ingrid stressed that mutual answers to the following questions were as important as the final curriculum deliverable. The questions were:
>
> 1. How do you identify a viable business?
> 2. Study microfinance clients—why do some succeed? Analyze the successful ones.
> 3. She called us to listen and absorb as much as we could.
> 4. Test out your curriculum—what conclusions can you derive?

Thus, some of the behaviors we enacted that helped in the embedding process related to our preparation pre-arrival. Other behaviors related to a literal embedding of ourselves in the local situation by co-locating in the dorms and jointly experiencing life. The latter could only be accomplished once we arrived in country. The first step in the sequence was to prepare beforehand by explicitly discussing the value of embeddedness. The second step in the sequence was to follow that preparation with physical co-location. By moving ourselves and the clients to the dorms with the ANU students, we removed barriers of physical distance as there were no meeting delays due to traffic, no us–them separation from staying in luxury hotels versus local accommodations. We were also available for (and able to promote) the serendipitous meetings and bonding that occur when people are co-located.

The UNC participants supported the quest for embeddedness even more fully once they arrived in-country. They cultivated the social cohesion with deliberate acts such as not sitting with the same people at meals/breaks and not sitting in U.S.-centric cliques (to their credit this was their instinct and was not a mandate). The students also instinctively enacted icebreaker activities. For example, they played "two truths and a lie" first with the ANU students and later with the microfinance clients. This was a highly portable game that needed no materials except a willingness to share and be creative.

The U.S. students continued to rely heavily on games throughout the process, as they brought and shared the game "Taboo" and they asked to be taught Kenyan games. Sports were also a universal language, and pick-up games of basketball happened almost every night. The ANU students showed great interest in coming to the U.S. student rooms to watch and join in the daily debriefs and project updates. Everyone also took local transportation together because that would be the way that future teachers would travel to future students.

In many ways, these decisions about physical relationships between people signaled more than a willingness to embed ourselves and to not be "special." They also signaled much about our mental state and our desire to be empathic and reflective about our own biases and norms.

Thinking Reflectively

Starting with our earliest preparation, the entire engagement was marked by a constant attempt on our part to replace our language of certainty with a language of inquiry (Yanow, 2009). This replacement was uncomfortable for all of us at first. For example, it required that I admit at the outset the uncertainty around the entire project rather than depict it as well-defined. Doing this in the leader role modeled a desired behavior—I wanted them to be able to discuss and embrace the ambiguity rather than pretend it away or ignore it. But more importantly, the language of inquiry required us to constantly ask ourselves about our assumptions: do we think a particular lesson is complete because we already understand basic accounting/marketing/business development? What would it be like to encounter this lesson if we were illiterate? What would it take to evolve this reading and make it into a play or a song? Are we reducing something too far? What if we were illiterate but very business savvy? What calculations do U.S. students do on their calculators that microfinance clients can do in their heads? What do we not know about the situation? And before our trip we asked: How can we find answers in the absence of information from the participants?

We slowly trained ourselves to ask these types of questions of each other, and more importantly to accept these types of questions from each other—not as criticism but as sincere attempts to help build a better result. As Yanow (2009, p. 581) points out, the language of inquiry requires "an interrogation of oneself, one's own assumptions, one's own attribution of motives to others, one's own ways of thinking and doing." Potentially, this type of reflective practice or "double loop learning" (Argyris & Schon, 1974;

Schon, 1983) intervenes and mitigates the self-sealing character of more traditional managerial practices. We found this to be true in our case, but it also made it difficult to ascertain when we were "done" with any particular deliverable we had set for ourselves. Additionally, this reflective practice extended all projects and complicated deadlines both pre-departure and post-arrival because it engendered constant redirection. This redirection and change occurred for all parties, as we also watched ANU students and Jamii Bora clients alter their plans and content suggestions based on our interactions. Similar to "adaptive" learning, which occurs after feedback (Edmondson, 1999; 2002), the process of reflection and reflective practice occurred because of feedback—or "backtalk" (Schon, 1983)—we received in-country *as well as* because of our internal dialogues.

The spirit of inquiry and the value of "backtalk" are illustrated in this comment:

> We came to Kenya with one curriculum despite earlier talks of creating various versions, but we knew certain activities needed to be tested upon arrival. Certain activities we threw in as placeholders (such as the visualization exercise). We were not sure if this would go over well in Kenyan culture. Also, we thought our business plan template was too long, but we were not sure how/where to cut it down. In the budgeting/accounting lesson we were not sure what to put as the inputs into the budget—what should be the line items. [KFBS student X] and [KFBS student Y] sat down with [Jamii Bora X] and [Jamii Bora Y] one evening to create together the budget lesson plan. The Jamii Bora members gave insights about their business and we used them as an example in this lesson.

As we considered post hoc why attempts at reflective practice did or did not yield changes and improvements, we concluded that a base of advance preparation was an important precondition for our co-created results—a fact which directly suggests the role of sequencing. The microcredit clients had been part of the Jamii Bora for some years/loan cycles and they had already been asked multiple times to describe to others why they were successful or not (Jamii Bora, 2010). For the U.S. students, they had prepared with their education-to-date, their personal histories and the selection process, and with a module of planning and preparation. All of this allowed both parties to come with some prior knowledge of the issues and of each other. This prior knowledge and long-term preparation served to both establish *and* expand the absorptive capacity (Cohen & Levinthal,

1990) of all parties—which enhanced everyone's ability to recognize valuable data, assimilate it, and apply it to routines.

Cultivating Humility

Certainly, calls to develop humility are more likely found in the context of theology rather than an MBA curriculum. However, we did attempt to cultivate humility in this engagement. While it might be more culturally acceptable to describe our behaviors as attempts at "trust-building" rather than as attempts at humility, in our case we were not in the position to build trust as much as we were in a situation where we wanted to eliminate distrust. This was more than an issue of semantics because we did not enter the relationships with any type of positive or even zero "balance" in our relationship reserves with which to commence trust-building activities. Instead, we knew that we entered the relationship with Jamii Bora and Ingrid with a negative balance. Since Ingrid was biased against business school students because of 25 years of past experiences with MBA-trained consultants and because of negative stereotypes about MBAs, one of the only ways for us to dislodge that bias was to simply not deserve it. Thus, we were motivated at the outset to cultivate humility. We needed to send strong signals about this to Ingrid, to mitigate any self-fulfilling prophecy effects based on her negative predisposition. Some of the requirements for physical co-location and shared physical experiences that helped achieve embeddedness also helped signal humility. As mentioned, it was part of the course structure to require that the U.S. students enact many obvious and physical choices such as living as equals with our partners under all of the same physical constraints.

Yanow (1997, 2009) defines "passionate humility" as "one's passionate conviction that one is right, wedded to the acknowledgement of the possibility that one might be wrong.... The willingness to consider the possibility of error is a requisite condition for its development" (2009, p. 587). The author purposefully focuses on how decision makers can enact humility while also remaining decisive. In our case, we fit the definition because we worked diligently during our preparation phase to be in a position to offer something to Jamii Bora and ANU that we were passionate and decisive about: for example, a revised curriculum, new exercises, updated and more appropriate examples, and additions and reductions to the original text. However, we designed it from inception with an awareness that one or more (or all) of our assumptions or suggestions could be "wrong" in one way or another. All along, we embraced the possibility (which was a reality) that we were making errors. For us, this mindset was in direct opposition to our training as faculty and as MBA students—we were all more accustomed to using a language of certainty and to maintaining an image of near omniscience.

However, we ultimately—and at times unknowingly—held to norms regarding the cultivation of humility in administrative sciences. Yanow (2009a, p. 593) explains that doing so "starts by asking: what, and whose, meanings—*other than mine*—are at play in this situation, in actuality or potential? How are they being conveyed? How are they being 'read?' How shall I treat my interpretation of events, especially when it is contradicted or denied by others? ...The practice relies on *deliberation* and *persuasion, not positional compulsion and fiat*" (italics mine).

Specific examples of how we cultivated humility include individual physical acts by some or all of the students, as well as collective acts of "deliberation and persuasion" on the part of the U.S. students. Structurally, we set up the norms supporting this idea from the first day of class. That day, I described the behaviors of one of Ingrid's favorite academics. This woman, named Anne, had hopped into a client chair in one Kenyan woman's beauty salon and promptly asked for and paid for a haircut—all this on her first visit to the worst slum in Kenya. We later called this the "Anne Effect" and spent several class sessions talking about what this behavior accomplished from a psychological and norm-setting, and norm-breaking, perspective for all parties—why did it impress Ingrid? What did it do for the confidence and sense of self-worth of the hairdresser? What was the psychological cost to Anne and what barriers did Anne likely feel? By giving significant time to these kinds of discussions through the pre-departure class structure, we signaled its importance to the project overall. Further, these discussions allowed us to practice new communication skills. We built the expectation that such behaviors were the ideal, but we left each student free to interpret how to enact the "effect."

Ultimately, we found that enacting the "Anne Effect" almost always required physical engagement, not just talk. Thus, it required our physical presence and could only occur later in the process. For example, one way it was invoked was when the U.S. students were willing to embarrass themselves in public. One student mentioned to the Kenyan group that she was able to clog dance and she broke into dance at that moment—she was brave enough to share, dance, and be laughed at. Certainly, this was an act of humility on several levels. Secondly, the students assigned different peers to watch for body language and other nonverbal and verbal information about how interviewees and partners might be feeling. They also directly asked about reactions and they invited comment, even criticism, from the supposed "learners" or "clients"—again, a behavior that is rarely modeled in our consulting curriculum. Such inquiries resulted in the team being told, despite all of their efforts to the contrary, that they were talking way too much and too fast, and that they needed to invite and let the Kenyans speak up more. The team attempted to incorporate this and other feedback rather than become defensive or entrenched in their behaviors. However, accomplishing this sometimes entailed long, late-night conversations as the MBAs grappled with the input and how to accept it. The UNC students admit that they were variously more or less skilled at this task of cultivating humility. In fact, they credit one individual on the team with exemplifying this behavior:

> [KFBS student X] was a huge asset to the team. She was very relational and spent countless hours just sitting and talking with the ANU students. Because her husband is African she knew the importance of quality time. Others on the team were more focused on project results, but having a team member that understands a bit about culture and relationship-building really helped.

Sometimes, the U.S. team did not wait to receive input from their partners in order to practice humility. Instead, the team held daily "conflict" meetings at the close of every day in-country, where each person shared their personal highest and lowest moment of the day as well as their opinions about what was working and what was not regarding the partnership and the ever-evolving lesson plan. Certainly, once the U.S. team decided to act on the information they received from the partners or from each other, they used the data to enact *care* in the process of knowledge creation and leadership development (von Krogh, 1998).

Enacting Care in Knowledge Creation

Management scientists have established that one of the enabling conditions which allows knowledge creation to occur is relationship-building using the value of care (von Krogh, 1998). "Care" is defined here as "serious attention (heed), a feeling of concern and interest" (von Krogh, 1998, p. 137). Potentially, care gives rise to trust, active empathy, lenient judgment, and real help. When knowledge creation is both highly social and enacted in a high-caring environment, the result is an effect called "indwelling" (Polanyi & Prosch, 1975). Defined as a commitment to an idea, an experience, a concept, or to a fellow human being, indwelling is also a change from "looking at" to "looking with" (Polanyi & Prosch, 1975; von Krogh, 1998). It is considered key in sharing tacit knowledge and in creating new concepts. A key tenet regarding care in organizations is that knowledge creation under high care happens among equals.

In our situation in-country, it was not until our partners started to believe that we saw them as equals and that we wanted to be treated as equals that meaningful progress occurred. Specifically, our consistency and the longer hours put in to every activity, as well as the students' willingness to volunteer for additional activities and to ask questions that respected feelings and norms helped to engender support and friendship from the partners. Other examples of "caring" behaviors included: walking slowly with the older Jamii Bora members, the sharing of gifts and thank-you cards after the Week 1 workshop, showing/sharing family pictures, exchanging equipment (one participant said: "I remember giving my iPod to [Kenyan] for the day—he really enjoyed listening to my music"), and in general doing things on others' terms.

It took the students nearly two weeks of 12-15 hour days of demonstrated and authentic "caring" before improved data came from the conversations. Over time, the U.S. suggestions were more thoroughly debated which enabled more real-time improvements to the curriculum. This data suggests again the important role of time, as some of these outcomes could not be rushed—or, if rushed, they would have had different effects.

Outputs—Relational Capabilities and Positive Social Changes at Multiple Levels

This case is a learning story about the simultaneous and bi-directional nature of knowledge creation under certain conditions as well as the importance of sequencing events to allow for relational capability building and co-created solutions. There was at least one physical deliverable or "output" from the process described here—the altered curriculum. By the time the students had interacted with all of the partners and befriended (or been befriended by) their colleagues, the "final" curriculum was altered and adapted and upgraded in real-time. The newer version included lesson plans that combined life skills with development skills, new trust building exercises and games, and improved and more culturally relevant examples throughout. There were new certificates, role-plays, and simulations in all lessons. The physical artifact of the training booklet enabled future positive social change for the Jamii Bora organization who had commissioned it.

However, in addition to this very tangible output there were also multiple intangible outputs that accrued to individuals and the organizations involved. These are outlined and briefly described in Table 19.2.

Relational Capabilities

Relational capabilities are discussed at different levels of analysis and have been variously defined as "the creation and management of the [firm's] overall network architecture" (Capaldo, 2007, p. 585) or the "capacity and competence for building high quality connections" (Dutton, 2003; Dutton & Heaphy, 2003). With few exceptions, relational capabilities are in the early stages of being discussed and analyzed in the strategy and management literature (Capaldo, 2007), and much of the extant work focuses on firm-level rather than individual-level competencies (Capaldo, 2007; Dyer & Hatch, 2006; Kale & Singh, 2007). Herein, I draw from both definitions as well as the social work literature to define relational capability as the ability to elicit and sustain relationships with others (Regehr, Hill, & Glancy, 2000, p. 334). This broad definition draws from the individual-level of analysis but can be applied at multiple levels. While Capaldo (2007) operationalizes relational capability at the firm level and within social network structure as a combination of the duration of a relationship, the frequency of collaboration, and the intensity of the collaboration, I argue here that relational capability reflects different elements. The process model in Table 19.2 illustrates the premise that relational capabilities can stem from: reflective thinking, cultivated humility, demonstrated caring, and contextual embedding. In short, I suggest that the capability is something

TABLE 19.2

Multilevel Outcomes from UNC-ANU-Jamii Bora Co-Learning Process

	Outcomes—Short Term	Potential Outcomes—Long Term	Explanatory Processes
Individuals-U.S. Students (U.S.)	Increased commitment to the business school, to the partner institutions, and to microfinance. Increased commitment to public service, change (for some) in career goals, interest in recruiting others for similar projects, desire for ongoing interaction with Kenyan colleagues. Desire to monitor impact and design measurement. Altered view of business and role of business in society. Increase in entrepreneurial and social entrepreneurial ventures.	Ethical decision-making (Detert, Trevino, & Sweitzer, 2008); proactive leaders; socially aware, emotionally intelligent (Boyatzis, 2001). Potential for lifetime involvement of self, families, and employers in microfinance and/or fighting poverty.	Empathy (Detert et al., 2008); students practice a high degree of autonomy and job-crafting (Wrzesniewski & Dutton, 2001). Program enables students to feel high perceived impact (Grant, 2007; Grant et al., 2007)—which likely activates competence and perseverance. Program also allows for reflection. Increased absorptive capacity.
Individuals-U.S. Faculty	Improved motivation and job satisfaction.	Increased experience with action-learning; possible negative implications for tenure.	Job enrichment (Hackman & Oldham, 1975, 1976); misaligned incentives for tenure (Bennis & O'Toole, 2005).
Individuals-International (Low-Wage Kenyan Microcredit Members)	Improved life skills Increased business profitability Increase in entrepreneurial behaviors Increased self confidence Wider world-view	Potential to improve living conditions, achieve greater savings, improved health outcomes	Benefits of entrepreneurship education (Karlan & Valdivia, 2007); benefits of contact with others (Allport, 1979)

continued

TABLE 19.2 CONTINUED

Multilevel Outcomes from UNC-ANU-Jamii Bora Co-Learning Process

	Outcomes—Short Term	Potential Outcomes—Long Term	Explanatory Processes
Individuals-International (Kenyan University Students)		Increased experience with action-learning; possible negative implications for tenure.	Job enrichment (Hackman & Oldham, 1975, 1976); misaligned incentives for tenure (Bennis & O'Toole, 2005).
Organizations-U.S. Business School	Increased portfolio of international projects; particular funders pleased; school commits continued funds.	Potential for increased reputation and for expanded recruitment options.	
Organizations-International (Jamii Bora MFI)	Received additional "staff" effectively for months-no cost to organization.	Open to additional partnerships, willing to engage with business schools (formerly hostile), willing to influence other NGOs. May roll out program at scale.	

people must feel as well as count. Certainly, there may be additional elements of relational capability not considered here and there are many possible ways to reconcile different operationalizations. For one, it may be possible to consider the four processes as explaining how to *elicit* relationships and the other measures may help describe how to sustain or describe the *quality* of relationships. While settling this issue is beyond the scope of this chapter, I agree with Capaldo when he states: "there is a rising field of relational capabilities" (Capaldo, 2007, p. 590). Ideally, the fact that all participants in the case enhanced the number and quality of their relationships with each other serves as an empirical contribution to this rising field.

Individual-Level Outputs

There were myriad other outcomes that accrued at the individual level besides improved relationships. Certainly, self-report data from the trained microfinance clients indicates that they experienced enhanced confidence and motivation because of the program. The processes suggested herein had immediate outcomes for the working poor involved in microfinance—they received tailored entrepreneurship training, they improved their skill sets, and they reported more confidence in their abilities. There is already a long history of desirable outcomes associated with microcredit and microfinance (Khandker, 1998; Morduch, 1998; Morduch, 2002), and the possibility that this training helped catalyze these and other benefits was powerfully motivating.

The program was also generative from the perspective of the MBA students because it expanded the role of student from that of being a passive recipient and consumer of information to one of being an actor and crafter of new information. Thus, for the duration of the project it is possible that task significance (Hackman & Oldham, 1976; 1980) of MBA student work increased exponentially. The same effect likely occurred for the ANU and Jamii Bora partners too. Evidence from organizational behavior and social psychology indicates that increased task significance also increases motivation (Grant, 2007) and identification with work (Fried & Ferris, 1987). It enables participants to feel high perceived impact (Grant, 2007; Grant et al., 2007)—which likely activates motivation and perseverance and potentially longer-term commitment to a cause such as microcredit or social change.

In contrast to other instructional methods utilized over the two years of full time education, such as a reliance on analyzing case descriptions of past business decisions, the MBA students in this course practiced a high degree of autonomy and job crafting (also related to task significance). There is the potential that the exposure and practice these MBA students experienced will enable them to desire and be able to lead future social change within organizations. The base of experience, as well as individual confidence from participating in a successful project, combine to make it likely that these participants will stay involved. We did not test this hypothesis, but it is an empirical issue that can be resolved with future experiments, particularly experiments tied to leadership development.

Regarding individual-level changes, one U.S. student reported: "This project was one of the most difficult projects I've ever worked on, but it was where I learned the most and where I feel we really helped make a difference."

Another student said: "This project opened my eyes to the value of education. The poor in Kenya desire to learn and appreciate any exposure to education. At the completion of our training session, the microfinance clients were eager to know when we would return to teach them additional skills."

Organization-Level Outputs

Certainly, both Jamii Bora and UNC experienced several beneficial outcomes: the business school increased its portfolio of international projects, which helps recruit top students and keep new students motivated about what they can do in the program. Certain funders were also pleased to see the school expand its international portfolio and the school thus received funds for additional work in Africa. The project also fit with the school mission and the dean's and faculty members' personal and public goals for the school.

The Jamii Bora organization also was affected through participating in the project. For several months they effectively received six to twelve extra staff members, as the MBAs worked from part- to full-time on the problems and concerns of Jamii Bora and its clients. Microfinance institutions, particularly those that maintain a focus on the very poor, tend to be radically understaffed—and the staff the organizations do have are typically extremely overworked and overcommitted (again, see Canales, Chapter 20). Thus, the monetary and psychic value of the MBA student involvement was not insignificant for Jamii Bora. Certainly, another benefit of project success is that Jamii Bora is open to additional future partnerships with UNC and with other business schools. This fact bodes well for future cross-cultural collaborations.

If this effort could be replicated at scale, then business schools could graduate leaders capable of co-creating new capabilities in partnership with more stakeholders. If the type of co-created and context-ready entrepreneurship curriculum described here is utilized in base of the pyramid locations, then more income-poor individuals can change their living conditions.

CONCLUSIONS AND IMPLICATIONS FOR FUTURE RESEARCH

Herein, I argue for the importance of contextual embeddedness, practicing reflective thinking, cultivating humility, and demonstrating caring. I suggest that these four activities—along with a conscious switching of roles from teacher to learner and back again—improve relational capabilities and knowledge outcomes. The premise is that enacting the processes and cultivating the role reversals enables capabilities borne from intentional and deeply personal interactions. The approach to change suggested herein offers ways to navigate through change-related uncertainty in the company of others while simultaneously building self, others, *and* the final products. The processes require participants to share physical and mental spaces and to engage in specific types of internal and external back-and-forth dialogues. The results of the co-location and the dialogues alter participants in ways that enhance individual and group outcomes. Participants cannot engage in these processes and remain the same as they were when they started—instead, the processes engender connected participants *and* stronger outcomes.

In this case, microcredit clients, Jamii Bora employees, ANU students, U.S. students, and U.S. faculty demonstrated relational capabilities in creating new approaches to poverty alleviation and entrepreneurship education. This work breaks new ground because it stands in stark contrast to many existing theories about strategy and knowledge creation for poverty alleviation. Current theories primarily focus on lopsided exchanges from the Western "expert" to the non-Western "recipient" (Hoskisson et al., 2000). Further, much of the current work on developing capabilities vis-à-vis poverty alleviation tends to "disappear" the *relational* nature of change in favor of considerations named more strategic. For example, much extant work focuses on less personal dynamics and capabilities such as "global efficiency," "national responsiveness," and "the explicit transfer of existing knowledge" (London & Hart, 2004). Even when research argues for "social embeddedness" (London & Hart, 2004), it does not describe *how* to achieve the embeddedness. In fact, London and Hart (2004) suggest that "future work in this ['base of the pyramid'] area could include examining *how firms understand and create competitive advantage in unfamiliar environments*" (London & Hart, p. 19; italics mine). This chapter offers such an examination and invites more study of human interactions in change processes.

Specifically, this chapter attempts to surface and illuminate the deeply human and personal nature of social change dynamics. I offer theory-based discussions of how to build relational capability—particularly in cross-cultural exchanges related to near-intractable problems such as poverty. Questions that remain to be tested are whether the model is replicable and whether it can—or should—be made more parsimonious. More importantly, questions remain as to whether one can measure changes in relational capabilities—if present, does such a capacity have carryover effects? Can the capability be lost with disuse? Like a newly discovered muscle, is it easier to revive once built? Is it transferable to other situations?

This project was generative in stimulating research questions in several other domains. While leadership development was not the raison d'être for the project, many of the outcomes relate to leadership capacity-building in business schools, and rich questions about how and when to adapt this process to alter pedagogical practice remain. Future research should also explore measurement issues, such as how to best measure changes in embeddedness, humility, reflective thought, or engaging with care. Intra-individual and group-level changes can be monitored, and it may be possible to isolate elements that have more impact than others. Researchers interested in building theory around positive social change could also be encouraged to test the co-creation process in other settings.

The most practical finding is that universities can be agents of immediate social change in contexts quite diverse from main campus (e.g., Kenyan entrepreneurship education was co-created and delivered in six months; income-poor people—non-enrolled students—in far-flung locales had more skills and income immediately). Ideally, the repercussions of these types of interventions range from improved services in microfinance to changing the way business school graduates lead or the way we structure and enact cross-cultural engagements. Professors of life may be all around us and likely have much to teach if we become individuals who are willing and *able* to engage. This chapter suggests theory-driven ideas about what it means to engage—it means building relational capability while co-creating actionable knowledge in change efforts. As the need for and pace of social change initiatives increase, the processes described herein may enhance the speed, effectiveness, and quality of future interventions.

REFERENCES

Allport, G. (1954). *The nature of prejudice.* Cambridge, MA: Addison-Wesley.

Argyris, C., & Schon, D. A. (1974). *Theory in practice: Increasing professional effectiveness.* San Francisco: Jossey-Bass.

Bennis, W. G., & O'Toole, J. (2005). How business schools lost their way. *Harvard Business Review, 83,* 96–104.

Beyond Grey Pinstripes (2010). Retrieved from http://www.beyondgreypinstripes.org/.

BoP (Base of the Pyramid) Protocol (2010). Retrieved from http://www.bop-protocol.org/.

Boyatsis, R. E. (2001). How and why individuals are able to develop emotional intelligence. In C. Cherniss & D. Goleman (Eds.), *The emotionally intelligent workplace: How to select for, measure and improve emotional intelligence* (pp. 234–253). San Francisco. Jossey-Bass.

Capaldo A. (2007). Network structure and innovation: The leveraging of a dual network as a distinctive relational capability. *Strategic Management Journal, 28,* 585–608.

Chambers, R. (1994). Participatory rural appraisal (PRA): Analysis of rural development. *World Development, 22,* 1253–1268.

Chambers, R. (1995). *Rural development: Putting the last first.* New York: Prentice Hall.

Cohen W., & Levinthal, D. (1990). Absorptive capacity: A new perspective on learning and innovation. *Administrative Science Quarterly, 35,* 128–152.

Cortese, A. D. (2003). The critical role of higher education in creating a sustainable future. *Planning for Higher Education, 31,* 15–22.

Detert, J. R., Treviño, L. K., & Sweitzer, V. L. (2008). Moral disengagement in ethical decision making: A study of antecedents and outcomes. *Journal of Applied Psychology, 93,* 374–391.

Dudley, S. C., Dudley, L. W., Clark, F. L., & Payne, S. (1995). New directions for the business curriculum. *Journal of Education for Business, 70,* 305–310.

Dutton, J. (2003). Fostering high quality connections through respectful engagement, *Stanford Social Innovation Review*, Winter, 54–57.

Dutton, J., & Heaphy, E. (2003). The power of high-quality connections at work. In K. Cameron, J. Dutton, & R. E. Quinn (Eds.), *Positive organizational scholarship* (pp. 263–278). San Francisco: Berrett-Koehler Publishers.

Dyer J., & Hatch, N. (2006). Relation-specific capabilities and barriers to knowledge transfers: Creating advantage through network relationships. *Strategic Management Journal, 27*, 701–719.

Edmondson, A. (1999). Psychological safety and learning behavior in work teams. *Administrative Science Quarterly, 44*, 350–383.

Edmondson, A. (2002). The local and variegated nature of learning in organizations: A group-level perspective. *Organization Science, 13*, 128–146.

Fried Y., & Ferris G. R., (1987). The validity of the job characteristics model: A review and meta-analysis. *Personnel Psychology, 40*, 287–322.

Gordon, M. (2008). Management education and the base of the pyramid. *Journal of Management Education, 32*, 782–791.

Granovetter, M. (1985). Economic action and social structure: The problem of embeddedness. *American Journal of Sociology, 91*, 481–510.

Granovetter, M. (1992). Problems of explanation in economic sociology. In N. Nohria & R. G. Eccles (Eds.), *Networks and organizations: Structure, form, and action*. Boston, MA: Harvard Business School Press.

Grant, A. M. (2007). Relational job design and the motivation to make a prosocial difference. *Academy of Management Review, 32*, 393–417.

Grant, A. M., Campbell, E. M., Chen, G., Cottone, K., Lapedis, D., & Lee, K. (2007). Impact and the art of motivation maintenance: The effects of contact with beneficiaries on persistence behavior. *Organizational Behavior and Human Decision Processes, 103*, 53–67.

Hackman, J. R., & Oldham, G. R. (1975). Development of the job diagnostic survey. *Journal of Applied Psychology, 60*, 159–170.

Hackman, J. R., & Oldham, G. R. (1976). Motivation through the design of work: Test of a theory. *Organizational Behavior and Human Performance, 16*, 250–279.

Hatch, J. (2004). *A brief primer on FINCA*. Berkeley, CA: University of California at Berkeley Press.

Hoskisson, R. E., Eden, L., Lau, C. M., & Wright, M. (2000). Strategy in emerging economies. *Academy of Management Journal, 43*, 249–267.

Islam, T. (2007). *Microcredit and poverty alleviation*. Aldershot, Hants, England: Ashgate.

Jamii Bora (2010). Retrieved from http://www.jamiibora.org.

Jones Christensen, L., Peirce, E., Hoffman, M., & Hartman, L. (2007). An analysis of ethics, CSR, and sustainability education in the *Financial Times* Top 50 international business schools: Baseline data and research directions. *Journal of Business Ethics, 73*, 347–368.

Kale, P., & Singh, H. (2007). Building firm capabilities through learning: The role of the alliance learning process in alliance capability and firm-level alliance success. *Strategic Management Journal, 28*, 981–1000.

Karlan, D., & Valdivia, M. (2007). Teaching entrepreneurship: Impact of business training on microfinance clients and institutions (working paper 107). Center for Global Development, Yale University.

Khandker, S. (1998). *Fighting poverty with microcredit: Experience in Bangladesh*. New York: Oxford University Press.

Khandker, S. (2001). Does micro-finance really benefit the poor? Evidence from Bangladesh. Paper delivered at *Asia and Pacific Forum on Poverty: Reforming Policies and Institutions for Poverty Reduction* held by the Asian Development Bank, Manila.

Kozlowski, S., Gully S., Nason E., & Smith E. (1999). Developing adaptive teams: A theory of compilation and performance across levels and time. In D. Ilgen & E. Pulakos (Eds.), *The changing nature of performance* (pp. 240–292). San Fransisco: Jossey-Bass.

London, T., & Hart, S. (2004). Reinventing strategies for emerging markets: Beyond the transnational model. *Journal of International Business Studies, 35,* 350–370.

MIX Market (2010). Microfinance information exchange. Retrieved from http://www.mixmarket.org/.

Morduch, J. (1998). Does microfinance really help the poor? New evidence from flagship programs in Bangladesh (working paper 198). Princeton University, Woodrow Wilson School of Public and International Affairs, Research Program in Development Studies.

Pearce, J. L. (2005). Organizational scholarship and the eradication of global poverty. *Academy of Management Journal, 48,* 970–972.

Pescosolido, B. (1992). Beyond rational choice: The social dynamics of how people seek help. *American Journal of Sociology, 97,* 1096–1138.

Polanyi, M., & Prosch, H. (1975). *Meaning.* Chicago: University of Chicago Press.

Prahalad, C. K., & Hammond, A. (2002). Serving the world's poor profitably. *Harvard Business Review, 80,* 48–58.

Prahalad, C. K., & Hart, S. (2002). The fortune at the bottom of the pyramid. *Strategy + Business, 26,* 1–14.

Regehr, C., Hill, J., & Glancy, G. (2000). Individual predictors of traumatic reactions in firefighters. *Journal of Nervous and Mental Disease, 188,* 333–339.

Schön, D. A. (1983). *The reflective practitioner: How professionals think in action.* New York: Basic Books.

Sen, A. (1999). *Development as freedom.* New York: Knopf Press.

United Nations Development Programme (UNDP). (2004). *Unleashing entrepreneurship: Making business work for the poor.* New York: Commission on the Private Sector and Development.

Uzzi, B. 1997. Social structure and competition in interfirm networks: The paradox of embeddedness. *Administrative Science Quarterly, 42,* 35–67.

von Krogh, G. (1998). Care in knowledge creation. *California Management Review, 40,* 133–153.

WBCSD (2004). *Doing business with the poor, a field guide.* Geneva: World Business Council for Sustainable Development.

Wrzesniewski, A., & Dutton, J. E. (2001). Crafting a job: Revisioning employees as active crafters of their work. *Academy of Management Review, 26,* 179–201.

Yanow, D. (1997). Passionate humility in interpretive policy and administrative analysis. *Administrative Theory and Praxis, 19,* 171–177.

Yanow, D. (2009). Ways of knowing: Passionate humility and reflective practice in research and management. *The American Review of Public Administration, 39,* 579–601.

20

The Stranger as Friend: Loan Officers and Positive Deviance in Microfinance

Rodrigo Canales
Yale University

INTRODUCTION

From its inception in the 1970s, microfinance—the provision of very small, productive loans to destitute populations—was envisioned as a tool to bring capitalism to marginalized groups and allow them to pull themselves out of poverty (Morduch, 1999; Morduch & Armendariz de Aghion, 2005). Through its early success, microfinance has increasingly captured the attention and resources of philanthropic and profit-driven investors alike. Today, the microfinance revolution has become the poster child for the notion that, in capitalism, we can do well while doing good. It is considered an indispensable tool in the fight against poverty and a tested mechanism to open social mobility to the poorest of the poor (Sachs, 2005; Yunus & Jolis, 2003). Yet, for all the resources devoted to microfinance and the publicity given to the most appealing success stories, there is shockingly little evidence that microfinance indeed generates the social changes it promises. In fact, the opposite is true. The most rigorous studies increasingly suggest that the average impact of microcredit is actually zero and can often be negative (Alexander-Tedeschi & Karlan, 2007; Banerjee et al., 2009; Canales, 2008; Morduch & Armendariz de Aghion, 2005). What are we to make of these conflicting images? Is microfinance best represented by the picture of the female micro-entrepreneur who pulled her family out of poverty? Or is it best captured in the oversubscribed initial public offering (IPO) of Compartamos (a Mexican organization) that led microfinance's moral leader, Muhammad Yunus, to claim that instead of eradicating moneylenders, microfinance institutions (MFIs) had turned into them?

At the heart of these contrasts lies a contradiction that increasingly pervades MFIs as they adapt to the market paradigm they now are expected to follow. The paradigm dictates that MFIs should be "sustainable," which means they should generate enough profits to cover their costs. Their ability to do so while serving poor populations is precisely what has attracted unprecedented amounts of funding to microfinance. Increases in fund sources have also brought additional competition among MFIs, resulting in strong pressures for operational efficiency through automation and standardization. But, as will be shown here, microfinance is inherently labor intensive, since destitute clients tend to live in remote areas and often face uncertain, unpredictable, and fragile circumstances. Increases in standardization, therefore, necessarily reduce an MFI's ability to attend to the special needs of the poorest clients, since their characteristics are much harder to codify. It is thus that the pursuit of operational efficiency pushes MFIs toward safer, easier to classify clients and away from the poorest of the poor. It pushes them closer to profitability and away from their stated core mission of poverty alleviation. It also risks transforming microfinance from a movement designed to bring capitalism to aid the poor into an additional mechanism of exploitation. The evidence suggests that both outcomes are present today, which changes the question of whether microfinance alleviates poverty to the more nuanced question of the conditions under which it can deliver on that promise (Morduch, 1999).

These contradictions are not only observed across MFIs. Rather, they are deeply felt, with varying levels of intensity, within each MFI. Not surprisingly, and given the nature of microfinance, the tensions created by organizational policies that seek to standardize decisions become most apparent on the field, where loan officers interact with clients (Heimer, 1992; Lipsky, 1980). Loan officers experience the contradictions between firm profitability and poverty alleviation each time they enact one of the many rules that pursue one goal at the expense of the other. While all loan officers are subject to similar structural pressures, each must resolve them individually. This is because the complexity of client situations is such that no amount of rules can anticipate all outcomes. Loan officers must therefore exercise discretion when enacting rules (Blau, 1955; Lipsky, 1980; Taylor, 1993). Thus, even though organizational rules are centrally and strictly defined, there is much agency in how and when individuals choose to enact them (Emirbayer & Mische, 1998; Feldman & Pentland, 2003; Howard-Grenville, 2005). Moreover, it is precisely through the varying strategies followed by rule enactors that organizational contradictions emerge, are negotiated, and are eventually resolved (Becker, 2004; Feldman, 2000; Feldman & Pentland, 2003; Howard-Grenville, 2005; Nelson & Winter, 1982).

This chapter shows how, in microfinance, certain loan officers seek to resolve their organization's contradictions through systematically bending organizational rules. Interestingly, even though the rules are designed to help loan officers do their work, rule-bending loan officers perform better and present a more uniform distribution of impacts among their clients. They deviate from rules, but they do so seeking to better accomplish the organization's stated goals (Feldman, 2003). In addition, they not only bend the rules, but they also seek to improve them in the process (Silbey et al., 2009). This chapter explores the structural conditions that lead to this positive deviance. It describes the strategies followed by rule-bending loan officers, the tensions and constraints that they face, and the impacts this can have in their organization. I argue that certain loan officers for cultural, social, and structural reasons tend to create deeper personal relationships with clients. These positive relationships expose them to richer client information and exhibit organizational contradictions in full relief. Positive client connections also generate an additional layer of resources, repertoires, and sources of value. At the same time, both the atypical relational style and the positive deviance that results from it place these loan officers in the position best described by Georg Simmel's concept of "the Stranger" (1950). This structural position is characterized by an increased structural fragility, which also pushes loan officers to generate deeper commitments to the organization's values. This chapter thus suggests that, rather than seek to blindly increase standardization to eradicate loan officer deviance, MFIs—and other service organizations that face similar inherent tensions—should embrace such discretion as an unavoidable consequence of their work and learn to see it as a potential source of learning to better resolve their internal contradictions.

BACKGROUND ON MICROFINANCE[1]

In the past three decades, microfinance has evolved into a global industry that disburses more than \$85 billion[2] in loans to more than 150

---

[1] This and other early sections of this chapter rely heavily on material I have developed elsewhere, particularly in Canales (2010).

[2] MixMarket (http://www.mixmarket.org) estimates an average loan balance per borrower of US\$557.

million low-income families per year (CGAP, 2008; Daley-Harris, 2007, 2009).[3] Success stories show that, contrary to previous theory, poor households can put small loans to highly productive uses—thus affording high interest rates[4]—and place a large value on the sustained access to liquidity—thus presenting remarkably low delinquency rates (Cull et al., 2007, 2009; Morduch & Armendariz de Aghion, 2005).[5] This combination of high loan productivity and low delinquency rates has fueled an aggressive proliferation of microfinance institutions (MFIs) throughout the world; has drawn increasing resources from international agencies, philanthropic donors, and profit-driven investors[6]; and has turned microfinance into one of the most widely used tools to address poverty. In addition, it has created intense competition for resources among MFIs which, coupled with an increased diversity of investors and international agencies interested in microfinance, has resulted in an increasingly clear paradigm of profitability and private investment (Cull et al., 2009). For donors, this paradigm has offered the promise of sustainability[7] while attracting vast, previously unavailable amounts of profit-seeking capital.[8] For MFIs, the paradigm has generated intense pressure to seek operational efficiency and comply with best practices and benchmarks (Armendariz de Aghion & Morduch, 2004; Christen, 2000; CGAP, 2008).[9] Investors and donors alike have come to rely heavily on these benchmarks to judge potential investments, and increasingly demand that MFIs comply with them across markets (Dugan & Goodwin-Groen, 2005).

As a result, MFIs increasingly rely on industry standard technologies that increase the reach and scope of their services while limiting operational

---

[3] Daley-Harris estimates that, in 2006, there were 133 million microcredit customers. By 2009, the number grew to 155 million. He also estimates that, all things remaining equal, the number should grow to 175 million by 2015.

[4] Globally, the average interest rate on microloans is around 30% for non-profit companies, it can be much higher in for-profit MFIs and in less developed markets.

[5] MixMarket reports an average portfolio at risk (loans with more than 90 days of delinquency) of 2% for its 1,242 affiliated MFIs.

[6] A recent, highly visible example is the successful IPO of Compartamos, a Mexican MFI that raised over US$400M in 2007.

[7] Note that sustainability here refers to a lack of dependence on donors for financial subsistence. It is different from other notions of sustainability, such as environmental or social.

[8] Returns have been generous. Compartamos, for example, has averaged annual returns on equity above 50% (BloombergBusinessweek, 2007).

[9] See http://www.mixmarket.org and http://www.accion.org as two of prominent examples of organizations that track such benchmarks.

costs (e.g., Dugan & Goodwin-Groen, 2005; Morduch & Armendariz de Aghion, 2005). These new tools include complex managerial systems; detailed credit-scoring models, statistical algorithms, and tools for actuarial judgment; as well as hand-held devices that loan officers can use in the field to access information in real time. MFIs have also favored a narrower focus on the most profitable services, such as microcredit (Dugan & Goodwin-Groen, 2005; Marulanda & Otero, 2005). Not surprisingly, the efforts have generated welcome and continuous improvements in efficiency.[10] At the same time, the investments have entailed important tradeoffs coupled with structural challenges for MFIs. At the most basic level, they have brought into full relief the inherent tensions, contradictions, and limits of the marriage between a social mission—in this case, the eradication of poverty[11]—and a commitment to profits (CGAP, 2008; Christen, 2000; Navajas et al., 2000).[12] They have also stretched MFI organizations at their core.

Regardless of their lending model,[13] MFIs serve clients who are low income, live in remote (often rural) locations, and are mostly unfamiliar with financial technology. As a result, MFIs are inherently labor intensive, since they must rely on loan officers to access and monitor clients (Morduch & Armendariz de Aghion, 2005). Loan officers constitute the primary point of contact between MFIs and clients. They find, recruit, and evaluate clients; they make lending decisions and disburse loans; and they are in charge of loan collections and renewals.

---

[10] According to MixMarket, average global return on equity (ROE) between 2003 and 2008 increased from 9% to 13% in for-profit MFIs and from 5% to 9% in non-profits. Operational expenses were reduced by 15% (informal data obtained by author from http://www.mixmarket.org, June 2010).

[11] This may seem like hyperbole. Consider this statement taken from the Compartamos Web site: "Our essence at Compartamos Banco is to generate development opportunities by giving access to financial services offering them to people in the lower economic segments."

[12] As an example, the average (global) loan amount increased from $264 to $567, while the average ratio of loan amount to client income *decreased* from 38% to 29%, which could suggest a shift to higher-income clients. It would certainly question the validity of the previous statement.

[13] There are three basic lending methodologies in microcredit: communal banks, solidary groups, and individual loans. Communal banks are by far the most widespread of the three and were promoted by the founder of the Grameen Bank in Bangladesh, Muhammad Yunus. They consist of joint-liability groups of 20 to 50 clients. The groups are self-regulating, self-enforcing, and are responsible for the distribution of loans—and the collection of payments—within the group. Solidary groups are smaller (from three to five, sometimes a few more) and are also jointly liable, but the loans are given directly to the individuals as opposed to the group, and the groups are not self-regulating. That is, each client in a solidary group undergoes a separate credit analysis and the interaction between the bank and the client is at the individual level. Individual loans are self-explanatory.

While the major dimensions of work—lending policies, incentive schemes, collection rules—are centrally defined, loan officers operate in situations that often require responses on dimensions that cannot be contemplated by formal rules—such as gauging the moral character of a client with no financial records. Employees in such complex, uncertain, and under-resourced settings tend to exercise great amounts of discretion in the application of rules (Hawkins & Thomas, 1989; Kadish & Kadish, 1973; Lipsky, 1980). Agency, therefore, becomes an unavoidable characteristic of rule enactment (Feldman & Pentland, 2003; Howard-Grenville, 2005; Pentland & Feldman, 2005; Taylor, 1993).

At the same time, any serious reduction in MFI costs must address the relative costs of loan officer work. The most immediate way to decrease the labor cost per loan, for example, is to increase the number of clients per loan officer.[14] Standardization and automation of decisions allow for this increase but also decrease the span of loan officer discretion. They require the codification, simplification, and filtration of contextual, complex, and strewn information. For example, a credit-scoring model may ask a loan officer to input the client's total household income. Low-income households, however, rely on a multiplicity of activities with varying levels of income stability. In most cases, clients can only offer verbal estimations of income sources. The loan officer, however, must provide a point estimate, knowing that it will dramatically impact the client's likelihood of receiving a loan, the amount of that loan, and the path that the client embarks on as a borrower. It is thus that standardization, ironically, often increases the structural tensions between loan officer work and organizational policies. Given the central role played by loan officers, it is important to understand how they resolve these tensions, how this can impact potential and existing clients, and the implications that it can have for organizational policies. Such understanding requires an approach that does not take written rules as facts but rather questions them and treats rules and practices as endogenously interrelated, while potentially decoupled (Becker, 2004; Ewick & Silbey, 1999;

---

[14] Consider that between 2003 and 2008, the average number of clients per loan officer increased by 25% to 250 (for MFIs reporting to MixMarket) (informal data obtained by author from http://www.mixmarket.org, June 2010).

Feldman, 2000, 2003; Feldman & Pentland, 2003; Howard-Grenville, 2005; Pentland & Feldman, 2005; Silbey, 2005).

DATA AND METHODS

This chapter and publications that have preceded it (Canales, 2009, 2010) are based on several years of data collection with three MFIs in Mexico. Throughout the process, I have placed particular emphasis on qualitative methodologies, following a grounded theory-building approach (Glaser & Strauss, 1980). I also explicitly straddle different levels of analysis, going from organization-wide rules and policies, to branches and branch managers, to interactions between loan officers and clients. Because the project explores how field-level practices vary, the research design seeks within-firm variation, or the mechanisms that explain differentials across branches and across clients of the same MFI, to later look for patterns across different MFIs. Accordingly, I selected three organizational sites (listed here as FR, FC, and CG)[15] that differed along important structural features to explore their field-level practices, how those practices depend on and influence structural features, and how they relate to MFI performance (see Table 20.1).[16]

I spent over five months collecting qualitative data within these companies, and several months doing periodic follow-up interviews. A majority of the time was spent with FC (around 60% of my total time), where the initial findings emerged. I repeated the methodology extensively with FR (around 30% of my time). Finally, CG was used as a validation case (the remaining 10% of my time). I divided the qualitative part of my work into two phases within each company. In the first phase, I interviewed MFI employees, starting with the CEO and slowly working my way down the organization until I reached the loan-officer level. I also observed several loan officer-client interactions and sat in internal meetings. Next, I interviewed branch managers and loan officers. I asked interviewees from the central office to place branches in three groups: good performers, average

---

[15] Organization and individual names are omitted to retain confidentiality.
[16] Note that the mixture of companies allows for the comparison across individual and group lending methodologies, as well as across urban and rural environments.

TABLE 20.1

Lending Methodologies and Geographic Focus by Company

	Lending Methodology			Geographic Focus	
	Communal Banks	Solidary Groups	Individual Loans	Urban	Rural
FC	No	Yes	Yes	Yes	No
FR	Yes	No	No	Yes (some)	Yes
CG	Yes	Yes	No	Yes	Yes

performers, and poor performers. The categorization was highly consistent across employees within each of the companies, and I corroborated it with company reports. I randomly selected between one and three of the branches from each group for each of the companies. I spent between half a day and a whole day visiting each branch, talking to the manager, attending committee meetings, and observing manager-client and manager-loan officer interactions. At the end of the branch visit, I selected a random sample of loan officers with the assistance of the branch manager. I spent an entire day, in some cases two days, with each of the officers, shadowing them on their route to learn how they interacted with clients, observing their lending and collecting methodologies, and asking the loan officers to narrate their actions after they had occurred. In this first phase, I interviewed just over 75 employees. In the second phase of the study, I performed client interviews. To pick clients, I asked loan officers to give me a list of their clients and I randomly selected four or five. I also asked officers to select one of their best clients and one of their worst clients to ensure variation. Moreover, I asked each officer to lead me to some program drop-outs, that is, clients who were no longer in the system.[17] In total, I performed just over 50 client interviews. I have performed over 50 follow-up interviews with MFI employees of different levels. The analytic strategy, not fully described here for brevity, was consistent with a grounded theory building approach (Glaser and Strauss, 1980).

---

[17] This is important because existing studies tend to neglect clients who terminated their relationship with the bank. This is problematic because it is impossible to determine whether a client dropped out because she "graduated" out of microcredit because she decided she did not want an additional loan, or because she experienced difficulties and was kicked out. This censoring is potentially significant, as it might grossly underestimate negative impacts of loans and only measure results based on the clients who have chosen to stay in the program.

WORK COMPLEXITY, GOAL STRAIN, AND POSITIVE DEVIANCE IN MICROCREDIT

Work Complexity and Loan Officer Practices[18]

The average loan officer in an MFI must serve around 250 clients.[19] For most of these clients, the loan officer was the first contact with the MFI—and with the financial sector, for that matter. During an initial client visit, the loan officer explains the characteristics of the loan and the requisites for approval and validates that the prospect is a viable candidate.[20] If possible, the loan officer gathers all the required credit information to avoid future visits. This information typically includes all relevant business metrics (e.g., sales, cost of sales, amount of inventory, supplier references), total family income, total family assets, desired uses of the loan, credit references, and credit history when available. Since prospective clients have not typically calculated this information, the loan officer helps clients by discussing daily sales, observing customer traffic, reviewing existing inventory, going over purchase receipts, and other means.

The loan officer is expected to perform an initial credit analysis and produce a credit recommendation. The loan officer then presents the case to a branch-level credit committee (typically composed of the branch manager and other loan officers), where she defends the recommendation. Should the loan approval require additional information, the commitment of cosigners, or other modifications the loan officer is responsible for obtaining them. Once a final decision is reached, the loan officer informs the client and provides all the necessary information for the disbursement of the loan.[21] A significant part of an officer's subsequent work entails educating first-time clients on how to manage a loan. Once a loan is approved and disbursed, the loan officer supervises its performance. This includes periodically visiting clients and reminding them of upcoming payments. Should a client miss a payment, loan officers decide the course of action.

---

[18] This section relies heavily on Canales (2010).

[19] See http//:www.mixmarket.com. These numbers are highly consistent with the three MFIs I studied, where the numbers fluctuated from 180 to around 280.

[20] In MFIs that lend through group loans, clients are advised to bring together a group of people they deem trustworthy and, once the group is large enough, to request a loan officer visit.

[21] Loan amounts typically range from the equivalent of US$50 to US$2,000 (with an average of around $400) and are granted for periods from four months to a year. Depending on client needs—and MFI preferences—the loans are repaid in weekly, biweekly, or monthly installments.

Ideally, missed payments are anticipated—loan officers who are close to their clients know when things are not going well—so a strategy can be devised before the payment is actually missed. Regardless, for the first 30 to 90 days of delinquency (depending on the MFI), loan officers are solely responsible for collections. During that time, loan officers can decide to collect directly from clients, collect from co-signers—or from other members of group loans—or even seize a client's assets. They can also choose to restructure a loan, send to the legal department for a more aggressive collection, or suggest writing the loan off as unrecoverable. As a loan reaches its maturity, the loan officer is expected to retain clients who exhibited good payment behavior and, ideally, increase their loan amounts.[22] In addition, in many MFIs the loan officer is increasingly expected to offer other products to the client—like home improvement loans, savings accounts, or insurance policies. But this also entails deciding how much of the client's cash flow to absorb while avoiding excessive indebtedness. On top of these client management activities, loan officers must attend all credit committees (and actively participate in them), keep all client information current in the MFIs' databases, and train incoming loan officers:

> You cannot overstate the role of loan officers.... They are our eyes and ears, they are our analytic team, they are our risk filters.... (They) are in charge of supervising that clients meet credit obligations.... They must keep close track of clients, their needs, and their payment capability, which means that they have to keep their hearts, their ears, and their noses on the ground, close to our clients. (Credit manager, FC)[23]

It is a complex job that demands a complex set of skills:

> Loan officers must be analytic, not just in their credit analysis, but also in creating needs for the client. For example, if a client complains about the interest rate, the officer can show that the loan is much more productive than the actual cost of the loan. They help us break paradigms that clients have. They must also be open. Things are constantly changing on the field, so loan officers must learn *everything*. They must be flexible to adapt to these changes.... Some officers think: "my job is just to present the loan, get it approved, and presto!" but no, you must finish the entire cycle. (Branch manager, FR)

[22] Many mechanisms have been proposed to explain the high repayment rates observed in microcredit. The best documented and proven of these is the promise that larger loans will follow a well repaid one.
[23] All quoted material comes from interviews conducted by the author or observation notes obtained through the author's fieldwork.

This description seeks to present a picture of the complexity, intensity, and importance of loan officer work. Loan officers not only bear a heavy responsibility for the welfare of their organization and its clients, but also must carry that responsibility with increasing constraints from a heavy workload, low professional status, and structural limitations. Consider, for example, that loan officers must perform all these activities in remote, difficult to reach areas with no transportation or logistic support from their organization. Thus, the average loan officer spends more than four hours a day commuting to work and between clients.[24]

Investors who increasingly expect MFIs to perform according to international benchmarks of profitability—and operational efficiency—only compound these pressures. As mentioned above, MFIs have developed an array of tools to help (and control) loan officers in almost every task. There are detailed credit manuals with specific instructions for most imaginable eventualities. Most MFIs have developed complex parametric credit models to automate lending decisions. Many have also equipped loan officers with handheld computers that allow them to capture client information and access company databases in real time. Each MFI has developed detailed training methodologies to orient and guide instructor loan officers. To coordinate the array of responsibilities and tools, there is an exhaustive set of policies that define the use of each, the specific decisions that should follow any eventuality, and the limits within which decisions are to be made. Moreover, loan officers, like many street-level bureaucrats (police officers, teachers, immigration officials, social workers, housing officials), routinely make decisions that directly—and dramatically—affect their clients' life chances. As a result, claims to impartiality are especially important, accountability to the public is ever present, and administrative officials are expected to shape policy accordingly (Lipsky, 1980; Thompson & Hoggett, 1996; Wilson, 1968).

Yet, the uncertainty of the situations faced by loan officers (and other street-level bureaucrats) is such that rules cannot possibly anticipate all of them and in fact often offer conflicting prescriptions. As a result, employees in such work settings exercise a great amount of discretion in how they enact policies, while managers must support—and often encourage—such discretion (Blau, 1955; Feldman, 2000; Hawkins & Thomas, 1989; Lipsky, 1980; Silbey, 1981; Silbey & Bittner, 1982; Taylor 1993).

---

[24] Around 2.5 hours between client visits, 1.5 hours commuting to and from the branch.

Accordingly, my in-depth observation of loan officer work revealed that loan officers relate to company policies in varying ways. Certain loan officers—labeled "spirit of the law" officers (SL) in Table 20.2—see policies as imperfect, incomplete, and narrow. They see policies as tools to facilitate their work that can and should be interpreted with some discretion. They often choose to bend policies or apply them partially. In contrast, other loan officers—labeled "letter of the law" officers (LL)—see policies as binding constraints, as prescriptions and recipes that must be followed closely. They make decisions based solely on policies and in so doing renounce their discretionary power. They choose to be bound by the rules, not because they don't think there is room for legitimate maneuver within them, but because rules reduce the uncertainty of decisions that have uncertain consequences. These LL officers assume rules are there for a reason and were made by people with experience, so they don't feel the need—or authority—to question them. The typology presented in Table 20.2 was developed inductively by observing all loan officers in my sample. Table 20.2 shows different rules and guidelines that are designed to shape loan officer interactions and the ways in which the two types of officers apply them.[25] It is not the case that *all* officers can be perfectly characterized by one type. Rather, each category can be thought of as one of two extremes in a continuum, with each officer placed somewhere within it.[26]

These differences are not just expressions of work styles that may produce similar outcomes. They reflect how different loan officers develop a work style that helps them manage the tensions and incongruity of their work. The work style can have deeper implications for company performance, loan impacts, and client loyalty (Canales, 2009; May & Winter, 2000; May & Wood, 2003). It is important to note, however, that although styles can lead to different client outcomes, both types of loan officers voice similar intentions. Both behaviors are driven by the pressure to perform under extreme uncertainty. Both types of loan officers, quite simply, seek to do their work well. What is different, therefore, is their understanding of what it entails to perform well under the uncertainty of microfinance.

---

[25] Note that, when I describe rule-bending or rule-breaking behavior, I refer to behaviors that are tolerated (indeed, sometimes encouraged) by management. There is a second type of rule-breaking that is not tolerated and is not described in this paper. For example, loan officers who are caught stealing, giving information away to competitors, or engaging in corruption with clients or government officials are immediately terminated.

[26] For more information on the typology and characteristics of SL vs. LL officers, see Canales (2009).

TABLE 20.2

A Typology of Loan Officers

Rule	"Spirit of the Law"	"Letter of the Law"
- Loan officers (LO) should maintain an institutional relationship with clients. Clients should see the LO as the institution, not as the person	- Relationships with clients at a personal level - Emphasizes personal character of relationship with client while constantly referring back to company as "the boss" or "company policies"	- Relationships with client at an institutional level - Emphasizes professional character of relationship, constantly highlighting the fact that he/she only represents the company and its investors
- LO should know the status of the client's business in terms of its profitability	- Close follow-up of business as well as personal activities, family issues, friendships, etc.	- Interaction mostly on a transactional basis, limits interaction to credit-related issues and business liquidity
- LO should know whether a client's referrals and guarantors exist and are trustworthy	- Knows a client's business and personal network and often refers clients to other clients, building wider networks	- Does not like to "get involved" with clients, prefers to maintain arms-length relationship and only checks on client's network to ensure potential pressure for repayment
- LO should not give business advice to clients due to liability issues	- Open to provide advice on business issues	- Afraid to provide advice on business issue with a "we could be liable" argument
- If a client is in trouble, negotiated agreements can be reached, but it is the LO's discretion	- Engages in joint problem-solving with client, especially in times of trouble	- No joint problem-solving, only interacts on contractual terms
- Loans must be collected upon and it is one of the most important measurement metrics	- Emphasizes trustworthiness of clients—"most clients want to pay"	- Emphasizes that clients can be devious—"most clients want to shirk"

"Spirit of the law" officers manage this uncertainty by gathering as much information about their clients as possible. To complement what they see as imperfect policies, they develop personalized relationships with clients as a source of information that enhances their judgment. Similar to accounts of government officials who are embedded in the contexts in which they provide services (e.g., Evans, 1995, 1996; Lam, 1997; Ostrom, 1996), these officers are embedded in their environment, have built personal connections with their clients, speak their language, and have developed a stake in their welfare. In contrast, "letter of the law" officers manage the uncertainty by deferring to policies and hierarchy. Since the rules are products of years of experience and thorough analyses, LL officers believe they will be better off, on average, strictly applying the algorithms. Policies are, after all, created to reduce uncertainty, make decisions easier, and reduce the biases of subjective judgment. LL officers choose to trust actuarial over personal judgment (Dawes, 1979; Dawes et al., 1989; Simon, 1988).

Goal Strain and Deviance

The different styles observed in loan officers should not be conceptualized without first considering the tensions created by the nature of their work. At the heart of those tensions lies a contradiction that increasingly pervades microcredit. The adoption of a market-centered paradigm has unquestionably brought desirable outcomes including managerial discipline, increased accountability, a more responsible credit culture among both lenders and borrowers, a more efficient use of funds, and a wealth of resources previously unseen in poverty relief efforts. It also has intensified the tensions between efficiency and fairness that are inherent in all service organizations (Canales, 2009; Heimer, 1992; Spitzer, 1975), but are especially present in those that provide life-altering services to the destitute (Lipsky, 1980). This is because any rule that categorizes clients makes it easier to classify them, but also rests on a set of assumptions that don't apply equally to all (Heimer, 1992). In microfinance, the increased efficiency translates to quicker, cheaper, and more reliable services to many—maybe even most—clients, but must also entail a reduced level of responsiveness or attention to others:

> Every time they give us new tools, they basically ask us to spend less time with our clients…. Take loan renewals, for example. In most cases, they

are automatic now. As long as the clients paid the first loan they are issued a second loan, no questions asked. (But) that second loan used to be when officers could really learn how the loans were working out for their clients. (SL officer, FC)

In a setting like microfinance, where a stated goal is to bring opportunities to the poorest of the poor, such a tradeoff has direct consequences:

For some people, the loans are incredibly productive.... But you need a certain level of stability and infrastructure to be able to make and manage those investments. The poorer you are, the less likely you will be to have those basic conditions and the harder it will be for you to make productive investments on your own on a consistent basis. (Operations manager, FR)

This may appear counterintuitive; first, because microfinance programs are supposed to be designed to help the poorest; second, because poorer people who start from a smaller economic base should be able to increase that base more rapidly than people who start from a higher base. The same manager, however, explained why this paradox exists:[27]

Poorer people have many problems beyond the lack of access to financial services. When you fix one of their issues by lending them money, they still have many other problems to deal with which are not solved by a loan. Sure, some people use the loans as a springboard, but you can't really use a springboard when it is under water, you know?

For some MFI administrators, these barriers have proven larger than the scope of their organizations:

From the early days of CG, I have been skeptical about actually helping the really poor, even though that was the claim.... Their problems are very complex. To really help them you need to provide a broader support structure, access to opportunities, access to business information, access to better networks, and some sort of cushion for difficult moments. All of this was the initial dream of microfinance, at least the way we understood it. But reality catches up.... It is impossible to provide all that to our poorest clients and still come out with black ink on our books. (Regional manager, CG)

---

[27] Among MFI employees, as well as academic circles, there is an understanding of the structural barriers that poorer people have to overcome beyond the lack of access to capital that make it difficult for them to benefit from loans (Collins et al., 2009; Hulme & Mosley, 1996; Morduch, 1994, 1999, 2000).

Most loan officers agree with this claim, with different levels of resigna-tion. More so in light of the rules and workload that constrain them. SL officers, however, view their roles differently:

> My biggest commitment is to my poorest clients. They are the ones who need me the most. Other clients can do well without me.... As an officer I have access to a lot of information. I know all my clients, and I know their families and their friends.... I also see hundreds of similar businesses and situations.... I know who does what and who knows who. So, I choose to use all that information to give my customers advice (and) extra support. (SL officer, FR)

> We are not just offering loans. We are offering life-long support, life-long opportunities.... You have to keep track of what your clients are doing, you have to stay on top of their needs. If you realize that your client is in a bad situation, you must give her a solution...even if that means working outside the written rules. (SL officer, FC)

For SL officers, their work goes beyond the manuals, the policies, and the algorithms:

> Policies are good, they are useful, but you also need to give them a personal touch.... For example, when you visit a prospect's grocery store, you could just begin asking questions following the policies.... It is much better to spend that time learning about the client, about her relationships, and sell-ing her on opportunities, like the purchase of a ham slicer and how much more money she can make with that and how productive the loan would be.... Or like putting her in contact with my other client who can be a bet-ter supplier. That's what helping my clients is about. (SL officer, FC)

This stands in stark contrast with LL officers, and more importantly, the companies' rules:

> My job is to recruit the new loan groups, train them on the methodology, do the credit analysis, and make sure that the whole process runs smoothly. It basically consists of applying the methodology strictly and making sure that the groups adhere closely to the policies. (LL officer, CG)

As shown in Table 20.2, SL officers relate to most of the companies' rules loosely. They often break, bend, or reify policies. In that sense—and from the LL officer's and some managers' perspective—SL officers could be seen as deviants (Canales, 2010). SL officers, however, do not see themselves as deviants or outsiders to the firm. Their identity is defined by a broader understanding of the organization, its goals, and its constraints rather than by their relationship to its policies. They deviate from policies not out of contempt or disrespect, but because their deeper knowledge of clients allows them to identify instances where policies might lead to undesirable outcomes. They see themselves as *more*, rather than less, identified with their organization and what it stands for:

> I am the eyes, the ears, the hands of the organization. We are the ambassadors of FR. To the clients, we *are* FR. And to FR, we *are* the clients. Yes, we promote and place loans, but that almost takes care of itself (through client referrals).... We also have to make sure that the company is doing the right thing, that it is truly helping our clients, and that our clients are being heard.... We have so much responsibility. (SL officer, FR)

It is precisely this higher level of identification that creates high levels of strain, as loan officers experience the tension between stated goals and the means provided to achieve them (Matza, 1969; Merton, 1968). In that sense, creating exceptions for a portion of their clientele is the only way to salvage the ideal conception of what their job should be (Lipsky, 1980, p. 151; Silbey & Bittner, 1982; Wrzesniewski et al., 1997; Wrzesniewski & Dutton, 2001). They see deviations from policy as a costly defense of their commitment to the company's mission, to their professional values:

> Me? I still visit my clients periodically, but it only means less free time, more work, and more stress.... I do it because I will not sacrifice the quality of my work, or what we stand for as a company.... there is too much at stake for my clients. (SL officer, FC)

The fact that SL officers consistently step beyond the boundaries of MFI policies, then, unquestionably classifies them as deviants. But what are we to make of the fact that, through their deviance, they are more effectively pursuing the organization's goals? In that sense, SL deviance cannot be understood in isolation. SL officers do not seek to be deviants; they *find themselves* as deviants in relation to a set of defined rules. We cannot understand their actions by looking at their outcome. We can only understand their relationship to rules by observing *the process* through which they became deviant; the day-to-day interactions with clients, managers, and other loan officers that gradually led to their position in relation to the rules as defined by others (Becker, 1953, 1991; Goffman, 1959, 1961, 1967; Matza, 1969; Spitzer, 1975). For, as will be seen below, SL officers don't set out to break rules. Rather, they learn through experience that the relationships they have established with their clients, the information they have gathered through those relationships, and the activities they see as *necessary* to perform their work with the quality that they aspire to happen to lie outside the written rules (Becker, 1991; Matza, 1969). With every new rule that automates an activity or creates a new classification for clients, a new set of SL behaviors is fenced out.

The Relational Origins of Positive Deviance

SL officers question organizational policies based on the information, trust, and commitment that they have obtained through deeper relationships with their clients (Canales, 2009; Heimer, 1992). In most cases, those relationships develop from a higher level of initial identification with clients. Often, SL officers were drawn to microfinance because they were once clients themselves or those close to them are past, current, or potential clients. In contrast, typical LL officers—as well as most other MFI employees, including managers—are normally hired out of college from economics-oriented majors or from more traditional financial firms, like commercial banks. These differences in background translate to differences in the loan officers' cultural toolkits, cultural "dialects," and perceptions of the clients' environment (Ambady & Bharucha, 2009; Elfenbein & Ambady, 2003; Marsh et al., 2003; Piaget, 1965; Swidler, 1986, 2001). They also translate to different understandings of the relative value and appropriateness of personal connections. Thus, from the initial moments of their interaction, SL officers establish, consciously and unconsciously, a different type of relationship with their clients.

LL officers typically see a personal relationship with a client as problematic, since it can lead to subjectivity in credit analyses, conflicts of interest should a loan become delinquent, and an overall devaluation of the MFI's institutional image. They basically code relationships with clients with a traditional view of particularism (Parsons & Shils, 1951). Thus, it is important to highlight that LL officers don't avoid establishing deeper relationships with clients out of contempt. Rather, they believe maintaining a "professional distance" from clients is necessary to ensure the quality of their work (see Canales, 2010, for more detail).

In stark contrast, SL officers learn to see personal relationships as indispensable work tools (McGinn, 2007). Ironically, they arrive at this conclusion not by disagreeing with LL officers on the core issues of their work, but rather by identifying exactly the same issues while disagreeing on the best means to address them. SL officers recognize the same complexity and uncertainty as LL officers do, but they see relationships as the best possible mechanism to manage them (Heimer, 1992). Whereas LL officers worry that a personal attachment might bring subjective information into already complex credit analyses, SL officers believe that by collecting rich ("soft") information that can only be gathered through a personal relationship they can parse through the messy, unstructured data presented by micro enterprises that, on paper, might all look the same (Berger et al., 2001; Berger & Udell, 2002). Whereas LL officers worry that a personal relationship might create a conflict of interest for collection efforts, SL officers see the relationship as the best mechanism to keep track of their clients, generate additional commitments for payment, and establish the kind of trust that can support creative problem-solving if something goes wrong (Sabel, 1993, 1994; Uzzi, 1996). Whereas LL officers worry that a personal relationship might devalue the professionalism of their work, SL officers see it as the only way to ensure that they provide a professional, customized service (Bearman, 2005; Canales, 2010). They use the relationship as a source of information about client needs and challenges so they can best use their own networks and knowledge to address them:

> My branch manager worries when I give business advice to my clients, he says if they listen to me and things go wrong they could blame CG.... This woman (who owns a small grocery store), for example. She is buying all her dairy products at the most expensive place. She is leaving so much money on the table and she does not know it. This other client of mine has a wholesale dairy business and gets amazing prices, so it only makes sense for me to put them in contact; they are both good people and they can help each other out. The same for her bakery goods, and for candy. I know *all* these people, how could I not use these connections to help my clients help each other?... I also learn a lot about business practices, for example, I know from seeing very successful stores that putting the dairy products where they are most visible is good for business, but she had them all the way at the back, so I tell her that and she will try it.... Precisely because I help them more than other (loan officers from other) companies would, they simply feel somehow indebted to me, in a good way, they value their

relationship with me and so they are always on time with their payments. (SL officer, CG)

Officers don't only disagree on the instrumental value of personal relationships. They also hold differing views on what determines client success and, more importantly, on the extent to which relationships can play a role in that success. As described in Canales (2010), LL officers believe that their most important work lies in the proper selection of clients, where actuarial models can best predict the probability that a client with a given set of observable characteristics will display good repayment behavior. This, naturally, reinforces the need to keep relationships "institutional." SL officers, on the other hand, believe models too often obscure reality, *especially* for clients who are in the lower part of the distribution. Thus, they believe their most important work lies in client *management* and in the *transformative* power that a positive relationship between the client and the MFI can have. For SL officers, most clients have the potential to become good clients, but some can only reach this potential if their special needs are met:

> Whenever my poorer clients tell me they can't make a payment because something bad happened to them, I have a policy of always trusting them.... Sure, some of my clients end up not being morally solvent, but I can tell you that of every ten clients I have helped, nine have made it and eight have become long-term clients. A restructuring is a great opportunity because then you develop a double commitment with your client. (SL officer, FR)

In that sense, SL officers are not simply using relationships instrumentally. Rather, they are able to *generate* new resources, opportunities, repertoires, and meaning through them (Dutton & Ragins, 2007; Ragins & Verbos, 2007). They see relationships not only as information-gathering tools as described earlier, but also as sources of new value that can put clients—specially the most vulnerable—on entirely different development paths (e.g., Rosenthal & Jacobson, 1968). Moreover, SL officers worry that such self-fulfilling expectations cannot be coded into rules and that rules that exclude these possibilities in fact create negative expectations that are equally self-fulfilling (Heimer, 1992; Lipsky, 1980):

> This officer is treating me as if I were a criminal, as if I were missing payments by choice.... I have missed some payments because I really have no

money right now. (The officer) figures that by trying to scare me with legal threats I will pay my loan … but tell me something: here is my neighbor who lent me money now that I was in trouble and here is (the officer) who has threatened me and insulted me. I am going to pay my debts to both of them eventually, as things improve, but which do you think I will repay first? (Client)

As described here, SL officers cannot relate to all their clients with equal levels of depth—they simply lack the time. They thus choose to develop and nurture relationships according to their own assessment of client needs and to the potential value they see in each relationship. Often, clients with "standard" needs can "take care of themselves." At the same time, while SL officers often have a preference for establishing relationships with clients, many times they do not seek such relationships, they simply find themselves in them. For it remains the case that SL officers are socially close to clients. From the language they choose to the subtle, involuntary nonverbal cues they send when they initiate a conversation, SL officers present an image that is familiar to and immediately interpretable by clients (Ambady et al., 2000; Heaphy, 2007). They also bring a cultural toolkit that allows them to better interpret clients' reactions (Elfenbein & Ambady, 2003; Swidler, 2001). From the very first interactions, then, a relational style is established between client and loan officer (both SL and LL) that defines not only those initial interactions but also future interactions between them as well as how the client learns to relate to the firm in general (Bearman, 2005; Canales, 2009). Especially for poorer clients, this can have dramatic, long-lasting consequences:

I had spent an entire morning visiting a client. She was the embodiment of a microcredit success case. She had no formal schooling beyond primary school and began working as a seamstress at a young age. She learned the trade successfully and saved until she was able to buy a single sewing machine…. She obtained a first microloan and purchased a second sewing machine. This pattern continued until the time of my interview with her, when she managed dozens of employees…. Both in her conversations with me and in the interactions I observed with her employees she came across as an extremely able, secure, and strong-willed woman who knew exactly what she was doing and had a firm sense of authority to back it. (She needed) to go to the MFI branch to discuss her loan (now a significant amount) with the branch manager. As we entered the branch, the strong, articulate, secure woman I had observed all morning suddenly became a quiet, stuttering, insecure client who cringed at every question posed by the manager. Only an actual loss in physical height would have been more dramatic to observe. It is not that she had things to hide—she was a good client, in good standing. She was simply intimidated by the formality of the MFI branch and the language the manager was using to address her; she was out of her element. The branch manager seemed completely oblivious to this. It struck me that all the manager had ever observed was this "version" of the woman, which surely affected both his image of her as a client and how future interactions were constructed. (Canales, 2008, pp. 261–278)

As each client relationship reveals additional information to SL officers and as they gain additional experience with company policies, they find increasing numbers of instances where policies don't seem to match reality well. The deeper perspective gained through interacting with clients reveals an entire layer of information that is not—indeed, *cannot be—* coded into existing rules. Each additional instance increases the desire and the sense of legitimacy to question, bend, or break rules when deemed necessary. This desire, however, only increases already high levels of structural strain.

THE STRANGER AS FRIEND

The backgrounds, relational styles, and experience of SL officers combine in mutually reinforcing ways to place them in a position best characterized by Simmel as that of a "stranger" (Simmel, 1950, p. 185).

> He is fixed within a certain (group boundary) but his position within it is fundamentally affected by the fact that he does not belong in it initially and that he brings qualities into it that are not, and cannot be, indigenous to it.

Put differently, while all loan officers are situated at the complex (cultural, social, and economic) boundary that separates MFIs from their clients, SL officers face the additional complexity of operating on one side while retaining a strong presence on the other (Lamont & Molnar, 2002). It is precisely the relative objectivity provided by this position as "strangers" that allows SL officers to question MFI policies with the understanding of an insider but the detachment and skepticism of an outsider. It allows them to act as "sociological citizens," challenging policies as the best way to improve them (Canales, 2010; Silbey et al., 2009):

> What am I supposed to do here? This client has been growing her business doing all the right things, she has followed every piece of advice I have given her and she has made incredible progress. Finally, after two years of steady work, she has a big opportunity, a big break. [A new supplier is offering her a radically better price, but it requires her to buy a much larger volume than she usually does, which requires a substantial increase in working capital.] I know she can sell the merchandise and she can make better margins.... Yet, the rule says I can only increase her loan by fifteen percent.... If we don't give her the full amount, it is like giving her nothing. So we are either pushing her to go to another MFI or, worse, to get an outside loan [from a moneylender]. So I have to find a way around the rules.... We just need to come up with a better rule. (SL officer, FC)

It is also this position that creates a deeper commitment to the organization and its values, for several reasons. First, the very fact that they are "strangers" to the organization signals that these loan officers do not come from the traditional paths that other loan officers do. Likewise, it signals that they are not following the traditional path of individuals with similar backgrounds. In this sense, a matching process between the organization and the individual on criteria other than traditional or superficial elements has already been exercised. Second, while a loan officer job may be a starting point of relatively low status and questionable appeal for a middle-class college graduate, it represents a rare path to social mobility for a community-bred microentrepreneur. In this light, the relative weight that loan officers from different backgrounds will place on their affiliation with the organization can be appreciated.

More profoundly, however, the same characteristics that allow SL officers to challenge MFI policies—their deep knowledge about clients, their embedded ties to the community, their relative objectivity—also put them in a position of constant fragility. For just like the policies—flaws and contradictions included—that others take for granted are more conspicuous to the "stranger," so the "stranger"—and any faults she may commit—can be more visible to others. In addition, since allegiance to the group cannot be claimed on the mere basis of identity, the "stranger" must demonstrate it more visibly and more frequently. Finally, while a SL officer can have a deeper understanding of the community she operates in and can build stronger ties in it than other loan officers, she can no longer claim to be a part of it. This combination of visibility, disputed identity, and dependence requires SL officers to show unquestionable commitment to the organization (Coser, 1974; Simmel, 1950). Accordingly, while SL officers may bend, question, or challenge the policies, they tend to do so with full knowledge of their branch managers[28] and with a strong rationale for how it can benefit the organization. Anything less would put their permanence in the organization at risk.

The skeptical reader might have questioned, at several points of this chapter, why more traditional forms of deviance—corruption, theft, graft—are absent from my description. In particular, there may be a concern that the findings are driven by selection bias on the loan officers in my sample. A first response is that, as described earlier, the loan officers I observed were selected at random. A second and important clarification is that I did observe or document instances of destructive deviance. However—and contrary to SL behavior—it was rarely observed, it was severely punished (often with dismissal) when discovered by the organization, and it was not systematically linked to other patterns of behavior. In that sense, there is indeed a bias in my sample of loan officers, but it is a survival bias inherent in the organization. Put differently, and in light of the previous discussion, it is not surprising that the SL officers *who remain* in the firm exercise a style of deviance that is deeply rooted in the organization's values. It is also unsurprising that these SL officers tend to work longer hours and be better performers, especially on metrics that relate to loan impacts or client retention. It is thus that, conditional on remaining in the firm, SL officers become an asset to the MFI. SL officers can help prevent negative outcomes for poorer clients; they can push their clients to perform better through higher expectations that clients live up to; they can generate tighter client retentions through reciprocity ties; and they can help the organization improve its rules by constantly challenging them (Canales, 2008, 2010). These benefits, however, come at a cost.

First, MFIs do not create rules on a whim. There are good reasons, external and internal, behind each new rule. It is hard enough to design, write, explain, and enforce a new rule without the constant pushback from a set of officers. Second, and not surprisingly, there are limits to SL effectiveness

---

[28] This is not at all uncommon in street-level bureaucracies. See Lipsky (1980).

and it is not always clear where those limits lie. It is for branch and regional managers to discover and enforce them:

> In some branches, all the loan officers are very analytic, so the (credit) committees become like pissing contests, officers just try to prove to each other who knows the policies better.... This can become counter-productive because then very few proposals are approved. (But) if all the loan officers are only thinking about pleasing clients, then the committees become like love fests, where everything is approved, and then the branch starts taking risks that it should not. Ideally, you have voices that push everyone to be rigorous in their analysis..., but you also want voices that put faces on to the files being presented. (Regional manager, FC, in Canales, 2009)

In fact, while the three firms I worked with acknowledge the value of SL behavior, managers in two of them expressed that they had to learn how to harness and manage that value. In these two firms, managers expressed previous frustration as they often lost some of their best loan officers because they could not find a way to "contain their energy" or "channel their disagreements" productively. Part of that learning came from finding managers who understood and related to SL officers. All three firms continuously struggle to find the right balance between company policies and service quality for all those clients that don't neatly fit into them, even as they acknowledge that SL officers are an invaluable source of information. They also believe firms who have "entered microfinance from the outside," such as large commercial banks who attempt to open microcredit arms, fail to see this value and tend to rely too blindly on the actuarial models that have proven successful for more traditional consumer credit models:

> The microfinance market is more complex, more uncertain. If you don't have eyes and ears on the ground, you miss out on environmental shifts and you fail to learn how the market is evolving.... There is something very appealing about a model that tells you that, based on thousands of observations, you have a risk lower than three percent. But we must remember that each element of those models is based on assumptions and incomplete data. Even if each assumption seems reasonable, we must be willing to question them based on new market information.... The fact is that our officers on the ground are the only source of that information. (Risk analyst, FC)

CONCLUSION

Microfinance—and indeed all poverty alleviation work—is a complex setting where it is unreasonable to expect organizational policies to anticipate all contingencies. In such settings, actors must exercise high levels of discretion in the enactment of rules. This is especially true for policies that seek to categorize clients, since the definition of a rule entails a set of assumptions about clients that do not apply equally well to all. In microfinance, where there is increasing pressure to comply with a paradigm of profitability, rules that seek to reduce operational costs through standardization often result in unintended discrimination against the poorest; a direct contradiction to MFI's stated mission. This chapter has shown that, consistent with other street-level bureaucracies, certain loan officers resolve contradictions inherent in MFIs through positive deviance in the enactment of organizational rules. These loan officers generate new organizational repertoires and resources through the positive relationships they establish with clients. In addition, they use their structural position as "strangers" and the deviance that results from it to improve organizational rules.

This chapter thus suggests that, rather than simply pursue standardization, MFIs should embrace the individual agency inherent in the nature of their loan officers' work. This perspective allows MFIs to channel the energy of positive deviance, capture the information and repertoires generated by it, and use them to better respond to client needs. It highlights the importance of hiring, retaining, and encouraging loan officers who are "strangers" to MFIs in their deep connectedness to the clients' world. It also hints at the difficulties of managing a more diverse workforce. Since not *all* loan officers can be expected to be positive deviants—the system would become untenable—then it is more reasonable to seek a degree of diversity in the loan officer population that incorporates more traditional, analytic, actuarial types of loan officers together with the socially embedded types. Such diversity can allow MFIs to balance exploration and exploitation simultaneously, but at the cost of increasing managerial complexity.

There is, of course, an alternative. MFIs could choose to continue on the path of standardization to further reduce operational costs without paying much attention to the conflicting information of the impacts this is having on their destitute clients. The argument can be (and is) made that providing a more efficient service to the "middle" poor creates enormous social value and that, if this comes at the expense of not serving the poorest of the poor then new poverty alleviation efforts should step in to fill that void. They could choose to increasingly rely on actuarial models to focus only on the most profitable clients. They could assume that these complex actuarial systems present a true picture of client risk and a full assessment of all relevant client traits. As actuarial models push them toward only the safest credit risks, however, MFIs should accept that, rather than a social mission of bringing capitalism to the destitute, they have now embraced the mission of learning how to best profit from the poor.

REFERENCES

Alexander-Tedeschi, G. & Karlan, D. (2010) Cross-sectional impact analysis: Bias from dropouts. *Perspectives on Global Development and Technology, 9*, 270–291.

Ambady, N., Bernieri, F. J., & Richeson, J. A. (2000). Toward a histology of social behavior: Judgmental accuracy from thin slices of the behavioral stream. *Advances in Experimental Social Psychology, 32*, 201–271.

Ambady, N., & Bharucha, J. (2009). Culture and the brain. *Current Directions in Psychological Science, 18*, 342–345.

Armendariz de Aghion, B., & Morduch, J. (2004). Microfinance. Where do we stand? In C. Goodhard (Ed.), *Financial development and economic growth: Explaining the links* (pp. 135–148) Basingstoke, Hampshire, UK: Palgrave Macmillan.

Banerjee, A., Duflo, E., Glennerster, R., & Kinnan, C. (2010). The miracle of Microfinance? Evidence from a randomized evaluation BREAD Working Paper No. 278, June 2010. Bureau for Research and Economic Analysis of Development. Durham, NC.

Bearman, P. S. (2005). *Doormen*. Chicago: University of Chicago Press.

Becker, H. S. (1953). Becoming a marihuana user. *The American Journal of Sociology, 59*, 235–242.

Becker, H. S. (1991). *Outsiders: Studies in the sociology of deviance*. New York: Free Press.

Becker, M. C. (2004). Organizational routines: a review of the literature. *Industrial and Corporate Change, 13*, 643–678.

Berger, A. N., Klapper, L., & Udell, G. F. (2001). The ability of banks to lend to informationally opaque small businesses. *Journal of Banking and Finance, 25*, 2127–2167.

Berger, A. N., & Udell, G. F. (2002). Small business credit availability and relationship lending: The importance of bank organisational structure. *Economic Journal, 112*, F32-F53.

Blau, P. M. (1955). *The dynamics of bureaucracy; a study of interpersonal relations in two government agencies*. Chicago: University of Chicago Press.

BloombergBusinessweek. (2007). Online extra: Yunus blasts compartamos. Retrieved June 7, 2010, from http://www.businessweek.com/magazine/content/07_52/b4064045920958.htm

Canales, R. (2008). *From Ideals to Institutions: Institutional Entrepreneurship in Mexican Small Business Finance* (Doctoral dissertation, Massachusetts Institute of Technology). Retrieved from http://hdl.handle.net/1721.1/44810

Canales, R. (2011). Weaving straw into gold: Rule bending, localism, and managing the inconsistencies in organizational rules (working paper), Yale University.

Canales, R. (2011). Rule-bending, sociological citizenship, and organizational contestation in microfinance. *Regulation and Governance, 5,* 90–117.

CGAP, Consultative Group to Assist the Poorest (2008). Foreign capital investment in microfinance: Balancing social and financial returns. Focus Note 44.

Christen, R. (2000). Commercialization and mission drift: The transformation of microfinance in Latin America. *CGAP Occasional Paper.* Washington, DC: The CGAP.

Collins, D., Morduch, J., Rutherford, S., & Ruthven, O. (2009). *Portfolios of the poor: How the world's poor live on $2 a day.* Princeton, NJ: Princeton University Press.

Coser, L. A. (1974). *Greedy institutions; patterns of undivided commitment.* New York: Free Press.

Cull, R., Demirguc-Kunt, A., & Morduch, J. (2007). Financial performance and outreach: A global analysis of leading microbanks. *Economic Journal, 117,* F107–F133.

Cull, R., Demirguc-Kunt, A., & Morduch, J. (2009). Microfinance meets the market. *Journal of Economic Perspectives, 23,* 167–192.

Daley-Harris, S. (2007). *State of the microcredit summit campaign report 2006.* Washington, DC: Microcredit Summit Campaign.

Daley-Harris, S. (2009). *State of the microcredit summit campaign report 2009.* Washington, DC: Microcredit Summit Campaign.

Dawes, R. M. (1979). Robust beauty of improper linear-models in decision-making. *American Psychologist, 34,* 571–582.

Dawes, R. M., Faust, D., & Meehl, P. E. (1989). Clinical versus actuarial judgment. *Science 243,* 1668–1674.

Dugan, M., & Goodwin-Groen, R. (2005). Donors succeed by making themselves obsolete: Compartamos taps financial markets in Mexico. *Case studies in donor good practices.* CGAP **20.**

Dutton, J. E., & Ragins, B. R. (2007). Moving forward: Positive relationships at work as a research frontier. In J. E. Dutton & B. R. Ragins (Eds.), *Exploring positive relationships at work : building a theoretical and research foundation* (pp. 387–400). Mahwah, NJ: Lawrence Erlbaum Associates.

Elfenbein, H. A., & Ambady, N. (2003). When familiarity breeds accuracy: Cultural exposure and facial emotion recognition. *Journal of Personality and Social Psychology, 85,* 276–290.

Emirbayer, M., & Mische, A. (1998). What is agency? *The American Journal of Sociology, 103,* 962–1023.

Evans, P. (1995). *Embedded autonomy: States and industrial transformation.* Princeton, NJ: Princeton University Press.

Evans, P. (1997). Introduction: Development strategies across the public-private divide and government action, social capital, and development: Reviewing the evidence of synergy. In P. Evans (Ed.), *State-society synergy: Government and social capital in development* (pp. 1–10; 178–210). Berkeley: University of California.

Ewick, P., & Silbey, S. S. (1999). Common knowledge and ideological critique: The significance of knowing that the "haves" come out ahead. *Law & Society Review, 33,* 1025–1041.

Feldman, M. S. (2000). Organizational routines as a source of continuous change. *Organization Science, 11,* 611–629.

Feldman, M. S. (2003). A performative perspective on stability and change in organizational routines. *Industrial and Corporate Change, 12,* 727–752.

Feldman, M. S., & Pentland, B. T. (2003). Reconceptualizing organizational routines as a source of flexibility and change. *Administrative Science Quarterly, 48,* 94–118.

Glaser, B. G., & Strauss, A. L. (1980). *The discovery of grounded theory: Strategies for qualitative research.* Hawthorne, NY: Aldine Pub. Co.

Goffman, E. (1959). *The presentation of self in everyday life.* Garden City, NY: Doubleday.

Goffman, E. (1961). *Encounters; two studies in the sociology of interaction.* Indianapolis: Bobbs-Merrill.

Goffman, E. (1967). *Interaction ritual; essays on face-to-face behavior.* Garden City, NY: Anchor Books.

Hawkins, K., & Thomas, J. M. (1989). *Making regulatory policy.* Pittsburgh: University of Pittsburgh Press.

Heaphy, E. D. (2007). Bodily insights: Three lenses on positive organizational relationships. In J. E. Dutton & B. R. Ragins (Eds.), *Exploring positive relationships at work: Building a theoretical and research foundation* (pp. 47–71). Mahwah, NJ: Lawrence Erlbaum Associates.

Heimer, C. A. (1992). Doing your job AND helping your friends: Universalistic norms about obligations to particular others in networks. In R. G. Eccles & N. Nohria (Eds.), *Networks and organizations: Structure, form, and action* (pp. 118–142). Boston: Harvard Business School Press.

Howard-Grenville, J. A. (2005). The persistence of flexible organizational routines: The role of agency and organizational context. *Organization Science, 16,* 618–636.

Hulme, D., & Mosley, P. (1996). *Finance against poverty.* London: Routledge.

Kadish, M. R., & Kadish, S. H. (1973). *Discretion to disobey; a study of lawful departures from legal rules.* Stanford: Stanford University Press.

Lam, W. F. (1997). Institutional design of public agencies and coproduction: A study of irrigation associations in taiwan. In P. Evans (Ed.), *State-society synergy* (pp. 11–47). Berkeley: University of California International.

Lamont, M., & Molnar, V. (2002). The study of boundaries in the social sciences. *Annual Review of Sociology, 28,* 167–195.

Lipsky, M. (1980). *Street level bureaucracy: Dilemmas of the individual in public services.* New York: Rusell Sage Foundation.

Marsh, A. A., Elfenbein, H. A., & Ambady, N. (2003). Nonverbal "accents": Cultural differences in facial expressions of emotion. *Psychological Science (Wiley-Blackwell), 14,* 373–376.

Marulanda, B., & Otero, M. (2005). Perfil de las Microfinanzas en Latinoamérica en 10 años: Visión y características. *Cumbre del Microcredito.* Santiago de Chile: ACCION International.

Matza, D. (1969). *Becoming deviant.* Englewood Cliffs, NJ: Prentice-Hall.

May, P. J., & Winter, S. (2000). Reconsidering styles of regulatory enforcement: Patterns in Danish agro-environmental inspection. *Law & Policy, 22,* 143–174.

May, P. J., & Wood, R. S. (2003). At the regulatory front lines: Inspectors' enforcement styles and regulatory compliance. *Journal of Public Administration, Research & Theory, 13,* 117–139.

McGinn, K. L. (2007). History, structure, and practices: San Pedro longshoremen in the face of change. In J. E. Dutton & B. R. Ragins (Eds.), *Exploring positive relationships at work: Building a theoretical and research foundation* (pp. 265–275). Mahwah, NJ: Lawrence Erlbaum Associates.

Merton, R. K. (1968). *Social theory and social structure.* New York: The Free Press.

Morduch, J. (1994). Poverty and vulnerability. *American Economic Review, 84,* 221–225.

Morduch, J. (1999). The microfinance promise. *Journal of Economic Literature, 37,* 1569–1615.

Morduch, J. (2000). The microfinance schism. *World Development, 28,* 617–629.

Morduch, J., & Armendariz de Aghion, B. (2005). *The economics of microfinance.* Cambridge, MA: MIT Press.

Navajas, S., Schreiner, M., Meyer, R. L., Gonzalez-Vega, C., & Rodriguez-Meza, J. (2000). Microcredit and the poorest of the poor: Theory and evidence from Bolivia. *World Development, 28,* 333–346.

Nelson, R. R., & Winter, S. G. (1982). *An evolutionary theory of economic change.* Cambridge, MA: Belknap Press of Harvard University Press.

Ostrom, E. (1997). Crossing the great divide: Coproduction, synergy, and development. In P. Evans (Ed.), *State-society synergy: Government and social capital in development* (pp. 85–118). Berkeley: University of California.

Parsons, T., & Shils, E. A. (1951). *Toward a general theory of action.* New Brunswick, NJ: Transaction Publishers.

Pentland, B. T., & Feldman, M. S. (2005). Organizational routines as a unit of analysis. *Industrial and Corporate Change, 14,* 793–815.

Piaget, J. (1965). *The moral judgment of the child.* New York: The Free Press.

Ragins, B. R., & Verbos, A. K. (2007). Positive relationships in action: Relational mentoring and mentoring schemas in the workplace. In J. E. Dutton & B. R. Ragins (Eds.), *Exploring positive relationships at work: Building a theoretical and research foundation* (pp. 91–116). Mahwah, NJ: Lawrence Erlbaum Associates.

Rosenthal, R., & Jacobson, L. (1968). Pygmalion in the classroom. *The Urban Review, 3,* 16–20.

Sabel, C. F. (1993). Studied rust: Building new forms of cooperation in a volatile economy. *Human Relations, 46,* 1133–1171.

Sabel, C. F. (1994). Learning by monitoring: The institutions of economic development. In N. Smelser & R. Swedberg (Eds.), *The handbook of economic sociology* (pp. 136–165). Princeton, NJ: Princeton University Press.

Sachs, J. (2005). *The end of poverty: Economic possibilities for our time.* New York: Penguin Press.

Silbey, S. S. (1981). Case processing—Consumer-protection in an attorney general's office. *Law & Society Review, 15,* 849–881.

Silbey, S. S. (2005). Everyday life and the constitution of legality. In M. D. Jacobs & N. Hanrahan (Eds.), *The Blackwell companion to the sociology of culture* (pp. 332–345). Malden, MA: Blackwell Publishing.

Silbey, S. S., & Bittner, E. (1982). The availability of law. *Law & Policy Quarterly, 4,* 399–434.

Silbey, S. S., Huising, R., & Coslovsky, S. (2009). The sociological citizen: Recognizing relational interdependence in law and organizations. *L' Annee Sociologique, 59,* 201–229.

Simmel, G. (1950). The stranger. In K. H. Wolff (Ed.), *The sociology of Georg Simmel* (pp. 402–408). Glencoe, IL: The Free Press.

Simon, J. (1988). The ideological effects of actuarial practices. *Law & Society Review, 22,* 771–800.

Spitzer, S. (1975). Toward a Marxian theory of deviance. *Social Problems, 22,* 638–651.

Swidler, A. (1986). Culture in action: Symbols and strategies. *American Sociological Review, 51,* 273–286.

Swidler, A. (2001). *Talk of love: How culture matters*. Chicago: University of Chicago Press.

Taylor, C. (1993). To follow a rule.... In P. Bourdieu, C. J. Calhoun, E. LiPuma, & M. Postone (Eds.), *Bourdieu: Critical perspectives* (pp. 45–60). Chicago: University of Chicago Press.

Thompson, S., & Hoggett, P. (1996). Universalism, selectivism, and particularism: Towards a postmodern social policy. *Critical Social Policy, 16*, 21–43.

Uzzi, B. (1996). The sources and consequences of embeddedness for the economic performance of organizations: The network effect. *American Sociological Review, 61*, 674–698.

Wilson, J. Q. (1968). *Varieties of police behavior: The management of law and order in eight communities*. London: Cambridge University Press.

Wrzesniewski, A., & Dutton, J. E. (2001). Crafting a job: Revisioning employees as active grafters of their work. *Academy of Management Review, 26*, 179–201.

Wrzesniewski, A., McCauley, C., Rozin, P., & Schwartz, B. (1997). Jobs, careers, and callings: People's relations to their work. *Journal of Research in Personality, 31*, 21–33.

Yunus, M., & Jolis, A. (2003). *Banker to the poor: Micro-lending and the battle against world poverty*. New York: Public Affairs.

21

Revealing Themes: Applying a Positive Lens to the Chapters on Poverty and Low-Wage Work

Jone L. Pearce
University of California, Irvine

Poverty also means dearth, and there certainly has been a dearth of attention in the organizational sciences to the organizations that grapple with the problem of poverty. Study of the causes and effects of poverty have been central to many of the behavioral and social sciences disciplines—with the glaring exception of the organizational sciences. Only recently have scholars from the range of organizational fields begun to bring their distinctive lens and knowledge to questions of poverty (e.g., Pearce, 2005, 2007; Spreitzer, 2007). Taking the positive organizational scholarship frame has been particularly valuable to this undertaking; with its focus on taking a positive stance toward participants, toward conflicts and barriers, and its emphasis on positive spirals of change, this framing has helped the early efforts to flower into a genuine movement, as is reflected in the mature research in the four chapters in Part V of this book. These works do not focus on changing organizations themselves, but on the organizations that are struggling to effectively change some of society's intractable problems. Organizations that address poverty struggle to be effective, and these chapters demonstrate the ways organizational scientists can help these organizations, as well as advance our organizational theorizing. There can be no social change more positive than effectively addressing the ancient scourge of poverty.

KNOWING THE CAUSES OF POVERTY IS NOT ENOUGH

Our colleagues in sociology and economics have carefully documented the causes of poverty, and each of these chapters reports research on the effectiveness of attempts to address some of these causes. However, sociologists and economists focus on large aggregates and mean differences that have limited the usefulness of their work. In positive organizational scholarship, positive deviance is important and each of these chapters seeks to understand that positive deviance. In Chapter 17, "Positive Change by and for the Working Poor," Carrie Leana and Ellen Kossek approach the problem of low wages from the fields of human resources management and organizational behavior. Their research has thrown into question the common public-policy assumption: that if we can get the poor into entry-level jobs, these jobs will serve as stepping stones lifting these workers out of poverty via promotions to higher paid jobs as these workers learn new skills. Leana and Kossek's research documents the ways in which this idea of organizations as bureaucracies with internal career ladders that entry-level employees can climb is increasingly a myth in the United States. More common are companies with business models based on high-turnover low-wage employees, jobs that rarely (and usually only if employees have obtained additional training at employees' own expense) allow upward mobility. The American economy is no longer dominated by large organizations with internal career ladders, and they propose that the stepping-stone theory needs to be updated. By focusing on the human resources employers actually do (or more accurately, do not) provide for low-wage workers, these authors have illuminated a public policy fiction with real implications for governmental policy for poverty eradication.

Christine Beckman and Brooking Gatewood, in their chapter, "Building Organizations to Change Communities: Educational Entrepreneurs in Poor Urban Areas," evaluate charter schools, one of the most popular interventions to address the failure of so many schools to provide their impoverished students with the skills they need to escape poverty. In the United States, with its decentralized local school districts, publically funded charter schools are seen as a way to avoid the organizational dysfunctions that many see as preventing schools with poor students from improving. They look behind the statistics showing that charter schools sometimes help (positive deviance) and sometimes do not help (negative deviance), and so on average have no effect on student mastery. Drawing on their knowledge of organization theory and entrepreneurship, they identify some surprises about which charter schools improve students' test performance and which survive. They identify formalization and the nature of the schools' network with outside organizations as key factors in their success. These are organizational practices that are unlikely to have been identified by policy makers examining only highly aggregated data and not familiar with what contributes to organizations' effectiveness.

In her chapter, "Navigating Change in the Company of (Dissimilar) Others: Co-Developing Relational Capabilities with Microcredit Clients," Lisa Jones Christensen describes the creation of a training program developed jointly by American MBA students working with fellow students and microfinance clients in Kenya. Drawing on the literature from organizational development, she provides a practical set of steps that can produce more effective business training for small-scale developing-country entrepreneurs. She addresses a widely identified cause of impoverishment—lack of sufficient voice to be able to influence what outside experts assume the poor need. It is an old cliché that outsiders come to poverty eradication with ideologically driven ideas about what must be done, but because they come with badly needed resources, the impoverished try as best they can to salvage something useable from these uninformed outsiders. Experiments with complete decentralization in America's War on Poverty in the 1960s helped demonstrate that simply handing over resources can lead to exploitation, so a combination of outside expertise and local knowledge is needed. This chapter has identified an approach that appeared to be a successful solution—intensive emersion of the outside experts with the local experts and clients, who lived together and worked as peers. Jones Christensen described Ingrid Munro, the founder of the Kenyan microcredit organization who was leery of yet more outside experts who would be more trouble than they were worth, but was ultimately won over by Jones Christensen's innovative program. Only by drawing on insights from organizational development's sensitivity to workplace emotion and dignity could she have developed practices that actually did enact care and cultivate humility among those who arrived from a rich country with technical expertise. Her approach to change suggests that the dominant organizational change model of unfreezing-change-refreezing (Lewin, 1951) is not only misguided but reflects a view of change participants as objects to be broken down and rebuilt by the all-knowing change agent.

Her foreign students' positive and respectful humility in approaching this task suggests a potentially radical reconceptualization of organizational change approaches. She developed a genuinely useful program, and can serve as a model for all of such experts seeking to do effective change work.

Finally, Rodrigo Canales' chapter, "The Stranger as Friend: Loan Officers and Positive Deviance in Microfinance," also examines the organizations behind aggregate statistics that show that microfinance sometimes helps, sometimes hurts, and on average has no effect on impoverished individuals' ability to build successful businesses. As an organization theorist, he examined the increasing standardization and rules these Mexican microfinance organizations faced arising from growing competitive pressures forcing efficiency in what is very labor intensive work. Microcredit clients often do not have the financial records, sales receipts, or documented credit histories that would allow them to obtain financing from traditional banks. Instead, the microfinance model depends on loan officers' detailed social knowledge of loan applicants, a knowledge that is increasingly difficult to obtain as loan officers must support ever more clients when pressured for greater efficiency. Focusing on within-organization comparisons (to control for policies and strategies) he found that not only do different loan-officer actions matter, but that the local organization makes a difference: even though loan officers who bent the rules to develop a more personal relationship with their clients made more profitable loans, they needed the check of colleagues at loan meetings who would ask tough questions, to enable sound loan decisions. This chapter identifies real risks in competition among those providing services to the poor, something underdeveloped in organizational theories.

In addition to the value of these chapters in identifying policy changes, taken together, these chapters also reflect some common insights for those conducting research in the organizational sciences. The dearth of research on organizations that address poverty has distorted our theorizing. Two of these are described here: knowing if your organization has been effective, and how to balance formality with flexibility in organizational practices.

HOW CAN WE KNOW IF WE HAVE BEEN USEFUL?

All four chapters help to highlight the value of a positive lens in identifying the difficulty of knowing what success is for something as complex as poverty eradication. By taking a positive stance toward clients and organizational participants they all note that knowing if change has been useful is more problematic than is usually assumed in the literature. For example, Leana and Kossek note that even in those cases where low-wage employees have climbed into higher paying jobs, some other low-wage employees will take that low-wage job. That is, even a successful individual solution may not be a successful societal one. In fact, managers learn how to manage low-wage employees more effectively (such as, with highly structured monitoring systems) allowing them to base their business models on a low-wage transient workforce, perpetuating the societal costs of poverty. In organizational behavior, scholars usually focus on the managerial objective of individual job performance, and assume that everyone benefits from better individual job performance. However, these authors demonstrate that a more productive individual is not necessarily better for that individual or our societies.

Beckman and Gatewood illustrate how the traditional organization-theory success measure of "organizational survival" does not adequately capture the effectiveness of charter schools. The schools in their study with a strong network of support from local organizations survived despite their low student performance. Their work illustrates the implicit assumption in studies of organizational survival: organizations that survive must be doing so because they are successful in their marketplaces. This ignores the fact that organizations may be poor performers with strong political support.

Jones Christensen directly addresses the uncertainty of knowing whether an organization has been useful, by clearly and heartbreakingly asking: how do we know if we have been useful? This is particularly uncertain for organizations such as hers involved in "training the trainers," leaving those doing the training removed from their clients. Similarly, Rodrigo Canales notes that microfinance originated to help the poorest of the poor, but that its very success has led many traditional financial institutions to begin new microfinance programs. This increased competition has forced all microfinance organizations to adopt efficiency and standardization practices that lead them to focus on loans for the less poor as these loans are more easily evaluated by standardized rules and are less labor intensive. Thus, efficiency, considered to be a good thing in business organizations, can undermine the effectiveness of poverty eradication organizations.

Of course, the problem of identifying effectiveness is not new to those who study non-profit organizations (e.g., Cameron & Whetten, 1983), and organizational psychologists have long lamented the "criterion problem" (for example, that our measures of job performance are much less accurate than we admit; Austin & Villanova, 1992). As these chapter authors all demonstrate, when addressing poverty all of these challenges are exacerbated and more complex than those that have been discussed in the organizational literature. The effectiveness problem with poverty eradication is not what to achieve (that is clear enough), but how best to address a problem with so many mutually reinforcing and interacting causes. When organizational scientists leave the simpler world of business, deciding how we know whether or not an intervention has been successful is challenging. Organizational scientists, led by these chapter authors, are now beginning to address this fundamental issue.

HOW CAN ORGANIZATIONS HAVE BOTH FORMALITY AND FLEXIBILITY?

The challenge of balancing formality (often called accountability) and flexibility (usually called decentralization or empowerment) is one of the most difficult practical problems in organizations. Organizational change involves simultaneously changing both, and that this precarious balance may be undermined in change programs is something that is insufficiently acknowledged. These problems are particularly acute for poverty eradication organizations that must balance the formality that gives funders confidence with the flexibility to meet clients' complex multiple needs. Beckman and Gatewood remind us that formality and standardization can be very valuable in contributing to organizational effectiveness, while Canales documents what superficially appears to be the opposite: that formality and standardization can undermine professional discretion, something that is critical to organizational performance. These authors' reliance on detailed observational and archival analyses of actual organizational practices provides several concrete examples of how formality can successfully coexist with flexibility.

Leana and Kossek contrast top-down (standardized and formal) and bottom-up (flexible and informal) approaches to positive organizational change. They highlight the work of those who have studied job crafting, in which lower-level employees alter their own jobs to make them more personally rewarding. The authors note that when employees can craft their own jobs they like those jobs more, but are silent on exactly how job crafting can be sufficiently constrained to ensure that coordinated performance is not sacrificed. Canales and Jones Christensen do provide specifics that show how these two can be balanced.

Canales describes how flexible loan officers, who have gotten to know their clients, have the tendency to want to help them in any way they can. This makes the loans better (more information), but can lead to bad loans too (loans made on the basis of attachment to clients). Only when loan officers' flexibility was balanced by other loan officers who would refer to standardized guidelines and who would raise concerns about the likelihood of repayment were successful loans made. He also addressed the risk of discretion that evolves into corruption: these microfinance institutions managed this threat with strong formal controls as well as strong values of honesty, such that those who used their discretion for corrupt purposes were rare, but when it happened they were identified by the extensive control system, and quickly fired. Jones Christensen also described specific organizational actions that can combine the advantages of formality with flexibility. Her American foreign experts arrived in Kenya with initial written outlines for the course they wished to develop, formulated in the full knowledge that it might all be abandoned once they had more information about client needs and abilities. This "provisional formal structure" of tentatively held written guidelines is an approach that merits further research.

By digging deeply into what actually happens in these organizations and focusing on the positive, these authors were able to provide real insights into how formality and flexibility can be successfully combined under difficult circumstances. Their work takes theorizing beyond simplistic slogans about empowerment and accountability. At present theorists focus on one or the other and do not treat them as the duality that they are. I hope these chapters help to spur new research that treats both of these together, rather than in isolation.

MORE EFFECTIVE POVERTY ERADICATION WITH ORGANIZATIONAL UNDERSTANDING

Organizational scientists, in particular, can bring unique insights to social problems usually dominated by the economists and sociologists advising governments. Governments in free societies prefer highly centralized solutions. It is hard for governments to let a thousand flowers bloom when they are providing the money. Misspent and wasted money creates headlines that make politicians agitated. Political leaders must be seen as "solving the problem," and often it is assumed that the only way they can accomplish this goal is to impose top-down controls and reporting requirements. Those responsible for governmental policies want them to be right the first time, and dread a flexibility that will inevitably result in damaging disclosures. This makes the social scientists who study large social aggregates—economists and sociologists—more congenial to policy makers. Organizational scientists (and everyone else) know the performance costs of large, highly centralized, inflexible organizations, but heretofore, these types of organizations were seen as the only politically safe way to address social problems. These chapter authors have helped illuminate the need for local flexibility, highlighting how a positive lens can lead to a fundamental re-examination of our theoretical assumptions. Leana and Kossek demonstrate that sweeping assumptions about low-wage work are inaccurate and identify both top-down and bottom-up alternatives. Beckman and Gatewood show how the very flexibility built into charters for schools allowed sufficient experimentation and innovation to identify differing pathways to survival. Canales documents the importance of allowing microfinance loan officers sufficient discretion to innovate. Jones Christensen's description of their highly flexible and innovative training program for poor entrepreneurs demonstrates what can be done when different organizations come together, on their own, without funding-driven guidelines.

By focusing on some of the most intractable change challenges using a positive lens, these chapters provide real insight into our theories of change. When our understanding of large-scale system change is dominated by the study of managers' interests in changing their subordinates in large business organizations, we produce only one model of change, and perhaps not even the most effective one for any organization. Undertaking difficult societal change highlights the fact that we may not have a clear idea of what the change should be or how we can know if it has been effective or not. All large-scale organizational change is complex, and it is more likely that the change agents are often as uncertain about whether or not they have been useful as these honest authors have been. In addition, poverty eradication is such a difficult task, usually funded by third parties that want accountability but must be responsive to clients' complex and changing needs. These are challenges that all organizations face, but the difficulty of the work of organizations seeking to eradicate poverty, and the excellent detailed data collection and analyses these authors have conducted help remind us that this is a duality insufficiently addressed in current theorizing. Scholars talk about accountability and about decentralization, but, unlike these authors, do not address how these two can be balanced in practice. These authors provide rich data and insights that can form the basis for powerful new theorizing on this important issue. These chapters are models of both, how organizational sciences can contribute to positive social change by bringing their frameworks and knowledge to the challenges of poverty eradication, and the organizational insights available to those who look beyond business.

REFERENCES

Austin, J. T., & Villanova, P. (1992). The criterion problem: 1917–1992. *Journal of Applied Psychology, 77*, 836–874.

Cameron, K. S., & Whetten, D. A. (1983). *Organizational effectiveness: A comparison of multiple models.* New York: Academic Press.

Lewin, K. (1951). *Field theory in social science.* New York: Harper.

Pearce, J. L. (2005). Organizational scholarship and the eradication of global poverty. *Academy of Management Journal, 48*, 970–972.

Pearce, J. L. (2007). Organizational behavior unchained. *Journal of Organizational Behavior, 28*, 811–814.

Spreitzer, G. (2007). Giving peace a chance: Organizational leadership, empowerment, and peace. *Journal of Organizational Behavior, 28*, 1077–1080.

Part VI

Conclusion

22

The Response: What Does This Book Contribute to the Understanding of Social Change and Organizations?

Karen Golden-Biddle
Boston University

Jane E. Dutton
University of Michigan

Elana Feldman
Boston University

We began this book with a belief that social change and organizations are deeply connected, and that a positive lens can be used to unlock new ways of understanding and enabling change processes. Along the way, the chapters portray and unpack this connection by disclosing new lines of sight on prevailing theories, for example, elaborating understanding of factors leading to organizational success and survival through analyzing dual pressures of legitimacy and accountability in charter schools (Beckman & Gatewood, Chapter 18), or by using practice theory in the empirical context of sustainability to propose an alternative view of change agency as a distributed phenomenon (Feldman, Chapter 9). The chapters also unpack the connection by excavating stories and the embedded wisdom that might otherwise not have been told, for example, Sawa Heroes (Branzei, Chapter 2), and by bringing forward important pathways for the analysis and practice of change, for example, alternative models of philanthropy (Meyerson & Wernick, Chapter 5).

As well, along the way, chapters not only affirm but also complicate the notion of *positive*. In affirming positive, the contributors explicitly detail or assume that tending to the positive does not mean overlooking or ignoring the negative, nor does it mean the absence of conflict or differences of opinion. Indeed, examining social change focuses attention squarely on very negative human conditions of poverty, environmental degradation, differential access to quality education, health care disparities, access to quality treatment, and so on. Rather than being ignored as occurs in society, these negative conditions are squarely faced as the chapter authors examine individual and collective action undertaken to create alternative and more desired scenarios. Additionally, some chapters (Sonenshein, Chapter 3; Riddell et al., Chapter 8; Pratt et al., Chapter 13) explicitly complicate the idea of positive by connecting differences of opinion and conflict with notions of generativity and intergroup harmony. Other chapters complicate the positive by suggesting that positive is not a universal condition in social change efforts. That is, even in change processes oriented to creating desired alternative futures, some actors can be disadvantaged, for example, in developing sustainable coffee production practices (Perez-Aleman, Chapter 10), without explicit efforts to build capability at the local level, farmers and economies would have been disadvantaged. The question of who benefits and who is disadvantaged or even harmed from efforts for desired social change is an important one. Similarly, the chapters also complicate the positive temporally, noting that what is positive at one point in time is not necessarily considered positive at another point. Thus, all of the chapters connect the positive and negative to illuminate new possibilities for human agency and theorizing the connection between social change and organizations.

Although no concluding chapter can fully traverse the terrain visited in the 16 chapters and four commentaries, we end this book by looking across these contributions. In particular, we explore the ways they add value to the field of organization studies through uncovering and enriching the theoretical elements of resources, processes, and outcomes that help to explain how social change is imagined, enacted, and accomplished in and of organizations and organizing efforts. We close with an invitation to you, the reader, to join us in further exploring this meaningful frontier of research that connects organizations and social change.

RESOURCES AND SOCIAL CHANGE: UNCOVERED AND ENRICHED

Resources are part of the currency through which change is accomplished. Some organizational researchers conceptualize resources as forms of wealth or forms of support that have economic, social, or emotional value (e.g., Rousseau & Ling, 2007). Other researchers think of resources as elements that are dynamically produced in the doing of activities (e.g., Feldman, 2004). Either way, resources fuel and enable change, which makes them central to theories of social change. Resources have been an important element in theorizing from a positive perspective on organizations as they help researchers see and theorize how new capabilities and capacities emerge and facilitate change processes (Dutton & Glynn, 2008). In addition, resource creation and resource use are critical elements in capturing the generative dynamics of social change.

The chapters illuminate two sets of insights about resources, social change, and organizations. First, they illuminate new resources and resource flows that differ from resources typically considered by organizational scholars. Second, the chapters embellish and elaborate how more "typical" resources might be central to social change processes and outcomes.

Highlighting the Power of "New" Resources

The book's chapters underline the importance of human-based resources in fueling and enabling social change processes. These are resources that are ephemeral in the sense of immediate measurability, but substantive in terms of their role in enabling and fueling social change at the individual and collective levels.

For example, one resource mentioned in many of the chapters is energy, or the sense of vitality or effervescence of an individual or group. A positive lens spotlights the role of energy as a critical resource for individual and collective activities (Spreitzer, Lam, & Quinn, 2011). When mentioned in the context of social change, one appreciates the role that various forms of this resource play in helping collectives stay engaged and dedicated to an alternative way of living (Rimac et al., Chapter 4), sustaining interest in making a difference with staff treating children struggling with mental health (Wells, Chapter 14), or in maintaining loan officers' dedication in working solutions with microfinance clients (Canales, Chapter 20). In all of these cases, energy is theorized and treated as a resource that importantly fuels the change process, which is particularly critical when change agents are confronting challenging and often depleting issues.

Hope is both an individual and collective resource that enables change. Several of the book's authors theorize hope as pivotal to creating and sustaining social change. Branzei (Chapter 2) elaborates how hope is produced and reproduced through three core relational processes that enable change agents to initiate and accelerate change. Golden-Biddle and Correia (Chapter 12) theorize how hope fosters change momentum that spreads and sustains change by loosening the hold on prior expectations, opening up possibilities, and cultivating trust. Together these chapters paint hope as a vital and dynamic resource that can be actively cultivated through both individual and collective actions. Both chapters build on the core idea of hope as relational accomplishment (Carlsen, Hagen, & Mortensen, 2011; Ludema, Wilmot, & Srivastva, 1997) and showcase the role of leaders in fostering hope that fuels action in dire and challenging situations.

Beyond energy and hope, the chapters point to personal worth (Rimac et al., Chapter 4) and identity security (Pratt et al., Chapter 13) as examples of states that alter the capacities of individuals or groups to think, feel, or behave in ways that enable openings for new practices and ways of thinking to emerge and movement toward change to occur. A positive lens allows glimpses into individual and collective states that take on new significance as enablers of change. At the same time that these resources fuel the change process, they are conditions that are valuable in and of themselves. Thus, expanding consideration of resources important to social change processes widens appreciation of psychological and social states that are beneficial human goods that have value independent of the outcomes that they produce.

Enriching Understanding of Resources Known to Be Important to Social Change

The chapters are replete with insights about resources that organizational scholars have identified as critical to social change. The chapters add nuance to these previous accounts by illuminating additional pathways by which these resources alter change processes and change outcomes. For example, several chapters affirm the importance of positive relationships as critical to change outcomes and processes. Positive relationships manifest themselves in various forms including high levels of intergroup trust, which, in the case of the Great Bear Rainforest (Riddell et al., Chapter 8), created a platform for developing innovative solutions around forest preservation. In Canales account (Chapter 20), trust was the resource that facilitated loan officers' customization of solutions for microcredit clients who were having a tough time meeting their obligations. In these cases, positive relationships functioned as resources that actors in the change process drew from in creating flexible and creative solutions on the ground, as part of the social change process.

Legitimacy, collective efficacy, and positive emotions are additional resources identified in various chapters as states that facilitate change by building strength and momentum and breaking down barriers that could arise in the change process. A positive lens helps us see how these resources function in social processes to build capability and broaden options that make change more achievable and thus more likely. So, for example, Sonenshein's (Chapter 3) description of issue selling illustrates how change agents can cultivate legitimacy of an issue's meaning by how they frame the content of an issue. His chapter reminds us that small moves and contextually appropriate actions can create resources that ease the change process. The Pratt et al. account (Chapter 13) of physician–administrator conflicts reminds us that not all positive emotions are unequivocally helpful in change processes as positive emotions can at times promote exclusion dynamics that retard change. Pratt and his coauthors identify what they call satisfied positivity, which contains elements of creative abrasion. These authors develop an argument for why this form of positivity is more facilitative of change in the context they were studying. Further, several of the chapters highlight how resources created in one phase of the change process can fuel and resource generation in another. Howard-Grenville (Chapter 11) notes in her commentary that this resourcing process fits an image of "unfolding and unpredictable emergence rather than replication." Thus, understanding resource dynamics in change processes—how they are created and what difference they make—is a critical contribution of application of a positive lens.

━━━━━━━━━━

PROCESSES AND SOCIAL CHANGE: UNCOVERED AND ENRICHED

The chapters in the book also add to what we know about processes and social change. Organizational researchers have created a large body of work that examines organizational change (Armenakis & Bedeian, 1999; Pettigrew, Woodman, & Cameron, 2001; Weick & Quinn, 1999). The process of change, central to effective implementation, has been conceptualized in two primary ways. Some organizational researchers conceive the change process longitudinally as unfolding over time through a series of steps or phases, and as requiring a significant break from the past (Lewin, 1947; Swidler, 1986). Other researchers think about change processually (Langley, 1999): change as itself comprised of processes that are temporally constituted and emergent (Tsoukas & Chia, 2002). Process has also been an important theorizing element from a positive perspective on change in organizations, as researchers disclose generative dynamics of organizing and theorize how they lead to human flourishing and capability development (Cameron, Dutton, & Quinn, 2003; Cameron & Spreitzer, 2011; Dutton & Glynn, 2008).

Yet, in focusing on the phenomenon of social change, the chapters in this book do not only detail process. They also show how people's desires, fears, and hopes for a better world inspire the creation of alternative possibilities for the common good. It is this grounding in desired future potential impact, regardless of problem domain and level of analysis, which enables the chapters to illuminate two sets of insights about processes of social change and organization. First, they affirm attention on human agency in social change, elaborating in particular the projective element (Emirbayer & Mische, 1998) and its significance in accomplishing social change. Second, they elaborate and extend understanding of generative dynamics in change.

Enriching Understanding of the Projective Element of Human Agency in Social Change

The book's chapters emphasize the significance of human agency, by which we mean, following Emirbayer & Mische (1998, p. 962), a "temporally embedded process of social engagement, informed by the past ... but also oriented to the future and toward the present." Given the emphasis on social change, many of the chapters highlight the future-oriented temporal dimension of human agency referred to as "a projective capacity to imagine alternative possibilities" (Emirbayer & Mische, 1998, p. 962) as a central process for generating and enabling social change. In particular, the commentary chapter by Reay (Chapter 16) highlights that paying attention to future alternative possibilities, instead of becoming distracted by barriers, unlocks capacities and processes that facilitate social change.

Some chapters disclose processes that enable consideration of future-oriented possibilities for social change at the individual and collective levels. Chapter 9 by Feldman shows how artifacts can act as important mediators of individual change agency by opening up individuals' attunement to, and exploration of, new possibilities for practicing sustainability. At a more macro-level, Chapter 7 by Hoffman et al. highlights how hybrid forms of organizations use their missions and views of their role in society in ways that call forth positive meaning that opens new possibilities for thinking about goals, engaging in practices, and partnering with others.

Other chapters disclose the deeply relational dimension of "experimental enactments" (Emirbayer & Mische, 1998, p. 988), defined as "alternative courses of action…tentatively enacted in response to currently emerging situations." Such experiments help to test and revise desired future scenarios enabling the accomplishment of social change. Branzei (Chapter 2) identifies three relational forms of agency (referencing, relating, and rotating) that infuse hope in emerging change situations people regard as hopeless. Christensen (Chapter 19) details the enactment of a three-way partnership of American and Kenyan universities and the founder of a microfinance organization, Jamii Bora, "to co-create something better than any party could create alone." Aware of their limits as experts, U.S. members sought "in general, to do things on their terms," a stance that involved simple everyday things like playing games and walking slowly with the older Jamii Bora members. In Chapter 12 by Golden-Biddle and Correia, trialing the new model of care enabled physicians to experience working in a "TRIO" with different clinical professions.

At a more macro level, these enactments are expressed through the creation of new associations by local coffee producers and government (Perez-Aleman, Chapter 10) in response to globally adopted standards for improving ecological sustainability; of two types of nontraditional philanthropic foundations (Meyerson & Wernick, Chapter 5) that, instead of funding large existing organizations, focus on funding local grassroots efforts or using venture capital to quickly scale start up efforts; and of the charter school movement (Beckman & Gatewood, Chapter 18), founded to create access to quality education for children in high poverty, urban communities. Finally, still other chapters disclose how these enactments can often be enabled by quite small moves, as in loan officers (Canales, Chapter 20) who bend rules to address client needs in response to emerging situations in their lives; or in supervisors who, after training about work-family issues (Leana & Kossek, Chapter 17), inquire about people's families and how these inquiries led to positive outcomes for low income workers.

Highlighting a Broader Repertoire of Generative Dynamics for Social Change

The chapters in this book are chock-full of generative dynamics, defined by organizational researchers as "life-building, capability-enhancing, capacity-creating dynamics in and of organizations that can explain human flourishing and the cultivation of strengths across levels of analysis" (Dutton & Glynn, 2008, p. 694). Generative dynamics are particularly important for understanding how challenging change is accomplished over time, as they highlight how elements in the change process are transformed in ways that increase or build capability or capacity.

Some chapters elaborate understanding of generative dynamics by situating accounts of personal development within collective projects for a common good. As a result, these chapters show how generative dynamics can transform individuals and, as discussed further in the outcomes section, how that transformation can positively alter the change process. For example, in Chapter 14 by Wells a "system of care paradigm" becomes the foundation for shifting the organization's control over care to the children and their caregivers. This loosening of control along with attention on strengths rather than deficits of the children enables managers to amplify support for frontline clinicians to take loving action toward the children. In Chapter 8 by Riddell et al., individual members of the ENGOs encountered situations "calling forth their own transformation" that enabled them to alter contentious relationship dynamics and enlist others "into collaboration toward a shared vision." Chapter 15 by Myers and Wooten describes a training session for health nurses and midwives about engaging patients as partners in co-creating health. In the session, practitioners themselves engage discovery learning while also being taught to facilitate a "discovery learning" group process that cultivates a safe space for patients to share problems.

Other chapters point to a new form of generative dynamic by highlighting the tensions that surface in the social change process, for example between economic and social goals, stakeholders' differing visions for the future, or hypothesized solutions. This form of generative dynamic complicates positivity by regarding tension as not only positive but generative because it holds the potential for opening up new possibilities. Tensions are not to be resolved, but rather the differences held so that they may generate and open up consideration of alternative actions and solutions for going forward (Howard-Grenville, Chapter 11). The generativity of tension emerges in holding rather than eliminating differences. For example, Sonenshein (Chapter 3) describes a process of "generative dialoguing," which is discourse about a social issue that widens and enriches conversation by enabling the airing of "productive differences" that can sustain debate. Similarly, two other chapters highlight the generativity of tension in retaining differing or oppositional views and forces for change. Pratt et al. (Chapter 13) use the idea "creative abrasion" to describe the importance of holding the tension in identities between physicians and administrators as a way to loosen up intractable identity conflicts. Rather than eliminating difference, they emphasize the need to build upon and retain differences "in the service of a greater whole." Riddell et al. (Chapter 8) use the idea of creative destruction to describe a "release" in the standstill among opposing views of stakeholders trying to reach a solution on the Great Bear Rainforest and the subsequent opening up of new possibilities for interacting. In this process, the ENGO leaders come to see their opponents differently.

Finally, some chapters disclose a form of generative dynamic that is other-focused, joining recent literature calling attention to other-focused psychological processes grounded in a desire to benefit others. For example, prosocial sensemaking (Grant, Dutton, & Russo, 2008, p. 903) reveals how employees interpret their own and their company's actions and identities in "more caring terms." Similarly, "perspective-taking" is an other-focused psychological process that, in enabling prosocial motivation, strengthens the association between intrinsic motivation and creativity (Grant & Berry, 2011). Other-focused social processes are similar to other-focused psychological processes in their basis in a desire to benefit others, but differ in their emphasis and explicit attention on organizing collective efforts. In our chapters, examples of other-focused social processes include the four deliberate processes constituting the engagement process that kept American students and faculty focused on "the men and women in Jamii Bora rather than our peers or a class grade" (Christensen, Chapter 19), and the "tollgate" mechanism in a new model of inpatient care (Golden-Biddle & Correia, Chapter 12) that keeps attention focused on the patient and on getting the patient well rather than organizational or clinician convenience.

In sum, the chapters raise new possibilities for exploring the underlying motives and core processes that inform, shape, and enable efforts to envision and create social change. The application of a positive lens focuses researchers on what in the process builds capacity and capability and it names these dynamics generative. The next section addresses how the lens opens up considerations around the outcomes associated with social change.

OUTCOMES AND SOCIAL CHANGE: UNCOVERED AND ENRICHED

Social change efforts are often undertaken with a specific, desired outcome in mind. For instance, those involved in the effort may seek to improve how they serve a deserving client base or to protect a particular environmental resource. However, the chapters in this book remind us that the positive effects of change efforts are not limited to single, narrow outcomes that are measurable at particular "endpoints." Instead, a host of beneficial outcomes flow from social change processes.

The authors of the four part commentaries (Steckler & Bartunek, Chapter 6; Howard-Grenville, Chapter 11; Reay, Chapter 16; Pearce, Chapter 21) all point to the broad scope of possible outcomes that may result from social change efforts. Commentators Steckler and Bartunek explain that such efforts often produce numerous beneficial effects because they create "ripples beyond specific target beneficiaries to strengthen and improve communities in proximity and society at large, both in the 'now' and into the future." This eloquent statement draws attention to two categories of positive effects beyond the focal outcome fueling the change effort. First, effects may be seen at multiple levels: society, the organization, and the individual. Second, although they may be less overt, strengths—at the level of the individual as well as the collective—may emerge and live on beyond the specific and intended change.

Multilevel Effects: Positive Outcomes for Society, the Organization, and the Individual

Looking across the parts of the book, there is ample evidence that social change efforts often produce positive effects at three levels: society, the organization, and the individuals engaged in the change effort.

Societal Level

First, social change efforts are often directed toward large-scale outcomes that represent amelioration of key social problems in areas such as poverty, the environment, and health care delivery. The chapters in the book broaden our thinking about these outcomes by providing new insights into the range and magnitude of positive societal outcomes that are possible, even in domains where problems have been characterized as intractable.

Examples of large-scale positive effects span the four primary parts of the book. In the *Change Agency*, Part II, we see positive outcomes in the form of reduced workplace discrimination or improved coordination for disaster relief efforts (Sonenshein, Chapter 3), greater diversity in philanthropic funding of social change initiatives (Meyerson & Wernick, Chapter 5), and a sense of inclusion and dignity for members of Sekem (Rimac et al., Chapter 4). In the *Environment and Sustainability*, Part III, strides are made in terms of increasing the availability of environmentally friendly products (Hoffman et al., Chapter 7), negotiating solutions to crucial issues of conservation (Riddell et al., Chapter 8), and shifting production practices to promote ecological sustainability (Perez-Aleman, Chapter 10). In the *Health Care*, Part IV, care is improved for hospital patients (Golden-Biddle & Correia, Chapter 12), children with mental health challenges (Wells, Chapter 14), and African-American women and their babies (Myers & Wooten, Chapter 15). Finally, in the *Poverty and Low-Wage Work*, Part V, progress is made in creating better working conditions for the poor (Leana & Kossek, Chapter 17), improving access to quality education (Beckman & Gatewood, Chapter 18), and alleviating poverty in Kenya and Mexico (Christensen, Chapter 19; Canales, Chapter 20).

The chapters in this book help us notice and identify less sweeping societal-level effects as well. These more micro outcomes, which seem to flow from the everyday "tweaking" of commitments and actions of those engaged in the change process, are powerful in that they offer "along the way" benefits as well as potentially adding up over time to create more measurable, meaningful change outcomes, such as those mentioned earlier. For example, in Chapter 14, Wells explains how single encounters between a mental health worker and child can become infused with loving actions, thus helping incrementally to improve children's mental health overall. Similarly, in Chapter 15, Myers and Wooten discuss how the co-creation of health approaches developed by Focus on Pregnancy and County Health Coalition led to better maternal and child health.

Organizational Level

There may be positive effects for the organization's internal "workings" (e.g., learning processes may become more sustainable, leaders may become more attuned to the importance of human agency) and/or external interactions (e.g., stronger relationships with external partners and customers). For example, hybrid organizations develop deep, mutually beneficial ties with their consumers because of their shared social values (Hoffman et al., Chapter 7), hospital physicians and administrators find new paths to collaboration and greater intergroup harmony (Pratt et al., Chapter 13), and front line mental health workers become not only more effective but also able to be more loving in delivering care (Wells, Chapter 14). In addition, Mexican microfinance organizations are better able to navigate inherent contradictions through the positive deviance in certain loan officers' enactment of organizational rules (Canales, Chapter 20).

Individual Level

Individuals involved in the change process also experience a range of positive outcomes. For example, in Chapter 3 by Sonenshein, a woman receives several major promotions because of her efforts to provide equal employment opportunities for women and minorities. In Chapter 10 (Perez-Aleman), the coffee industry's shift to more sustainable production practices leads to the inclusion rather than exclusion of poor coffee producers in learning and using more environmentally friendly growing practices. Similarly, in Chapter 13 (Pratt et al.), physicians and health care administrators, who often clash over resources and identity, come to see each other as well as themselves in new ways. Other positive outcomes at the individual level include an improved work environment and opportunity to undertake more meaningful work for health care employees at ThedaCare (Golden-Biddle & Correia, Chapter 12), increased engagement for mental health front line staff (Wells, Chapter 14), and greater job satisfaction and expression of prosocial motivation for business school faculty (Christensen, Chapter 19).

Enduring, Strength-Based Outcomes

Looking across the chapters in this book, we also noticed the humanity evidenced during the change processes. The stories in these chapters are not only about hope; in their reading they inspire hope that social change benefiting the common good can be accomplished. In paying closer attention to these stories, we began to see change as itself bolstering human strengths, commonly defined as good or beneficial qualities of a person. In psychology, Peterson and Seligman (2004) have developed a "VIA" classification of six character strengths that emerge with consistency across a wide range of philosophical and religious discussions. In addition to changes occurring in individual expressions of these strengths, we saw glimpses in the chapters of changes in collective strengths as well.

In some of the chapters, these strengths were called forth explicitly and named, while in others they were quietly implicit. Regardless of whether they were trumpeted or whispered, three particular strengths embedded in the chapter stories caught our attention: humility, compassion, and courage. Such strengths are particularly significant in that they are enduring—that is, they "last" beyond the so-called "end" of a specific change process. The existence of these strengths reminds us that change efforts rarely have a fixed endpoint, but rather involve an ongoing—and sometimes cyclical—process.

Humility

This strength, which "entails a deeply held belief of shared human limits and worth that shapes how individuals view themselves (objectively), others (appreciatively) and new information (openly)" (Owens, Rowatt, &

Wilkins, 2011, p. 262), is bolstered in change as when individuals or collectives embrace the possibility of being wrong and the need to rely on others' wisdom. In some instances in the chapters, humility was an intentionally sought outcome. For example, Christensen (Chapter 19) explains how the faculty and students from the U.S. business school cultivated collective humility. From the outset, they acknowledged they would make mistakes and underscored the need to learn from their local Kenyan partners by living and interacting with them. The students amplified the development of individual humility in affording each other "room" to enact humility in his/her own way.

In other chapters, the development of humility was not an intentional goal but rather a beneficial byproduct of the change process. Based on their experiences over the course of multiple interventions, the Sawa Heroes (Branzei, Chapter 2) came to realize they needed help from local partners to effect change, thus demonstrating their individual humility. In Chapter 7 (Hoffman et al.), Bena Burdá became a successful leader and majority-owner of Maggie's Organics, but remained personally humble: she knew she had to maintain "lasting friendships with employees" and "supplier partnerships based on interpersonal connections" because she could not achieve her social mission alone. Finally, in Chapter 13 (Pratt et al.), the hospital physicians and administrators gained humility as a group as they worked through the change process. As they began to identify not just with their separate professional groups but also with an inclusive, superordinate group, they accepted that, despite differences of opinion, each group had something worthwhile to contribute to solving common problems.

Compassion

This strength centrally involves the noticing, feeling, and responding to others' suffering (Lilius, Kanov, Dutton, Worline, & Maitlis, 2011). In addition to the individual-level expression, it is the "reliable capacity of members of a collective to notice, feel, and respond to suffering" (Lilius, Worline, Dutton, Kanov, & Maitlis, 2011, p. 874). In the contributions to this book, the augmenting of compassion as strength results from seeking to care more effectively or fully for deserving populations.

Given that compassion emerges often most vividly in settings where the focus is on delivering care to others, it is not surprising that the most compelling instances of compassion emerge in *Health Care*, Part IV of the book. Indeed, we see strong evidence of compassion as a reliable and last-ing strength in three of the healthcare chapters. In Chapter 15 (Myers & Wooten), two agencies serving pregnant African-American women devel-oped care approaches that went beyond addressing issues of health, thus encouraging providers to cultivate and express compassion in their rela-tionships with patients. Focus on Pregnancy's model emphasized the need to help with psychosocial as well as medical needs, while County Health Coalition's directed attention toward issues related to racial disparity. In both organizations, caring for patients shifted from transactional "visits" to com-passionate "healing relationships." Similarly, by making the patient more central to effective health care delivery, the ThedaCare collaborative care model (Golden-Biddle & Correia, Chapter 12) encouraged and bolstered col-lective compassion, as providers shifted to view each patient as a human with unique care needs, rather than as a medical condition. Finally, in Chapter 14 (Wells), managers enabled front line staff to develop and express collective compassion, in the form of "loving actions," for mentally ill children.

Courage

The strength-based outcome of courage, or "the ability to do something that frightens one" (Oxford Dictionaries Online, 2011), is portrayed in several chapters. Courage has been classified by psychologists (Park & Peterson, 2003, p. 35; Peterson & Seligman, 2004) as a character strength; it is defined as "emotional strengths that involve the exercise of will to accomplish goals in the face of opposition, external or internal." When scholars consider courageous individual action in the context of organi-zations, they note that while action on the one hand is constrained by organizational rules and form, it at the same time remains possible for individuals to express "principled action that violates the status quo" (Worline & Quinn, 2003).

While collective courageous action is possible, in the chapters of this book, courage is depicted as an individual strength bolstered in change processes. Issue sellers (Sonenshein, Chapter 3) are good examples of why courage may result from involvement in change. Individuals who engage in issue selling are often motivated by passion, but this motivation may not be enough to persevere in the face of adversity and initial failures. In order to push forward, past ineffective attempts, issue sellers must build deep stores of courage. For instance, one issue seller's first attempt to secure domestic partnership benefits for gay and lesbian employees at HP was a failure because of her tactics. However, rather than accepting defeat, she drew on her courage to try again, this time with a different (and more successful) approach.

Another example of courage resulting from social change lies in Chapter 20 (Canales). The "Spirit of the Law" loan officers at the microfinance organization in Mexico are likely to rely on courage more than their "Letter of the Law" counterparts because, by bending the rules of their employer, they expose themselves to greater risk in case of defaulted loans. Even though their flexible approach enables them in many situations to be better at their jobs, they are likely to be aware that their less orthodox approach will come under scrutiny should something go awry. Their courage likely develops iteratively: each time they apply discretion with successful results, they add to their reserve of courage for future discretionary actions.

Additional Strengths

Although we elaborated only three strength-based outcomes—those we saw as appearing consistently throughout this book—there are hints in several chapters of other strengths that need further exploration in future research. For instance, in Chapter 4, Sekem's daily circle practice leads to a strength centered on inclusivity. In this chapter, the participation of Sekem's members in the daily circle practice seems to spur the development of a collective participatory strength that "trickles down" to the individual level as well. Similarly, in Chapter 7 (Hoffman et al.), there appears to be a symbiotic, hybrid organization-customer strength that bears additional elaboration. We see the positive lens as inviting further inquiry into how the accomplishment of social change relies on and builds human strengths that help us explain how a social change process unfolds and how it leaves residues that live on beyond the immediate change effort.

CONCLUSION

The field of organization studies is starting to pay more attention to the connection between organizations and social change. It is represented in the various streams of research described in the introduction. It also is represented in the vision of the Academy of Management (n.d.): "We inspire and enable a better world through our scholarship and teaching about management and organizations."

As we move forward, we are enthused and inspired by the contributions in this book made by applying a positive lens in the study of social change and organizations. The stories told, themes revealed, and theories explicated herein at once reveal explanation and dare us to imagine how organizations might better serve the common good. Importantly, the chapters, in the detailing of resources, processes, and outcomes associated with social change, help enrich and uncover new ways of understanding and enabling change processes. We end by inviting you to join in the growing and deepening inquiry into the connection between organizations and social change, and the use of a positive lens to open up new ways of thinking and theorizing that have been overlooked. Just imagine the difference our collective inquiries could make for our field's work and our world.

REFERENCES

Academy of Management. (n.d.). Vision. Retrieved October 19, 2011, from http://strategic plan.aomonline.org/

Armenakis, A. A., & Bedeian, A. G. (1999). Organizational change: A review of theory and research in the 1990s. *Journal of Management, 25*, 293–315.

Cameron, K. S., & Spreitzer, G. M. (2011). *The Oxford handbook of positive organizational scholarship*. New York: Oxford University Press.

Cameron, K., Dutton, J., & Quinn, R. (2003). *Positive organizational scholarship*. San Francisco: Berrett-Koehler Publishers.

Carlsen, A., Hagen, I. L., & Mortensen, T. F. (2011). Imagining hope in organizations: From individual goal attainment to horizons of relational possibility. In K. S Cameron & G. Spreitzer (Eds.), *Handbook of positive organizational scholarship*. Oxford: Oxford University Press. Oxford Dictionaries Online. (2011). Courage. Retrieved from http://oxforddictionaries.com/definition/courage?region=us

Dutton, J. E., & Glynn, M. A. (2008). Positive organizational scholarship. In J. Barling, C. P. Cooper, S. R. Clegg, & C. L. Cooper (Eds.), *The SAGE handbook of organizational behavior* (Volume 1, pp. 693–712). London: Sage Publications Ltd.

Emirbayer, M., & Mische, A. (1998). What is agency? *American Journal of Sociology, 103*, 962–1023.

Feldman, M. S. (2004). Resources in emerging structures and processes of change. *Organization Science, 15*, 295–309.

Grant, A. M., & Berry, J. W. (2011). The necessity of others is the mother of invention: Intrinsic and prosocial motivations, perspective taking and creativity. *Academy of Management Journal, 54*, 73–96.

Grant, A. M., Dutton, J. E., & Rosso, B. D. (2008). Giving commitment: Employee support programs and the prosocial sensemaking process. *Academy of Management Journal, 51*, 898–918.

Langley, A. (1999). Strategies for theorizing from process data. *Academy of Management Review, 24*, 691.

Lewin, K. (1947). *Field theory in social science: Selected theoretical papers.* New York: Harper & Row.

Ludema, J. D., Wilmot, T. B., & Srivastva, S. (1997). Organizational hope: Reaffirming the constructive task of social and organizational inquiry. *Human Relations, 50*, 1015–1952.

Lilius, J. M., Worline, M. C., Dutton, J. E., Kanov, J. M., & Maitlis, S. (2011). Understanding compassion capability. *Human Relations, 64*, 873–899.

Lilius, J. M., Kanov, J., Dutton, J. E., Worline, M. C., & Maitlis, S. (2011). Compassion revealed: What we know about compassion at work (and where we need to know more). In K. S. Cameron & G. M. Spreitzer (Eds.), *The Oxford handbook of positive organizational scholarship*. New York: Oxford University Press.

Owens, B. P., Rowatt, W. C., & Wilkins, A. L. (2011). Exploring the relevance and implications of humility in organizations. In K. S. Cameron & G. M. Spreitzer (Eds.), *The Oxford handbook of positive organizational scholarship*. New York: Oxford University Press.

Park, N., & Peterson, C. M. (2003). Virtues and organizations. In K. Cameron, J. Dutton, & R. Quinn (Eds.). *Positive organizational scholarship*. San Francisco: Berrett-Koehler Publishers.

Peterson, C., & Seligman, M. (2004). *Character strengths and virtues: A handbook and classification* (1st ed.). New York: Oxford University Press.

Pettigrew, A. M., Woodman, R. W., & Cameron, K. S. (2001). Studying organizational change and development: Challenges for future research. *Academy of Management Journal, 44*, 697–713.

Rousseau, D. M., & Ling, K. (2007). Commentary: Following the resources in positive organizational relationships. In J. E. Dutton & B. R. Ragins (Eds.), *Exploring positive relationships at work: Building a theoretical and research foundation* (1st ed., pp. 373–386). Mahwah, NJ: Lawrence Erlbaum.

Spreitzer, G. M., Lam, C. F., & Quinn, R. W. (2011). Human energy in organizations: Implications for POS from six interdisciplinary streams. In K. S. Cameron & G. M. Spreitzer (Eds.), *The Oxford handbook of positive organizational scholarship*. New York: Oxford University Press.

Swidler, A. (1986). Culture in action: Symbols and strategies. *American Sociological Review, 51*, 273–286.

Tsoukas, H., & Chia, R. (2002). On organizational becoming: Rethinking organizational change. *Organization Science, 13*, 567–582.

Weick, K. E., & Quinn, R. E. (1999). Organizational change and development. *Annual Review of Psychology, 50*, 361–386.

Author Index

Subject Index

Mobilization, 33, 40–41
Modeling, 30, 31, 34, 35–36, 39
Moral dialogue, 32, 37–38
Moral vision, 32, 38
Morphing, 31, 36
Munro, Ingrid, 403–405, 406–409, 413, 416, 417, 465
Mutuality, 33, 39–40

N

Nakaseke Community Development Initiative (NACODI), 27
Narratives, 28
  personal, 168–170
National Committee for Responsive Philanthropy, 94
National Institutes of Health, 311
National School Lunch Program (NSLP), 384
National Work-Family and Health Network, 363, 373
Negotiations, in Great Bear Rainforest case, 159–160
Nestle, 207
Network creation to build know-how and resources, 210–214
Neumann Kaffee, 206
New Leaders for New Schools, 99
NewSchools Venture Fund, 95–96, 97–100
Nicaragua, 213, 218
Nike, GreenXchange, 229
No Child Left Behind, 298–299
Non-profit organizations, 94, 97, 102, 134, 145, 380, 467
North Star Fund, 102, 104
Nurse(s)
  partnering with pharmacists, 259–260
  partnering with physicians, 260
Nurse-midwifery ideology, 318, 326
Nursing leadership, 248–249; see also Leadership

O

Oakland Unified School District (OUSD), 384, 385
Obama, Barack, 273
One World Award, 75

Organizational boundaries, bridging, 131–132
Organizational change
  positive, by and for working poor, 353
Organizational development (OD) specialist, 259–260
Organizational practices, visibility of, 371
Organizational scientists, 468, 469–470
Organizational sociologists, 94
Organizational stratification gaps, 371
Organizational support, 363–364
Organizational virtuousness, 291, 301
Organization for Economic Cooperation and Development, 355
Organizations
  balancing formality and flexibility in, 468–469
  effectiveness of, 466–468
  intractable identity conflicts in, 271–283
  social change, 4
Outcomes, and social change, 484–490
  in individual level, 486–487
  in organization level, 486
  in societal level, 485–486
  strength-based outcomes, enduring, 487–490
Outgroup tolerance, 275; see also Tolerance

P

Participatory rural appraisal (PRA), 412
Partnership(s), 321–324
  organizational, 388, 392, 394, 396
  in public health ideology, 318–319
  for resource acquisition, 325–326
Passionate humility, 416
Patient(s)
  empowerment, 328–330
  positive outcomes for, 343–344
Paul Revere General Hospital, intractable identity conflicts in, 273–275
Payroll, 358
Personal worth, 478
Perspective-taking, 483
Pharmacist(s), partnering with nurses, 259–260